Forging Nations

Forging Nations

Currency, Power, and Nationality in Britain and Ireland since 1603

DAVID BLAAZER

Great Clarendon Street, Oxford, OX2 6DP,
United Kingdom

Oxford University Press is a department of the University of Oxford.
It furthers the University's objective of excellence in research, scholarship,
and education by publishing worldwide. Oxford is a registered trade mark of
Oxford University Press in the UK and in certain other countries

© David Blaazer 2023

The moral rights of the author have been asserted

All rights reserved. No part of this publication may be reproduced, stored in
a retrieval system, or transmitted, in any form or by any means, without the
prior permission in writing of Oxford University Press, or as expressly permitted
by law, by licence or under terms agreed with the appropriate reprographics
rights organization. Enquiries concerning reproduction outside the scope of the
above should be sent to the Rights Department, Oxford University Press, at the
address above

You must not circulate this work in any other form
and you must impose this same condition on any acquirer

Published in the United States of America by Oxford University Press
198 Madison Avenue, New York, NY 10016, United States of America

British Library Cataloguing in Publication Data

Data available

Library of Congress Control Number: 2022948831

ISBN 978–0–19–288702–3

DOI: 10.1093/oso/9780192887023.001.0001

Printed and bound in the UK by
Clays Ltd, Elcograf S.p.A.

Links to third party websites are provided by Oxford in good faith and
for information only. Oxford disclaims any responsibility for the materials
contained in any third party website referenced in this work.

To Renata, at last.

Acknowledgements

This book has taken a very long time to plan and write, and many people have helped me along the way. Colleagues too numerous to mention at UNSW campuses in Canberra and Sydney have provided stimulating, supportive, and congenial working environments. Among them, Eleanor Hancock and Alison Bashford commented helpfully on draft chapters. Laura Stewart, formerly of Birkbeck and now at the University of York, brought her expertise to bear on an early draft of Chapter 2, while Philip Bull, my friend and former teacher at La Trobe University, read late drafts of the entire manuscript and not only saved me from errors but worked hard to encourage me to be kinder to my readers, especially those with little knowledge of monetary history. OUP's expert reviewers devoted much time and thought to produce constructive and insightful reports that have made the book far better than it otherwise could have been. OUP's editors, especially Neil Morris, have worked with care and skill to save readers from confusion and to save me from various embarassments. Of course, its shortcomings and errors are entirely my responsibility.

The work of historians relies absolutely on the professional expertise and helpfulness of archivists and librarians. I owe gratitude to many staff of UNSW libraries in both Canberra and Sydney, but especially Anna Rutkowska for her speedy acquisition of essential e-books as I worked through Sydney's long Covid lockdown in 2021. I also thank Andrew Sergeant and the staff of the Petherick Reading Room at the National Library of Australia for their friendly and efficient assistance over the years while I snatched time from other responsibilities to work in that oasis. Staff at the British Library (including the newspaper library at Colindale before its closure), the National Library of Scotland, and the Senate House Library, University of London, also provided valuable assistance and guidance.

While working on this book (including the versions of it that never got written) and other related projects, I paid several fruitful and enjoyable visits to the Bank of England Archive. I owe thanks to the staff there, especially successive chief and deputy archivists Henry Gillet, Sarah Millard, and Mike Anson for their unfailingly good-humoured advice and efficient assistance. Their knowledge of the archive is truly remarkable, as is their readiness to help all kinds of researchers, including those—like me in my early visits—with less than half-formed ideas about what they are doing. I also received great help during various flying visits to the HBOS (now Lloyds Banking Group) Archives and RBS (now NatWest Group) Archives. The wonderfully efficient operations at the UK National Archives, National Records of Scotland, and National Archives of Ireland were, of course, indispensable to completion of the work. Visits to the Coins and Medals Department of the British Museum were made far more rewarding than they would otherwise have been thanks to the scholarly insights and encouragement of its former curator of paper money, Virginia Hewitt. Mara Caden and Hiroki Shin were each kind enough to provide me with copies of their respective PhD dissertations.

While developing the ideas in this book I have given numerous papers at conferences and seminars in various countries. My thanks are due to all involved in organizing them and to everybody who made encouraging comments or asked questions—particularly the difficult ones. I would also especially like to thank Tim Alborn, Mara Caden, Chris Desan, and Carl Wennerlind for their participation in a panel I organized for the 2018 North American Conference on British Studies. It was a rare opportunity for me to spend a little bit of time in the company of fellow monetary historians, who remain a rare breed in Australia.

I have also been fortunate to benefit from visiting fellowships at the Humanities Research Centre and the History Program in the former Research School of Social Sciences at the Australian National University, and the Department of History, Classics and Archaeology at Birkbeck, University of London. These visits, as well as attendance at conferences and other research visits to the UK have been supported by periods of leave, and small grants and allowances from UNSW Canberra and the Faculty of Arts and Social Sciences at UNSW Sydney. Without them I would have been unable to do essential archival research.

Finally, there is nothing I can write to properly acknowledge the support of my family. My daughters, Harriet and Liliana Blaazer-Grossi, now grown women, cannot remember a time when I was not working on, or thinking about, some version of this book. As well as enriching my life by being the wonderful people they are, they have been nothing but supportive and encouraging for as long as they have been aware of the book's demands and its importance to me. But it is to my partner, Renata Grossi, that I owe by far the greatest debt. She has lived with this work, and with me doing it, for far too long—all the while managing the challenges of her own academic work and the demands of everyday life. In that time she has given boundless love and support, and patience that has only worn thin when it really needed to. More than this, she has maintained a steadfast faith not only that I could complete this book but that it would be worthwhile, pushing me through periods of serious and debilitating self-doubt. In that sense the book is hers as much as mine, and I dedicate it to her with all my love and gratitude.

Contents

List of Illustrations   xi
List of Abbreviations   xiii
Note on Dates   xv

Introduction   1
   What Is Money? Defining the Subject Matter   2
   Money and the Nation in Three Kingdoms   9
   Money and History   15
   Road Map   19

1. 'I will make them one nation': 1603–1660   23
   Money in England, Scotland, and Ireland before the Regal Union   23
   Uniting the Nations: Regal, Political and Monetary Unions   36
   The Fracturing and Remaking of the Monetary Order   41

2. The Decline of the Old Monetary Order: 1660–1689   46
   1660: Restoring Difference   47
   Crises, Credit, and the Origins of Modern Money   50
   Ireland: Managing Monetary Catastrophe   58
   Scotland: the Uses and Abuses of Monetary Autonomy   67
   The Price of Revolution: the Monetary Consequences of 1689   73

3. Money and Revolution—the Case of England: 1690–1697   78
   Monetary Revolution I: the Case for the Concept   78
   Monetary Revolution II: Banks   80
   The Coinage Crisis: Judicial Terror and Popular Resistance   90
   Monetary Revolution III: Coins   98

4. Revolution, Union, and Divergence—from Scotland to North Britain: 1689–1772   105
   Storms from the South: Scotland's Money and England's Revolution   106
   A Failed Revolution? Bank of Scotland and the Company of Scotland   108
   Exporting Revolution? The Union of the Coins   114
   Converging Diversity: Scottish and British Money after the Union   125

5. Engines of State, Emblems of Nation, Tokens of Trust: 1695–1796   135
   Monetary Standards, New and Non-Existent   135
   Struggles over Credit I: the South Sea Bubble   141
   Struggles over Credit II: Banking in Ireland 1721–82   144
   Ireland: Struggles over Coin   153
   Ireland: towards a Sterling Standard   158
   Credit and Counterfeits: Managing the Scarcity of Money   161

6. The Only True, Intelligible Standard: 1793–1822 166
   The Suspension of Cash Payments 166
   Paper against Gold: the Push for Resumption 178
   The People's Money 189
   The Price of Gold 195

7. The Limits of Perfection: 1825–1914 202
   Uniformity and Its Discontents: the 1825 Crisis and Its Aftermath . . 202
   Uniformity Bungled: the Assimilation of the Irish Coinage 211
   Orthodoxy and Heterodoxy: the Unequal Struggle over Gold 215
   No Failure Like Success: the Banking Acts of 1844 and 1845 222
   The Golden Age 227

8. Things Fall Apart: 1914–1931 236
   The First World War: Remaking the Monetary Order 237
   'Back to Sanity': the Price of Orthodoxy 243
   'A Golden Gallipoli': the Return to Gold and Its Critics 249
   Union (Partially) Undone: Creating an Irish Currency 255
   1931: Power, Patriotism, and the Discourse of Catastrophe 263

Epilogue: The Burdens and Uses of the Past 272
   Memory, History, and the 'Decline' of Sterling 273
   Money, Sovereignty, and Identity in Ireland and the UK 280
   History and Forgetting in the Scottish Currency Debate 284
   Final Thoughts: the Global Financial Crisis and Its Aftermath . . . 289

Select Bibliography 293
Index 317

List of Illustrations

6.1. William Pitt reinvents Midas by suspending cash payments, 1797 — 177
7.1. A Provincial Bank of Ireland note, 1825 — 209
8.1. A third-series currency note, 1917 — 242
8.2. A Bank of England one-pound note (reverse), 1928 — 254
8.3. An Irish Currency Commission note, 1929 — 260
8.4. John Bull faces the crisis in the *Daily Herald*, 1931 — 268
8.5. John Bull faces the crisis in the *Daily Express*, 1931 — 268
8.6. A sardonic comment on Saorstát Éireann's sterling peg, 1931 — 270

List of Abbreviations

BE	Bank of England Archive
BLN	British Library Newspapers
BNA	British Newspaper Archive
CMO	Calendar of the Manuscripts of the Marquess of Ormonde preserved at Kilkenny Castle
CSPD	Calendar of State Papers Domestic
CSPI	Calendar of State Papers Relating to Ireland
CTB	Calendar of Treasury Books
CTP	Calendar of Treasury Papers
DIB	Dictionary of Irish Biography
GFC	Global Financial Crisis (2007–)
HPHC	History and Proceedings of the House of Commons (Great Britain)
HPHCI	History and Proceedings of the House of Commons (Ireland)
ILP	Independent Labour Party
INA	Irish Newspaper Archive
JHC	Journal of the House of Commons (England/Britain)
JHCI	Journals of the House of Commons of the Kingdom of Ireland
JHL	Journal of the House of Lords (England/Britain)
JHLI	Journals of the House of Lords of the Kingdom of Ireland
LBGA	Lloyds Banking Group Archives
LJI	Lords Justices of Ireland
NAI	National Archives of Ireland
NRS	National Records of Scotland
ODNB	Oxford Dictionary of National Biography
POB	Proceedings of the Old Bailey 1674–1913
RCS	Robert William Cochran-Patrick, *Records of the Coinage of Scotland, from the Earliest Period to the Union* (Edinburgh, 1876), 2 vols
RPS	Records of the Parliament of Scotland
SPC	Scotland Privy Council
TNA	The National Archives (UK)

Note on Dates

In England and Ireland, the New Year began on 25 March until 1 January 1752. For the sake of clarity, I have shown English and Irish dates between 1 January and 24 March in the years before 1752 thus: 18 January 1691/2, where 1691 is the year in the old style.

Introduction

> Money does not exist in a vacuum. It is not a mere lifeless object, but a social institution. Without its background it has as little meaning as a verb divorced from its context.
>
> Paul Einzig, *Primitive Money in Its Ethnological, Historical and Economic Aspects* (1966)

This book is a study of the relationships between money, power, and nationality in Britain and Ireland since the faltering beginnings of monetary union between Scotland, England, and Ireland and the concomitant emergence of early modern credit money in the seventeenth century. It examines how the changing architecture of money in each country affected the monetary order of each of the others as the United Kingdom was created. More particularly, it focusses on differing and changing attitudes to relationships between money and the nation, and how money was, or was not, seen as a critical element in national identity, prestige, and 'honour' over the course of three centuries in England, Ireland, Scotland, Britain, and the United Kingdom. The main narrative ends with the partial dismantling of the monetary union following the foundation of the Irish Free State in the 1920s, and the United Kingdom's final departure from the gold standard in 1931. The book concludes with an epilogue reflecting on the possible significance of this long history in structuring responses to more recent monetary events and debates, including the 'decline' of sterling, the creation of the euro, debates over the future of Scotland's currency in the event of independence, and responses to the Global Financial Crisis that began in 2007.

The central process examined in the book is the creation of a unified monetary order in the United Kingdom. By this I mean not just the unification of the currency that loosely attended the forging of England and Wales, Scotland, and Ireland into a unitary state but also the development of a particular kind of monetary system, specific to capitalism, which incorporated virtually the entire population and commanded widespread support across the boundaries of nations, economic sectors, social classes, and political ideologies. From three kingdoms, each exhibiting its own version of early modern monetary instability and conflict, there was eventually created a single monetary order exercising an intellectual hegemony so profound that its central assumptions could barely be identified, let alone challenged—even by those who were in principle hostile either to the capitalist economic order or to the political union of which the pound sterling formed an indispensable part. The creation of this monetary order can only be properly understood as a set of overlapping, asynchronous, and sometimes dissonant processes, each of which took place in its own specific historical context. Like money itself, these processes were simultaneously economic, political, social, and cultural.

What Is Money? Defining the Subject Matter

These claims require elaboration. While the statement that money is economic is a tautology, the way money works in the economy is anything but straightforward. It is also obvious that money is political. The production of money has long been a prerogative of the state, and the creation of national money has been a foundational task of most nation states for as long as nation states have existed.[1] The claim that money is a social and cultural phenomenon is less immediately obvious. I will therefore attempt to justify that claim first, before considering the implications of money's economic and political nature.

While this is a work of history, it must begin with some theoretical discussion, for it is impossible to write meaningfully about the history of money without first coming to grips with what money is. This is notoriously difficult, and many authors who attempt it draw from a stock of well-worn quotations to illustrate the point. For our present purpose the most useful of these is provided by Charles Dickens in an exchange between the 4-year-old Paul Dombey and his father, which does more than merely point to the fact of perplexity:

'Papa! what's money?'...

'What is money, Paul?' he answered. 'Money?'

'Yes', said the child, laying his hands upon the elbows of his little chair, and turning the old face up towards Mr Dombey's; 'what is money?'

Mr Dombey was in a difficulty. He would have liked to give him some explanation involving the terms circulating-medium, currency, depreciation of currency, paper, bullion, rates of exchange, value of precious metals in the market, and so forth; but looking down at the little chair, and seeing what a long way down it was, he answered: 'Gold, and silver, and copper. Guineas, shillings, half-pence. You know what they are?'

'Oh yes, I know what they are', said Paul. 'I don't mean that, Papa. I mean what's money after all?'...

---

[1] Helleiner, *National Money*.

'What is money after all!' said Mr Dombey, backing his chair a little, that he might the better gaze in sheer amazement at the presumptuous atom that propounded such an inquiry.

'I mean, Papa, what can it do?' returned Paul....

Mr Dombey drew his chair back to its former place, and patted him on the head. 'You'll know better by-and-by, my man', he said. 'Money, Paul, can do anything.'[2]

This passage encapsulates four common ways of approaching our question. First, Mr Dombey considers delivering a lecture on the different kinds of 'money-stuff'[3] (circulating medium, currency, paper, bullion) with some words about factors affecting the value of money (rates of exchange, value of precious metals, depreciation). Realizing that this is far too arcane for his audience, he falls back on the simplest possible reference to the money-stuff Paul knows: the coins he sees handed over shop counters. Paul sees not only that this is no answer at all but also, perhaps, that his father is struggling. He tries to help by reframing his original, ontological question ('What is money?') as a functional one ('What can it do?'), in the way beloved of the economics textbooks. Mr Dombey's answer to this new question ('Money can do anything') moves the conversation even further from Paul's starting point, for it is not about money itself but about the distinct (although related) topic of wealth. In any case he is wrong, as Paul soon shows by asking why money cannot bring back his dead mother.

Mr Dombey's difficulties stem from more than the fact that an adequate answer to Paul's question is beyond the grasp of a 4-year-old, for even the complex response that first comes to his mind could not have answered the question, no matter how thoroughly expounded. Of all the headings that Mr Dombey considers, only 'circulating medium' and 'currency' (which are essentially different words for the same thing) appear to have even the potential to lead to a definition. As an adherent of nineteenth-century economic orthodoxy Mr Dombey would probably, on reflection, have wanted to add some other points to this suggestion: that money is a means of payment, a store of value, and a unit of account. To his mind, as to the minds of most writers on the topic then and now, this should have served as an adequate answer.

Nigel Dodd has shown the deficiencies of this kind of answer by showing that not all things that clearly are or have been money have necessarily had all of these functions.[4] The most obvious of these is the money in our own bank accounts. As a store of value it is seriously deficient: even at very low rates of inflation it steadily loses value over time; and being almost totally dematerialized as electronic

---

[2] Dickens, *Dombey and Son*, pp. 98–9.   [3] Ingham, *Nature*, p. 33.
[4] Dodd, *Sociology*, p. vi.

impulses, it can hardly be described as a circulating 'medium'. Without doubt, however, it is a unit of account, enabling us to calculate the relationship between assets and liabilities, incomings and outgoings, desire and fulfilment. It is also indisputably a means of payment. It can be used to pay any debt or to buy any good or service, usually without needing to be converted into the notes and coins that clearly are a circulating medium (although they are no better than the electronic money as a store of value).

These are not exclusively modern problems. As we shall see, early modern coins rarely functioned as units of account, and were characterized by complex relationships of inverse proportionality between their various functions. The more a coin circulated, the more likely it was to lose bullion content through wear and tear and clipping; the less reliable it would therefore become as a store of value, or even as a means of payment. Conversely, a coin that was intact would serve well as a store of value, making it correspondingly more likely to be hoarded and therefore less likely to circulate.

These remarks about early modern money may be disorienting for the contemporary reader owing to the profound differences between early modern money and our own. As one eminent writer put it in the 1950s, 'Prior to the French Revolution, the monetary system of most European countries was based on altogether different principles.... [Its] strange terminology causes us, who live in a different world, to wander for a while in a dark forest.'[5] Despite this, it is important to find a stable definition of money that will be equally valid across the centuries spanned by this study. To understand what has changed, we need to grasp what has remained constant.

In this book, money is understood as a numerically measured means of final settlement of transactions, universally recognized and generally accepted as such within a given time and place. When money is considered in this way, the need to understand it as a social, cultural, and political phenomenon becomes clear. Nothing is money unless it is generally recognized as such: it thus takes its place, with language and the family, as one of the central social institutions and cultural practices of almost all human societies.

Almost all, but not quite. There have been human societies that have had no money, although there have been none that have had no language, and (if the term is defined broadly) none that have had no families.[6] This alerts us to the cultural nature of money. Unlike language and the family, money can make no claim at all to have some basis in nature compelling its existence. Money is entirely a human invention, relying—like language—on shared understandings about its meaning to function. If our understanding of the function and value of banknotes or coins was not generally shared, they would become mere commodities: pieces of

---

[5] Einaudi, 'Imaginary', p. 235.   [6] Martin, *Money*, pp. 33–7.

decorated paper or metal worth no more than their raw materials could fetch in exchange for other commodities. That these complex meanings are politically and culturally constructed and reproduced is obvious when one considers paper (or polymer) money or base-metal token coins. But contrary to one of the most durable popular myths about the history of money, the same could equally be said of a solid gold or silver coin. Admittedly, the metal in the coin also had a market value, in variable proportions to its monetary value, but market value was also a cultural fact, determined not only by the market value of gold or silver as a raw material for conspicuous consumption (another cultural fact) but also, to complete the circle, by the fact that it had the capacity to be turned into money.

Further consideration of bullion coins will help clarify matters. Medieval and early modern mints accepted bullion from members of the public and returned freshly minted coin in exchange. But mint charges, including production costs and, more significantly, a royal 'seigniorage', ensured that the monetary value (or value by 'tale') of a coin was always greater than the market value of the bullion it contained.[7] (Whenever the reverse was true, the coin would be melted for profit almost as soon as it was minted.) Moreover, coins were notoriously liable to be clipped, filed, and 'sweated' to obtain bullion, either for sale or to assist in counterfeiting.[8] The bullion value of a circulating coin was therefore often significantly less than its tale value. Despite this, clipped coins circulated freely, and were almost universally accepted and counted as money. Once they deteriorated past a certain point, however, people became increasingly reluctant to accept them by count and insisted on weighing them and giving, not their bullion value, but the tale value that such a weight of coins should represent.[9] At this point they almost ceased to be money and became a commodity—widely but not universally accepted in settlement of transactions, and, crucially, weighed rather than counted. In many jurisdictions it was an offence to refuse a coin by tale unless the state had determined that coins at a specified state of deterioration were to be so treated. Once this happened, the coins had been 'demonetized'.

While a demonetized bullion coin did not become valueless, it did lose the capacity to effect the transfer of abstract units of account from one party to another. That capacity is what constitutes the 'moneyness' of any given object; but it is the abstract units—universally recognized claims on infinitely commensurable, socially produced goods and services—that constitute money. Unsurprisingly, the abstract units have been far more durable than the objects used to transfer them. Museums and private collections are full of things that once were pounds—or multiples or fractions of pounds—and are no longer; but the

---

[7] The implications of the relationship between bullion and tale value in the English context are examined in Desan, *Making Money*, chs. 2–3.

[8] Sweating mimicked the effects of normal wear by putting coins in a bag together and shaking them vigorously to make them shed some of their metal as dust.

[9] Muldrew, 'Midas': p. 90.

pound itself remains.[10] The abstract system of monetary values thus logically precedes and temporally transcends any of its specific, concrete representations.

The creation and maintenance of this abstract system require the existence of concentrated political authority. As an anonymous thirteenth-century author put it, 'in the first place then, before there is any money, there must be a statute'.[11] Such authority requires a stable system of values in order to proclaim and to calculate what is owed to it and what it owes. It also determines what passes as money, and at what value, by proclaiming what it will accept and give for its own payments and what others must accept. Within the bounds of this study, that authority has taken the form of various states, whose power to turn bullion or anything else into money is often taken to be one of the defining elements of sovereignty.

The extent to which the state shares or delegates the power to make money reflects the extent to which the state shares power generally, and with whom. Some modern states have jointly delegated it to transnational bodies like the European Central Bank. Some feudal states authorized bishops and great aristocrats to mint coin, in the same way and in much the same proportion as they authorized them to raise armies and to exercise justice.[12] Likewise, capitalist states try to set parameters within which they allow banks to create money; parameters which, historically, have loosened or tightened according to prevailing ideologies and the balance of power between those actors.

The state plays a decisive role in fostering the general social recognition that constitutes money. This is typically experienced and reproduced culturally, but it depends originally on political decision and relies ultimately upon legal enforcement. Monetary history therefore cannot be written without close and continuous attention to the operation of state power. The latter, however, is inseparable from social power, and it is that to which we will now turn.

The proverb that 'money is power' is true in ways that are seldom fully realized. It is usually intended in the same sense that Mr Dombey claimed that money can do anything, confusing money itself with wealth. Important as wealth is, however, our concern is with something different: the power of the monetary system itself— the processes and institutions that create money and determine its value—to shape social structures, influence collective belief, determine individual and societal destinies, and, indeed, shape the distribution of wealth.

One way of thinking about monetary power is to consider how decisions about money affect different groups in society. At one level the national currency, like the nation itself, is everybody's property, creating a common interest that often

---

[10] This point is highlighted by the current meaning of the 'promise to pay' on Bank of England notes. An old, demonetized note cannot be used to buy goods and services, but it can be exchanged at the Bank of England for current notes or coins which can be so used.
[11] *De Moneta*, p. 66.   [12] See, for example, Spufford, *Medieval*, pp. 75–6.

transcends other social and political differences. Everybody's prosperity depends in large measure upon money's reliability and availability. Changes in the value of money, both in terms of its local purchasing power and its foreign exchange value, have real and significant consequences for people of all occupations and all social classes. But such consequences are neither equal in degree nor similar in kind for different people. Inflation or deflation harm some people a lot and others only a little, but benefit still others. Similarly, a change in the exchange rate will unequally advantage some economic groups and unequally disadvantage others in the short term, while unequally advantaging and disadvantaging others as its consequences work their way through the system. In short, while everyone has a stake in the currency, not everyone's stake is of the same size or the same kind.

Not everybody's capacity to influence monetary decisions is of the same size or kind either. Rather like the nation itself, a few people exercise power over the currency in ways that the vast majority do not. As we will see, the monetary decisions and beliefs of the mass of people do occasionally have some impact on the working of the currency, and on the decision-making of the financially powerful, just as the decisions and beliefs of the mass of voters and/or subjects sometimes have consequences for those who wield political power. But there is no disguising the imbalances of monetary power between, for example, the ministers planning a recoinage and the labourer left holding coins whose purchasing power has halved as a result, or the bonus-taking executive of a bank stocked with 'toxic assets' and the family made homeless by the foreclosure of their securitized home loan.

Matters such as interest rates and foreclosures lead us at last to money as an economic phenomenon. As these examples imply, money is a powerful economic force that has serious, real effects on people's lives. That this is not entirely obvious to those of us living with the seemingly endless consequences of the 2007 Global Financial Crisis is due to a failure to properly understand the nature of money in a capitalist society. Most commonly, the crisis is attributed entirely to illegitimate manipulation of exotic financial instruments such as securitized mortgages and hedge swaps, made possible by lax regulation.[13] All that is wanting to prevent such a crisis recurring is the restoration of prudent regulation and rigorous enforcement to bring money and credit back to their proper, inoffensive roles. Underlying this view is firstly an assumption that money and credit are separate phenomena, and secondly a belief that money is, or at least should be, a mere servant of the 'real' economy: nothing more than a convenient mechanism for overcoming the enormous barriers to sustaining even the simplest network of market exchanges on the basis of barter.

---

[13] See, for example, Lanchester, *Whoops!*

Such views rest crucially on the 'barter myth' as an account of the origins of money, as propounded by every orthodox writer since John Locke and others mobilized this Aristotelian fable to support their monetary views during the debate over the 1696 recoinage in England.[14] Its most obvious problems should be briefly noted.[15] First, it presupposes the existence of specialized economic agents (butcher, baker, brewer, in Adam Smith's example) who could not conceivably exist prior to a monetary economy, and sets them to work to invent one; second, it is inconsistent with every empirical account we have of pre-monetary or proto-monetary societies.[16] Such accounts consistently show that the indispensable actor in money's creation was the ruler rather than autonomous traders in a state of nature. Ethnographic accounts also undermine the widespread notion that credit follows money after money has followed barter. Instead, they suggest that money typically originates not in market exchange but in the need to calculate and settle not only debts owing to the state, but also those arising from injuries to the person, affronts to status or hierarchy, and marriage.[17]

The history examined in this book reveals an even more complicated relationship between money and credit. Contrary to orthodox stories reviewed in Chapter 3, modern banknotes originated in 1694 with the Bank of England, which issued them as loans to individuals and the government on the basis of loans it had made to the government in exchange for pledges of future revenues. This, in a vastly elaborated form, remains the model of money creation to this day. As Ingham explains, modern money is constituted by webs of indebtedness between the issuer, the issuer's creditors and debtors, and the holder. In the case of the cash and electronic balances circulating in contemporary societies, this web involves the state-owned central bank that issues the money, holders of government debt in various forms, and taxpayers.[18]

There is a further complication. Bank of England notes at first circulated almost entirely within London and only among the commercial and mercantile classes and between them and the government. In times of crisis they were not always accepted at face value. But even long after the notes circulated widely throughout England, they were not regarded as money but as its representative, convertible into actual money in the shape of gold coins. At this point in their development, they were an example of what is now called 'near-money': circulating credit instruments that are part of the money supply but whose value derives ultimately from their capacity to be converted into legal tender money, which in times of crisis can be open to question. The centuries since the Bank's foundation have

---

[14] See Chapter 3, below, and Desan, *Making Money*, p. 350. It was reiterated influentially by Smith, *Wealth*, 1, pp. 24–30.
[15] Ingham, *Nature*, p. 12, provides an incisive discussion.
[16] Einzig, *Primitive Money*, pp. 378–80; Graeber, *Debt*, pp. 21–41; Martin, *Money*, pp. 9–10. See also Desan, *Making Money*, ch. 1.
[17] Graeber, *Debt*, ch. 3.   [18] Ingham, *Nature*, p. 135.

seen a proliferation of such instruments, principally cheques and different types of bills of exchange in the period covered by this book but evolving into a plethora of private and public securities arising from ever more baroque webs of credit in our own day. The creation of these instruments, along with the 'retail' lending activities of banks, are the principal drivers of central banks' money creation in a modern economy.[19]

Since the very beginnings of the Bank of England, these structures have given rise to periodic crises, which at their most severe have in one way or another annihilated ordinary people's money or threatened to do so. Such crises, and their aftermath, have commonly involved long periods of high unemployment, low wages, violent changes to money's purchasing power, and, in more recent times, severe reductions of government social expenditure.

The legitimation of the system in such times of crisis, while obviously a major feat, has historically been achieved with surprisingly little difficulty. Like other forms of power, monetary power depends on ideology to sustain and reproduce itself. Just as political power simultaneously derives from and confers the capacity to shape public and political discourse, so too monetary power both enables and requires those who wield it to propagate plausible representations of the nature, meanings, and roles of money. These representations are as multifaceted as money itself, and include such things as the metaphors deployed to convey the meaning and causation of inflation, deflation, and movements in exchange rates; the visual rhetoric of banknotes and coins; the moral and legal framing of public and private debt, monetary crime and malpractice; public discourse concerning the activities and motives of the individuals and institutions that wield monetary power; and, underpinning all of these, accepted beliefs concerning the nature of money itself. These representations, and contests over them, will loom large in this book.

Money and the Nation in Three Kingdoms

The process of creating a monetary union was deeply entangled with the making of the United Kingdom.[20] Eric Helleiner's work on 'the making of national money' therefore provides a useful starting point for consideration of this relationship. Helleiner—a cultural geographer—examines the process whereby monetary systems were created which were monopolistic within a national territory in the sense that no other monies circulated—whether foreign or issued by a non-official source—and which were unified in the sense that all types of monetary instruments had a consistent, legally specified relationship with the unit of account.[21]

---

[19] McLeay, Radia, and Thomas, 'Money Creation', p. 2.
[20] This paragraph is derived from Blaazer, 'Mainstreaming', p. 60.
[21] Helleiner, *National Money*, p. 326.

The process was both geographic and socioeconomic: geographic in the sense that local and private currencies of various kinds had to be superseded and suppressed (along with the use of foreign currency) so that the boundaries of the nation state were coterminous with the currency zone; socioeconomic in that it saw the creation of a monetary system that unified the different types of currency used by all classes. While it remained true that the common people in England hardly used currency instruments such as banknotes at all before the twentieth century (the story in Scotland and Ireland is different), the system was unified before the middle of the nineteenth century in the sense that the state had established viable terms by which each type of instrument was reliably convertible into any other.

Helleiner has examined this process as a global phenomenon, arguing that it generally took place well after the establishment of the relevant nation state, as a result of deliberate nation-building projects with both economic and propagandist objectives.[22] A case study for this kind of process will appear near the end of this book with the Irish Free State's creation of a new currency in the 1920s. Otherwise, the United Kingdom's experience followed a different pattern. The making of the United Kingdom's national money was a gradual and uneven process imbricated in the creation of the state itself, a fact that may go some way to explaining the depth of feeling that attached to the 'good old British pound'—at least in England—when the euro appeared briefly to pose a threat to its continued existence.[23]

It is now approaching fifty years since John Pocock made his famous plea for 'British' history as a new subject, by which he meant the study of relations between the nations of the Atlantic archipelago, and the ways in which that complex of relationships has shaped the political, cultural, and social formations that have developed there.[24] Pocock's plea was not widely heeded until the 1990s, when a rash of historical and historiographical studies under the aegis of the 'New British History' appeared.[25] And while the rate of such programmatically explicit publications dwindled sharply thereafter, Pocock's plea has had lasting effects, well beyond the welcome fact that it is no longer possible for a professional historian to use the terms 'Britain' and 'England' interchangeably. This approach has not only yielded valuable insights into its mid-seventeenth century *locus classicus*, it also continues to enrich historians' approaches to the genesis and consequences of

---

[22] Helleiner, *National Money*, pp. 8–11.
[23] The term was used in 1992 by Boris Johnson, in an interview on the Australian Broadcasting Corporation's current affairs television programme *Lateline*, during John Redwood's 'Eurosceptic' challenge to John Major's leadership of the Conservative Party.
[24] Pocock, 'Plea'.
[25] The exceptions concern the period before 1603 and make little or no reference to Pocock. See, for example, Ellis, 'Crown, Community'. Later works include Asch, *Three Nations*; Grant and Stringer, *Uniting*; Bradshaw and Morrill, *British Problem;* Kenyon, Ohlmeyer, and Morrill, *Civil Wars*; Roberts and Bradshaw, *Consciousness*; Burgess, *New British History*; Connolly, *Kingdoms United*; and Ohlmeyer, 'Seventeenth Century Ireland'.

such obviously 'British' phenomena as the Scottish and Irish Acts of Union (of 1707 and 1801, respectively).

More generally, the four-nations approach has prompted 'both the decentring of historical accounts and the refashioning of a "British" metanarrative'.[26] The most influential such narrative remains Linda Colley's *Britons: Forging the Nation 1707–1837* (1992), whose subtitle I have deliberately chosen to echo in the title of this book. Colley argues persuasively that 'Britishness' was founded on Protestantism and hostility to France, both Catholic and Revolutionary. The implications of this construction for Ireland were, of course, deeply problematic. Colley's insight that Britain had to be constructed—or 'forged'—is obviously a point of departure for this work, although, interestingly, Colley makes not a single reference to money.

The archipelagic approach has been subject to some telling lines of critique, especially in its 'New British History' manifestation, and especially from historians of Scotland and Ireland. It will be helpful to review some of these to help clarify how and why I have attempted to take an archipelagic approach to monetary history.

The first problem concerns terminology. Just as the creation of Great Britain 'left Ireland out on a limb', so too has Ireland been left out on a lexical limb, bereft of any convenient term with which to include it with Britain.[27] Many proponents of the 'New British History' have dealt with this problem by relying on ancient usages to justify describing their enterprise as 'British' history and calling their subject 'the British Isles', thus avoiding the clunkiness of 'Britain and Ireland', or 'British and Irish' history. If nothing else, however, clarity and analytical precision prohibit such loose terminology in the context of monetary history. To give one example, the political union of England and Scotland in 1707 created a single 'British' coinage. It had no effect on Ireland, whose monetary regulation and monetary practices remained as distinct as ever from those of England and Scotland. Not even the creation of the United Kingdom of Great Britain and Ireland in 1801 did away with Ireland's unique units of account. In this book, therefore, the terms 'England', 'Scotland', 'Ireland', 'Britain', 'Britain and Ireland', 'the United Kingdom' (of Great Britain and Ireland), and, later on, the 'Irish Free State', 'Republic of Ireland', and 'Northern Ireland' will need to be used precisely, depending upon which features of which monetary jurisdictions are under discussion, which in turn depends largely on which period we are concerned with. Unavoidably, the terminology will be unwieldy, especially when discussing the periods of 'multiple monarchy' that preceded the political unions of 1707 and 1801, when the monetary relationships between the kingdoms were at their most untidy.[28]

---

[26] Lloyd-Jones and Scull, *Approaches*, p. 4.
[27] Burgess, *New British History*, p. 2; Morrill, 'British Problem', p. 5.
[28] For a discussion of the diverse ways that the problem of 'composite monarchy' or 'multiple kingship' could be managed, see Elliott, 'Composite Monarchies'. See also Wormald, 'Creation'.

Wales is conspicuous by its absence from the preceding discussion. Largely for reasons of euphony, I will use 'England' as shorthand for England and Wales, meaning that the book is a study of three kingdoms rather than four nations. The justification for this proceeding is the inverse of my insistence on not using 'Britain' as a shorthand for 'Britain and Ireland'. Since long before the chronological beginning of this study there has been no *nationally* distinct Welsh monetary history, any more than there has been a Cornish monetary history. In a monetary context, both can be considered within the framework of regional rather than national variation.

Another problem concerns Anglocentrism. Historians of Scotland and Ireland especially have cautioned against a tendency to adopt a 'cut-and-paste British history' that slots Scotland or Ireland into a narrative that 'presumes the importance of those events which have featured prominently in conventional English history'.[29] A closely related criticism is that much New British History has been so centrally preoccupied with the process of the formation of the British state that it 'risks taking us back to old-fashioned Anglocentric constitutional history'.[30] Such approaches can easily ride roughshod over the historical complexity of the rest of the archipelago. Toby Barnard has made this point forcefully, arguing that 'historians of Britain...in the main, have preferred the most coherent but simplistic evocations of Ireland' which ignore its 'strong regional variegation', and have therefore contented themselves with accounts of that country that are 'jejune, unsubtle or simply inaccurate'.[31] The same point could equally be made about Scotland.

These concerns alert us to the 'extremely powerful professional and historical reasons pressing us towards the continuation of the Anglocentric perspective' acknowledged by Pocock in his original essay.[32] The historical reasons arise from the obvious fact of England's political, military, and economic dominance (and aggression) within the archipelago, such that 'British [*sic*] history can be written largely in terms of English conquest, colonization and influence, as the result of which the periphery became the passive recipients of English institutions or the equally passive victims of the English quest for hegemony and power.'[33] While it would be a serious error to assume Irish or Scottish passivity, we need to face England's quest for power squarely and consider its causes and consequences

---

[29] Brown, 'Scottish Clio', p. 241; Canny, 'Anglicization', p. 49. Conrad Russell's work explaining England's descent into civil war in 1641 is often cited as the most conspicuous example of this tendency. See, e.g., Russell, 'British Problem'; Russell, *Fall*.

[30] Brown, 'Scottish Clio', p. 242; Macinnes, *Union and Empire*, p. 49, goes further, questioning 'whether the "new British histories" have marked a distinctive shift in focus away from Whiggish concerns with nation building'.

[31] Barnard, 'British and Irish', pp. 220-2.   [32] Pocock, 'Plea', p. 613.

[33] Asch, 'Obscured', p. 16. The point has been discussed by various writers. See, for example, Brown, 'Scottish Clio', p. 242. Pocock, *Discovery*, p. 59, suggests that Scots writers since the early modern period have grasped the point clearly.

carefully.³⁴ As an eminent Irish historian who was one of the keenest early critics of the New British History observed, 'the attempted Anglicisation of Ireland (and also of Scotland) must become the central theme of any subject called British History if this subject, as it has been defined by its advocates, is to have any credibility'.³⁵

Much of the monetary history of the three kingdoms can easily be boiled down to a tale of how the English pound sterling superseded the separate currencies of Scotland and Ireland, so that by the time modern central banking began to evolve in the United Kingdom, it was inconceivable that its functions would be exercised by any institution other than the Bank of *England*. But as Pocock points out, 'the fact of a hegemony does not alter the fact of a plurality'³⁶—a plurality which survives, albeit in highly attenuated forms, in the currency arrangements of the United Kingdom to this day, as anyone who tries to spend Scottish or Northern Irish banknotes in England will discover. Nor does the fact of an outcome obliterate the complexity of a process. While the outcome of the process to be examined here was a unified (although not entirely uniform) monetary order throughout the United Kingdom, much of its form will remain invisible or inexplicable without a nuanced account of those complexities, contextualized in an account of the changing nature and distribution of monetary power. Failure to understand these processes will also leave us powerless to understand salient features of the more recent past, including divergent responses in England, Scotland, Northern Ireland, and the Republic of Ireland to the proposal to surrender monetary sovereignty to the European Central Bank, or the inability of the Scottish National Party to mobilize any aspect of Scotland's monetary history to counter the damage done to its 2014 referendum campaign by the debate over an independent Scotland's currency arrangements.

However historians negotiate the historical forces pushing them towards Anglocentrism, the professional reasons steering them towards one or another national specialism will remain very powerful. As Colin Mason has observed, 'historians of England, Scotland, Wales and Ireland, while doffing their caps to Pocock's British and archipelagic agenda, have by and large remained historians of England, Scotland, Wales and Ireland.'³⁷ The most obvious reason is that it is beyond the reach of any single person to attain mastery of even a fraction of the historiographies, much less the relevant primary sources, across the archipelago— a problem which multiplies with every decade we add to the chronological span of any study. While I cannot claim to have overcome the problems besetting a study spanning the three kingdoms across more than three centuries, my focus on the history of a core institution—money—which evolved into its modern form as

---

[34] Adamson, 'English Context', pp. 23–4.   [35] Canny, 'Anglicization', p. 50.
[36] Pocock, 'Plea', p. 605.   [37] Mason, 'Debating Britain', p. 3.

relations between the constituent nations of the archipelago took *their* modern form, provides a thematic focus that mitigates many of these difficulties.

It does not, however, immediately resolve the question of what type of history to write. Lloyd-Jones and Scull have identified two broad types of four-nations history—comparative and supranational—while Burgess divides the latter into 'holistic' (concerned mainly with the history of state-building) and 'episodic' (concerned with episodes when the history of one nation illuminates the history of another).[38] To these we can usefully add another by adapting Armitage and Braddick's notion of 'cis-Atlantic' history—by which they mean national or regional history written within an Atlantic context (for example, the integration of the economy and society of an English village into Atlantic networks of exchange). 'Cis-archipelagic' history in the present study will consider monetary developments and their consequences within England, Scotland, and Ireland (and regions within them) in the context of the changing monetary structures of the archipelago.[39]

In conception, this book is both holistic and comparative. Holistic in that is concerned with the formation of a monetary union in Britain and the United Kingdom, with the failures and reverses of that process, moments of resistance to it, and, finally, its partial dissolution and current prospects; comparative in that it is concerned with similarities and differences in the development and structure of monetary institutions, practices, and attitudes. Above all, it will compare expressions of monetary patriotism and monetary nationalism across the three kingdoms and consider why certain critical developments took place in one kingdom but very differently (or not at all) in another. Both episodic and 'cis-archipelagic' approaches will be required. To take one example, in the mid-1690s England and Scotland each underwent their own monetary revolutions, arising from their respective structural monetary crises. A comparison of these will need to take account of cis-archipelagic issues such as each kingdom's place in the multiple monarchy, and the monetary consequences for Scotland of being England's neighbour in a time of monetary turmoil. As we will see, the fact that no such monetary revolution took place in Ireland at that time was partly due to cis-archipelagic factors affecting Ireland's long-term economic development and monetary structures.

The 'socioeconomic processes' of monetary unification pose different challenges to the historian. They are much more difficult to pinpoint than the geographical processes. While there are certainly critical episodes, it is impossible to say definitively that any part of the process was 'complete' at any moment or, indeed, what it might mean to describe such a process as complete. We are dealing

---

[38] Lloyd-Jones and Scull, 'New Plea', p. 7; Burgess, *New British History*, pp. 3–5.
[39] Armitage and Braddick, *Atlantic World*, p. 3; Sacks, *Widening Gate*, provides an example of a cis-Atlantic history.

with something multifaceted and nebulous, involving not only material objects and transactions, and (often submerged) struggles around the distribution of wealth and power, but also cultural practices and social beliefs—*mentalités*, to borrow the useful term of the *Annales* historians. Moreover, not only did the socioeconomic processes unfold in very different ways in each country, they were not even synchronous within each country: for example, the changing monetary experience of three generations of peasants in Galway was vastly different not only from that of their landlords but also from the experiences of the labouring poor of Dublin, Belfast, Edinburgh, and London, and different again from that of the rural poor of the English home counties or the west of Scotland. The monetary experience of all of these differed significantly from the rather more geographically uniform experience of their respective national elites.

Money and History

A history of this kind necessarily draws on different kinds of primary and secondary sources. The relevant primary sources include royal decrees, parliamentary debates, and committee reports; bank correspondence and records; Treasury and mint archives; books, pamphlets, and leaflets addressed to audiences ranging from the elite to the plebeian; journalism ranging from eighteenth-century broadsheets to twentieth-century tabloids; cartoons, literary fiction, and verse; court reports, accounts of trials and public executions; and the text and images on coins and banknotes.

Despite a surge of interest in the field in the last twenty years or so, the kind of work on money presented here, using these kinds of sources, is still unusual. For almost the whole of the twentieth century non-economists left the study of money—past and present—to economists, whose heavily quantitative work became increasingly inaccessible to anybody outside their own specialism. Geoffrey Ingham has suggested that this was one of the regrettable results of the theoretical *Methodenstreit* of the early twentieth century, in which those economic thinkers who claimed a special scientific status for economics quarantined economic inquiry from the other social sciences.[40] This separation has restricted our view of money, and thereby impoverished the social sciences.

The failure of the other social sciences to study money has been self-reinforcing. Orthodox economics posits money as an essentially neutral instrument that exists to overcome the inconvenience of barter by means of tokens. Apart from 'mistakes' in its management, or wrong-headed, ideologically inspired, and inevitably doomed attempts at monetary engineering by deluded or impecunious

---

[40] Ingham, *Nature*, pp. 9–10.

governments, money does not, or at least should not, have any effect on the 'real economy', but should merely respond to its ebbs and flows. In this view the history of money can only be teleological: a history of the 'discovery' of the laws of its management, culminating in the present situation where monetary decisions have been removed from government control and placed in the hands of central banks' panels of 'neutral' experts, who determine their policy in response to recent or projected conditions in the 'real economy'.[41] If such a view of money is correct, it can barely be seen as a fitting object of any but technical analysis by economists.

This is not to suggest that there are no older historical accounts of money, monetary institutions, or monetary thought, nor even that there have been none that have developed critical perspectives. There are valuable surveys of the history of sterling by Sir Albert Feavearyear (1963) and, at the beginning of the current resurgence of monetary history, Nicholas Mayhew (1999). Glyn Davies's general history of money (1994) also discusses sterling at length.[42] There are also numerous histories of banking and of particular banks of issue, some of which have reflected on the nature of the money those banks have produced, the politico-economic relationships in which they have been embedded and the social consequences of their issuing practices and policies.[43] There is also a substantial body of work on regal coins (and the mints that produced them) and unofficial and local tokens.[44] Most of these are concerned with periods near the beginning of this book's chronological span, and there is much more work on these topics concerned with still earlier periods.[45] By no means all of these works are guilty of the tendency identified by Felix Martin to conflate money with the physical objects that constitute the primary source materials of numismatic historians.[46] Still more valuable for this study are a number of works by economic historians—mostly from the 1960s and 1970s—on the history of critical monetary episodes and their attendant theoretical and political debates that look beyond the narrow paradigms of professional economics.[47]

More striking than the relative paucity of specialist works in monetary history is the tendency of most non-specialist historians to ignore money altogether in contexts where its relevance should be obvious.[48] As I have shown, one such context is work on relations between the three kingdoms, whether written from an

---

[41] For examples of such teleological approaches see Sargent and Velde, *Small Change*; John H. Wood, *Central Banking*.

[42] Feavearyear, *Pound*; Mayhew, *Sterling*; Davies, *History of Money*.

[43] To confine ourselves to monographs and edited collections, some of the more conspicuous examples are Saville, *Bank of Scotland*; McGowan, *Money and Banking*; Lyons, *Bicentenary*; Checkland, *Scottish Banking*; Roberts and Kynaston, *Bank of England*; Sayers, *Bank*, 1; Pressnell, *Country Banking*.

[44] Boyne, *Tokens*; Dolley, 'Coinage'; Whiting, *Trade Tokens*; Challis, *Mint*.

[45] Bolton, *Medieval*; Wood, *Money Matters*; Spufford, *Medieval*. [46] Martin, *Money*, p. 19.

[47] Appleby, *Economic Thought*; Dickson, *Financial Revolution*; Fetter, *Orthodoxy*; Hilton, *Corn, Cash*; Horsefield, *Experiments*.

[48] I discuss this point at greater length in Blaazer, 'Mainstreaming', pp. 54–5.

English, Irish, Scottish, or even 'New British' perspective. Until recently almost the only exceptions to this rule concerned Scotland.[49] It is also striking that in the histories of sterling cited earlier, the key episodes in the creation of the UK monetary union are mentioned only in passing, if at all.[50] The full title of Feavearyear's survey, *Sterling: a History of English Money*, typifies this issue. Most surprising of all these lacunae is the almost total absence of currency issues from historical studies of modern Ireland, which has only begun to be corrected by the recent emergence of work dealing mainly with the eighteenth century and with an avowedly archipelagic or Atlantic frame of reference.[51]

Most of the early impetus to understand money as a social, cultural, and political phenomenon came from outside the discipline of history, even when the focus was on the past. As Deborah Valenze has pointed out, it was scholars in literary and cultural studies who in the late twentieth century performed the invaluable service of leading the way in 'illuminating [the] subtle reticulation of economy and culture'.[52] By doing so, they paved the way for historians, including Valenze herself, to carry out some of the key aspects of the research agenda implied by the insights of sociologists such as Ingham and Nigel Dodd. As Dodd put it in 1994, 'The uses made of money, the institutions associated with its control and acquisition, and the ideas people have of its nature and functions, are compelling features of contemporary life.... [T]o understand what is distinctive about money requires reference to the network of social relationships which makes its transaction possible.'[53] Since then, a small number of important works by scholars in a range of disciplines have added substantially to our knowledge of these uses, institutions, ideas, and networks.

As well as from literary scholars, much of the initial impetus in this field came from social and cultural geographers. Helleiner's work on the making of national money has already been mentioned, but the stimulating contributions of Andrew Leyshon and Nigel Thrift should also be noted. All three scholars contributed in 1999 to a collection on *Nation-States and Money*, which included contributions from other geographers, two sociologists, a numismatist, a literary scholar, an economist, and a political scientist, but, remarkably, no historian.[54]

The first major work by a historian to tackle the broad questions and approaches pursued by these scholars was Valenze's *The Social Life of Money in the English Past* (2006). Valenze presented a series of interconnected but discrete essays to develop an argument about the changing 'repertoire of concepts and

---

[49] Galloway, *Union*; Hamilton, *Economic History*; Watt, *Price*.
[50] Feavearyear, *Pound Sterling*; Mayhew, *Sterling*; Sinclair, *Pound*.
[51] The conspicuous exception is the work of the economic historian L. M. Cullen. The main recent collections are McGrath and Fauske, *Money, Power*; Carey and Finlay, *Empire*. See also Walsh, *Bubble*.
[52] Valenze, *Social Life*, p. 15. For a sense of the work Valenze had in mind, see the essays in Woodmansee and Osteen, *New Economic Criticism*.
[53] Dodd, *Sociology*, pp. vi, xxiii.
[54] Helleiner and Gilbert, *Nation-States*; Leyshon and Thrift, *Money/Space*.

techniques for understanding and using money' in the period 1640–1770.[55] Key to her argument was the idea that the customary accepted boundaries between monetary relations and other kinds of social relations were much less distinct at the beginning of her period than they became at its end, when anti-slavery campaigns insisted that human beings could not be given a monetary value. At the same time, the growth of a relatively stable monetary economy had helped to refashion older hierarchies around measures of wealth, and to make money the legitimate focus of social aspiration.

Valenze's work offers us a way into monetary worlds that are fundamentally alien to our own. The plural form is important, for her work echoes Dodd by emphasizing that people in early modern England did not all occupy the same monetary world or think about money in the same ways. Her argument concerning changing views of money also suggests an important corollary: as money retreated from the human, so it became dehumanized, and thus was seen increasingly as independent of human volition and subject to 'laws' which human beings could attempt to discover, but could not make. The developments Valenze discusses can reasonably be seen as preconditions for the separation of economics in general, and the study of money in particular, from the purview of the humanities and social sciences.

Before Valenze, Craig Muldrew's work on the complex social consequences of the growth of networks of credit obligations in early modern England offered a variety of insights, not only into the diverse monetary worlds of people of different classes and milieux but also into the nature of money itself.[56] In another vein, Carl Wennerlind's work on 'The Death Penalty as Monetary Policy' helped to provide a conceptual frame in which to place other work on monetary crime and punishment by Malcolm Gaskill, John Styles, and, dealing with a later period, Randall McGowan.[57] Wennerlind's later *Casualties of Credit: the English Financial Revolution, 1620–1720* provides valuable insights into a range of English monetary developments during a crucial period and brings into focus the connections between abstract theoretical arguments, political and judicial decision-making, and the lived experience of a variety of people whose lives were profoundly affected by monetary change.[58] More recently, Christine Desan, a legal historian, has done for the medieval and early modern period some of what I am trying to do for the early modern and modern period. Her *Making Money: Coin, Currency, and the Coming of Capitalism* advances a richly rewarding argument about the development of the legislative framework of the monetary order and the ideological and theoretical debates that underpinned it.

---

[55] Valenze, *Social Life*, p. 2.   [56] Muldrew, *Obligation*.
[57] Gaskill, *Crime*; McGowen, 'Gallows'; Styles, 'Money Makers'; Wennerlind, 'Death Penalty'.
[58] Wennerlind, *Casualties*.

A striking feature of the recent work just discussed is its strong focus on the period before the French Revolution. While specialists in literary Romanticism have developed interesting insights into the monetary politics and culture of the late eighteenth and early nineteenth centuries, the seam gets much thinner thereafter, possibly because of the towering presence of Mary Poovey's *Genres of the Credit Economy* (2008), which brings profound literary scholarship to readings of work on money and credit to develop important arguments about the development of a nineteenth-century canon of economic writing.[59] Among historians, Timothy Alborn, who deftly combines the insights and techniques of cultural studies with a deep understanding of financial institutions and processes, seems to be almost alone in the later Victorian period.[60]

This book is intended to build on this growing body of work through an analytical narrative, by which I mean simply an argument embodied in a story, which is still the characteristic form of most history books. This remains the most appropriate form for explaining a complex set of interrelated processes over a long period of time, which arrived at identifiable points of crisis whose resolution shaped ensuing developments. The book proceeds by analysing and interpreting episodes, which are discussed mostly in the same sequence as they took place. The book makes no pretence, however, to offer a narrative of every significant event or development in the monetary history of the British Isles. As noted above, we already have several such works. Rather, in its endeavour to develop an argument about changing structures and locations of monetary power and their role in the formation of the United Kingdom, the book presents a 'lumpy' narrative, which drills down only into the episodes and processes most salient to its purposes.

Road Map

It may be helpful to the reader to have an outline of how the argument unfolds. The first chapter describes the origins and ultimate failure of James VI and I's attempt to unify England's, Scotland's, and Ireland's money shortly after he inherited the English and Irish thrones. Scrutiny of the attempt and its ultimate failure reveals much about the state of currency in early modern England, Scotland, and Ireland, and the monetary relations between them. It also provides a vantage point to help us to understand the nature and increasing instability of early modern money. These points will help us understand the transformations examined in later chapters.

Chapter 2 traces the paths taken from dysfunction to crisis by the monetary orders of the three kingdoms, as theoretical debates over monetary problems

---

[59] Rowlinson, *Real Money*; Dick, *Romanticism*. Poovey, *Genres*.
[60] Alborn, 'Moral'; Alborn, 'Coin and Country'; Alborn, 'Money's Worth'; Alborn, *Glittered*.

raged in the final decades of the seventeenth century. It identifies differing attitudes to relationships between money and national prestige in the three kingdoms. While distinct, these developments cannot be understood in isolation from each other. In particular, Scotland and Ireland were often obliged to respond to monetary challenges resulting from English developments and policies within the constraints of a royal prerogative exercised primarily in English interests.

Chapter 3 focusses almost entirely on England, where the fiscal demands of war led to the collapse of the government's credit and the near breakdown of the monetary system. This crisis precipitated a monetary revolution that included the foundation of the Bank of England (1694) and the great silver recoinage (1696). Together, these transferred significant monetary power from the state to mercantile and monied interests, while widening the gulf between the monetary worlds of the elite and the rest of society. The crisis also established monetary ideas that would endure for centuries. Crucially, they cemented the belief that an unchanging monetary standard was essential to England's prestige and 'honour'.

Chapter 4 examines the destabilizing effects of England's monetary turmoil on Scotland and Scottish attempts to alleviate its economic and monetary problems. I examine the distinctive implications of the foundation of Bank of Scotland for Scotland's social relationships, power structures, and popular beliefs about money. I scrutinize the monetary union of the two countries that accompanied the political union of 1707 for what it reveals about Scots' attitudes to money and nationality and English attitudes towards Scotland. The chapter ends with the development of Scotland's banking system in the eighteenth century, highlighting both its distinctiveness and the ways it became ever more deeply linked with London-centred networks of public and private credit.

Chapter 5 outlines the consolidation of the post-revolutionary monetary order in England, including the establishment of an effective gold standard from 1717 and the elevation of the Bank of England to a largely unquestioned position as a key component of the state apparatus. In parallel, it examines Ireland's ongoing monetary problems throughout the century, and critical struggles over coinage and banking. These were framed largely by the complex and ambivalent relationship of resentful and mistrustful dependency of the Irish Protestant elite on the British government. The chapter also considers the consequences of chronic shortages of coin in Britain and Ireland as well as the growing importance of paper money and credit throughout England.

Chapter 6 considers the monetary consequences for Britain and Ireland of wars with France, especially the crisis of 1797 which triggered the 'bank restriction', a twenty-four-year period when the Banks of England and Ireland were prevented from paying gold for their notes and circulated low-denomination notes for the first time. This episode provoked key debates concerning not just the politics and morality of money but also money's relationship to national honour and patriotism. I differentiate the experiences of England, Scotland, and Ireland and challenge conventional claims that the common people's monetary experience in this period was wholly negative and produced an enduring hostility to paper money.

In Chapter 7 I examine the consolidation of the gold standard to the eve of the First World War, including the final 'assimilation' of the Irish currency into the UK and Scottish resistance to complete monetary uniformity in the 'small notes' controversy of 1826. In the last half of the century, everyday experience of the monetary system throughout the UK became almost wholly unproblematic, with an adequate supply of coins and notes of stable value. The system appeared both natural and timeless, accepted and even admired by people of all nations, classes, and political persuasions. Despite some ambivalence, the internationalization of the gold standard and the global financial hegemony of London helped to make the system a source of patriotic pride.

Chapter 8 deals with the long monetary crisis that began with the outbreak of the First World War and ended with the UK's departure from the gold standard in 1931. It highlights the use of patriotic appeals and arguments to enjoin specific monetary behaviours during the war and to enlist support for efforts to restore and maintain the gold standard after it, even when these came at significant economic cost. For most people, the gold standard had become an end above all others, essential to national well-being, power, and honour. This consensus embraced the leaders of the newly established Irish Free State, who, in constructing a new currency, saw the UK gold standard as the embodiment of 'sound' monetary internationalism. They therefore willingly tied their new currency to sterling on a pound-for-pound basis.

Despite its narrative structure, the book is not teleological. On the contrary, it aims to challenge a teleology in which the rise of money is seen as part and parcel of a narrative of triumphant modernization, whose central processes are the rise of free markets based on autonomous and rational self-seeking actors.[61] Nor does the book subscribe to any Marxist teleology—whether of class struggle or of the rise and fall of capitalism. Nothing in this book, including the crisis with which it ends, was preordained. The book is not intended to explain or to trace any single process leading to a singular end. Rather, it aims to explicate diverse and even contradictory processes that interacted with each other in complex ways at every point. The synopsis of its argument is necessarily somewhat schematic; the book itself, in all its varied and messy detail, is not.

While a few of the episodes discussed will be unfamiliar in their details and others will be presented with an emphasis on aspects which have received only fleeting attention, most will be fairly familiar even to many non-specialists. The book's claims to originality do not rest primarily on the production of new

---

[61] See Reddy, *Money and Liberty*, pp. 1–2, 14.

nuggets from previously unmined primary sources; nor do they rest on any methodological innovation. Rather, the book tries to afford a fresh angle of vision on a number of important historical processes and episodes by using a variety of approaches to synthesize them in novel ways. I will count the book as successful if it helps readers to become more aware of the importance of money in British and Irish history and to think about its role in the formation of the United Kingdom along new and fruitful lines. If it provokes further research into the episodes it discusses, even if only to refute my arguments, then it will be an even greater success.

1
'I will make them one nation'
1603–1660

> Nothing is more appropriate to the Soveraigne dignity of Princes then the ordering of their Moneys.
>
> King James VI and I (1604)

During the evening of 26 March 1603, James VI of Scotland learned that he had at last inherited the Kingdoms of England and Ireland from his cousin Elizabeth. Almost the first concrete problem he faced as ruler of a composite monarchy concerned money. On 8 April, as he passed through England on his way to his new capital, he discovered—as he would explain a year later—that it was 'impossible for Our Nobilitie and other subjects attending us in our journey hither, to be provided of currant Moneys of this Realme for their expenses so soone as Our Speed required'.[1] In only his second proclamation as King of England, he therefore decreed 'that the Quoyne of Scotland called the Sixe lib. Piece, of golde... shall bee from henceforth Currant within his Majesties Kingdome of England, at the value of Tenne shillings Sterling', and that the Scottish 'Quoyne of silver called the Marke piece, shall be from henceforth Currant within the sayde Kingdome of England at the value of Thirteene pence halfe-penny'.[2] The proclamation solved a pressing but purely local difficulty: James's suite were now able to buy what they needed with their Scottish coins. So far, so simple. But closer scrutiny of the proclamation and its monetary context reveals not only some of the monetary differences between two of James's three kingdoms but also the radical disparities between our own monetary concepts and practices and those of the early modern period.

Money in England, Scotland, and Ireland before the Regal Union

James's valuation of the Scots six-pound piece at ten shillings sterling was based on the accepted 12:1 exchange rate between the two countries. The valuation of

---

[1] [James I,] *A Proclamation for Coynes* (London, 16 Nov. 1604).
[2] [James I,] *A Proclamation declaring at what values certaine moneys of Scotland shal be currant within England* (London, 8 Apr. 1603).

the 'marke piece', however, is more complicated. The silver 'marke', or 'merk', as it was known in Scotland, was a Scottish coin worth two-thirds of a Scots pound, or 13s. 4d. (160 pence). Together with the half merk of 80d. it constituted a significant part of the Scottish currency. But James's value of the merk at 13½d. sterling, when multiplied by twelve, produces a value not of 160d. Scots, but 162d. By virtue of the vagaries of the value of bullion, the merk did not conform to the accepted exchange rate. As it transpired, neither did the gold Scots coins. As James was compelled to admit eighteen months later, while his valuation of the Scots £6 coin was accurate in terms of English silver money, 'the English Coynes of Golde are not in regard of the Silver Coynes, of the true proportion betweene Gold and Silver accustomed in all Nations'.[3] These proclamations, dealing with only two Scottish coins, provide a small window on the complexities of early modern money.

Varying bullion content, and the changing market values of silver and gold, are only the beginning of this complexity, for the value of the bullion it contained was only one element constituting a coin's value. With rare exceptions, a coin's value 'by tale' (or 'face value', as it would be called later) was higher (usually by around 5–10 per cent) than its bullion value.[4] Indeed, on the rare occasions when the bullion value of a type of coin exceeded or even equalled its value by tale, the coin would disappear from circulation—exported to be melted and reminted elsewhere on more favourable terms. The difference arose from the price people were willing to pay for converting bullion into coin. That price had two elements: mint charges to cover the actual costs of minting and—the larger element—the 'seigniorage' charged by the Crown. The right to sell bullion (including foreign coin) to the mint at the price ordained by the Crown was in principle open to everyone. In practice it was exercised overwhelmingly by merchants, who were willing to exchange a larger quantity of bullion for a smaller in order to gain the enormously greater utility and convenience of coin.[5] As Christine Desan has put it, a coin's value by tale was a 'compound' composed of 'its commodity value enhanced by its advantage as cash'.[6]

As Desan explains in detail, the relationship between the elements of the compound was not constant or stable. Obviously, a change in the market price of the precious metals would change the commodity value of every coin containing them, while leaving the tale value unaffected. Seignorage and mint charges could vary from metal to metal and denomination to denomination, or even according to whether the bullion supplied was in the form of old English coins or foreign silver.[7] Moreover, manual minting techniques meant that coins could not be minted to precise weights, meaning that even officially 'identical' coins

---

[3] [James I,] *A Proclamation for Coynes* (London, 16 Nov. 1604).
[4] Mayhew, 'Money in England', p. 185.   [5] Mayhew, 'Regional', p. 83.
[6] Desan, *Making Money*, p. 111.
[7] Challis, *Mint*. Tables 3 and 10 (pp. 134 and 196), collectively covering 1278–1526, show how great the variations could be.

could contain different quantities of bullion. Once the coins went into circulation, the variability increased as the gap between bullion value and tale value widened through normal wear and tear, and—more drastically—through the theft of the precious metal in the coins by clipping, filing, and sweating. These problems apply to any system of commodity money, but from the late Middle Ages they were further complicated by the fact that, although the monetary standard was silver, the official legal tender in many jurisdictions, including England, Scotland, and Ireland, consisted of a mixture of silver or gold coins, whose relative values varied across time and place and even—in some contexts—between different types of transactions.

For most people, whose transactions were both small and local, these complexities were largely beside the point. Tale value was what mattered; a coin was worth what the monarch said it was worth. Indeed, to attempt to tender or accept it at any other value was a criminal offence.[8] In England, and by extension Ireland, the handful of relevant lawsuits brought during the Middle Ages and early modern period made it crystal clear that any money payment specified in a contract was to be paid in coins to that legal value at the time payment was due, regardless of any changes to the relationship between their bullion content and their valuation since the contract was made.[9] Thus in 1250 the court found in favour of Maud de Pavely, who sued Richard Basset demanding that he pay a debt owing to her in new pennies which, as a result of a change in the standard, contained more silver than pennies had contained when the debt had been incurred.[10] Basset had not incurred a debt for a quantity of silver, but for something different: a sum of money. As David Fox points out, the paucity of such cases, and the fact that they only arose when something else had gone wrong with the process or timing of payment, suggests that this principle was so strong that disputes were generally 'not seen as raising a legal problem worth arguing'.[11]

The consistent application of these principles meant that few people had reason to care about the bullion content of the coins they received, secure in the knowledge that others were likewise obliged to accept them. As very few had the equipment or expertise to truly ascertain the bullion content of their coins, this was just as well. Indeed, the fact that there was no need to assess its weight or purity was one of the great advantages that money had over bullion, and therefore why it carried a premium. Moreover, the legal valuation was the rate at which the Crown would accept coins in all payments due to it, ensuring that those who had taxes, rents, or other dues to the Crown were willing to accept them at that rate in payment of rents and fees owing to them, as well as in market exchanges. In all sorts of ways, it was sovereign power that made money circulate.

---

[8] Fox, 'Enforcement', pp. 209–10.
[9] Desan, *Making Money*, pp. 133–8; Fox, 'Enforcement'.
[10] Desan, *Making Money*, pp. 134–5.
[11] Fox, 'Enforcement', p. 221.

While Mayhew's contention that historians have worried much more about the bullion value of coins in this period than most contemporaries ever did is clearly correct, this does not mean that bullion was of no consequence.[12] When coins crossed borders, the sovereign authority of their issuer counted for nothing; what their bullion would fetch in the market or at the local mint became their most important attribute. And unlike most of their contemporaries, merchants engaged in foreign trade had the capacity to find this out.

Even in international transactions, however, the value of currency was significantly more complicated than any simple correspondence of bullion content to value. To begin with, although outstanding balances ultimately had to be settled with coin, it was cheaper, more convenient, and far less risky to transact business with international bills of exchange, and exchange rates were typically expressed as the prices of bills denominated in one currency in the coin of another.[13] This sometimes had to be expressed in terms of specific denominations of coins: not only did different rulers' mints price gold and silver differently (as we have seen in James's proclamations), but even within a single jurisdiction different denominations of coins of the same metal could have different proportions between their bullion and tale value.[14]

At their simplest, bills of exchange were documents instructing a third party in a foreign centre of trade to pay a given sum in a specified currency (usually the local currency) on a given future date. Thus an Edinburgh merchant who wanted to pay for a consignment of wine in Rouen would purchase in Edinburgh a bill or bills 'drawn on' a Rouen banking house to the value of the consignment in local currency. But bill transactions were often more complex than this: before it matured, a bill in one currency might be traded for bills in another rather than be exchanged immediately for coin, meaning that a greater net volume of transactions could be sustained than a simple transfer of coin would allow. The level of demand for bills in a given currency in a given place could affect their value. Such demand was driven by trade balances. Heavy demand for, say, wine for export to Scotland that was not balanced by demand for Scottish goods would create a demand for Continental bills in Edinburgh, sending them to a premium there. By the same token, foreign demand for Scottish bills would be small, meaning that they would typically be cashed at face value on maturity without any intervening transactions. If such an imbalance persisted, it could be met only by the ongoing export of bullion (often in the form of coin or melted coin, although this was illegal) from Scotland, diminishing the supply of bullion and thus of coin in Scotland, with the recessionary effects that a contraction of the money supply is bound to have. As we will see shortly, governments could attempt to counter these effects in a number of ways, all of which presented problems of their own.

---

[12] Mayhew, 'Money in England', p. 189.   [13] Lloyd, 'Investigations', p. 60.
[14] Lloyd, 'Investigations', p. 61; Einzig, *Foreign Exchange*, p. 77.

Moreover, bills of exchange were credit instruments, deferring cash payment until a future date in return for an interest payment. The amount or rate of interest of the bill was never specified. Rather, the interest payment was incorporated into the value of the bill, which would be greater than the bare exchange of coins in relation to the value of the goods being purchased would afford. While merchants were quite capable of deriving the amount of interest embedded in a bill based on calculations of the price of the commodities being purchased and the prevailing rates of exchange for coin, this way of charging interest placed another difficulty in the path of anyone attempting to calculate the relative values of currencies.[15] Indeed, it was impossible to state any single definitive exchange rate between currencies. One official inquiry into the sterling exchange rate in 1576 used different methodologies to come up with answers that varied by as much as 16 per cent, while earlier inquiries in the middle decades of the century produced still different figures.[16] Modern scholars in the field have dealt with this problem by listing different rates for different kinds of exchange, ranging from the direct exchange of coins to official rates, to the 'abstract' rates found in merchants' accounts.[17]

The balance of trade was not the only factor influencing demand for bills or coin. Not all foreign coins went straight to the melting pot or the mint. Coins that enjoyed a reputation for stable weight and purity (or 'fineness') of their bullion found wide acceptance among European merchants and could be used in a range of international transactions. The most important was the Florentine gold florin, but English silver pennies and gold 'angels' were also widely accepted.[18] Moreover, some coins circulated more generally in domestic markets outside their jurisdiction of issue. This could happen with or without the blessing of the local ruler. Typically, monarchs attempted to ban the circulation of foreign coin, preferring it to be recoined at their own mints, where seignorage could be extracted. In those cases, certain familiar foreign coins could pass at a socially accepted rate in terms of local units of account, subject to fluctuation and negotiation, and always prone to refusal. On other occasions, however, monarchs would incorporate foreign coins into their own money supply by giving them an official valuation in terms of local units, calibrated to their bullion value on much the same terms as indigenous coins. Such coins then became lawful money as surely and completely as the products of the monarch's own mint.[19]

It was through the mechanisms of international exchange—above all flows of bullion in the medium and long term—that the value of the units of account of the different countries of Europe progressively parted company from one another

---

[15] Lloyd, 'Investigations', p. 61.
[16] Einzig, *Foreign Exchange*, p. 77; Lloyd, 'Investigations', *passim*.
[17] Spufford, *Handbook*, pp. l–lii *et passim*.
[18] Mayhew, 'Economy', p. 214; Nightingale, *Enterprise*, p. 7.   [19] Fox, 'Enforcement', p. 211.

during the Middle Ages, reflecting differential reductions in the bullion content of their coins, driven by trade imbalances in a context of endemic shortage of silver and consequent increases in its price.

One of the most extreme such partings was between Scotland and England. The coinages of those two countries for centuries conformed to what was effectively a European standard based on the minting of 240 pennies from a pound weight of silver. The unification of England during the tenth century enabled King Athelstan to decree that his type of these pennies would be the only coins to be minted there. Indigenous and foreign rulers of Scotland, Ireland, and Wales also used the same standard. In the twelfth century, David I of Scotland coined pennies identical to those of his English counterparts in all but design, as did the Norse in their Irish settlements, and as had Hywel of Wales in the tenth century.[20] Such coins circulated readily throughout the British Isles and beyond, with English coin more likely to be found than any other, not only in England but everywhere else in the archipelago, amounting to what Nicholas Mayhew has described as 'a Sterling Area which extended throughout the British Isles, and also exercised very great influence in Northern Europe'.[21]

Beginning in the later fourteenth century, however, the Scots, Irish, and English authorities, in common with others in Europe, began to reduce the silver content of their pennies, either by making them lighter or by adding base metals, or both. While this process has sometimes been presented by English writers as a Scottish and Irish departure from an English standard, it is far better understood as part of the systemic breakdown of currency standards, caught between the scissor blades of an expanding monetary economy and the exhaustion of crucial mines.[22] England remained closer to the former standard, not because it possessed uniquely prudent or virtuous monarchs, but for more prosaic economic and political reasons. Firstly, for much of the Middle Ages England had less need to reduce the silver content of its coin because it enjoyed a very strong balance of payments owing to the enormous demand for its wool for European looms, ultimately paid for by the importation of foreign coin. Secondly, and of great future import, English officials had stumbled across a way of using government debt to economize on the use of coin through the use of wooden tallies.[23]

Originally used to record payments to the government, tally sticks began to be issued as credit instruments by the government as early as the twelfth century, signifying claims by the holder on revenues that had yet to arrive at the Exchequer. This practice expanded rapidly in the later fourteenth century, and, although the picture is unclear, there is 'cumulatively persuasive' evidence that the tallies

[20] Chart, *Economic History*, p. 151; Jack, *Medieval Wales*, pp. 198–9.
[21] Mayhew, 'Money in Scotland', p. 90; Allen, 'Sterling Area', develops the concept further.
[22] Spufford, *Medieval*, pp. 339–62.
[23] Mayhew, 'Economy', p. 216. For a description of how tallies worked, and of the early growth of markets in tallies, see Steel, *Receipt*, pp. xxx, xxxiv, xxxvi, 364.

circulated as currency, principally among 'those who moved in the court's radius, including... government officials, royal lenders, soldiers, and others performing services to the crown, public creditors from large suppliers to small vendors'.[24]

Finally, as Desan has argued in detail, English monarchs during the fourteenth century reached a unique political settlement with the elite which 'paired strong money with regular and significant taxation', reflecting 'an alliance between landholders and the Crown and an allocation of authorities between them' in which the Crown exercised its unquestioned prerogative over the coinage so as to ensure infrequent and relatively modest reductions in the weight of the coin, and even rarer changes to its fineness.[25] This suited landlords, whose rents in money terms were typically fixed for long periods. As Spufford notes, unlike most of their European counterparts, 'the English landlord... could expect to receive the same rents [in bullion terms] for the same lands as his father and grandfather had done. If his rents fell, it was not because he received them in debased coin.'[26] For as long as the elite sitting in Parliament were willing to grant adequate taxes—which they ensured bore heavily on the lower orders—this arrangement also suited the monarch.[27]

More than many of their counterparts, English monarchs' military expenses were for the most part incurred and paid overseas, where the benefits of a 'strong' currency were at their greatest, as was a high bullion content in the coin received as taxes. Thus, for example, it was because of the high bullion content of his coin that Edward I did not have to raise even more than £750,000 in taxation in 1294–7 in order to provide £550,000 to his allies.[28] Finally, those involved in international trade also valued a coinage that travelled well, for reasons we have already considered. We will have reason to note this confluence of interests between government, landlords, and the most internationally oriented sections of the capitalist class many times in later chapters.[29]

Scotland, by contrast, with its persistent balance of payments deficits, experienced the silver shortage more acutely than many other countries, and much more acutely than England.[30] Under this pressure, and with nothing resembling the English political settlement, Scottish monarchs reduced the silver content of their coin more sharply than most other European princes, and far more sharply than the English.[31] In 1373 the English legislated an official exchange rate between

---

[24] Desan, *Making Money*, pp. 81, 85–6, 153.
[25] Desan, *Making Money*, p. 153; Spufford, *Medieval*, p. 317.   [26] Spufford, *Medieval*, p. 318.
[27] Desan, *Making Money*, p. 158. Maddicott, *Demands*, p. 52.   [28] Bolton, *Medieval*, p. 159.
[29] This confluence corresponds to the later formation that Cain and Hopkins call 'gentlemanly capitalism'; *British Imperialism*, vol. 1, esp. ch. 1.
[30] Grant, *Independence*, pp. 80–1. Gibson and Smout, *Prices*, p. 5.
[31] See Spufford et al., *Handbook*, pp. ix, 211–12. These tables show that from parity in the early fourteenth century, the Scottish currency's value against sterling decreased by a factor of 3.5 by 1500. This represented a decline against the Florentine florin by a factor of 5.9. This was a greater decline than all but three of the twelve major currencies Spufford lists. Sterling declined against the florin by 1.7—the smallest decline in the list.

Scots and English pennies of 4:3—a significant undervaluation of the Scottish coins, which eventually required weekly proclamations by English sheriffs against taking them at any higher rate.[32] Once again, despite the prerogative powers of the Crown, bullion content still mattered when coins crossed borders, especially when they might easily cross back.

This undervaluation was temporary. Continued reduction in the precious metal content of Scottish coins, the intermittent overproduction of silver alloy ('billon money') and base metal coins ('black money') led to further devaluations in terms of the units of account over the following two centuries, resulting in an exchange rate of 6:1 by the accession of James VI in 1567.[33] Within another four decades the exchange had halved again, culminating in the proclaimed rate of 12:1 we have seen at the regal union.[34] The cause of this rapid change was an almost continuous policy of devaluation intended to yield a rich stream of revenue from the mint, which from 1573 'became firmly harnessed to the government's fiscal policy', just as the English mint had been forced to serve Henry VIII's fiscal needs in Ireland and England during the 1530s and 1540s.[35] Between 1579 and 1604, the Edinburgh mint yielded approximately £293,000 for the Crown, dwarfing the sums received from that source at any earlier time.[36] In Scotland the means used to extract these sums were usually coercive. Existing coin was frequently demonetized, leaving people with little choice but to take it to the mint, where it was restamped or reminted into coin of a higher tale value. On one occasion, people who did not comply were threatened with outright confiscation of the demonetized coin.[37]

The effects of this naked use of monetary power were not wholly negative for Scots. The low-value, readily available, small denominations provided an official means of making small payments that was chronically lacking in England and Ireland, where the high value of the penny made it almost useless for most everyday transactions. Roughly equal to a day's wage for an unskilled labourer in the late thirteenth century, the English penny left such workers in the position of a UK worker on the minimum wage in 2022 if she were to be paid each day with a £76 note and nobody was able to give change when she needed a loaf of bread or a bottle of dishwashing liquid. Even the widespread practice of cutting pennies into halves and quarters provided only a partial solution when ale sold for four cups per farthing and a penny bought between four and eight pounds of bread.[38] More helpful was the circulation of some of the small Scottish coins, which were officially tolerated.[39]

---

[32] Einzig, *Foreign Exchange*, p. 105; Gemmill and Mayhew, *Changing Values*, p. 117.
[33] Gemmill and Mayhew, *Changing Values*, pp. 123–8, 138–9.
[34] Gilbert, 'Usual Money', p. 142.   [35] Challis, 'Debasement', p. 190.
[36] Challis, 'Debasement', pp. 186, 190.   [37] Challis, 'Debasement', p. 192.
[38] Desan, *Making Money*, p. 193.   [39] Dyer, *Making a Living*, p. 219.

This problem became more severe in England from the fourteenth century, with the introduction of larger denominations of silver coins, and, crucially, the regular minting of gold coins from the 1340s. As well as being more convenient and lucrative for the mint, high-denomination coins were especially useful for those who needed money for international trade, high-value domestic trade, and large payments to and from the government.[40] Accordingly, as a result of deliberate policy, the minting of gold massively outstripped that of silver for the remainder of the era of bullion coin.[41] Combined with the endemic shortages of bullion that characterized late medieval Europe, monetary policy and minting practice left most people in England chronically short of means of payment for the small transactions of everyday life. This problem would persist throughout the three kingdoms—in differing forms and degrees—until the nineteenth century.

Shortages of coin, especially small coin, required people in all three kingdoms to make extensive use of credit or to make payments in kind—usually, although not always, calculated in terms of the monetary value of the goods or services exchanged. Thus wages might be paid in goods of a specified monetary value instead of, or as well as, coin. To give one example, in the early seventeenth century labourers in Fife—a relatively monetized part of Scotland—had their recompense calculated in money, but this was often reduced by half if food was provided during the work. Even the remaining monetary sums were likely to be paid largely or even wholly in oats, fuel, or other commodities.[42]

Credit sustained networks of commercial exchange far larger and more complex than the available coin could have allowed. While historians are now generally agreed that obligations expressed in monetary terms typically required ultimate settlement in coin, such settlement could be long deferred and represent only a tiny proportion of the money values represented by the transactions.[43] Thus, for example, in 1514 John Heritage, a Gloucestershire wool merchant, 'sat down with William Mansell and reviewed their various exchanges probably over a number of years, and reached the conclusion that Heritage should pay Mansell 20s'. Sometimes the use of cash could be reduced even further: 'when Thomas Palmer reckoned with Heritage in 1507, part of Heritage's payment to Palmer consisted of 3 loads of peas and 4 sacks of oats, and in 1509 it was concluded that Palmer could put his lamb flock onto Heritage's summer pasture, four cows were allowed to graze at Coldicote in Moreton, and a colt was put onto a winter pasture, all of which were substituted for money owed to Palmer'.[44]

---

[40] Postan, *Medieval Agriculture*, p. 9, follows Marc Bloch in holding that gold was reserved for international trade. There is plenty of evidence to support the intuitive idea that it was also used for domestic transactions of high value. See, for example, Nightingale, 'Gold', p. 1085.

[41] Mayhew, 'Wages and Currency', pp. 214–17; Challis, *Mint*, pp. 684–94. Nightingale, 'Gold', p. 1082.

[42] Gibson and Smout, *Prices*, pp. 265, 278.

[43] Mayhew, 'Money and Economy', pp. 203–15; Briggs, *Credit*, pp. 200, 211.

[44] Dyer, *Country Merchant*, p. 98.

Despite the widespread use of such expedients, the fact that payment could legally be demanded in money for debts expressed in monetary terms meant that the availability of coin directly affected the availability of credit. Rather than, as some historians have argued, credit expanding to fill the void when coin was most scarce, it now appears that people became less willing to give credit when they feared that their prospective debtor might have no means to repay.[45] Often having monetary obligations of their own, creditors in these circumstances demanded repayment more urgently, with potentially devastating consequences for their debtors. As Desan shows, those with least access to coin paid most dearly for these risks: not only did debtors lose most actions for recovery and have to pay the attendant fees and penalties as well as the loan, but scarcity of money had a general deflationary effect which made the money they repaid more valuable than the money they had borrowed. Finally, the need to repay could be ruinous—requiring the sale of livestock or land in bad market conditions. Far from being a panacea for the shortage of coin for everyday life, credit, being most constrained when coin was hardest to find, largely reproduced or even amplified the social effects of England's peculiar monetary order.[46]

Such problems were less prominent in Scotland and Ireland than in England, largely because their market economies were less developed. Both also suffered from chronic scarcity of coin. This was especially severe in Ireland, where English dominion—although often patchy and contested—made the pursuit of monetary policy to suit Irish needs impossible in all but exceptional circumstances. Indeed, the relationship between English and Irish currency maps so precisely to the contours of the ongoing struggles over sovereign power between English, indigenous, and settler forces that it serves as a case study of the point that money and sovereign power are inseparable.

Following the Hiberno-Norse coinage in the late tenth and early eleventh centuries, virtually all Irish coins between the 1180s and the 1920s were struck by English rulers in a form and to a value that was (as we shall see) usually more conducive to their own political and economic interests than to those of the people of Ireland. Unlike the Danes, the Normans—having a far more ambitious programme of conquest and settlement—made the coinage a central tool of government: 'Their sheriffs exacted money fines from delinquents, the royal taxation was collected by assessments made in money, customs charges were payable in money, a great financial department, the Exchequer, came into being, keeping its accounts in pounds, shillings and pence.'[47]

---

[45] See Bolton, 'Crisis of Credit?'; Nightingale, 'Crisis?'; Bolton, 'Reply'. The consensus among specialists now appears to rest with Nightingale's position. Desan, *Making Money*, pp. 205–29, takes this view in her discussion of the 'social stratigraphy' of credit in the peculiar English monetary context. Muldrew, *Obligation*, provides a thorough account of the use of credit in King's Lynn 1550–1700, based heavily on actions for recovery of debt occasioned by shortages of coin.
[46] Desan, *Making Money*, pp. 227–8.   [47] Chart, *Economic History*, p. 152.

First minted by Henry II's son John, in his capacity as Lord of Ireland, Irish coins were of the same standard as English until 1460. The main purposes of minting in Ireland, rather than exporting coin from the London mint, were the straightforward ones of making a profit for the Crown and extracting Irish silver to fund the military and diplomatic ventures of English kings.[48] Apart from the designs, the only difference was that round halfpence and farthings were minted in Ireland between the twelfth and fourteenth centuries, whereas the English had to make do, until 1279–80, by cutting pennies into halves and quarters.[49] In 1460, the Drogheda parliament, exploiting the chaotic state of English rule resulting from the beginning of the Wars of the Roses, asserted Irish independence under the (Yorkist) Crown in a number of ways, not least by initiating a separate coinage containing only three-quarters as much silver as English coins.[50] In doing so they acted in their own interest, attempting to remedy a particularly severe local instance of the chronic late medieval shortage of silver coin, which had been aggravated by the continuing depredations of the English Crown. Reflecting the uncertainty of the dynastic struggle in England, these coins bore neither the name nor the portrait of the king.

Despite strenuous efforts by successive English kings to bring the Irish mints back under control, and Irish coins back to the English standard, the parity, once lost, proved impossible to restore.[51] By the reign of Henry VII the tables were turned. Henry, determined to keep light Irish coin out of England, oversaw—or at least allowed—the minting in Ireland of coin of such poor quality that the Anglo-Irish soon began to ask for good quality Irish coin—although lighter and smaller than the English—to be minted at the Tower in London if necessary.[52] After a prolonged three-way struggle between the interests of the Anglo-Irish, the Crown, and more or less venal moneyers operating under only tenuous regal control, the matter ended with victory for the Crown. After reasserting English control over the Irish administration under the Lord Deputy, Sir Edward Poynings, in 1494–6, Henry at first compromised with Anglo-Irish interests by minting coins of the three-quarter weight standard proclaimed by the Drogheda parliament, but readily distinguished from English issues by the shoddiness of their workmanship. By the end of his reign he had closed the mint altogether and ceased any separate issue for Ireland.[53] The pounds, shillings, and pence of Irish account remained for the time being at three-quarters of their English counterparts, consistent with the Irish Act of 1460. When the first English shillings (or testoons) were minted in 1504, they therefore circulated at 12d. in England but 16d. in Ireland.

---

[48] Ellis, 'Struggle', p. 17; Dolley, 'Coinage to 1534', p. 819.
[49] A few English round halfpence were minted in the reign of Henry I (1100–35).
[50] Ellis, 'Struggle', pp. 19–20.   [51] McDowell, 'Devaluation'.
[52] Ellis, 'Struggle', pp. 30–3.   [53] Dolley, 'Coinage to 1534', p. 825.

The closure of the Irish mint was one precondition for Henry VIII's massive debasement of the Irish coinage from 1534 onwards. Ten years before commencing his somewhat milder debasement of the English currency, Henry began, in a separate establishment within the Tower, a process that would see the silver content of Irish coins fall to not much more than a quarter of that of a sterling silver coin of the same weight by 1546. The purpose of the debasement was one that would recur: a straitened treasury needed to find the money to pay the troops necessary for the suppression of an Irish revolt. In the case of the Geraldine revolt of 1534–6, the sum required was £40,000.[54] Ironically, this act of English suppression and exploitation was accompanied by a major contribution to the symbology of Irish nationalism, when Henry chose to put a crowned harp on the reverse of the coins.[55]

While the Irish debasement might be seen as a dummy run for the debasement of the English coinage after 1544, there were some crucial differences.[56] The English currency was never as debased as the Irish: at the nadir of both debasements the 3:4 ratio of the 1460 coinage reasserted itself, although this time via a difference in purity rather than weight. More importantly, Irish monetary policy during the reigns of Henry's children abundantly reiterated Ireland's status as a subordinate colony, despite Henry VIII's elevation of the Lordship to a Kingdom in 1541—a change duly proclaimed on the coins themselves. Both Mary I and Edward VI made attempts to restore the English currency to its previous value, and even attempted some improvements in the Irish currency, but the latter were repeatedly abandoned in order to meet English priorities. In 1552 and 1554, large quantities of English base coin were dumped in Ireland, the first time as Edward's government offloaded pennies that had become surplus to English requirements, the second time as Mary conserved bullion for English purposes.[57]

But it was Elizabeth's reign that most clearly showed that the Crown's Irish monetary policy was not simply subordinate to English needs but could be used actively as an instrument in Ireland's subjugation. Rightly credited with restoring the English silver coin to its former purity, Elizabeth made a gesture in that direction towards Ireland in the third year of her reign with a small issue of distinctive Irish coins of close-to-sterling fineness. This made little impression, and until 1601 there was no distinctive Irish money. To the existing cacophony of old English and Irish coins of varying values and qualities were added the old, debased English coins (which, having been demonetized in England to allow for the reintroduction of a sterling standard, were introduced in Ireland at their bullion value) and current English coins still rated at 4:3 in terms of Irish units of account. A report of December 1600 shows the cumulative effects of a century

---

[54] Pawlisch, *Davies*, p. 145.   [55] Pawlisch, *Davies*, p. 145.
[56] Dolley, 'Irish Coinage', p. 409.   [57] Dolley, 'Irish Coinage', p. 412.

of exploitation, neglect, shoddy expedients, half-hearted reforms, and outright malpractice by the Irish state's English rulers:

> The coins now current in Ireland besides the English standard. First, the base coins are of most esteem, for that they contain more silver by at least 12d. in the pound, than the value they go for, viz.:– The teston coined at 12d., and now current for 4d. sterling. The white groat coined at 4d., and now current three at 4d. sterling. The red-harp coined at 4d., and now current at 1d. sterling. Dominic groats, Galway pence, and other like ancient coins. They be not so much embased as the other, and are better than their common value. But they are not greatly material, for there is small use of them, but in Connaught only, and there the store of them is not great. The harp shilling coined for 12d. goeth for 9d. sterling, and is of the English standard. But the Spanish gold and silver is the coin that most aboundeth, and is chiefest reckoned on in that realm, specially in Connaught and Munster.[58]

By the time of this report, the Anglo-Irish Nine Years War (1594–1603)—easily the most expensive military venture of Elizabeth's reign[59]—was at a crisis. Concerned that Hugh O'Neill was using the English sterling coin to purchase weapons abroad, and desperate for money to pay the troops she needed to defeat him, Elizabeth attempted in 1601 to withdraw sterling from Ireland and flood the country with so-called 'mix'd money' as debased as the worst of her father's reign. Perhaps to pre-empt this move, O'Neill, who had earlier sought papal authority to 'be made King of Ireland, and to have authority to coin money', proclaimed that Spanish money would be accepted in the territories he controlled on pain of death.[60] Acceptance of the queen's new money was also forced: it was a criminal offence to refuse it by tale, or to discriminate in favour of sterling. Even in an age of absolutism, however, the state could not simply make it so if people saw only serious financial loss in accepting the coin by tale. A series of edicts aimed at withdrawing the sterling money from circulation and moving it to England failed in their aim but succeeded in inflating prices and all but stopping the import of goods, giving rise to severe shortages, and disturbances and revolts among otherwise loyal subjects in Dublin and other places during the last months of Elizabeth's reign.[61]

---

[58] 'The coins now current in Ireland besides the English standard', [Dec.] 1600, TNA, SP 63/207/6 f. 321.
[59] Pawlisch, *Davies*, p. 144, gives a figure of £1,845,696, compared with the £1,419,16 spent in the Low Countries in 1585–1603.
[60] Burgh to Cecil, 10 Sept. 1597, TNA, SPI 63/200 f. 302; F. King to Sir George Carey, 2 April 1601, TNA, SP 63/208/2 f. 0003; 'James Tobin's advertisements', [December] 1598, TNA, SP 63/202/4 f. 99.
[61] Pawlisch, *Davies*, pp. 148–51; Simon, *Irish Coins*, pp. 39–41.

Uniting the Nations: Regal, Political and Monetary Unions

In March 1603, James VI and I thus found himself ruler of three quite divergent monetary realms. His ways of dealing with them reflect those differences, but also, more broadly, the differences between their political and social systems, as well as the different contours of their historical relationships. In Ireland, his immediate aim was to conciliate discontented supporters and contain recently defeated rebels in what was to remain a tributary kingdom—at least for the time being. In England and Scotland, his aim was no less than to bring about a complete political union. We shall begin by considering the latter project.

James's proclamation of 1603 concerning the values of Scottish coins in England was, as we have seen, no more than an expedient to solve a passing problem. It was also entirely in keeping with centuries of monetary practice. The periodic disappearance of usable indigenous coin led to the widespread use of exotic coins in every jurisdiction. Monarchs periodically decreed these coins' value in terms of their own units of account—partly to facilitate everyday exchange, sometimes to try to manipulate the flow of coins across borders, and always to ensure that it was possible to collect taxes. While the state was often willing to accept exotic coins as payment, it was obviously necessary to be clear about the terms on which it would do so.

More than its practical content, the rhetoric of the proclamation's preamble made James's attitude and agenda clear when it claimed that 'the realms of England and Scotland are amongst others by the providence of God Almighty, & lawfull right of descent united and incorporated together under the Imperiall Crown of the high and mightie Prince James'.[62] Coming fifteen days after the Union of the Crowns, this reference to a single 'imperial' Crown is James's earliest public claim that the regal union represented something more than a mere dynastic acquisition. His first English coins gave a small sign of things to come. Before the end of 1603, as befitted a new monarch, James had issued a new series of coins for England. These were identical to their predecessors in both weight and fineness, but significantly different in design. The coins featured the traditional bust of the monarch on the obverse, and the royal coat of arms on the reverse, with the latter incorporating the arms of Scotland and Ireland for the first time. The obverse of the sovereign and half-sovereign bore the circumscription 'EXURGAT DEUS DISSIPENTUR INIMICI' ('Let God arise and let his enemies be scattered')[63]—a legend familiar on Scottish coins for over a century, but entirely novel on English coins. Equally telling, the mint mark of all the coins was a thistle,

---

[62] [James I,] *A proclamation declaring at what values certaine moneys of Scotland shal be currant within England* (London, 8 April 1604).

[63] Psalm 68:1. Images of James's coins held in the British Museum can be viewed at https://www.britishmuseum.org/collection/search?keyword=coin&agent=James%20I,%20King%20of%20England%20%28James%20VI%20of%20Scotland%29&view=grid&sort=object_name__asc&page=1.

imposing a practice of the Edinburgh mint on that of England. The reverse of the gold crown and half-crown bore the legend 'TUEATUR UNITA DEUS' ('May God guard these united [Kingdoms]').

James's first English coins thus articulated the key issues of the early part of his English reign. On the one hand the new king was determined to turn the regal union into something much deeper and wider. On the other hand, his way of approaching the question gave English politicians good reason to fear that to let him have his way would be to acquiesce to a Scottish takeover.[64]

By the latter part of 1604 it was clear that James was going to have a major struggle on his hands to achieve anything like the political union he desired.[65] Frustrated at every turn in his desire to procure legislation to promote political or economic union, James had little choice but to fall back on areas where he could exercise his prerogative powers. Coinage was clearly one such. As James himself proclaimed, 'nothing is more appropriate to the Soveraigne dignity of Princes then the ordering of their Moneys'.[66]

James's mandate for such a claim had been powerfully reinforced a few months earlier in the case of Brett of Drogheda, when the Privy Council found that contracts made before the introduction of the Irish 'mixed' money could be paid only with that money for as long as it remained the current money of Ireland. Brett had concluded a contract with Gilbert, a London grocer, which obliged him to pay £100 'sterling, current and lawful money of England' in Dublin.[67] The contract was agreed in April 1601, the month before Elizabeth decreed the currency of the 'mixed money', and the debt fell due before James's reforms of the Irish currency began. Naturally, Brett sought to pay in mixed money, while Gilbert demanded English coin. Crucially, the case determined that money derived its value from the prerogative of the Prince alone, regardless of its intrinsic value.[68] Relying on a selective reading of leading European civil law authorities, as well as existing English case law and established constitutional principles of the royal prerogative, the case for the first time provided 'an explanation of the substantive reasons why monetary obligations should be enforced on a nominal basis'.[69] Bizarrely, the Privy Council also found that the phrase 'current and lawful money of England' applied to Irish money, not only because Irish money was minted in England but also because 'this the king's land of Ireland is a member appendant, and rightfully belongeth to the imperial crown of the realm of England, and united unto the same'.[70] This did not, however, make the currencies interchangeable. Elizabeth's decree demonetizing English coins circulating in Ireland made it positively unlawful for Brett to pay Gilbert in English coins.

---

[64] Galloway, *Union.*, esp. ch. 1; Cuddy, 'Anglo-Scottish Union'.
[65] Wormald, 'Brave New World', pp. 24–5, 29–32.
[66] [James I,] *A Proclamation for Coynes* (London, 16 Nov. 1604).
[67] Davies, *Cases*, pp. 48–9. The reasoning in Davies's *Report* is analysed fully in Fox, 'Mixt Money'.
[68] Davies, *Cases*, pp. 55–7.   [69] Fox, 'Mixt Money', p. 225.   [70] Davies, *Cases*, pp. 72, 69.

Armed by an Irish case with the strongest possible statement of his monetary power in each of his kingdoms, James made the fullest use of it in his scheme for Anglo-Scottish union. In November 1604 he decreed the replacement of the two countries' respective currencies with a single coinage based around a gold coin worth 20s. sterling to be known as the 'unite'. The coins themselves carried a weight of propaganda far heavier than any regular coins of either kingdom before or since. Earlier coins had done little more than proclaim the monarch's existence and divine authority; these coins articulated a political programme, and an unpopular one at that. Pictorially conventional, the coins presented a range of slogans justifying union. The unite itself proclaimed James's determination with 'FACIAM EOS IN GENTEM UNAM', which can be translated as either 'I will make them one nation' or 'I will make them one people'. Like many numismatic circumscriptions, this was biblical, and the passage from which it is drawn imparts a significance that would have been understood by any educated person: 'I will make them one nation in the land upon the mountains of Israel; and one king shall be king unto them all: and they shall be no more two nations, neither shall they be divided into two Kingdoms any more at all.'[71] The half-unite expressed James's project as historical destiny: 'HENRICUS ROSAS REGNA IACOBUS' ('[As] Henry the roses, [so] James the Kingdoms') connected James's succession to the English throne with Henry VII's ending of the Wars of the Roses by uniting through marriage the houses of York and Lancaster—a marriage which had also produced James's great-grandmother, Margaret Tudor, whose own marriage to James IV of Scotland had in turn made possible the Union of the Crowns in James's own person. The notion that the union itself was a marriage was promoted on the reverse of the silver crown with 'QUÆ DEUS CONIUNIXIT NEMO SEPARET' ('What God hath joined together let no man put asunder').[72] While these slogans could be seen as harmlessly aspirational or even fanciful, the obverse of almost all of the coins contained a direct negation of the will of the English Parliament. James's first English coins described him as King of England, Scotland, France, and Ireland. Yet despite Parliament's earlier defeat of James's proposal to rename the newly united kingdoms as 'Great Britain', King of Great Britain was the title he took both on the unite coins and in the proclamations that heralded them.[73]

While the coins were intended to circulate on identical terms throughout the two kingdoms, the proclamations introducing them were strikingly different in Scotland and England, perhaps reflecting James's perception of contrasting attitudes to his union project in the two countries. The English proclamation, after affirming James's prerogative in the matter of coinage, proceeded to narrate the

---

[71] Ezekiel 37:22.   [72] Matthew 19:6.   [73] Galloway, *Union*, pp. 20–2.

inconveniences stemming from separate currencies and the problems arising from the idiosyncratic valuation of English gold and silver coins, which had led to a large quantity of the undervalued English gold coins being exported despite heavy penalties.[74] A wholesale reform was thus justified. The Scottish decree took a completely different tack. While it referred to the commercial expediency of a common coinage, it placed the reform in a far more ambitious framework, asserting it to be 'not only necessar preparation for the union of the saids Kingdomes, bot ane essentiall pairt of the samen'—a suggestion conspicuously lacking from the English proclamation.[75]

James's project for a complete union of England and Scotland lay in ruins by the beginning of 1608.[76] Despite this, when the second issue of the unite coinage appeared in 1610, it made only the most trifling distinctions between coins minted in Edinburgh and London. The coat of arms, for example, included the English or Scottish arms in either one quarter or two as appropriate. Nor did it matter that most of the coins went by different names in each kingdom, reflecting the 12:1 exchange rate between their units of account that was now consistently reflected in the uniform coinage. Given that coins in this period almost never stated their denomination (in order to allow for the possibility that their value might change) it was of little importance that the same coin was called a crown in England and sixty shillings in Scotland.

While there is no evidence that James sought to include Ireland in a political union, he appears to have initiated an abortive attempt to incorporate it into the monetary union. In 1603, he took the highly unusual step of introducing sterling silver coins to Ireland while proclaiming that they were only 75 per cent pure.[77] Coins of that standard would have accurately reflected the established 3:4 exchange rate between the countries, but, in the absence of any definite evidence of the governments' reasoning, the decision to understate their value only makes sense in the context of a plan to assimilate the two currencies. With such coins circulating, it would not have been difficult to do away with the exchange rate by revealing their true value and crying them up from 9d. to 12d. sterling. It did not work out that way, perhaps because it cannot have taken long for clippers and counterfeiters to discover the true standard of the silver, at which point the inducement to melt them would have been clear. The true value of the Irish silver coins was never revealed, only being discovered by numismatic scholars in the

---

[74] [James I,] *A Proclamation for Coynes* (London, 16 Nov. 1604); Lipson, *Economic History*, pp. 531–3.
[75] SPC, *Proclamation of the new Coinage* (Edinburgh, 15 Nov. 1604), RCS 1, p. 210.
[76] Cuddy, 'Anglo-Scottish Union', p. 116.
[77] Dolley, 'Irish Coinage', p. 414. Dolley suggests that the misvaluation of the coins was part of an elaborate preparation for the withdrawal of the mixed money. This would, of course, have been a necessary precondition of any assimilation of the currencies.

1970s.[78] In May 1607 James stopped minting separate coins for Ireland, and decreed that English coin was legal tender in Ireland at the now-traditional rate of 4:3 in terms of Irish units of account.

Alone of James's schemes for union, the union of the English and Scottish currencies survived to the end of his reign, and even some way into the next, but it could not survive the opening stages of the turmoil of the middle of the century. By the time the monarchy was restored in 1660, the English, Scottish, and Irish currencies were no more unified than they had been under Elizabeth. As early as 1609, the Edinburgh mint—perhaps unilaterally—had begun to fiddle with the designs in small ways to make the Scottish coins more distinctive.[79] But the first significant step away from union was initiated by Charles I on his accession. While continuing with 'FACIAM EOS IN GENTEM UNAM' ('I will make them one nation') on the unites minted in Scotland, he chose to change the circumscription on the English unite to 'FLORENT CONCORDIA REGNA' ('United kingdoms flourish'). This could, of course, refer just as easily to unity within kingdoms as between them, presaging many of Charles's later difficulties. Indeed, of the many new legends introduced on his English coins, most suggest a preoccupation with some of the tragically intractable problems of Charles's reign: the relationship between prince and people, and the nature of the prince's claim to authority. 'AMOR POPULI PRAESIUM REGIS' ('The love of the people is the King's protection'), 'JUSTITIA THRONUM FIRMAT' ('Justice strengthens the throne'), and 'CHRISTO AUSPICE REGNO' ('I reign under the auspices of Christ') were all new. Apart from 'ROSA SINE SPINA' ('A rose without a thorn'), there was only one legend from his father's coinage that Charles appears to have found relevant. Last seen on James's short-lived English issue of 1603, 'EXURGAT DEUS DISSIPENTUR INIMICI' ('Let God arise and his enemies be scattered') reappeared on coins minted in Bristol during the first year of the English Civil War.

If nothing else, Charles's early willingness to vary the legends on the 'flagship' coin of the series shows that effecting a total union of the currencies simply was not the priority it had been for his father. By the time of his second Scottish issue of gold coins in 1637, his distance from the union project was clear, reflecting not only the complete desuetude of James's precious scheme but the growing difficulty Charles was having in merely keeping control of his northern kingdom. The unite in this issue bore a legend that had nothing to do with unity. 'HIS PRÆSUM UT PROSIM' ('I am set over them, that I may be profitable to them') was a boast about the active role Charles had played in reforming the Scottish currency by calling in and recoining the overvalued foreign coin which had effectively replaced the domestic coin by the time he ascended the throne.[80] But this reform itself appears to have provided a basis for Charles to reintroduce the uniquely Scottish half-merk coin in 1636. With a value of 80*d*. Scots, the half-merk was awkward in

---

[78] Dolley, 'Irish Coinage', p. 414. [79] Craig, *Mint*, p. 136.
[80] The relevant proclamations can be found in *RCS* 1, pp. 48–54.

English terms (6⅔d.). Along with the similarly untranslatable 40d. and 20d. coins of the same issue, these coins were obviously not minted with English circulation in mind, making them the first such coins to be produced since the Union of the Crowns. As if to emphasize the point, Charles on these coins was described as King of Scotland, England, France, and Ireland, while continuing as King of Great Britain, France, and Ireland on the sixty-, thirty-, twelve-, and six-shilling coins, which conveniently translated to the corresponding number of English pence. Even when, in 1642, the minting of half-merk, 40d., and 20d. coins was ordered to cease, all new coins specified Scotland and England rather than Britain in the king's titles.

While the first attempt at Anglo-Scottish monetary union was thus slowly dissolving, Anglo-Irish monetary relations were converging—albeit temporarily. In 1637, Charles ordered that all 'the accompts, receipt, payments and issues of his majesties moneys' in Ireland would henceforth be calculated in sterling rather than the Irish money of account.[81] The declared purpose of this step was to protect the integrity and repute of the revenue by preventing abuses by collectors, who, it was alleged, were falsely claiming that sterling values were meant when collecting monies, and pocketing the difference when they paid the Crown in Irish units of account of three-quarters of that value. Versions of this problem would recur for centuries. At the same time, however, the proclamation provided that all monetary contracts 'shall be understood and interpreted to be English'[82]—a step hardly justified by the problem that the proclamation was ostensibly intended to solve. Had this new dispensation persisted, it would undoubtedly have led to the complete supersession of separate Irish units of account, especially as the distinct Irish coinage was also being superseded by English sterling. Anglo-Irish monetary union would thus have been completed long before Anglo-Scottish. That the former actually took place more than a century after the latter, and that it was not completed until a quarter of a century after the political union of Britain and Ireland in 1801, was thus anything but inevitable. We can only speculate about whether monetary union at this stage might have reduced the ever-widening gap between England's and Ireland's trajectories of economic development over the ensuing centuries, and what effect this might have had on their cultural differences and political relationships. Alternatively, the disparities of wealth and economic structures between the two nations in the seventeenth century may have made any such union unsustainable.

The Fracturing and Remaking of the Monetary Order

Such questions remain speculative because all manifestations of monetary union between the kingdoms were destroyed by the same fissiparous forces that

---

[81] Wentworth, 1637, reproduced in Simon, *Irish Coins*, p. 117. [82] Simon, *Irish Coins*, p. 117.

produced the wars between and within them in the middle of the seventeenth century. Indeed, the wars themselves provide yet another example of money's symbiotic relationship with the state: as their shared allegiance to their single head waned, so too did the English, Irish, and Scottish states' production and use of the common money that circulated under his authority. As multiple political crises descended to civil war, with rival claimants for political authority in each state, their respective monetary systems fractured, with multiple mints operating in England and Ireland, and no minting at all taking place in Scotland after 1642. And while pounds, shillings, and pence continued as the units of account in all three countries, the values of the Irish and English units were to part company once again.

In 1642 the English Parliament seized control of the Tower mint. Fortunately for King Charles, a new mint had been established at Aberystwyth five years earlier in order to exploit silver deposits in the Welsh mountains that had allegedly been neglected in the past.[83] This allowed Charles to continue minting after he had lost control of his capital, although the moneyers and their equipment were moved from place to place repeatedly while the war raged. Charles understandably made maximum use of the coins' propagandist possibilities. Most famously, the coins first minted at Shrewsbury in 1642 featured a scroll with Charles's declaration of the principles for which he claimed to fight, and an implicit repudiation of the most serious charges levelled against him by his opponents:

RELIG: PROT   LEG: ANGL   LIBER: PARL
[Religion: Protestant   Law: English   Liberty: Parliamentary]

Parliament continued to mint the established regal designs until 1646. In this it followed the practice of the Scots covenanters, who had taken control of the Edinburgh mint in 1639 and had encouraged (and later forced) people to bring in gold and silverware for minting, but had decided to continue to produce coins identical to the king's in every respect in order to ensure their universal acceptance.[84] In doing so, they also emphasized their own legitimacy and their allegiance to the existing constitutional order, from which the king, by implication, had deviated. The English Parliament did not introduce new designs until after the execution of the king and the declaration of a republic in 1649, when it began to produce coins that displayed an unprecedented level of chauvinism. The coins were apparently intended to circulate only in England and Ireland. Apart from the smallest silver coins, which bore no legend, coins of different denominations varied only in size and metal. The legends were—for the first time ever—in English. The obverse carried a cross of St George on a shield, with the

[83] Craig, *Mint*, p. 150.   [84] Stevenson, 'Scottish Mint', pp. 95–6.

circumscription 'THE COMMONWEALTH OF ENGLAND'. The reverse conjoined the St George shield to one bearing an uncrowned Irish harp and was circumscribed 'GOD WITH US'.

The protectorate devised a new, quasi-regal coinage, complete with a portrait of Cromwell and Latin circumscriptions, including the Orwellian 'PAX QUÆRITUR BELLO' ('Peace is sought through war'), and a blunt threat to clippers: 'HAS NISI PERITURUS MIHI ADIMAT NEMO' ('Let no one remove these [letters] from me under penalty of death'). The English legend on the copper farthing—'CHARITIE AND CHANGE'—suggests that Cromwell's administration had no more democratic notions about who the state's money was made for than had its royalist predecessors. For the vast bulk of the people who used them, 'our daily bread' would have been a more pertinent description of the coins' function. Thomas Violet, the author of the report to the council that recommended their introduction, took this view, citing 'the accommodation of all sorts of people who buy or sell small wares' as his first reason for minting farthings. As for charity, the main benefit of the farthing would be to encourage almsgiving by people who might not be 'disposed to give a [silver] penny or twopence, or to lose time in staying to change money, "whereby they might contract a noisome smell or the disease of the poor"'.[85]

The annexationist union imposed by the English Protectorate in 1654 made English coins the legal tender of all three kingdoms. In the case of the Protectorate's own coins this was largely hypothetical. Dies were made for the copper farthings, but only a few were struck, and they were never actually issued. The other 'Cromwell' coins were struck in very small quantities. Indeed, the total quantity of gold and silver minted in the eleven years from the execution of Charles I in 1649 to his son's restoration in 1660 was just over 11 per cent of the total in the previous eleven years, and all of it took place in London.[86] Few coins can have circulated in Ireland or Scotland. Those that found their way much beyond south-east England presumably did so as soldiers' wages, and as these were chronically in arrears, this can only have been a very weak vector of transmission. The Cromwellian monetary union was, if anything, even more specious than the political union that failed to underwrite it, and, as we shall see in the next chapter, just as easy to dissolve.[87]

Tudor and Stuart assertions of the absolute monetary power of the prince notwithstanding, the whole episode of the Cromwellian union demonstrates that a monetary union could not simply be called into existence by fiat in the absence of the necessary political and economic preconditions. It is perhaps conceivable that a monetary union could have withstood even the powerful

---

[85] *Reasons submitted by Thomas Violet to the Mint Committee to prove the necessity of making farthing tokens* (10 August 1651), reproduced in Boyne, *Tokens*, 1, p. xxxix.
[86] Challis, *Mint*, p. 689.   [87] Macinnes, *Union and Empire*, pp. 78–9.

centrifugal forces present at the Restoration (which we will consider in the next chapter), had the state ever been able to establish a viable unified monetary order in the first place; but the scarcity of bullion had made this impossible, even independently of the other forces at work. The structure of the trading relationships of each kingdom with the others and with the rest of the world, together with the excessive bullion content of the English silver coinage, made it impossible to prevent coin from gravitating towards England or from leaving the archipelago altogether. These were chronic problems, which made successive seventeenth-century governments largely incapable of producing sufficient coin for England, let alone Scotland and Ireland. The added difficulties presented by wars and revolutions left the Cromwellian regime even more helpless in this respect than its predecessors, ensuring that its ambitious scheme of monetary union remained a dead letter. This made the task of doing away with it extremely easy. When, in November 1661, a decree of the Scottish Privy Council banned outright the circulation of any coins minted by 'the late usurpers', and offered to exchange them at full value at the 'Minthouse which is to be instantlie set up',[88] the fact that there can only have been a handful of such coins in Scotland meant that it hardly mattered that no mint was actually established there for another two years. There was no possibility of anything corresponding to the surge in mint production in London in 1661–2, which appears to have absorbed the whole of the Cromwellian silver coinage and a good proportion of its gold, even though the mint was offering an extremely uncompetitive price for the latter.[89]

Given the length and severity of the fighting in Ireland, it is unsurprising that the monetary order there broke down more completely, and for longer, than it did in England or Scotland. The defeat of the royalist forces took longer in Ireland, giving rise to an even greater proliferation of the improvised 'monies of necessity' and siege monies which also appeared in royalist strongholds in England. Uniquely, the Lords Justices of Ireland minted a number of silver crowns and half-crowns in the name of Charles II for circulation in the territories they controlled immediately after the death of Charles I.[90] While old official coin supplemented by an increasing proportion of foreign coin continued to make up the bulk of higher denominations in circulation, the devastation caused by the wars was so complete that the market economy in most parts of Ireland had all but ceased to function after 1651, leaving minimal demand for any but the smallest coins.[91]

The gap left by the state's inability to provide small coins was filled in England and Ireland by the production of 'tradesmen's tokens' and 'town pieces'. Such tokens had been seen previously, but in the three decades following Charles I's

---

[88] SPC, *Proclamation anent the value of current Gold*, 26 Nov. 1661, RCS 2, pp. 145–6.
[89] Challis, *Mint*, pp. 689, 337–8.   [90] Yeates, 'Coinage of Ireland', pp. 217–20.
[91] Dolley, 'Irish Coinage', p. 417; Corish, 'Cromwellian Regime', p. 357.

execution they appeared on an unprecedented scale. According to the most comprehensive catalogue, no fewer than 11,942 different types of token were issued in England and Wales, and 779 in Ireland.[92] In Scotland, on the other hand, the need for small money appears to have been met by the continued circulation of the old black money and the post-union Scots copper farthings of James and Charles. In the whole country only one type of token was issued in the seventeenth century, and that appeared eight years after the restoration of the monarchy.[93]

Apart from some of the town pieces, which had government sanction, these all infringed the royal prerogatives concerning money, which had passed to the republican government. Technically, they were not money but tokens of personal credit. Almost all bore the initials and stated the business of the person or married couple who issued them, usually with the husband's name in full on the other side. Many explicitly promised that they would be redeemed on demand. In practice, however, they were accepted and circulated not on the basis of their exchangeability for non-existent official coin, but on the basis that others would accept them to effect transfers of value expressed in the official units of account. Moreover, although they mostly circulated within a small radius of their issuers' business, evidence from hoards suggests that many travelled well beyond, and presumably had currency in places where the issuer was completely unknown. In this, the English tokens were probably helped by the fact that the bullion value of the copper they contained was only slightly below their halfpenny or farthing tale value.[94] Irish tokens were physically much smaller, and many Irish penny tokens contained less copper than English farthings. This, as well as the economic ruin of the country in the 1650s and 1660s, presumably prevented their circulation outside their immediate localities.

By the 1660s, then, the monetary differences between the kingdoms were no closer to being overcome than were the differences between the monetary worlds of different strata and sectors of the population within each of them. In monetary terms, James VI and I had no more made his kingdoms 'one nation' than he had made his subjects 'one people'. As James's grandson settled on the throne his son had lost, his aspirations for monetary union moved further from realization than ever, as the coinage deteriorated still further and as the respective monetary orders of his three kingdoms each moved towards its own collapse.

---

[92] Boyne, *Tokens*, 1, p. 1429.   [93] Boyne, *Tokens*, 1, p. 953.
[94] Boyne, *Tokens*, 1, pp. xxiv–xxv.

2
The Decline of the Old Monetary Order
1660–1689

> The intrinsick value of the English coyn surpasses most nations and may very probably be ane error from their vanity.
>
> [Sir Robert Gordon] (1683)

The restoration of the monarchy in 1660 and the return of a degree of political stability did little to solve the chronic problems in the respective monetary orders of any of the three kingdoms. The odd windfall aside, supplies of bullion at the Tower mint remained close to the disastrously low levels they had plumbed throughout the 1650s.[1] The Edinburgh mint did not resume until 1664, and Ireland remained mintless and therefore dependent on trade for its supplies of coin. The resulting scarcity of money—aggravated by other factors we will consider shortly—thus remained a constantly pressing concern for parliaments and administrations in London, Dublin, and Edinburgh throughout the reign of Charles II and long afterwards.

Ongoing scarcity was symptomatic of the fact that the needs of both the state and commercial society in early modern England had long outgrown what remained in essence a medieval monetary order. And while the demands of the state and the requirements of commerce were less intense in Ireland and Scotland, their geographical proximity and close trading relationships with England, together with their shared monarchy, ensured that they would hardly be less affected by the deepening monetary crisis.

It is not merely the duration of this monetary instability but its intractability that suggests that the problem was structural. Virtually every attempt by monetary authorities to solve or alleviate monetary problems ended up aggravating them, often by increasing opportunities to turn monetary dysfunction to private advantage in the short term, while progressively surrendering the state's monetary power to private interests or impersonal 'market forces' in the long term. Eventually, as we shall see in later chapters, the ongoing, multifaceted crisis was to lead to complete transformation of the monetary order in each of the three kingdoms.

---

[1] Challis, *Mint*, pp. 312–13, 40, 42, provides figures for the London mint. Scotland's problems will be discussed below.

The prolixity of the debates provoked by the ongoing monetary crisis in England, and their importance in the development of early modern political economy, have ensured that England's monetary dilemmas have attracted a significant body of historical scholarship.[2] But Scotland's and Ireland's monetary tribulations during the period have been largely overlooked.[3] Still less has there been systematic attention given to the differences between English, Irish, and Scottish monetary experience in this period, the relationships between them, or the long-term consequences of those differences.

This chapter takes a step towards refocusing our view of the problem by examining the diverse monetary trajectories of Ireland, England, and Scotland from the immediate aftermath of the Restoration to the eve of the latter two countries' respective monetary revolutions at the end of the seventeenth century. It identifies differences that ensured not only that Ireland's transition to a modern monetary order would be later and more gradual than the revolutionary transformations experienced by Scotland and England but also that the latter kingdoms' respective revolutions were bound to differ from each other in many important respects. As we shall see in subsequent chapters, the consequences of these differences were long-lasting, not only for each individual kingdom but for the multifaceted and prolonged processes of creating a monetary union in Britain and eventually extending it throughout the United Kingdom.

1660: Restoring Difference

These divergent paths were enabled in the first instance by the crucial monetary decision taken at the Restoration to undo not only the monetary changes made by the protectorate but also many of the most significant unifying developments since the Union of the Crowns. Not only was Cromwell's monetary union of the three kingdoms reversed, but even those vestiges of monetary union between England and Scotland that had still existed before the outbreak of hostilities in 1639 were abandoned. Fifty-six years after it was begun, James VI and I's partial monetary union might as well never have happened.

The new dispensation was clearly registered on the face of the coins. Charles II's English coins, in essentials, restored the status quo ante bellum, although the name 'unite' or 'unit' was often dropped in favour of 'laurel', referring to the laurel

---

[2] Wennerlind, *Casualties*; Appleby, *Economic Thought*; Horsefield, *Experiments*; Desan, *Making Money*.

[3] Lenman, *Economic History*, pp. 22–3, notes the proliferation of payments in kind in Scotland in the Restoration period, but does not specifically discuss monetary problems or policy. Cullen, *Economic History*, pp. 30–3, briefly mentions fluctuations in the Anglo-Irish exchange, which he treats as entirely dependent on developments in the 'real' economy. Gillespie, *Irish Economy*, pp. 55–9, is almost alone in dwelling on Ireland's lack of a mint, and its monetary powerlessness, as a factor in its economic problems in this period.

wreath on the king's head on the obverse of the coin.[4] Circulation of these coins in Ireland was extremely limited for reasons we will consider shortly, and took place on the same basis as English coins had circulated before 1603: with a value or rating in terms of Irish units of account, differing from other foreign coin only in that the official rating was determined by the sovereign authority that minted it. From the Restoration, the only official coins minted specifically for Ireland were copper halfpennies and farthings.

Beginning with Charles II's first issue of 1664, Scotland saw the full restoration of a separate currency, with the pre-union denominations and distinct designs from the English coins. Like most of the coins in the last days of his father's effective control of the country, the coins of Charles II's first Scottish issue were clearly not intended to be of any particular use for easing transactions between his northern and southern kingdoms. The highest-value coin was the silver four merk piece, stamped with its value in terms of Scottish units of account, 'LIII/4' (53s. 4d.), which, at the 12:1 exchange rate, corresponded to the inconvenient English value of 4s. 5⅓d.[5] The two merk, one merk, and half-merk pieces would have been no less awkward south of the border. The copper 'turners' or 'bodles' with a value of 2d. Scots were clearly intended solely for local use. Alone of the issues of Charles II's reign, the sixpence, or 'bawbee', translated to the value of an English coin (a halfpenny), but this was hardly calculated to oil the wheels of trade.

The Scottish coins of the Restoration almost completely abandoned legends other than the simple statement of the king's titles. These once again included King of 'Great Britain', although even this gesture towards the idea of union was abandoned in 1676 with Charles's second issue, when the four merk—redesignated as the 'dollar', with the other coins designated as fractions of dollars—described Charles as King of England, Scotland, Ireland, and France.[6] The only other text to appear on any coin was 'NEMO ME IMPUNE LACESSET' ['No one shall hurt me with impunity'], on the low-denomination copper coins.[7] Although in Latin, this text would have been familiar to anyone who could read as the ancient motto of the Scottish royal house. It thus cleverly emphasized the importance of the Stuart monarchy to the preservation of Scotland's identity and dignity as a separate nation.

The drivers of this rapid monetary separation were largely political. Given the levels of distrust and hostility subsisting between England, Scotland, and Ireland on most questions in the aftermath of war and revolution, complete reversal of the monetary union was almost inevitable. The legacy of the wars for the kingdoms of the British archipelago was to obliterate whatever small signs of unity and amity

---

[4] See https://www.britishmuseum.org/collection/object/C_1935-0401-7975.
[5] See https://www.britishmuseum.org/collection/object/C_E-2757.
[6] See https://www.britishmuseum.org/collection/object/C_E-2768.
[7] See https://www.britishmuseum.org/collection/object/C_E-2784.

may have developed in the first decades of the century and to remove any appetite for closer union among the politically powerful.[8] This included the king himself, who preferred 'the freedom of action that came from ruling his three kingdoms as separate entities'.[9]

But the desire for separation also had more directly economic and monetary imperatives. Conscious that their monetary needs continued to be neglected under the Commonwealth, Scots had begun to demand the reopening of the Edinburgh mint as early as 1652, and the Scottish Privy Council appears to have begun preparations for such a reopening shortly after the Restoration.[10] For their part, English politicians were in no mind to seek closer economic integration with a kingdom they saw chiefly as a financial burden.[11]

There were additional reasons why the three kingdoms took divergent monetary paths after 1660. Most obvious was their differing rates and levels of economic development. Whatever intermittent economic growth took place in Ireland and Scotland was dwarfed by rapid growth of commerce, trade, and industry in England, especially in and around London. These differential rates of development amplified the difference in the sheer size of the three kingdoms' respective economies, reinforcing the Anglocentric monetary priorities of the crown.[12]

Although coinage remained unambiguously a royal prerogative, the Crown's monetary power was far from absolute. Apart from the constraints imposed by the perennial shortage of bullion, there were historical, economic, and political limits on how that problem could be dealt with. In England, any kind of debasement—anathema for centuries—had been rendered virtually unthinkable by the depredations of Henry VIII.

Just as importantly for this discussion, royal monetary authority was exercised differently in each kingdom. Scotland's separate coinage allowed its administration—albeit officially under royal auspices—to run a distinct monetary policy, and even its tightly managed Parliament could at times assert its monetary wishes. Moreover, the extensive powers of the Master of the Mint allowed him to run an alternative, covert monetary policy for his own personal benefit, with disastrous consequences. In Ireland, the lack of both a mint and a parliament with meaningful autonomous power in theory afforded the royal government in London much more direct monetary power through the instrument of the Lord-Lieutenant. In practice, matters were somewhat more complicated.

---

[8] Morrill, 'British Problem', pp. 35–7; Harris, 'Autonomy', p. 269.
[9] Smith, *Double Crown*, p. 210.
[10] *Anent False Coyne*, 21 Dec. 1652, RCS 2, p. 135; *Ratification in favours of the Officers of his Majesties Minthouse*, 1 Jan. 1661, RCS 2, p. 135.
[11] Ferguson, *Scotland's Relations*, p. 142; Patrick, 'Union Broken?', p. 119.
[12] Cullen, *Economic History*, pp. 13–25; Lenman, *Economic History*, pp. 23–4, 33–43; Cullen and Smout, *Comparative Aspects*, pp. 3–4.

Crises, Credit, and the Origins of Modern Money

Despite these differences, the focus of all monetary decision-making in London, Dublin, and Edinburgh revolved around the tension between maintaining an adequate supply of money on the one hand and stable values on the other. This took place in the context of wide-ranging public discussion of monetary questions. These debates were most intense in London, as the centre of political power, economic activity, and literary production. Indeed, Irish and Scots contributions to monetary debates in this period are surprisingly meagre, perhaps in tacit acknowledgement of where the most momentous decisions were likely to be made.

Carl Wennerlind has shown that a number of writers recognized that England's monetary problems were structural rather than contingent, and that any lasting solution would therefore require the development of new forms of money to add to the total stock. As early as the 1620s, members of the Hartlib Circle concluded that 'wealth was potentially infinite' and that 'expanding the money stock was therefore no longer about solving a temporary scarcity of money, but rather about the introduction of a monetary mechanism that could facilitate change and growth, ad infinitum'. Being steeped in alchemical thinking, the Hartlibians at first sought solutions in the transmutation of base metals into silver and gold.[13]

By the second half of the century, however, advocates of the need for continuous expansion of the money supply began to turn to ways of circumventing the chronic shortage of bullion through the circulation of signifiers of debt with no 'intrinsic' value. These schemes depended to varying extents upon state action. All of them required laws to help confer a degree of 'moneyness' by making the proposed credit instruments assignable: that is, to confer legal responsibility for payment on the issuer alone, rather than any intermediate holders.[14] This would not only enable people to spend them with the assurance that they would not later face legal action as a result of someone else's insolvency; it would also give the bearer a clear path of legal redress, should the issuer fail to cash the instrument according to the terms specified on its face. Such assignability underpinned the widespread acceptance indispensable to any object's status as money. More importantly, almost all schemes required or assumed that the instruments would be accepted in payments to the state.

The schemes themselves varied significantly, from John Bland's and Andrew Yarranton's suggestions that all credit instruments should be enabled to circulate by being made infinitely assignable to Samuel Lambe's scheme for a bank to create 'imaginary money' in the form of commercial credit secured by what later periods would call a 'fractional reserve' of coin, to William Potter's combination of

---

[13] Wennerlind, *Casualties*, p. 45.
[14] Desan, *Making Money*, p. 337. For a discussion of the emergence of assignability in various monetary instruments, see Richards, 'Evolution', pp. 383–7.

elements of both of those ideas, or Hugh Chamberlen's rival scheme for a bank whose credit instruments were founded on pledged goods and merchandise, to Sir William Killigrew's proposal for circulating government bonds secured by claims on future revenue.[15]

While the specifics of only a few of these schemes ever saw the light of day, currency based on circulating signifiers of debt—already foreshadowed by wooden tallies and commercial bills of exchange—evolved rapidly in the latter part of the seventeenth century and would be central to the revolutionary monetary order that came into being near the end of the century. They therefore warrant their prominent place in accounts of the intellectual origins of the modern, credit-based monetary system.

They also justify the Anglocentrism of the historiography of this topic in this period. Like the growth of circulating credit itself, proposals for its development were confined largely to England before the 1690s. In Ireland, Richard Lawrence and William Petty—leading members of the government's Council of Trade—each argued during the reign of Charles II in favour of a national land bank whose bills, in Lawrence's words, would 'become current in all places, and to all persons where, and to whom assigned', but this appears to have been the extent of such discussion.[16] In Scotland, although there was considerable debate about the coinage—much of it focussed on Scotland's relationship with England—the absence of any surviving texts suggests that Checkland's conclusion that 'Scotland seems to have had little part' in discussions of banking and credit in this period is, if anything, to overrate the Scottish contribution.[17]

For many writers, including advocates of circulating credit, the coinage remained a central preoccupation, as it did for the government. Indeed, for some, one of the major benefits of circulating credit was that it would free up coin for the king's use.[18] The reasons for this preoccupation are obvious. Coin remained the means of final settlement, and while some writers could envisage a monetary system entirely divorced from the 'intrinsic worth' of bullion coin,[19] these represented a small minority of monetary thinkers and, we may safely presume, a still smaller minority of the population at large, for whom the payment or receipt of coins remained the fundamental monetary transaction. Moreover, as credit instruments could only be made legally assignable within the king's jurisdiction, international transactions would continue to depend ultimately on bullion. This included the governments' overseas remittances, mainly for soldiers' wages and military supplies. The importance of this international dimension meant that the problem was not just the quantity of coins available but also their quality, measured by the reliability of their bullion content.

---

[15] Wennerlind, *Casualties*, pp. 96–106. Potter, *Jewel*, esp. pp. 7–8.   [16] Lawrence, *Interest*.
[17] Checkland, *Scottish Banking*, p. 13.   [18] Ford, *Experimented Proposals*, p. 5.
[19] For example, Ford, *Experimented Proposals*.

It is a measure of the intractability of the chronic monetary crisis that the government's adoption of an entirely uncontroversial innovation to solve the quality problem immediately made the quantity problem worse. As a result of the permanent adoption in the English mint of Pierre Blondeau's machinery for pressing coins with the mill, coins minted after 1662 were much more even in weight and thickness, more consistent in appearance, and therefore more difficult to counterfeit than older coins. Above all, their edges were engraved so as to make any clipping or filing immediately obvious.[20] These improvements ensured that the bullion content of the new coins was far more uniform than previously. Paradoxically, however, this made them more vulnerable to fluctuations in the absolute and relative market values of silver and gold. If the market price of silver rose, the bullion value of the coin would rise with it. If it rose too much, the bullion value of the silver coinage would become greater than its face value, thus providing an incentive to melt the coin to realize the price of its metal, either in 'legitimate' markets or to networks of counterfeiters, who would use it in their trade.[21]

This problem had previously been alleviated by clippers, who diminished the weight of the coins so that their bullion value remained well below their tale value, thus removing the incentive to melt them. The counterfeiters' work in using the clipped metal relieved the domestic shortage by augmenting the money supply with coins that were inherently unsuitable for foreign transactions and so unlikely to be exported. Domestic transactions could therefore continue for as long as the state and the people were willing to accept clipped coins and counterfeits as signifiers of the same abstract value as their scarce, unclipped, authentic counterparts.

Given that silver was undervalued at the mint, the consequences of the new perfection of minting for the Restoration coinage were immediate and dramatic. The new English silver coins, being undervalued in relation not only to gold coins but also to the price of silver bullion in foreign markets, remained in a gratifyingly pristine state as they made their short way from the mint to the crucible and thence abroad, or disappeared into hoards. In 1695, despite more than thirty years' steady production of the milled coins, the Secretary to the Treasury, William Lowndes, could observe that the coins of Elizabeth and her two immediate successors 'make up the bulk of our present cash'.[22] And while the new coins were far harder to counterfeit, the prevalence of the old, hammered money meant that counterfeiters simply imitated that, even down to the clipped edges.[23]

The removal of restrictions on the export of bullion, also in 1662, may well have made the problem worse. While both exporting and melting English coin

---

[20] Challis, 'Hastings to Recoinage', pp. 329–31, 41–7.   [21] Gaskill, *Crime*, p. 132.
[22] Lowndes, *Report*, p. 100; Feavearyear, *Pound*, pp. 121–4. This problem was not finally solved until 1817. See Chapter 6, pp. 189–92, below.
[23] Gaskill, *Crime*, p. 132.

remained offences, in practice the latter crime was very difficult to detect, and there was no way of knowing whether a consignment of bullion consisted of melted English coin, despite the exporter being required to swear an oath on the matter.

The case for the free export of bullion had been set out most clearly in 1623 by Thomas and John Mun, who argued that the only way for the nation to acquire 'treasure' was through a trade surplus, and that the use of money was essential to the successful conduct of international trade.[24] William Petty pointed out that those countries which did not ban the export of coin were more prosperous than those that did. Writing twenty years after the lifting of the ban, Petty pushed further, suggesting that England's remaining laws against the export of coin itself were not just impracticable but 'against the laws of nature'.[25] Whatever the merits of these enduringly influential arguments, the relaxation of the laws against the export of bullion under a monetary dispensation that offered a handsome profit to the exporter of coin as a commodity was bound to aggravate the scarcity of money.

In the mind of one critic, the loss of its power over the export of bullion constituted an existential threat to the monarchy. Thomas Violet, who had been employed to detect and prevent such export under Charles I, and who spent a lifetime in the vigorous pursuit of his own self-interest, argued that once merchants were freely permitted to export bullion and foreign coin they would 'for their private profit... leave neither gold nor silver in the nation'. The proposal to treat gold and silver as 'a free merchandise' rather than as 'a kingly merchandise' whose management was 'one of the prime flowers of your Majesties crown' was a 'Jesuitical, Fanatick design' to put the monarchy in thrall to the merchants and moneyed men of the City. Violet articulated a very traditional idea when he argued that money was previously held to be 'the blood and sinews of war and peace' and that its management should be 'for the honour of the king, and safety of the people, and to maintain trade and commerce in the kingdom, to pay rents, customs, excise and subsidies, to be a strength and honour to the kingdom'.[26]

England's international trade was beginning to grow massively even as Violet wrote. Between 1620 and 1660, for example, imports of tobacco from Virginia increased by a factor of 250, much of it to be re-exported to Europe. Imports of other colonial produce such as cotton and sugar also grew dramatically, as did exports of woollen textiles to the Iberian peninsula.[27] Meanwhile, the European thirst for luxuries from the East continued to mushroom. Ideas like Violet's therefore appeared increasingly old-fashioned in the face of writers like Mun and Petty.

---

[24] Mun and Mun, *England's Treasure*, ch. 4. Appleby, *Economic Thought*, p. 37.
[25] Petty, *Quantulumcunque*, p. 6.   [26] Violet, *Cæsar*, pp. 10, 11, 16, 9.
[27] Wennerlind, *Casualties*, pp. 27–8.

The government's next attempt to overcome the scarcity of money, by removing disincentives to bring bullion to the mint, was much more in keeping with the spirit of the age. The 1666 'Act for Encouraging of Coinage' abolished seignorage and shifted the costs of production from the person bringing bullion for minting to the public purse, funded by an additional tax on wine and spirits. As Feavearyear notes, this was highly significant because it was the third and final step—following the introduction of the mill and the removal of restrictions on the export of bullion—of the 'great steps towards the establishment of a completely decontrolled and automatic metallic standard'.[28] Desan sees a still deeper significance: the removal of mint charges effectively 'submerged the difference between coin and bullion in the common perception', which she argues was to be a critical issue in later debates over the recoinage of the silver.[29] The points are closely related: the Act was a crucial step in the development of a monetary system that was to rest much of its claim to be 'natural' on the notion that it operated 'automatically'. Together, these became crucial to its legitimacy.

As we have seen, the premium money carried over silver had always been much more important in domestic transactions than in international trade. In an environment where the volume of international trade was growing, and where the mint price of silver was lower than the price available abroad, that premium lost much of its meaning. Now, the only value of a bag of minted coins over the same weight of bullion was the fact that its purity was reliably warranted by the state. The fact that the increase in minting that followed the introduction of free coinage failed to alleviate the scarcity of money in circulation suggests that its main effect had been to turn the mint into a free assay and weighing service for the merchant class, and its coins into little more than miniature ingots. As Desan has shown, this was a crucial development in the reconceptualization of money.[30] It would have profound consequences for the key monetary debates and decisions of the ensuing quarter-millennium.

Seventeenth-century writers on monetary questions focussed on two problems posed by monetary scarcity and instability: the increased difficulty of collecting taxes, and the obstacles to international trade. Pressing as these problems were to the governmental and mercantile elite, they were not the principal concerns of the vast bulk of the population, and should not obscure the more prosaic problems the scarcity of money posed beyond the elites: for people like the farmer who struggled to put together enough passable silver sixpences or shillings to pay a few labourers their wages, or the labourers themselves who might have to rely on credit to buy their weekly provisions or accept payment or part payment in kind; the artisans who lacked the cash to buy raw materials; and the small traders who

---

[28] Feavearyear, *Pound*, p. 96. [29] Desan, *Making Money*, p. 238.
[30] Desan, *Making Money*, pp. 236–9.

had no choice but to extend credit to their customers, but whose suppliers demanded cash.

While the government also had to grapple with these problems in its small dealings, including the payment of wages, its most serious problems sprang not merely from a deficiency of available currency but from an absolute shortage of funds. The trader, the artisan, and even the labourer had to rely on networks of personal or impersonal credit and were at risk of ruin if they could not obtain cash in time to meet a commitment. Common prudence therefore dictated that they keep their ongoing assets and liabilities in balance, if not in surplus.[31] The government was in a very different situation. Even if a sufficiency of good, full-weight coin had made collecting the taxes straightforward, they would not have been sufficient to meet the government's commitments.

The answer was borrowing, and it was in the process of borrowing that the government created and shaped the emergent monetary order. The government's urgent need to borrow was the driver of the adoption of those proposals that started from a premise of a structural inadequacy of the money supply. This is not to suggest that monetary decisions of the period were often the result of calm reflection and analysis of the competing arguments of theorists aimed at developing coherent, long-term solutions to structural problems. Rather, most of the measures taken by successive governments in the later seventeenth century bear the hallmarks of expedients chosen in desperation.

The Restoration government's earliest innovations in borrowing had little effect on either the supply or the nature of money. The purchaser of a tontine, life annuity, or lottery ticket lent the government silver or gold coin in exchange for an interest-bearing security. The first two expired on the death of the purchaser or their nominee, and were thus a wager on longevity. Tontines were also a wager on the longevity of others, as the dividend pool was divided annually between the surviving holders. The lottery tickets differed from modern lotteries in that they bore interest as well as the promise of a large dividend if matched to a prize coupon at one of the periodic draws.[32] While some of these securities were then traded in the market, and even became accepted as a means of payment in certain limited contexts, they did not constitute new forms of money.[33]

By contrast, the government's expanded use of tallies, the issue of tallies with repayment orders, its use of debentures in payment for services, and, above all, the issuing of exchequer orders and similar instruments not only eased the government's fiscal difficulties but increased the money supply by adding what became new forms of currency circulating chiefly among the merchant classes.[34] In addition, the government's intermittent acceptance of goldsmiths' notes in payments facilitated the expansion of yet another novel monetary form. Taken

---

[31] Muldrew, 'Midas', p. 94.   [32] Dickson, *Financial Revolution*, pp. 50–7, 77–8, 506–7.
[33] Horsefield, *Experiments*, p. 159.   [34] Horsefield, 'Paper Money', pp. 119–20.

together—along with the king's extensive loans of coin from goldsmiths and other rich merchants—these borrowing practices in the latter part of the seventeenth century included key elements of a recognizably modern monetary order 'held together'—to borrow Ingham's formulation—'by networks of credit/debit relations... underpinned and constituted by sovereignty'.[35]

In the Restoration period, these networks were small and fragile, and many of the monetary instruments they generated were correspondingly provisional. This state of affairs stemmed variously from the state's inconsistency about accepting them, lack of clarity about their assignability, and—most corrosive of all—well-placed scepticism about the government's capacity to meet its obligations.[36]

The most straightforward instance of a new form of government borrowing adding to the money supply was the use of interest-bearing tallies with repayment orders as a means of payment, introduced in 1665 by George Downing, then a Member of Parliament and teller to the Treasury. Rather than simply anticipating revenues yet to be received at the Exchequer, as tallies had originally done, the new tallies were used by the government to pay for goods and services, or sold to raise cash. In accordance with Downing's plan, the relevant legislation made them assignable by endorsement, thus allowing them to circulate as a means of payment. Often called treasury orders or exchequer orders, or just 'assignments', as they assigned payment from a particular revenue stream to the bearer, they were issued in large numbers between 1667 and 1671 as Charles II struggled to finance his wars with the Dutch.

While the orders circulated in commercial circles, thus providing additional liquidity and easing the scarcity of money, they were not themselves money according to the definition put forward in this book.[37] Not only did they have a price, but they were not universally acceptable in payments. Indeed, the government that issued them would not even accept them as tax payments, as to do so would be to contradict the spirit of the promise that they would be repaid 'in course', that is, in a particular order on nominated dates.[38] This is no mere theoretical point. As we shall soon see, the difference between assignments and money could pose severe difficulties for government officials. The tallies are therefore best regarded as an early example of 'near-money', of which we will see more in later chapters.

Many of the new tallies were acquired by goldsmith bankers, who held them as investments. To that extent they became, in effect, a mechanism for goldsmiths to

---

[35] Ingham, *Nature*, p. 10.   [36] Desan, *Making Money*, p. 243.
[37] There has been some controversy over whether the treasury orders were money. Shaw, 'Order Book', p. 40, argued that they constituted 'the origin of official paper money in England'. Horsefield, 'Paper Money', p. 119, challenges this view. Desan, *Making Money*, p. 261, argues that they were not money on similar grounds to those I mention here, adding that their high denominations also made them unable to function as cash. Some of these points could be made about Bank of England notes in their early years.
[38] Desan, *Making Money*, p. 261.

lend money to the government, in addition to the loans that they made directly. They thus became part of the goldsmiths' working capital—a reserve which allowed them to issue more of their own notes than they might have otherwise. Those notes in turn formed another element of the expanded currency.

Goldsmiths had begun to issue notes as early as the 1650s on the principle of what later came to be called fractional reserve banking, although the notes did not become common until around 1670.[39] Being possessed of strong safes to store their stock-in-trade, goldsmiths offered their customers—at first for a fee—secure storage for their own gold coin or bullion earned in the course of trade. Over time—and greatly aided by a legal decision in 1666 'that the custom of merchants was part of the law of the land'—the receipts issued for the gold and other assets held by the goldsmiths became negotiable, passing from hand to hand before returning to the issuing goldsmith as a claim on gold or coin he held.[40] When the bearer was another goldsmith, the process took the form of a bilateral clearing of debt between the two. When the bearer was also a customer, the transfer of ownership represented by the note could be performed by a simple book entry.

The practice of issuing notes became seriously lucrative when goldsmiths began to issue receipts, or 'running cash notes', as interest-bearing loans—that is, for cash that they were yet to receive. Given that in the normal course of a week or a month only a small proportion of customers would call for their gold, it was possible to issue notes to a value far greater than the metallic assets actually held. The goldsmiths were thus able to earn interest on money that they did not possess for as long as they were able to pay promptly in exchange for any of their notes presented. Alternatively, they could lend their customers' assets at interest to third parties—chiefly the state—while the notes representing the gold continued to circulate.

The 'stop of the exchequer' in 1672 demonstrates the symbiotic relationship between the goldsmiths' notes and treasury orders—two very different types of near money. It also shows the simultaneous dependence of the whole structure on the creditworthiness of the state and the assets of the goldsmiths. The stop occurred when the government, pressed by the financial demands of war, unilaterally deferred payment on certain categories of outstanding exchequer orders. At that time almost £1.3 m of the orders were in the hands of fourteen goldsmith bankers. Sir Robert Vyner, the king's goldsmith, held £416,724, while two others each held around a quarter of a million pounds.[41] The stop left them stuck with large amounts of now illiquid assets, while rendering their own notes useless for payments, including payments to the government, which no longer accepted them. Several goldsmiths were obliged to 'stop payment'—that is, refuse to

---

[39] Quinn, 'Goldsmith-Banking', pp. 411, 413; Horsefield, 'Paper Money', p. 121.
[40] Horsefield, 'Paper Money', p. 119.   [41] Horsefield, 'Stop', p. 516.

exchange their notes for coin—within days of the government's announcement.[42] Their credit was thus severely undermined, and while none failed immediately, their businesses were fatally damaged. Eleven goldsmiths, including Vyner, would fail within a few years.[43]

The stop did enormous damage to the government's creditworthiness, and in particular its capacity to use exchequer bills. The only foundation of the assignments' value—like that of tallies—had been the confidence people felt that the government would eventually honour the financial commitment written on them, which in turn underpinned people's willingness to buy them for coin or accept them in exchange for goods and services. In the last analysis, as John Brewer has argued, this confidence depended on people's confidence in the government's capacity to collect sufficient taxes to meet its obligations, and its resolve not to overcommit itself by issuing more of such instruments than it could pay.[44] The stop of the exchequer shattered this confidence, leading the circulation of the government's paper to stop immediately. The stop therefore not only demonstrated how the growth of government debt had locked the government into a symbiotic relationship with large dealers in money; it also killed off any possibility of 'a pure state fiduciary issue of paper money' evolving, thus ensuring that the state's dependence on private interests for the operation of the monetary order would soon be total.[45]

Outside the socially and geographically circumscribed networks of credit in which exchequer notes circulated, their value rested on an even narrower foundation: the belief that it would be possible to exchange them readily for the bullion coin necessary to purchase life's necessities. Such a belief depended on the presence of individuals who not only had enough confidence in the assignments to accept them but also had a use for them. It also depended on the actual existence, somewhere, of the necessary coin.

Ireland: Managing Monetary Catastrophe

In Ireland, these conditions were often absent. When requesting subsidies to pay the army in 1663 and in 1667, the Duke of Ormond, the Lord-Lieutenant, felt he had to spell out that assignments would not do. On the latter occasion, having heard that the treasury was planning to pay with assignments on funds granted to the king by the Irish parliament, he explained that it was 'not possible in this kingdom, where the want of coin is so great, to raise any money upon that fund'.[46]

---

[42] Horsefield, 'Stop', p. 513. [43] Horsefield, 'Stop', pp. 522–5.
[44] Brewer, *Sinews*, pp. 88–9. [45] Clapham, *Bank*, 1, p. 12.
[46] Lord-Lieutenant to the King, 7 Feb. 1663, *CSPI* (1663–5), p.18; Lord-Lieutenant and Council to Secretary Arlington, 2 Aug. 1667, *CSPI* (1666–9), p. 415.

Other evidence suggests that this was not merely the hyperbole we might expect in a begging letter. Writing privately some months earlier, Viscount Dungannon, military governor of Ulster, reported that 'the army have lately received assignments for six months pay.... Whether money can be got for this it is hard to tell; for I never knew a dearth of money so great here, or so likely to increase.'[47] Ormond's plea to London to 'let me not have an imaginary instead of a real supply'[48] reveals an important truth not only about the ambiguous monetary status of assignments but also about the difference between the monetary worlds of London and Ireland.

Ireland's monetary system in the seventeenth century was little more than an impoverished subsidiary of England's. Its government, being possessed of no mint, and its Parliament, subordinated to the English Privy Council by Poynings' Law, had little scope to exercise power over the currency. For higher-denomination coinage Ireland had to make do with whatever English or other foreign money it could earn in the course of trade, which was insufficient to support the basic requirements of the money economy. The only elements of the Irish monetary system that could be regarded as indigenous were extra-legal tradesman's tokens and—at a very long stretch—base-metal coins which from time to time were produced either at the London mint or by private contractors. Like their counterparts in England, the former had purely local circulation and could not in any sense be regarded as 'national'. The latter, while minted expressly for Ireland and enjoying a national circulation, were produced in England under patents granted in London—an arrangement that was to be a recurring source of grievance for Ireland's people and problems for its government.

The ravages of war in the middle of the century had dealt severe blows to this intrinsically feeble system, leading George Rawdon in 1658 to complain to his brother-in-law, Viscount Conway, that he had never seen 'money so scarce... and the market so dead' in his three decades in the country.[49] For Rawdon, the shortage of coin posed an immediate practical problem: as overseer of Conway's estates it was part of his role to remit money as required to the Viscount, who was often in London—a common enough scenario, which also aggravated Ireland's scarcity of money and was a topic of frequent complaint.[50] And while Ireland's economy recovered quite rapidly at the end of the 1650s, the scarcity of money persisted: the difficulty of collecting money rents, selling the products of the estate, or even obtaining advances of cash on reasonable terms—all because of the scarcity of money—were steady refrains in Rawdon's letters throughout the 1660s.[51]

---

[47] Dungannon to Conway, 5 Jan 1667, *CSPI* (1666–9), p. 268.
[48] Lord-Lieutenant to Secretary Arlington, 22 June 1667, *CSPI* (1666–9), p. 383.
[49] Major Rawdon to Conway, 20 Mar. 1658, *CSPI* (1625–70), p. 665.
[50] Petty, *Anatomy*, p. 71.
[51] Cullen, *Economic History*, p. 10; Rawdon to Conway, 5 July 1667, *CSPI* (1666–9), p. 392; 4 Jan. 1665, *CSPI* (1663–5), p. 523.

In this context it was clearly impossible for the Restoration Irish government to overcome their country's monetary problems, especially while the English government was wrestling with formidable monetary challenges of its own. Not only were Ireland's difficulties inherently more severe, but all efforts to deal with them were nobbled by the subordination of Ireland's economic interests to those of England as a matter of royal policy. Instructions to successive viceroys were explicit about this from the Restoration onwards: 'You shall in all things endeavour to advance and improve the trade of that our kingdom *so far as it shall not be a prejudice to this our kingdom of England*, which we mean shall not be wronged how much soever the benefit of that our other kingdom might be concerned in it.'[52] The problem was aggravated by an ongoing losing struggle on the part of the Dublin administration to exercise a modicum of monetary autonomy. As a result, efforts to remedy Ireland's monetary problems were contradictory and for the most part utterly ineffective.

This is not to suggest that both parties did not sincerely wish to overcome Ireland's monetary problems; indeed, both saw the problem as urgent. There was, after all, a revenue to secure. But the institutional obstacles to improvement became clear almost immediately after the Restoration. In November 1660, the king instructed the Lord-Lieutenant not only to consider adjusting the value of foreign coin in Ireland in view of the 'great scarcity of coin' but also to suggest any other ways of encouraging the import of coin.[53] In January 1661, the government accordingly proclaimed new rates for sixteen of the twenty different types of foreign gold and silver coin then generally in circulation[54] The intent of the rerating appears to have been to bring all the foreign coins as near as possible to parity with sterling in terms of their bullion content. This was no answer to Ireland's monetary difficulties. Silver coin rated at the relatively low valuation of the English mint would find its way into European bullion markets from Ireland as quickly as it would from England. Indeed, the imposition of a sliding scale of actual weight to value on the foreign coins made it profitable to melt and export them for their bullion value even when clipped, unlike their English counterparts, which, for domestic transactions, retained their value by tale regardless and could thus be saved from the crucible by the shears.

The government was nevertheless determined to press on towards a uniform standard. In January 1662 the English Privy Council recommended that a Royal Mint be established in Ireland. Full instructions, specifying that the coins 'be of the exact standard of those in England' as well as the same denominations, were sent to the Lord-Lieutenant in May.[55] At the same time, however, the government

---

[52] Instructions for Lord Robartes, [July] 1660, *CSPI* (1660–2), p. 16 (emphasis original).
[53] [King] to [Lords Justices], Nov. 1660, TNA, SP 63/304 f. 337.
[54] Simon, *Irish Coins*, pp. 51–2, 126.
[55] Instructions to the Lord-Lieutenant for erecting a Mint in that Kingdom, 14 May 1662, *CSPI* (1660–2), p. 544.

agreed to a measure that directly contradicted this policy. In March, the king granted a patent to a small syndicate to mint silver coins in Dublin ranging from halfpenny to fourpenny pieces. In addition to the big Dublin goldsmith Daniel Bellingham, the syndicate comprised two of the richest men in London: Robert Vyner and Sir Thomas Vyner, his step-uncle and business partner. Sir Thomas at this point was easily the king's biggest creditor and a significant presence at court. He was also a major lender to the Irish government, as well as to the chronically impecunious Lord-Lieutenant personally.[56]

Unsurprisingly, the terms of the patent were extremely generous. The patentees were to coin silver at the rate of seventy shillings per troy pound, as against the English mint rate of sixty-two shillings. And although the patent expressly forbad them from importing English coin to recoin in Ireland, the substantial profit to be gained, even after paying the king a shilling for every pound of silver minted, makes it certain that even if the patentees could have resisted temptation, others would have found ways of supplying them with melted English coin.

The Irish government supported the petition on the grounds that it would 'bring bullion into the country, thus enriching the country in general and enabling it to pay taxes'.[57] After the patent had been granted in March 1662, however, the Master of the Mint persuaded the English Privy Council to suspend the project immediately, arguing that minting on these terms in Ireland would rapidly drain coin from England.[58] The original proposal and the modified version in the patent were then submitted to the officers of the mint in London, who responded with a thorough condemnation of both. Central to their critique was the obvious point that if the plan were to go ahead, it would severely aggravate the shortage of money in England. As the committee appointed to consider the matter put it, 'the preserving of a single standard of weight and fineness all over the King's dominions is very much to their advantage, and...the debasement of this standard, especially in the cases of small silver coins which are the common measures given to your Majesty by the people [i.e. how most people pay their taxes], cannot be practiced or allowed in any one of the King's kingdoms without eminent prejudice to all the rest'.[59] Ireland's scarcity of money problem was not to be resolved by making England's worse, nor by depriving the Crown of a fraction of the bullion due to it. Confronted with this opposition, the goldsmiths had little choice but to undertake not to proceed.

---

[56] Caden, *Mint Conditions*, pp. 155–7. Aylmer, 'Vyner'. The following year Vyner advanced Ormond £5,000 for his purchase of Moor Park in Hertfordshire: Earl of Anglesey to Ormond, 3 Nov. 1663, *CMO*, vol. 3, pp. 101–2.
[57] LJI to Secretary Nicholas, 14 Aug. 1661, *CSPI* (1660-2), p. 399.
[58] Earl of Anglesey to Ormond, 3 May 1662, *CMO*, vol. 3, p. 18.
[59] Report of the Committee appointed to discuss Vyner's patent, 14 Nov. 1662, *CSPI* (1660-2), p. 621.

The committee's words would be quoted in ensuing decades in response to attempts by the authorities in the American colonies to establish their own mints, with the opposition being led on each occasion by the officers of the mint. These colonies, which suffered at least as grievously as Ireland from shortages of coin, repeatedly sought permission to establish their own mints, usually to coin money lighter than the English standard. On each occasion they were rebuffed on the principle that 'any deviation from the English standard of currency across its dominions would pose an intolerable danger to the integrity of English money', which clearly trumped any considerations of the colonists' well-being.[60]

In agreeing to withdraw, Sir Thomas Vyner conceded that the scheme was inconsistent with the king's earlier decision to establish a mint in Ireland to produce coins to the English standard.[61] The point could hardly be more obvious: the government had almost simultaneously ordered the minting of silver pennies, threepences, groats (4d.) and half-groats at 62 shillings to the pound and at 70 shillings to the pound—providing an obvious opportunity for anyone to melt coins from Dublin's Royal Mint to feed that of the goldsmiths.

Although such an absurd state of affairs might be explained in part by the Lord-Lieutenant's admission that he was 'the most unskilful man in the world in the mystery of coins and exchange', it also points to the unsustainable tension between the conflicting objectives of simultaneously maintaining an adequate supply of money and stable monetary values.[62] The whole episode also reflects sharp struggles for authority. As the Earl of Anglesey put it to Ormond, that 'an act of your Lordship's relating to your own government' should so easily be reversed as soon as Ormond's back was turned clearly indicates the weakness of the Lord-Lieutenant's position.[63] More seriously, it points to a general dysfunction in Ireland's governance. As the Irish Lord Chancellor argued, responding to another pair of contradictory instructions from London, 'if the business of Ireland do not pass through one hand there will be much disorder in His Majesty's service and I need not tell you the ill consequences that will follow thereupon'.[64] The government's failure to make any reasonable arrangements for Ireland's money should be counted as one such ill consequence.

The instruction to mint coin to a sterling standard and the Bellingham–Vyner patent can both be seen as attempts to regain some sort of governmental control of the monetary system—or at least to delegate control to the government's chosen creditors. This too was a recurring theme of monetary policy in England and Ireland, although much less conspicuous in Scotland. A declared aim of the

---

[60] Caden, *Mint Conditions*, p. 165 and ch. 4 *passim*.
[61] Report of the Committee appointed to discuss Vyner's patent, 14 Nov. 1662, *CSPI* (1660–2), p. 621.
[62] Ormond [to Secretary Bennet], 16 July 1663, *CSPI* (1663–5), p. 174.
[63] Anglesey to Ormond, 3 May 1662, *CMO*, vol. 3, p. 18.
[64] Lord Chancellor Eustace to Secretary Bennet, 31 Dec. 1662, *CSPI* (1660–2), p. 670.

goldsmiths' patent was to deal with the ongoing problem of low-denomination, base-metal tradesmen's tokens, which had proliferated owing to successive governments' inability to provide the necessary coins, and which successive Lords Lieutenant throughout the 1660s were directed to suppress.[65] The tokens were a problem, it was alleged, because the issuers sold them in bulk for higher-value silver coins, which they then exported for spectacular profits before making themselves scarce to avoid having to repay.[66]

Another attempt to counter such unauthorized plebeian monetary initiative was equally abortive—at least initially. As well as licensing Bellingham and the Vyners to issue small coins in silver, the king also issued a patent to Sir Thomas Armstrong to mint copper farthings for Ireland, at a profit to both Armstrong and the Crown. But in a rare victory for the Dublin administration, perhaps scandalized at the fact that the new farthings were to contain even less bullion than most of the tokens they were intended to replace, Armstrong was not permitted to proceed.[67] Once this patent lapsed, however, Dublin Castle did not stand in the way of Armstrong's issue of proportionately much weightier halfpence from 1680.[68]

Whatever the shortcomings of the two governments' Irish monetary policy, the English Parliament's actions could be positively malign. In 1666, it passed an act to ban outright the import of Irish cattle to England, extending a partial ban imposed a few years earlier.[69] As the Lord-Lieutenant explained to the king when the complete ban was first proposed, even the partial ban had sunk every part of Ireland into 'so sad a degree of poverty and scarcity of money' that the 'misery' was 'felt by all persons of all qualities and professions'.[70]

This severely aggravated the hardships of many Irish people. For Viscount Conway's tenants, it made the business of finding the rent simply impossible. As Adam Leathes, one of Conway's agents, explained in 1668, 'money is so scarce... that unless I grant those gentle forbearances which the general part of the tenants require, they will be brought to a very low condition'. But even when Leathes granted the tenants 'a general releasement of their cattle before our fair last week, that they might make a little money by their dealings', he 'did not get in 20s from them all'.[71]

From the Lord-Lieutenant's perspective, the ban had made it impossible for the government to pursue 'just and honourable means... for bringing money into the kingdom for encouraging improvement of men's estates and for increasing the

---

[65] See [July] 1660, *CSPI* (1660–2), p. 16; 19 June 1669, *CSPI* (1666–9), p. 741; Feb 1670, *CSPI* (1625–70), p. 81.
[66] Proclamation by the Lords Justices and Council, 17 Aug. 1661, *CSPI* (1660–2), p. 401.
[67] Simon, *Irish Coins*, pp. 50–2. Dolley, 'Irish Coinage', p. 417.
[68] The farthing was to weigh 25 grains, the halfpenny weighed 115 grains—i.e. 100 grains to the penny as against 230. Herbert A. Grueber, *Handbook*, pp. 239–40.
[69] Cullen, *Economic History*, p. 17.
[70] Lord-Lieutenant and Council to the King, 15 Aug. 1666, *CSPI* (1666–9), p. 183.
[71] Adam Leathes to Viscount Conway, 18 July 1668, *CSPI* (1666–9), p. 630.

ways and means of trade and commerce'. This inability to monetize the economy would not only prevent the Irish rising from their state of 'barbarism' by means of industry but also force the English in Ireland either to sink to the same level of barbarism as the native Irish or to return to England with their assets.[72]

After taking counsel among Ireland's leading merchants, the Lord-Lieutenant requested permission to trade with the king's enemies in order to bring in bullion, and, echoing a theme of a number of pamphleteers, to ban the import of luxury goods, which 'take away from us even that little base and foreign coin which now supports the small trade and commerce we have'.[73] At the same time he requested permission to raise the value of the foreign coin above the sterling standard in order to try to keep it in Ireland. The king granted all of Ormond's requests, even down to permitting Ireland to trade with the enemy to obtain bullion. In short, the English government permitted the Irish government to implement a set of mercantilist responses to the English Parliament's act of mercantilist aggression. In doing so, it once again allowed Ireland's monetary policy to diverge from that of England's.

By the winter of 1667, the Irish government's fiscal and monetary difficulties once again came back to bite the English treasury, as economic hardship led to disorder and an increased need for military force to maintain the peace. Coming on top of the need to build expensive fortifications as a result of the Second Anglo-Dutch War, this placed the Irish government between the blades of a rapidly closing pair of scissors, which made it impossible for it to live off its own resources. As Ormond explained, 'Some who cannot live now by their labour maintain themselves by the spoils of others, and we have too much cause to believe the numbers of such bad people will daily increase as their wants do, whereby while there is need (both at home and from abroad) to augment your Majesty's army, the treasure which should pay it lessens.' The army in Ireland would therefore have to be paid with 'treasure sent out of England'. To that end the Irish government needed £60,000 immediately, 'if not in English coin...in such foreign coin as is current amongst us'.[74] On 23 March the king agreed to send £50,000 in foreign coin 'to meet the emergencies which the disjoined condition of that kingdom and the present state of affairs must necessarily occasion'.[75] This was familiar ground. Four years earlier, fearing that 'general discontent' might become disturbance, Ormond had also required a cash subsidy to pay the army, having 'nothing in the Treasury to draw or keep it together'.[76]

---

[72] 'Copy of Memorandum by the Lord-Lieutenant and Council containing reasons to be offered to His Majesty against passing the Act to prohibit the importation of Irish Cattle into England', 15 Aug. 1666, *CSPI* (1666–9), pp. 185–8.
[73] Lord-Lieutenant and Council to the King, 15 Aug. 1666, *CSPI* (1666–9), pp. 183–5.
[74] Lord-Lieutenant and Council to the King, 9 Feb. 1667, *CSPI* (1666–9), pp. 290, 292.
[75] King to Lord-Lieutenant, 23 Mar. 1667, *CSPI* (1666–9), p. 329.
[76] Lord-Lieutenant to the King, 7 Feb. 1663, *CSPI* (1663–5), p. 18.

Such entreaties highlight the problem we have identified as the most serious posed for governments as a result of the general scarcity of money: it made it enormously difficult, and sometimes impossible, to pay and supply the armed forces. But it also illustrates specific nuances of the problem arising from the structure of the Anglo-Irish composite monarchy. While the issue was complicated in varying degrees in Scotland and Ireland by the fact that a substantial military presence was required to suppress internal dissent, and because money was scarcer in those kingdoms than in England, it was nevertheless the English government for whom the problem was most difficult, and the English government which ultimately had to find a lasting solution.

Ormond's entreaties, and the English government's response, demonstrate why this was so. Ultimately, the English government had no choice but to raise what funds it could in England to send subsidies to Ireland to ensure that the king's forces there were paid. Moreover, the navy and those elements of the army engaged in foreign wars were paid for by the English treasury, regardless of the national origin of their officers and men.[77]

Ireland's monetary state clearly provided barren soil for the articulation of any kind of monetary patriotism of the kind that began to appear increasingly in English discourse. The nearest we can observe to such a thing in the seventeenth century is Richard Lawrence's *The Interest of Ireland in its Trade and Wealth Stated*. Lawrence was born in England and arrived in Ireland as a senior officer in Cromwell's New Model Army in 1648, where he managed not merely to survive but to prosper in a variety of important roles through the vicissitudes of Commonwealth, Protectorate, and Restoration politics. By the time he published *The Interest of Ireland* in 1682, he was a substantial businessman and landowner, and the leader of Ireland's Baptist community. He also enjoyed Ormond's patronage, and had been a member of the Irish government's Council of Trade for twenty years.

Lawrence articulated a strong settler patriotism.[78] He maintained that the interests of the English Crown and people would best be served by promoting 'the English interest of Ireland', encouraging Irish economic development and ensuring that Irish civilian and military offices were filled by the Anglo-Irish rather than by 'foreigners' (that is, people normally resident in England).[79] Only the former had the direct stake in Ireland's prosperity to impel them to manage the economy, and the necessary understanding of the country's customs and culture to enable it to maintain the peace.[80] The common English fear that a

---

[77] Murray, 'Administration', p. 34.
[78] See Barnard, 'British and Irish', pp. 202–6, for a discussion of the complexity of the identities and varied flavours of patriotic sentiments among Irish protestants.
[79] Lawrence, *Interest*, part I, pp. 51, 78–91.   [80] Lawrence, *Interest*, part II, ch. 3.

prosperous Ireland was a potential threat had been rendered anachronistic by the dispossession or conversion of Ireland's Catholic elite.[81]

Lawrence advanced no specific argument for Irish monetary autonomy beyond his general claims that 'Ireland be governed by its own members'.[82] Rather, he appeared to take it as given that the valuation of the coin was for 'the Government of Ireland' to decide. This was clearly not so either in theory or in practice; the English Privy Council concerned itself with even the most minor aspects of currency in Ireland. In 1683, for example, to the consternation of both Ormond and his son the Earl of Arran, the latter, deputizing while Ormond was in London, felt obliged to withdraw a proposal to adjust the Irish ratings of pistoles and ducatoons 'since such a business was made of it' at Westminster. Naively perhaps, Ormond had expected the proposal to meet with 'no difficulty' and was surprised that the English politicians had been influenced by 'some apprehension that the regulation of coin [in Ireland] may have some influence upon trade here'.[83]

Reflecting on the incident the following week, Ormond's frustration is clear: 'If the raising of pistoles and the reducing of ducatoons be of advantage, I know not why it should be declined. Sir Wm Petty and Col Lawrence have showed their skill in tumbling the argument of coins up and down, but with little edification to the hearers.'[84] The withdrawal of Arran's proposal thus marks the failure of another attempt by the government of Ireland to establish a degree of monetary autonomy, this time by bringing to bear the intellect of the two most persuasive members of its Council of Trade. Ormond's encouragement of the publication of Lawrence's book may be seen as a part of this effort, as might Lawrence's somewhat disingenuous assumption that Irish Government already possessed monetary power.[85]

It can hardly have helped the Irish case in Westminster that Lawrence and Petty disagreed on key principles regarding the valuation of coin. Indeed, on Lawrence's own admission, 'this one Question' had 'been more controverted with less agreement in the Council of Trade than any other point'. In *The Interest of Ireland* Lawrence set out all the reasons put forward by opponents of devaluation, listing first the claim that it 'would be a dishonour to the Government, Coyn being the Standard or Measure of all other things, it would weaken our Credit in our foreign Traffique'. The remaining reasons he summarized thus: 'if our Mony, which must rule the price of all things, be mutable and uncertain, no man can make a sure and clear estate of what he hath; Contracts, Bargains, Rents, Taxes, Wages will all be uncertain'.[86] Petty advanced almost every one of these arguments in his various writings on money. In his view, the only explanation that 'many wise states' had ever 'practised this artifice' was 'the stupidity and ignorance of the people'.

---

[81] Lawrence, *Interest*, part II, pp. 47–51.   [82] Lawrence, *Interest*, Part II, pp. 96.
[83] Ormond to Arran, 3 Apr. 1683; Arran to Ormond, 11 Apr. 1683, *CMO*, vol. 7, pp. 7, 11–12.
[84] Ormond to Arran, 17 Apr. 1683, *CMO*, vol. 7, p. 14.
[85] Ormond to Arran, 15 May 1683, *CMO*, vol. 7, p. 27.
[86] Lawrence, *Interest*, Part II, pp. 173–4.

Fundamentally, it was nothing but 'a very pitiful and unequal way of taxing the people; and 'tis a sign that the state sinketh, which catcheth hold on such weeds as are accompanied with the dishonour of impressing a Princes effigies to justifie adulterate commodities, and the breach of public faith, such as is the calling a thing what it really is not'.[87]

Lawrence conceded that the arguments against devaluation were 'very sound, as to a well-settled Commonwealth'; but there were exceptions to the general rule because 'for sick States as well as sick Bodies Physick is more necessary than food'. He believed that devaluation was 'not only expedient but necessary' in certain circumstances. Two of them clearly obtained in Ireland—scarcity of bullion and a chronic trade deficit. Lawrence rested much of his argument on the European historical precedents Petty dismissed, including English ones. In his view, if 'England had not enhanced their Coyn as Bullion rose... it is not reasonable to believe England would have had a Silver spoon or a sixpence left: and if Bullion should yet increase in value to six or seven shillings per Ounce, if we enhance not our Coyn proportionably, it is not rational to believe we shall have a penny left'.[88]

Petty and Lawrence not only weighed 'honour' differently in their calculations but also had a different sense of whose honour was at stake. For Petty it was the honour of the Prince—the King of England and Ireland; for Lawrence it was the honour of the Irish government, which, for all that it was the king's government, Lawrence seems to have conceived as belonging, in principle at least, to 'the English interest of Ireland': people like himself, Petty, and Ormond. Given the chronically disordered and weak state of Ireland's money, however, it is not surprising that Lawrence was willing to sacrifice the demands of 'honour' in favour of a resolutely pragmatic approach to the problem of the valuation of Ireland's currency.

Scotland: the Uses and Abuses of Monetary Autonomy

Such questions of 'honour' hardly figured at all in the monetary discourse of Scotland. Notwithstanding that Scotland possessed significantly greater quasi-autonomous monetary powers than Ireland, much Scottish monetary policy following the Restoration necessarily consisted of reactions to English developments—a state of affairs that significantly narrowed the scope for the development of any nationalistic discourse around money. Indeed, both long-term and short-term factors led many Scots increasingly to question whether Scotland's limited monetary autonomy held any real benefits at all. Even before the Scottish elite seriously considered merging their political sovereignty with

---

[87] Petty, *Treatise*, pp. 65, 68. [88] Lawrence, *Interest*, Part II, pp. 174–5, 77.

England's, decades of monetary dysfunction, aided by shocking levels of aristocratic corruption, led many to conclude that Scots' best use of their monetary autonomy would be to bind their currency as closely as possible to the more stable and powerful currency of their king's richer domain.

The push and pull between Scotland's competing needs for autonomy and uniformity with England was demonstrated shortly after the Restoration, when delays in reopening the Edinburgh mint and pressures from its southern neighbour severely exacerbated the country's shortage of coin. An English proclamation of 26 August 1661 raising the value of English gold coins by 6.7 per cent required urgent imitation by the Scottish Privy Council to prevent the 'transportation of all that is in this kingdome, by reason of the great advantage that will aryse therefra'.[89] But because such questions remained the exclusive prerogative of a distant king, eight precious weeks passed between the Council resolving to request the king's permission to make the change and the issue of the relevant proclamation in Edinburgh on 26 November—three full months after the English proclamation. Unsurprisingly, by the time the Scottish government was able to act, the 'stock of gold and money' in Scotland was 'reduced to a great ebbe and scarcitie'.[90]

At the same time as it sought the king's pleasure regarding the valuation of the coin, the Privy Council also begged the English government to equip the Master of the Edinburgh Mint, then waiting in London, to be furnished with the stamps of the king's image necessary for minting to resume in Edinburgh. This apparently took some time, as did the production in London of new trial pieces necessary to ensure the standard fineness of coins. The originals had been produced to facilitate James VI and I's monetary union, but had been lost 'in the tyme of the late troubles'.[91]

But the resumption of minting in 1664 did little to remedy Scotland's shortage of money. According to a report of a committee to examine the coin at the end of 1667, 'by farre the greatest part' of the money in Scotland consisted of foreign coin because certain Spanish coins had been overvalued relative to Scottish coin by previous proclamations. This encouraged not only the importation of the foreign coins, at a profit of between 3 and 5 per cent, but also the melting down of the king's 'weighty coyne' to make counterfeit foreign coin. Indeed, as the committee shrewdly recognized, this might also be one of the reasons 'why the kings new weighty coynes in England are caryed beyond the sea'. The committee considered various options for overcoming these problems, each of which came at a cost and was likely to cause a 'great clamour', before deciding to revalue every coin then in common circulation—including Scottish coin—on the basis of its relationship to

---

[89] SPC, Letter to the Lord Secretary, 2 Oct. 1661, *RCS* 2, p. 143.
[90] SPC, *Proclamation anent the value of current Gold*, 26 Nov. 1661, *RCS* 2, p. 145.
[91] SPC, Letter to the Secretary anent the Standart [sic] Weight, 1 Dec. 1663, *RCS* 2, p. 151.

the English standard at the now 'traditional' Anglo-Scottish exchange rate of 12:1.[92] In effect, the government put Scotland onto what the twentieth century would call a 'sterling peg'.

While many regarded this as Scotland's least bad monetary option in the circumstances, it left the Scots with exactly the same problem as the English in that any full-weight, good silver coin rapidly disappeared from circulation. Together with the decision to stop minting copper in 1668, this had serious effects on the money supply. Early in 1677 the Scottish government received petitions from the royal burghs bemoaning the shortage of all kinds of coin. The shortage of silver, they argued, had led to a decay of both foreign and domestic trade and had forced traders to rely almost entirely on credit. The lack of copper had severely prejudiced not only 'the meaner sort' of traders, small dealers, and fisherfolk but also beggars, for whom copper 'in former tymes used to be their stock wherewith they were supplyed'.[93] No doubt well aware of the futility of trying to remedy the scarcity of heavy silver coin by minting more of it, the government attacked the shortage of higher denominations by making current, at attractive rates, some of the most important, high-quality silver and gold coins of Scotland's major trading partners.[94] This, the Privy Council argued, would be a more effective way of keeping out coarse foreign coin than would any attempt to ban it, a step they were unwilling to take given the extreme shortage of any coin at all.

This was to take one step away from the sterling peg. In 1681, following representations from merchants, the government abandoned it completely by raising the value of its silver coin to reflect the value of silver not at the English mint, but elsewhere in Europe. The government justified this step by reasserting Scotland's historical monetary independence, citing specific occasions on which Scottish kings had raised the extrinsic value of the coinage in response to changes in 'neighbouring kingdoms and states'. This had once again become necessary because most of the coin had been exported and made 'merchandise', to be 'melted down by foreign mints and goldsmiths, and imported again in foreign species, much below our own coyn, both in weight and fineness whereby our Authority has been contemned, our people cheated and abused, and the trade and commerce of this Kingdom highly prejudged'.[95]

But the situation was far worse, and the processes at work more sinister, than the government knew, or at least than it was prepared to admit in 1681. In fact, the main site for manipulation of the nation's silver coin for private gain was the Edinburgh mint itself, which since its reopening had become a racket for the

---

[92] SPC, *Report anent the Coyne*, 19 Dec. 1667, RCS 2, p. 156.
[93] SPC, *Act for Coyning of Two Penny and Sex Penny Peices of Copper Coyne*, 27 Feb. 1677, RCS 2, p. 168.
[94] SPC, *Act anent the value of some Forraigne Species of Gold and Silver Money declared currant*, 27 Feb. 1677, RCS 2, pp. 169–70.
[95] [Charles II of Scotland,] *A Proclamation Concerning the Coyn*, 5 Mar. 1681.

corrupt enrichment of its officers, most especially its 'Generals', Lord Haltoune (Charles Maitland) and his son Richard, and its Master, Sir John Falconer. Haltoune, as the brother and frequent deputy of the Duke of Lauderdale, who was Scotland's most powerful politician for much of his tenure at the mint, exerted an absolute control, buttressed by the extraordinary powers and indemnities traditionally afforded the Master of the Mint, as well as by his willingness to make his subordinates complicit in his frauds, and to threaten, bully, and even imprison them whenever necessary.

Haltoune's criminality came to light in 1682, in the context of a 'ruthless gladiatorial contest' in the Scottish Privy Council following Lauderdale's decline and fall from power.[96] On the evidence of Falconer and other implicated officials, who hoped to find favour with their testimony, a Commission of Inquiry found that Haltoune and others had committed seven specific abuses.[97] The most serious boiled down to two distinct frauds: first, they had kept for themselves the revenues allocated for the purchase of bullion, and instead had produced adulterated and underweight silver coin by melting down current good coin; second, instead of minting 3,000 stone of copper in each of the periods in which they had been authorized to do so, they had used the mint's resources to purchase and mint a total of 29,600 stone, at significant profit to themselves. Not counting the unquantifiable sums they had made from minting adulterated silver coin, the Generals and the Master had made illegal profits of no less than £699,873 Scots, or £58,322 sterling.

Given these facts, and the levels of corruption in Lauderdale's regime more generally, it is difficult to accept claims that any given decision regarding the Scottish currency in this period was taken for the public good.[98] While it was almost certainly true, for example, that the coining of copper after a nine-year pause was a boon to the poor, it was obviously an even greater boon to Lauderdale's brother and his henchmen. Similarly, the raising of the value of the silver coins in 1681, while possibly helping to keep coin in the country, also presented an opportunity for the mint officers to profit from the increased value of the stocks of silver bullion they had accumulated at the mint before the decision was publicly announced.

Modern analysis has shown that while the silver coin minted under the Haltoune regime was consistently significantly underweight, the charge of adulterating the coin was almost certainly untrue: Haltoune's and Falconer's coins contained at least as high a proportion of silver as the coins produced before and after.[99] Indeed, the charge is inherently implausible in the absence of other contemporary evidence. Any discernible adulteration would have been detected

[96] Lynch, *New History*, p. 296; William B. Gardner, 'Maitland', pp. 118–20.
[97] Laing, *Scottish Affairs*, p. 355.   [98] Lynch, *New History*, p. 291.
[99] Photos-Jones, Jones, and Bateson, 'Light', pp. 173, 175.

by foreign merchants soon enough, and caused the coins to go to a discount, yet there is no reason to believe that this occurred. The most remarkable feature of this charge is perhaps that Lauderdale's and Haltoune's enemies were willing to uphold it, given the potential it had to damage their country's monetary reputation. The mint and the coinage had become a mere tool for pecuniary and political advancement, with little regard for the national well-being, however that may be conceived.

The Haltoune regime can be regarded as Scotland's most outrageous abuse of monetary power until the banking disasters of the early twenty-first century. Like anyone in a position to abuse monetary power in a serious way, Haltoune was also close to political power, and, like his twenty-first-century successors, he escaped with little more than disappointment of his highest ambitions and a relatively trivial financial penalty, eventually paying a fine of £20,000 sterling after it was reduced by King Charles from the original £72,000. Initially stripped of all public offices, he was readmitted to the Privy Council in 1686 after an absence of only a few years. The heaviest price Haltoune paid was that the king barred him from inheriting the dukedom to which his brother had been raised in 1672, leaving him to live out the years following his brother's death as a mere earl.[100] The Scottish people paid a much heavier price. The mint was closed as a direct response to the scandal, and was not to reopen for six years, leaving Scotland almost helpless to alleviate its chronic scarcity of money.[101]

Even before the mint was officially closed, the commissioners who had investigated the scandal were asked to report and make proposals for the future of Scotland's coinage. Their reports were unequivocally in favour of near-complete monetary assimilation with England, even—understandably in the circumstances—down to imitating key aspects of governance of the mint. Citing a series of statutes from David II in 1367 to James VI in 1604 which had commanded that the Scottish coinage should be of the same weight and fineness as the English, and itemizing the costs and inconveniences to commerce and travel of any variation, the commissioners recommended not only that Scotland adopt the English standard but also that, in addition to the existing denominations, it mint sixpences, shillings, half-crowns and crowns identical to those of England, except with the arms of Scotland in the first quarter of the shield. These new coins were to be produced by recoining the foreign coin then in circulation, which was to be demonetized.

The final imitation of English practice recommended by the commissioners was the adoption of free coinage, which they believed had 'exceedingly enriched' England since its introduction in 1666.[102] Unlike their other proposals, which lay entirely within the royal prerogative, this required Parliament to vote the taxes

---

[100] Jackson, 'Maitland'.
[101] Letter from the King to the Privy Council, 8 June 1683, *RCS* 2, pp. 169–70.
[102] 'Report of the Commissioners appointed for tryall of the Mint', 1683, *RCS* 2, p. 204.

necessary so that the state, rather than the individuals who brought metal to be minted, would foot the bill. The commissioners were confident that the next parliamentary session would happily grant the necessary supply, and the Privy Council accordingly decided that the mint should remain closed until after Parliament had met. Their confidence was almost justified: the supply was granted in 1686—in the second parliamentary session following the report—by means of taxes on a long list of commodities, including wine, steel, lemons, leather, window glass, prunes, and trees.[103]

A memorandum among the relevant papers, probably by Sir Robert Gordon of Gordonstoun, who was one of the commissioners, gives some insight into the thinking behind these recommendations. Noting the damage done to both trade and the landed interests by the recent troubles in the mint, the memorandum claimed that 'we had no such disorders or any want of money' in the past when Scotland had observed uniformity with England. Against the view that Scotland should maintain a lower standard to prevent the export of its coin, the paper argued not merely that Scots would be great losers whenever they attempted to use such money abroad but, strikingly, that however Scotland valued its money, it 'must still continue under the slavery of the English exchange'. But the most remarkable observation was reserved for an addendum: 'Although I confess that the intrinsic value of English coyn surpasses most nations and may very probablie bee ane error from their vanity, yet a mater of that consequence having the authority of so rich and wyse a nation ought to make a man diffident of his owen private opinion.'[104]

It is a measure of the desperate monetary mess that Scotland was in that England's monetary order of the 1680s could look so successful as to command imitation, even when its policies seemed to defy the dictates of reason. The Scots were clearly long past any of the 'vanity' that Gordon detected in English policy. The 'honour' that concerned Lawrence and Petty, as well as many writers in England, was almost entirely absent from the monetary discourse of Scotland, whose leaders had come to see its currency arrangements in wholly pragmatic terms.

Pragmatism does not always entail a single conclusion, and the commissioners' pragmatic recommendations were, for equally pragmatic reasons, implemented selectively. Although the new coinage was not decreed until after free coinage had been voted, minting resumed before the latter policy was implemented. The new silver coins of 1687 and 1688 imitated English practice only superficially. Symbolically, they told a tale of something like complete monetary subordination to England, with the king referred to by his English title, James II, and wearing the English rather than the Scottish crown. The coins were also minted to the same standard of fineness as English, and in multiples of shillings rather than the

---

[103] *Act anent the Mint*, RPS, 1686/4/54.
[104] [Sir Robert Gordon,] 'Memorial anent the Mint', 1683, *RCS* 2, pp. 202–3.

Scottish denominations. This would have made the highest value Scots silver coin of 60s. conveniently equal to its English counterpart, the crown, had the commissioners' keystone recommendation to assimilate the standard at a par of 12:1 been followed. Instead, however, the Scottish coins had only 93 per cent of the recommended bullion weight, giving an actual proportion of bullion between the two countries' coins of 13:1.[105] In substance, and without fanfare, Scotland chose for the time being to retain its monetary difference from England, allowing it to make its own coins less vulnerable to melting and export than their English counterparts. As we shall see in Chapter 4, this limited monetary autonomy gave Scotland at least some capacity to protect itself from the monetary turmoil that was shortly to engulf its sister kingdom.

The Price of Revolution: the Monetary Consequences of 1689

By 1688, as James VII and II's reign approached its terminal crisis, Scotland and Ireland were, for different reasons, in states of acute monetary distress: Ireland still under the burdens of war and revolution; Scotland just emerging from the long shadow of the crimes of its own monetary authorities. England, although still plagued by its chronic shortage of standard coin, was at least not in the grip or immediate aftermath of any specific monetary crisis. But it did not have long to wait. The inevitable consequence of the accession of William and Mary was war with France, whose unprecedented cost, and consequent massive export of silver by the government, would rapidly overwhelm the coinage.

But it was in Ireland that the consequences of the Williamite revolution were the most immediate and serious. In March 1689, within a few months of fleeing England and even before the Scottish Parliament had declared his abdication, James II and VII landed in Ireland, hoping to establish it as the base from which to reclaim the English throne. Among the disasters the ensuing war was to bring to Ireland was the wreck of its monetary system. Even before hostilities between James and the English revolutionary government had begun, money in Ireland became even scarcer than usual as Protestant merchants left the country (or hid their money).[106] Accordingly, one of James's first acts on establishing himself in Dublin was to raise the rates of both foreign and English coin in the hope of keeping them in the country. While the rating of English coin above the official rate in England was a reversion to a pre-Stuart practice, his raising of foreign coin above bullion equivalence to sterling was simply a continuation of an older practice the Irish government had tried unsuccessfully to reintroduce as recently as 1683.[107]

---

[105] Grueber, *Handbook*, p. 207.   [106] Simon, *Irish Coins*, p. 58.
[107] Simon, *Irish Coins*, p. 50. See p. 66, above.

But James's monetary problems in 1689 were far greater than such expedients could overcome. His need for money to equip and pay his army was desperate, and there was almost none he could lay his hands on. Accordingly, he invoked such sovereign authority as he exercised in Ireland to create a currency of token money using whatever scrap metal he could get hold of, commanding that it be paid and accepted at the values he decreed. Those who refused them at these rates were to be regarded as 'contemners of the king's royal prerogative', to be punished to the utmost extent of the law.[108] Like O'Neill before him, James finally resorted to the death penalty to enforce the circulation of the coin at the rate he desired, in this case by enforcing a maximum price (in his token money) that could be asked or paid for gold or silver money. His only concession to the market was that these rates were not at par, but at 158 per cent and 138 per cent for gold and silver, respectively, of the rates he had proclaimed in 1689.[109]

The only pretence James could make that the value of his money derived either from a 'backing' of bullion or the 'credit' of the government was a promise that the token money would be short-lived, and that those left holding it when it was demonetized would be allowed to use it to pay any debts owing to the government, or would be repaid in full-weight, precious-metal coin. His increasingly strident threats of force may be read as an inverse measure of the confidence of his Irish subjects in his ability to honour those promises when balanced against their need for circulating coin of any description. In the event, those left holding such coin after James's defeat by William III lost out severely. Claiming that almost all the token coins were now in the possession of 'the Irish who are in rebellion', William immediately reduced James's token coins to something approximating their bullion value.[110] Most spectacularly, the value of the half-crown was reduced by more than 95 per cent to one penny, while various shillings and sixpences were reduced to halfpennies and farthings.

This was the monetary state of Ireland at the beginning of the 1690s—the decade in which England and Scotland were to embark upon their respective monetary revolutions. No such revolution was to take place in Ireland, clearly not because the monetary order there was less in need of fundamental change but because it could not furnish the conditions for the creation of a new one. We will consider the consequences of this predicament in Chapter 5.

The effects of war and revolution on Scotland's monetary system were less direct but nevertheless significant. Fighting to establish the new regime in Scotland, although neither as widespread nor as long-lasting as in Ireland, was severe enough to lay large sections of the country to waste.[111] Moreover, resistance

---

[108] [James II,] 'Whereas for Remedy of the Present Scarcity of Money...' (16 June 1689).
[109] [James II,] 'Whereas we are informed that several covetous persons...' (15 June 1690).
[110] LJI, 'Whereas their Majesties...', in Simon, *Irish Coins*, p. 165, Appendix 92.
[111] Whatley, *Scots and Union*, p. 149.

to the new regime and the ever-present threat of a renewed Stuart incursion meant that Scotland had to maintain large forces at home, adding significant pressure on a treasury that already received less revenue than it spent, and helping to bring its management into 'an increasing state of confusion'.[112] The war with France, however, was far less fiscally challenging for Scotland than for England, as Scottish regiments serving abroad were a charge on the English rather than the Scottish Treasury. As we will see in Chapter 4, the more serious monetary consequences of 1689 came a little later and less directly, as Scotland—severely weakened by years of intermittent but severe famine—was buffeted by the force field generated by England's monetary revolution.[113]

In England, the rapidly worsening scarcity of money caused by military expenditure abroad meant a general 'decay of trade', thus eroding that part of the revenue derived from customs and excise by reducing the volume of imports and cash transactions. The government had to collect a diminishing tax bill from a country starved of the means to pay it, in order to make ever-larger payments ranging from a few silver shillings at home to thousands of pounds abroad for naval and military supplies, usually paid in Spanish silver dollars, or 'pieces of eight', borrowed from its own citizens.[114] As silver was still the standard, and as the rating of the silver coins was a sign of royal authority, collectors of the revenue could not refuse to take the king's silver coins by tale, no matter how much silver had been clipped from them, meaning that the government could only spend its own coins overseas at an enormous loss. Despite this problem, the situation was so desperate that receivers of revenue were instructed to take coins in almost any state, including plausible counterfeits.[115]

The rating of gold coins was a different matter. As gold was not the standard, the price of guineas could be allowed to fluctuate in line with market forces. When borrowing guineas from London merchants and goldsmiths, for example, the Treasury had to specify their rate in sterling, which by 1694 could vary from week to week, and occasionally required some haggling.[116] The only certainty was that the price would be higher than the nominal 20*s*. at which the coin had been issued in 1663, and which remained its 'official' rating in successive mint indentures until 1718. The value of Spanish dollars also had to be established in loan negotiations, although it remained more stable than the value of the guinea at 4*s*. 6*d*. by tale or 4*s*. 9*d*. by weight, or for 'weighty pieces'.[117]

---

[112] Murray, 'Administration', pp. 33–4; Murray, 'Treasury', p. 104.
[113] Whatley, *Scots and Union*, pp. 154–70.   [114] Jones, *War and Economy*, p. 76.
[115] 'Entry Book 1689', *CTB* (1689–92), p. 317.
[116] See, for example, 'Minute Book, July 1689', *CTB* (1689–92), p. 44.
[117] 'Entry Book: July 1689', *CTB*, (1689–92), p. 55. For examples of the relative stability of the price of dollars, see, 'Minute Book, 4 May 1668', *CTB*, (1667–8), p. 311; 'Entry Book, 15 Oct. 1684', *CTB*, (1681–5), pp. 428–9.

Unstable coin prices presented splendid opportunities for unscrupulous politicians and officials. Sir William Harbord, while paymaster of William's forces in Ireland, was the subject of complaint from soldiers and officers whom he had paid in guineas and dollars at the rates of £1 4s. and 5s., respectively, rather than the £1 2s. and 4s. 9d. the government had paid for them. While this was 'taken as hardship' by the recipients, who could not spend them at that value, it was good business for Harbord, who turned a profit of 10 per cent on the gold and 5 per cent on the silver.[118] These transactions could be doubly lucrative, as the guineas were sometimes lent at interest to the Treasury by Harbord himself, who was then immediately issued them 'at the same rate' for use in Ireland. But while Harbord was considered corrupt even by the standards of his day, his appears not to have been an isolated case.[119] Many records of loan agreements ended with the injunction that 'the Treasury Lords will take care to have the money issued at the same price'.[120]

Such strictures are testimony not only to a routine expectation of peculation but to the government's difficulties in controlling the relationship between the various non-standard media of exchange and the units of account. Naturally, the treasury borrowed guineas and dollars at the lowest value at which wealthy men would part with them. Unless effectively constrained by the treasury or their consciences, however, government officials spent the same coins at the highest price people would take them, often—as with soldiers' wages—in a 'take it or leave it' situation. In this dynamic, government activity presented a Janus face to the markets in guineas and foreign silver coin.

Receivers of revenue were in a different situation again. As we have seen, they had no choice but to take English silver coins at their face value. To do otherwise would amount to demonetizing what remained the only legitimate money in circulation—a step the government did not take until the recoinage of 1696. We can only assume that, knowing this, people saved their very worst coins for the tax collectors, just as they kept their best coins in hoard whenever they could afford to, or—if they had access to the right markets—sold them to silversmiths and goldsmiths, or directly to clippers and counterfeiters for something higher than their tale value.

While the collection of silver coin was made difficult by its scarcity, the collection of gold was complicated by the uncertainties surrounding its price. Collectors had little choice but to accept guineas at something close to their local market price and hope that the treasury would be willing to take them at the same price or better. The government periodically instructed receivers of revenue not to

---

[118] 'Entry Book, October 1689', *CTB*, (1689–92), p. 248.   [119] Handley, 'Harbord'.
[120] 'Minute Book, July 1689', *CTB* (1689–92), p. 44.

accept guineas at above a given rate. This could not stop their price from rising eventually to as high as thirty shillings—150 per cent of the original rating.[121]

But even if there had been enough good, stable coin to make collecting the taxes straightforward, there could never have been enough to meet the unprecedented fiscal strains of the Nine Years War. The government had no choice but to borrow on a large scale using the accustomed short-term securities—principally tallies secured by specific streams of revenue. But as the government kept deferring payment, and as the number of tallies in the market mushroomed, they lost credit to the point where it was almost impossible for their holders to use them as means of payment, even at crippling rates of discount. The government's existing credit instruments would therefore no longer circulate, placing even more pressure on the availability of coin, and helping to push up the price of guineas. In such an environment it was inevitable that new tallies would eventually be spurned, as happened early in 1694 when the government could find nobody willing to take them in exchange for the supply of naval stores.[122]

While none of these problems was new, their severity in the wake of 1689 was unmatched. Moreover, the government had, in effect, used up any comparatively easy solutions to its monetary problems, leaving its options 'limited to levying taxes and raising voluntary loans'.[123] The government energetically pursued both of these options, although, as Brewer reminds us, no amount of innovation with credit instruments would have had any chance of success if taxation had not been increased to provide sufficient revenue to instil confidence in the government's ability to service its debts.[124] Indeed, it was precisely a loss of such confidence that had frozen the market in tallies in early 1694. But the government's capacity to raise such taxes, and thus to underpin whatever other financial measures it might take, was severely constrained by the shortage of good coin. The government's efforts to solve its fiscal problems would therefore remain hamstrung until it could find some way to overcome or circumvent the same scarcity of money problem faced by the people at large. The alternative was not merely military defeat and the failure of the regime, but the likely end of England's capacity to project power not only in Europe and the wider world but possibly even within the Atlantic archipelago. As I will argue in the next chapter, the solutions the government found would amount to a monetary revolution.

---

[121] 'Minute Book, May 1689'; 'Minute Book, June 1690'; 'Minute Book, July 1690', *CTB* (1689–92), pp. 26, 398, 406; Feavearyear, *Pound*, pp. 130–1.
[122] Jones, *War and Economy*, p. 11.   [123] Brewer, *Sinews*, p. 73.
[124] Brewer, *Sinews*, pp. 88–9.

3
Money and Revolution—the Case of England
1690–1697

> What fatal consequences may not happen, where so great a trust is reposed in private hands.
>
> Robert Murray (1695)

A structural crisis of the depth and scope we have seen besetting England, Ireland, and Scotland for much of the seventeenth century could not end without a fundamental transformation of existing monetary institutions and relationships. In England this took the form of a monetary revolution. The process was attended, in varying degrees, by many of the features generally observed in a revolutionary crisis: febrile and often incoherent debates, with proposals for (sometimes outlandish) innovation matched by attempts to recover (generally mythical) past stability; governments lurching from one inadequate expedient to another; various manifestations of popular discontent and resistance; the increased use of force as the state struggled to maintain control, and finally, the creation of novel institutions and processes with largely unforeseen long-term ramifications.

Monetary Revolution I: the Case for the Concept

I follow Christine Desan in using the concept of an English 'monetary revolution' because it helps to make sense of the events themselves over the short, medium, and longer term, and because it helps to bring into view processes and relationships which otherwise might remain obscure.[1] Specifically, it helps us to see the foundation of the Bank of England (1694); the clipping crisis (1693–5), and the silver recoinage (1696) as elements of a process that was much more than the sum of its parts.

To use the term 'revolution' is not to suggest that a new monetary order emerged fully formed and functioning from the ruins of the old in the space of

---

[1] Desan, *Making Money*, p. 1 *et passim*.

a few years. While the tipping point of revolution—the decisive events that determined the contours of England's new order—can be pinpointed to a few years in the middle of the 1690s, the structural crises that precipitated them were, as we have seen, a long time brewing, and important features of the new order took significant time to stabilize and still longer to mature. From the foundation of the Bank of England in 1694 to the great silver recoinage in 1696 was a short span of time but the Bank of England did not stand unquestioned even in its English (let alone British) role until after the South Sea Bubble had burst in 1720; and its revolutionary paper money, issued on the basis of government debt, continued intermittently to cling to the legitimation of its supposed commodity basis until 1931 (and indirectly until 1970). The English monetary standard, meanwhile, took decades after 1696 to move from silver to a *de facto* gold standard (by which time it was a British standard), and it took another century, and another major crisis, for this change to be enshrined in law.

Historians are already well accustomed to the idea that England experienced a *financial* revolution during this period. Since its publication in 1967, the key concept of P. G. M. Dickson's *The Financial Revolution in England* has become an indispensable part of early modern historians' conceptual toolkit—even of those who otherwise display little interest in monetary or financial questions.[2] The development of public credit, which Dickson traced from the political revolution of 1688–9, is now rightly part of the stock-in-trade of discussions of England's (and Britain's) development as a 'fiscal-military state' during its ultimately successful struggles against France and its emergence as a great imperial power, as well as accounts of the preconditions of the Industrial Revolution.[3]

The value of focussing on *monetary* revolution rather than just the English financial revolution is that it has the potential to bring a wider set of social phenomena into focus and to understand the relationships between them, to offer a broader perspective on the political issues at stake, and, as I show in later chapters, to provide a better vantage point for consideration of developments both within and between the three kingdoms.[4] Finance was a matter for the government and those who funded it as lenders or taxpayers. And while taxes on assets like hawkers' and pedlars' licences, and on commodities like beer, not to mention the hated poll taxes of 1689–98, obviously affected people a long way outside the elite, the general effect of the English financial revolution on the great mass of English people was simply to increase the size and change the incidence of existing burdens, as more revenues were required to fund the government's newly created long-term debts.[5] To that extent, the English financial revolution could even be

---

[2] Dickson, *Financial Revolution*.
[3] See, e.g., Jones, *War and Economy*; Brewer, *Sinews*; Dickinson, 'Sword'.
[4] Wennerlind, *Casualties*, p. 124, notes, for example, that 'few scholars have examined the relationship between the Financial Revolution and the great recoinage'.
[5] Dowell, *History of Taxation*, pp. 48–55; O'Brien, 'Taxation', pp. 2–4.

argued to have narrowed the gap between the elite and the common people on the basis of a more widely shared liability for taxes. The effects of monetary revolution, on the other hand, were generally more ubiquitous and more socially disruptive. We have already seen that rich and poor, elite and common people lived in different monetary worlds in the early modern period. The English monetary revolution—by creating a new form of money that was centrally important to the state and the elite, but which the great mass of the people never handled, and by effectively removing from circulation the ostensible standard coin of the kingdom—widened the gulf between those worlds even as it brought growing numbers of people into the ranks of those with a direct interest in the government's credit. As we will see in the next chapter, the Scottish monetary revolution also created new money, but on a different basis to that in England and with different effects on money's 'social stratigraphy'.[6]

It is also important to note that the *financial* revolution was in essence an affair of the English government and its creditors, with Scotland and Ireland doing little but add to the financial burdens the English government had to manage. Monetary crisis, on the other hand, was manifest in all three kingdoms, but took distinct forms in each of them, with varied consequences for each of the others as well as for the monetary lives and relationships of their respective peoples. The lens of monetary revolution therefore provides a fresh view of the history of each of the three kingdoms and the relationships between them. It also affords a fresh perspective on the struggles between elite groups vying for hegemony within the new political and financial dispensation. Tracing the distinctive course of such struggles in each kingdom will allow us to see more clearly the forces that led to the development of a governing consensus around their respective new monetary orders, and—as we shall see in later chapters—the unified monetary order that would emerge in the following centuries. For the remainder of this chapter, however, our focus will be on England, whose monetary revolution would have profound ramifications not only for its sister kingdoms but for the world.

Monetary Revolution II: Banks

England's rapidly deepening monetary crisis added urgency to long-running debates about possible remedies for the chronic scarcity of money. Pamphlets proposing various kinds of banks proliferated by the dozen after 1690, adding only minor variations to the basic types outlined in Chapter 2.[7] Some of these were considered by the government or Parliament, and two were eventually endorsed,

---

[6] I have borrowed the term from Desan, *Making Money*, p. 191.
[7] The most detailed analysis of the proposals remains Horsefield, *Experiments*, pp. 93–220.

although only one, the Bank of England, founded in June 1694, was to succeed. It would permanently change the structure of monetary power not only in England but ultimately in Ireland and Scotland as well.

The story of the Bank's foundation has been told from many perspectives and need not be recounted in detail here.[8] The Bank was constituted by a charter (sanctioned by Act of Parliament), issued on condition that it lend the government the sum of £1,200,000 for an indefinite period at 8 per cent interest and that half the sum be raised by subscription no later than 1 August 1694. The subscription was filled within two days, largely on credit in that only 25 per cent was paid up. Accordingly, most of the loan to the government was paid with paper credit instruments issued by the Bank itself, rather than with cash. Almost all of this sum consisted of the Bank's 'sealed bills': bills of exchange bearing the Bank's seal, for which the bearer received interest at 3 or 4.5 per cent, and which could be cashed or deposited at the Bank's office.[9] The government was willing to receive them because its other creditors were willing to accept them as payment owing to the confidence they had in the Bank's ability to pay.

From the point of view of a desperate government, the chief significance of the foundation of the Bank was the conversion of a great deal of unsustainable short-term debt into more manageable long-term debt, and the establishment of an effective agency to manage both. This not only provided new funds in the form of the long-term debt itself but also, more importantly, dramatically boosted confidence in the government's capacity to meet its commitments, and thereby thawed the flow of short-term funds which, as we saw in the previous chapter, had frozen two months earlier.[10] This marked the birth of public credit in its modern form. Previously based on moneyed people's confidence (or at least hope) that the Crown would meet its obligations to them directly, it was now based on moneyed people's confidence in an institution founded and owned by moneyed people, underwritten by the symbiotic relationship between that institution and the state.

The shift was neither instant nor absolute. Willingness to accept the Bank's sealed bills was aided immeasurably by the fact that the government itself was willing to accept them as payment of taxes at their face value—the key political decision that usually suffices to confer 'moneyness' on any given object. It is difficult to overstate the radicalism of this arrangement. It put money into the hands of the government's lenders by the extraordinary expedient of allowing them to create it. But the sealed bills circulated only among the commercial elite, and tended to return very rapidly to the Bank, either directly or via the government. They can therefore be viewed as money in only a limited sense. Their

---

[8] Clapham, *Bank*, vol. 1, ch. 1; Andreades, *Bank*, part 2; Richards, *Early History*, ch. 5; Desan, *Making Money*, ch. 8.
[9] Clapham, *Bank*, vol. 1, p. 22.
[10] Feavearyear, *Pound*, pp. 127–9; Jones, *War and Economy*, pp. 13–15.

greater significance was their role in underpinning part of the Bank's issue of another form of paper credit: the 'running cash note', also known as the 'cashier's note', or more simply the 'bank note'. Some of these notes had made up the last £44,335 18s. 9d. of the Bank's £1.2 million payment to the government.[11] They bore no interest and were payable in coin on demand at the Bank's office. Like the sealed bills, they were accepted by the government's creditors owing to their confidence in the Bank, although it took some months before the government itself was willing to accept them in all payments.[12] Once this was done, however, they rapidly became an important part of the currency—at least among those who handled sums as great as five pounds, which was the smallest denomination available. Issued in smaller denominations than sealed bills, and free of the need to negotiate a premium at each exchange to account for the prospect of collecting interest, the running cash notes were a far more convenient medium of circulation.[13]

The quantity of these notes in circulation increased rapidly as the Bank used them, in effect, to convert still more short-term government debt into long-term. Holders of tallies, which had, as we have seen, become completely illiquid, were doubtless relieved to sell them to the Bank at a discount in exchange for the Bank's new notes, which would circulate freely. By 1696 the Bank had bought up £585,000 worth of short-term tallies with its notes.[14] The fact that the bank had revived a market in tallies restored their value to something above par by August 1694 and thus made it possible for the remaining tallies to circulate once more, alongside the new notes. At the same time it increased the market value of what had become a major part of the Bank's assets.

The issue of notes on this basis enabled the Bank to circumvent what would otherwise have been important restrictions on its capacity to make money—in both senses of the term. The Bank had been empowered to lend the government only the £1.2 million specified in the Act and to issue sealed bills to that amount. The issue of notes in exchange for sealed bills, together with the use of banknotes to purchase government debt from third parties and thus allow the government to issue more debt, was an easy way to sidestep both of these restrictions.[15]

By these means the Bank added £1.6 m of new money to a total circulation of less than £18 m by the end of 1694. Moreover, its revival of the market in tallies, and the return of the tallies to par, enabled the government to place £1 m worth of new tallies in August 1694, and ensured that they would circulate within the commercial sphere. The Bank's note issues thus did a great deal very quickly to alleviate the scarcity of money problem, at least in the form it pressed hardest on the government and the mercantile community.

---

[11] Clapham, *Bank*, vol. 1, p. 22.
[12] Desan, *Making Money*, pp. 312–14.
[13] Clapham, *Bank*, vol. 1, p. 22.
[14] Clapham, *Bank*, vol. 1, p. 43.
[15] Feaveayear, *Pound*, p. 129.

Despite their description as 'running cash' notes, it was clear to contemporaries that the Bank of England's notes were not the same as notes of the same name issued by the goldsmith bankers. Rather, the Bank's notes are best understood as combining the notional convertibility on demand into bullion coin of the goldsmiths' notes on the one hand with the claims upon government revenues embodied in tallies and assignments on the other. Like the goldsmiths' notes, the Bank's notes bore a promise to pay the bearer a given amount. It went without saying that this meant payment in coin. Paradoxically, however, the Bank did not at first maintain a fractional reserve, for which at that time 'there was neither theory nor practice'.[16] The notes' promise to 'pay the bearer' was a necessary fiction—true most of the time, but no more a guarantee that every note represented bullion in the Bank's vaults than was the image on the Bank's seal of Britannia sitting on a pile of coins, which appeared in the notes' top-left corner. Despite the promise of convertibility, the Bank's capacity to issue notes was not based primarily on its stocks of coin but on its holdings of government debt in various forms.

The tension created by the disjuncture between the real and imagined basis of the Bank's notes' value manifested itself even before the Bank was established. In order to get parliamentary approval for their scheme, the Bank's promoters were obliged to engage in systematic evasion and obfuscation about the nature and extent of its proposed notes. An initial proposal which made it clear that the proposed Bank intended to issue legal tender notes based solely on government debt was rejected by a Commons committee 'appointed to receive proposals for raising a sum of money towards the carrying on the War against France upon a fund of perpetual interest' on 18 January 1691/2. The Scottish proposer, William Paterson, representing a group of City merchants, was told by the committee that they were not prepared to 'receive any Proposal which required the making the [subscribers'] Bills of Property current, so as to force them on any without their Consent'. Although Paterson assured the committee that his backers would not regard this as an insuperable obstacle, it appears that for the time being it was, as Paterson advised the committee the following day.[17] It would be two more years before the same group was to make another proposal, this time without any suggestion that the deal depended on Parliament making their notes legal tender. The Act that brought the Bank into being made no such provision. Instead, it made the Bank's bills 'assignable by indorsement', which was merely to give a legal assurance that the bills were perfect signifiers of the debt incurred by the Bank at the moment of their issue and could therefore pass securely from hand to hand as property.[18] Important as this was, it was a good step short of obliging people to accept them in payment of any debt.

---

[16] Clapham, *Bank*, vol. 1, p. 34.   [17] JHC, vol. 10, pp. 631–2 (18 Jan. 1691/2).
[18] Desan, *Making Money*, p. 308.

Once his legal tender proposal had been rejected, Paterson was at pains to deny that it had ever been made. This was necessary partly to reassure the members and the public that the intended Bank wanted no such monstrosity, and partly in order to attack the projectors of land banks. In *A Brief Account of the Intended Bank of England*, he suggested that a bank scheme he had promoted earlier had been scuppered because 'no sooner was this Proposal stated by a Society of considerable Persons, but the notion of *Currency* was started, and carried so far before it was well perceived or understood by some, that it then proved of pernicious consequence'. Some promoters, it seemed, had even intended such currency to be forced on the public, 'the effect of which would have been, to turn the Stomachs of Mankind against it'.[19]

Disowning a key aspect of his original proposal was not enough for Paterson's purpose. It was also necessary, if the 'stomachs of mankind' were to return to equilibrium, for the public to be in no doubt of the pure monetary orthodoxy of its promoters. According to the *Brief Account*, the key belief that must underlie any proposal for legal tender paper, 'that the Stamp or Denomination gives or aids to the value of Money', was simply an old mistake, and those who advocated legal tender paper or tokens were asking for 'the power of an *Act of Parliament...to conjure every Man's imagination into the attitude of theirs*'.[20] On the contrary, according to Paterson, the intended Bank of England was premised on the purest principles of bullion coinage, the first of which was 'That all Money or Credit not having an intrinsic value, to answer the Contents or Denomination thereof, is false and counterfeit, and the loss must fall one where or other.' It therefore followed that 'all Credit not founded on the Universal species of Gold or Silver, is impracticable, and can never subsist either safely or long'.[21]

While there was no chance that a seventeenth-century Parliament would approve any scheme whose promoters did not propound these sorts of principles, their main functional purpose was to disguise the radicalism of what had just happened. Despite the pretences of the Act, the Charter, the Bank's notes, and Paterson's pamphlet, the Governor and Company of the Bank of England, in exchange for rescuing the new regime from financial collapse and consequent military defeat, had been ceded a substantial part of what had hitherto been a royal prerogative. The monarch's sovereign authority over money was thus partially surrendered to a corporation of moneyed citizens.

This did not go unnoticed, especially by proponents of rival schemes. Enmeshed in general complaints that the Bank was, or would soon become, too powerful were specific objections to its usurpation of royal power. These were articulated chiefly in arguments that the existence of a Bank was a distinguishing feature of republics and was therefore incompatible with monarchical

---

[19] Paterson, *Brief Account*, p. 5.   [20] Paterson, *Brief Account*, p. 3 (emphases original).
[21] Paterson, *Brief Account*, pp. 9–10.

government.[22] This argument was set out most fully in an anonymous pamphlet of 1694. Around the edges of the argument was a suggestion that most of the directors and subscribers to the Bank were known as people with little 'zeal for kingship'. Even if this were not already the case, the pamphlet argued, it would be an easy matter for the many cashed-up 'warm Republicans in the nation' to acquire a majority shareholding if they so wished. This was a problem because 'money being the sinews of war', the Bank's control of 'most of the money of the nation' created a massive vulnerability. The argument was impervious to the simple observation that the list of original subscribers to the Bank was headed by the king and queen, who had subscribed £100,000. It was equally possible that some future despotic king might use funds from the Exchequer to gain a controlling interest in the Bank and untrammelled access to its funds, thus removing the dependence on the 'frequent parliaments which are the *guardians* of our laws and the *barrier* against oppression and tyranny'. Inevitably, 'either the King will swallow up the Bank, or the Bank supplant the King'.[23]

These arguments did not seem far-fetched to a generation which had endured life-and-death struggles between monarchy and republic in a country that was yet to stabilize in the wake of its most recent revolutionary conflict. And there can be no disputing the author's complaints regarding the Bank's very rapid extension of its interest in the state's financial management, including its large-scale purchases of tallies and its desire to take responsibility for paying the army; nor of its issue of unsealed bills on no security to circumvent the limitations of its incorporating Act of Parliament.[24]

On the face of it, the critics were clearly wrong: the Bank eventually prospered, while the monarchy was never again to experience the existential threats of the seventeenth century. But just as the structure and operation of political power—including the role of the monarchy—were radically transformed by the upheavals of the seventeenth century so as to set England on the path to a parliamentary system with an almost entirely ceremonial monarchy, so the establishment of the Bank marked a critical moment in an equally momentous shift in the structure and distribution of monetary power from the state to its creditors.

At least one opponent of the Bank of England appears to have had this kind of process in view, rather than a republican revolution, when he accepted the gist of Paterson's point, but argued that 'Such politicians as could not allow of Banks here (because 'tis no Commonwealth) mistook the English constitution very much, for, till the time of King Charles the Second, nobody was ashamed to call it a

---

[22] Pincus, *1688*, pp. 393–6, considers many of these arguments in the context of his persuasive challenge to the views of Pocock and others regarding the significance of classical republicanism in the political discourse of the period.
[23] Anonymous, *Considerations*, p. 2.   [24] Anonymous, *Considerations*, p. 3.

commonwealth.'²⁵ For this writer, as for other advocates of a land bank, the questions were not whether England should have a bank, nor whether it might become a commonwealth, but, rather, what kind of bank England should have, how this choice was likely to effect what kind of commonwealth it would be, and how power would be distributed within it.

With these points in mind, some of the arguments of the Bank's opponents take on greater salience. The author of *Reasons against the Continuance of the Bank of England* advanced a line of criticism that went beyond suspicion of the proprietors, hypothetical future scenarios, or some possible coincidence regarding where banks had and had not prospered. Ignoring arguments about which other banks in Europe were truly banks, he insisted on a different point of distinction between the Bank of England and the banks in republics and crypto-republics. Unlike the Bank of England these were true *state* banks, with the whole of their respective polities therefore responsible for their solvency. This made them perfectly secure despite 'their being indebted ten times more than they are really and intrinsically worth', because 'whilst those Governments stand, every man's money is there safe'.²⁶ By contrast, the English state was not responsible for the Bank beyond paying the interest it owed on the perpetual loan.

The author's ostensible concern on this point was for the security of the investors' funds, so it is ironic that for many investors this distance from the state was one of the Bank's major attractions, as the former had given little grounds for confidence in its custodianship of creditors' funds. According to one contemporary commentator who was no friend to the Bank, the nation in 1694 was generally 'treated like a bankrupt', with its paper 'signed by their Majesties Commissioners, being less esteemed than a note under the hand of an ordinary tradesman'.²⁷ As Feavearyear has noted, it was the Bank rather than the subscribers who lent the £1.2 million to the government, and the subscribers did not come forward with such alacrity because they saw an opportunity to lend to the government at 8 per cent, but because they seized a chance to invest in a concern got up by some of the wealthiest and shrewdest men in the City.²⁸

Other writers were also concerned about the mismatch between the Bank's public power and responsibilities and its private basis. Robert Murray, another land bank proponent, also stressed the contrast between the Bank of Amsterdam and other schemes being proposed:

> Ours begin on narrow and private foundations... and do intrust the keeping and dispose [sic] of cash in the same hands, under a private management,

---

²⁵ [Chamberlen,] *Useful Reflections*, p. 3. Pincus, *1688*, p. 395, mistakenly attributes this view to a defender of the Bank of England.
²⁶ Anonymous, *Considerations*, p. 3.   ²⁷ Briscoe, *Late Funds*, p. vii.
²⁸ Feavearyear, *Pound*, p. 125.

uncontrolled by public authority: this is a method so unsecure and impolitic, that one may equally wonder, that men could hope to impose such thing upon the public; and that any could be found so unthinking, as to credit them.... What fatal consequences may not happen, where so great a trust is reposed in private hands, who naturally contract private and separate interests, divided and distinct from that of the republic.[29]

These critics had identified an important structural tension in the relationship between the Bank and the government, which we will see played out through critical episodes over the best part of the next quarter-millennium. While neither the Bank nor the king 'swallowed' the other, the Bank's unmistakeable but undefined public responsibilities meant inevitably that the government and the Bank very rapidly evolved a symbiotic yet indeterminate relationship. As Broz and Grossman have put it, the government and the Bank's proprietors 'remained mutual hostages to an initial incomplete contract'.[30] Given that the central concern of that contract was the terms on which the state had conceded one of its traditional sovereign prerogatives to a private body, it is little wonder that it would periodically become a major preoccupation of politics and public debate for generations to come.

In the 1690s some of that concern was articulated through support for the establishment of a land bank in addition to or instead of the Bank of England. The core idea underlying schemes put forward under the land bank label was to create money on the security of landed property rather than on stocks of debt. Like all bank proposals, however founded, their central claim was that they would help to overcome the desperate scarcity of money for the benefit of both the government and the people at large. But proponents of land banks also sought specifically to benefit landowners. In addition to their constitutional criticisms of the Bank of England, they argued that it provided opportunities only for the monied interest, whereas a land bank would also provide opportunities for cash-poor landed proprietors to profit from supporting the government. A land bank would benefit landowners in other ways. By absorbing so much capital, the Bank of England had pushed up interest rates, decreasing the value of land and making mortgages harder to obtain and more onerous to service.[31] Accordingly, a prominent feature of all proposed land banks was the provision of mortgages on attractive terms to those who subscribed to the bank by pledging their land as security.

Such proposals were clearly intended to appeal to the traditional landed classes, but it is noteworthy that none of the proponents of land banks came from such backgrounds. The most prolific, Hugh Chamberlen, was a medical doctor. His rival promoter, John Briscoe, was a merchant, inventor, and entrepreneur. Of

[29] Murray, *National Bank*, p. 3.   [30] Broz and Grossman, 'Privilege', p. 58.
[31] Carruthers, *City*, pp. 140–1.

Briscoe's partners in the National Land Bank eventually approved by Parliament, John Asgill was a lawyer and Nicholas Barbon (son of a radical, anti-restoration MP) made his money as a builder and the founder of fire insurance.

'Pure' land bank proposals received little support from any quarter. Posturing as a counter to the subversive radicalism of the Bank of England and its monied Whig supporters, most land bank schemes were themselves too radical to attract significant support from the conservative country gentlemen who were the mainstay of the Tories. Like the first version of Paterson's Bank of England proposal, these schemes included a wholly unacceptable stipulation that their notes be made legal tender on the grounds that their basis in land made them completely secure.[32] Later versions dispensed with this requirement but failed to include any satisfactory provision for a cash reserve. As Paterson came to understand, such a reserve—enabling the claim that notes were representative of 'real' money—was an indispensable condition of parliamentary approval and public acceptance.

It was not until they came up with their 'National Land Bank' scheme in 1696 that Briscoe, Barbon, and Asgill were able to enlist any significant political support and ultimately win parliamentary endorsement. Given the composition of this support and the content of the scheme, it is difficult to attribute divisions over the National Land Bank to any conflicting principles of political economy, as some scholars have suggested.[33] Indeed, although some Tories posited an opposition between landed and moneyed interest to 'make political argument', and although the rancorous party-political conflicts of the day were often enacted within and between chartered companies, it is difficult even to locate the land bank neatly in that dynamic, except insofar as it brought together strands of opposition to the ruling 'Junto' Whigs who were aligned with the Bank of England.[34] As the most thorough study of the struggle shows, the leading parliamentary supporters of the scheme were a mixed bag of moderate Tories, Whigs of various stripes (including some who were on their way to becoming Tories), and moderates with no clear allegiance. As a group, moreover, they were no more inclined to support the 'country' interest against the court politicians than was the Parliament as a whole.[35] The commissioners appointed to take subscriptions were mostly London-based and had connections with all the leading companies. Indeed, until the land bank's enabling legislation made their position untenable, sixty-four of the commissioners—about one-fifth—had substantial holdings in the Bank

---

[32] Horsefield, *Experiments*, pp. 158–64, 74–8, 82, 89.   [33] Pincus, *1688*, p. 460.
[34] Hoppit, 'Landed Interest', p. 84, Carruthers, *City*, esp. ch. 6; De Krey, *Fractured Society*, esp. pp. 22–39.
[35] Rubini, 'Battle', p. 703, suggests that the National Land Bank should be understood as a 'country' project. While this is an improvement on the 'Tory' label offered by earlier historians, Rubini's own evidence suggests that the alignments were not clear enough to allow even this categorization.

of England itself.[36] Insofar as the struggle over the National Land Bank took on a clear party-political complexion, it was due to the Junto Whigs' desire to crush any rival to the Bank of England, on whose success their influence and political fortunes largely depended.[37] This is not to dismiss the importance of party politics, sectional interests, or even political principles in conflicts over finance and commercial ventures during this period; rather, it is to suggest that these things had shallower resonances in debates about money and finance than is sometimes suggested, and that lines of cleavage on monetary questions were less coherent than any intellectually pleasing scheme of classification will allow.

Like the Bank of England, the National Land Bank's first business, and the chief condition of its charter, was to lend a large sum of money to the government. It also undertook to provide a cash reserve to ensure the convertibility of its notes, although it is not completely clear where this was to come from once the government had its money.[38] Far from being 'fully committed to the notion that land, and only land, was the basis of wealth',[39] the National Land Bank, like the Bank of England, relied on very substantial subscriptions of cash, prompting Chamberlen to complain that the promoters had actually set up a 'Money-Bank' though calling it a 'Land Bank'.[40] It was thus bound to rely on the confidence of monied people at least as much as that of landowners.

It won parliamentary approval because the king was too desperate for money for ministers to openly resist any reasonable prospect of raising it. As Godolphin wrote to the king, it was 'the only way...of establishing anything like a credit toward the supplying of the army'.[41] The bank failed to realize this hope. Launched at the height of the silver recoinage, when money was scarcer in England than it had ever been, the land bank was required to raise half of the £2,564,000 it was to lend to the government by 1 August 1696. By that date it had managed to raise a total of £2,100 from three subscribers (as well as £5,000 from the king), with only 25 per cent paid up.[42] Naturally the Junto Whigs did nothing to help. As its promoters became increasingly desperate, the Lords of the Treasury refused all their requests to help get it off the ground, including one to accept clipped coin in subscriptions and another to give every encouragement 'for the passing of their Bills in all his Majesty's general Receipts and Payments, as was done in the case of the Bank of England'. Exchanges over these questions were acrimonious, leading to a caustic pamphlet by Asgill after it was wound up.[43]

---

[36] Rubini, 'Battle', p. 705. It is not clear why the relevant clause was inserted, or by whom.
[37] Rubini, 'Battle', pp. 694–6.
[38] Horsefield, *Experiments*, p. 204. Rubini, 'Battle', p. 700, gives a more favourable account of the scheme's provision for a cash reserve.
[39] Pincus, *1688*, p. 460.   [40] Chamberlen, *Remarks Upon a Libel*, p. 3.
[41] [Godolphin] to the King, 29 May 1696, *CSPD* (1696–1696), p. 202.
[42] Rubini, 'Battle', p. 709.
[43] 'Minute Book', May 1696, *CTB* (1696–7), pp. 311–12; Asgill, *Remarks*.

The Treasury Lords' indifference to the fate of the National Land Bank stood in marked contrast to their approach to the government's next attempt to raise money. The Chancellor of the Exchequer, Charles Montagu, had ensured that the Act establishing the land bank had also provided for the creation of exchequer bills—interest-bearing paper money issued by the government in exchange for loans. The first issue began while the land bank was still in its death throes. This was unsuccessful, partly because of the extreme shortage of cash that crippled the land bank, but also because the government's credit had ebbed to a new low under the ongoing pressure of the war. As Aaron Graham has shown, this initial failure only led the Treasury Lords to redouble their efforts to make the next issue succeed. Crucially, and in marked contrast to the land bank's notes, the bills were made payable in taxes, increasing people's willingness to accept them in payments and less likely to run to the Treasury to cash them. At the same time, the government used every kind of inducement and pressure on members of the political and financial elite to establish a fund to support the credit of the bills, including making such support a question of loyalty. While this active, ongoing support for the bills allowed them to succeed well enough to tide the government's finances over, it was a precarious enterprise, tottering on the brink of failure until the prospect of peace began to revive the government's credit in August 1797. Like the Bank the previous year, the exchequer bills saved the state from financial and hence military and political catastrophe.[44]

Despite the fiasco of the National Land Bank's launch and the scepticism of many contemporaries and some historians, there is no reason to think that it could not have succeeded in more favourable circumstances.[45] Banks on similar lines founded in the first decades of the next century were successful in numerous American colonies.[46] More significantly for our study, Bank of Scotland, founded in the year between the Bank of England and the National Land Bank, although never styling itself a land bank, rested on similar foundations to the latter, and—despite attacks from rival ventures—was able to prosper. Before turning our gaze northward, however, it is time to consider the English monetary crisis that not only ensured the failure of the National Land Bank but very nearly undid the Bank of England.

The Coinage Crisis: Judicial Terror and Popular Resistance

It is not clear how the foundation of the Bank affected the monetary problems facing that great majority who passed their entire lives without ever holding a sum

---

[44] Graham, 'Exchequer Bills', esp. pp. 65-7, 69, 71-3, 76-7.
[45] See Rubini, 'Battle', p. 693. Horsefield, *Experiments*, p. 205, concedes the point, despite his generally sceptical approach to Land Banks and their promoters. The Land Bank was a favourite target of 'Whig' historians: see Rogers, *First Nine Years*, ch. 2; Macaulay, *History of England*, vol. 2, pp. 576-7.
[46] Rubini, 'Battle', pp. 700-1, 713; Caden, 'Mint Conditions', p. 284.

so large as to require the use of the five-pound notes which were the smallest the Bank produced. On the one hand, there is little scholarly support for the frequently made claim (first advanced a priori by the 1810 Bullion Committee) that the Bank's money creation fuelled the inflation which aggravated already serious levels of economic distress in 1694–5.[47] On the other hand, at a national level the additional money the Bank provided for domestic circulation more than filled the gap left by the rapidly diminishing supply of silver, enabling a sharp acceleration of silver exports in 1694–5, which might otherwise have led to an economic slump sufficient to destabilize the regime and destroy its capacity to wage war.[48]

Thus enabled, the government's insatiable demand for silver for foreign remittances began gradually to push up the market price of silver from shortly after the foundation of the Bank until November 1694, from which it rose a further 18 per cent in the course of the next ten months.[49] This was merely one element of a complex dynamic of monetary disorder—mediated by war and the pursuit of profit via various legal and illegal routes[50]—which was ultimately to finish off the silver standard as the basis of the monetary order while, paradoxically, cementing as official doctrine a novel definition of money in terms of an eternally fixed value of silver.

The rising price of silver made coin clipping more attractive, especially in the context of high prices and unemployment that characterized London life in the 1690s, and especially 1693–4[51] For as long as people knew that others, including the government, would accept severely clipped coin, and hence were willing to accept it themselves, clipping was highly lucrative. For the perpetrators, it was also much less dangerous and difficult than most other kinds of property crime. The size and weight of the coin fell vertiginously. In 1686 a random bag of circulating silver coins contained 89 per cent of its legal weight, which might be regarded as wear and clipping as usual. It took six years for that figure to fall to 73 per cent; but only two more years to reach 60 per cent. In the course of the next twelve months, it lost 16 per cent of that weight, to fall to 51 per cent of legal weight by 1695.[52]

Clipping bore unevenly on different participants in the monetary order. For the common people, the direct effects—so long as the authorities let the situation run—were not immediately obvious. Until 1695, when it became apparent that the government intended to do something about the clipped coin, by far the most important currency problem for most people was the absolute shortage of money rather than the quality of the coins they could obtain. For these people, clipping, by enabling counterfeiting and removing the profits of melting and exporting, did

---

[47] Cannan, *Paper*, pp. 38–9; Feaveayear, *Pound*, p. 127; Appleby, *Economic Thought*, p. 218. The claim is refuted in Li, *Recoinage*, pp. 11–14, and more thoroughly by Horsefield, 'Inflation'.
[48] Kelly, *Locke*, Table 3.   [49] Rogers, *First Nine Years*, p. 171, Table V.
[50] Quinn, 'Arbitrage', provides a case study of a single London goldsmith to illustrate the drivers and mechanics of this process in detail. See also Kleer, 'Diana', pp. 537–8.
[51] Waddell, 'Distress', p. 324.   [52] Kelly, *Locke*, Table 3.

the great service of keeping currency in circulation. On the other hand, it certainly increased the price of imported goods, and probably also contributed to general inflationary pressures by pushing up prices in terms of the more heavily clipped silver coin.

But the benefits of clipping went far beyond the quotidian. As Dwyryd Jones has pointed out, 'Where trade failed, [England] survived by clipping the coin. It was by clipping that she obtained the bullion needed to pay her debts. Normally such bullion export would enforce an intense monetary squeeze, but clipping provided an escape.'[53] Gilbert Heathcote, a founding director of the Bank and importer in the Baltic trade, was one contemporary who recognized clipping's functional role:

> When we first began this war our kingdom was full of merchandise and silver, and our coin was near its due weight, but our goods and silver have been gradually exhausted, which together with, perhaps a million of clippings, that have been shipt out, have enabled us to continue the expense in Flanders.[54]

But for people in Heathcote's position, as for all of those involved in the payment of money abroad, the negative consequences of clipping were far more direct and obvious than any macroeconomic need it might serve. Overseas balances eventually had to be settled in bullion by weight, with its value dependent on its capacity to be coined into the money of the jurisdiction in question. A significantly greater tale value of clipped coin than full-weight coin was therefore required to settle a foreign balance. As well as importers, this problem pressed particularly hard on the government and on the Bank of England, which lost £128,000 in twelve months after it took over the management of the government's remittances in early 1695.[55]

Despite the deep and tangled roots of England's monetary disorders, clippers soon came to be burdened with all the blame. The Bank of England's first governor, Sir John Houblon, was in no doubt that 'clipping and counterfeiting' was the cause of all problems affecting the currency, both foreign and domestic.[56] Accordingly, the clipping crisis called forth a full-blooded judicial assault, supported by the entire political and monetary elite, on those directly responsible. As Wennerlind argues, the death penalty became an instrument of monetary policy.[57]

The assault began in 1693, when there were sixty-nine prosecutions at the Old Bailey for currency offences, one more than in the previous five years put

---

[53] Jones, *War and Economy*, p. 228.
[54] 'Mr Gilbert Heathcote about the coyn', Goldsmith's MSS 187, iv, f. 20.
[55] Dickson, *Financial Revolution*, p. 346.
[56] 'Sir John Houblon's Proposall about the Coyn', Goldsmiths MSS, 158, ff. 28–9.
[57] Wennerlind, 'Death Penalty'; Wennerlind, *Casualties*, ch. 4.

together.[58] Prosecutions in the provinces, where money was even scarcer, also rose significantly.[59] This level was sustained, on average, over the following four years. Coining prosecutions not only rose in absolute terms but, despite a sharp spike in prosecutions for all offences in 1693, made up a significantly higher proportion of total prosecutions in this period, rising to over a quarter in the peak year of 1695, compared with less than 5 per cent in 1688–92. While increases in prosecutions for a given offence in the seventeenth century were just as likely to reflect levels of official anxiety about the crime in question as they were to reflect an actual increase in offending, there is little doubt that in this episode they reflected both.[60]

The judicial assault was a conspicuous failure. Despite the enormous skill and energy devoted to detection and prosecution—not least by Sir Isaac Newton as Master of the Mint[61]—there were disconcertingly few convictions. In the 1690s less than 37 per cent of the 337 Old Bailey trials for coining offences resulted in convictions, compared with just over 60 per cent for all types of offences.

One response to this problem was an invitation at the end of 1694 by the Lord Mayor and Aldermen of the City of London to William Fleetwood, chaplain-in-ordinary to Their Majesties, to preach a sermon in the Guildhall chapel against clipping.[62] The sermon, which was immediately published, provides insights into the monetary crisis by setting out a didactic exposition of what were rapidly becoming conventional, official ideas on the nature of money, the monetary crisis, and the threat presented by clipping. It therefore illuminates not only the authorities' judicial response to the clipping crisis but also the way they were to approach the recoinage, which was, above all things, their attempt to put a permanent end to clipping. At the same time, Fleetwood's counterarguments illuminate the authorities' beliefs about the popular attitudes standing in the way of any solution, and hence shed some light on the differences between popular and elite attitudes to the nature and significance of money.

The sermon was addressed to anyone involved in the administration of justice. As Fleetwood put it, his key task was to 'wean [men] from that soft pernicious tenderness, that sometimes, certainly, restrains the hand of Justice, slackens the care and vigilance of magistrates, keeps back the under-officers, corrupts the juries (for passions and affections bribe as well as gifts) and withholds the evidence [i.e. witnesses], both from appearing and from speaking out, when they appear'.

Although many prosecutions for currency crimes failed because they were weak, one unique and striking feature of such trials lends weight to Fleetwood's claim that the low conviction rates were in fact due to jurors' reluctance to subject

---

[58] Crime statistics cited in this section have been derived via the statistics functions of the 'Proceedings of the Old Bailey, 1674–1913' (POB), https://www.oldbaileyonline.org/forms/formStats.jsp.
[59] Gaskill, *Crime*, p. 187.   [60] Beattie, *Crime*, pp. 192, 491.
[61] Craig, *Newton*, esp. 20–1; Wennerlind, 'Death Penalty', pp. 148–52.
[62] Handley, 'Fleetwood'.

people to the full rigour of the law for these types of offences. Considering all Old Bailey prosecutions during the 1690s, conviction rates for men and women are very similar: 61.6 per cent and 58.9 per cent, respectively, but this small difference in the overall figure is virtually entirely accounted for by a dramatic gender difference in conviction rates for currency offences, where 46.6 per cent of men were convicted, and only 23.3 per cent of women. These figures did not change noticeably in the peak years of the crisis, except for a small drop in the conviction rate for men. The thirty-four trials for coining offences involving women and men together in 1693–7 underline juries' reluctance to convict women. The evidence in such trials usually centred on people being found together with the trappings of currency crime such as shears, clippings, stamps, crucibles, or freshly clipped coins. The co-accused therefore almost invariably received the same verdict. Those verdicts suggest that juries' reluctance to convict women for these offences withstood the presence of a man in the dock: the conviction rate for the thirty-five women in such trials was identical to that of women tried alone or with other women, while the conviction rate for the thirty-seven men was less than two-thirds the rate for men lacking a female co-accused.

This difference in verdicts is best explained by the almost unique gender difference in the punishment of these crimes. Clipping and coining were high treason and attracted the standard penalties for that crime: drawing, hanging, and quartering for men; drawing and burning at the stake for women. In practice, however, quartering was rarely included in the men's sentences, and when it was, it invariably took place post-mortem, and by the 1690s it had long been the practice that women sentenced to burn were strangled at the stake before the fire was lit.[63] These were small mercies, especially for the women, as violent destruction of their corpse was a truly terrifying prospect for most people at that time.[64] By the seventeenth century the women's punishment was almost uniquely dreadful: meted out otherwise only for a tiny number of rarely committed offences. These differential acquittal rates in coining trials, in the context of a low rate of convictions generally, suggest that Fleetwood was correct to believe that juries were reluctant to send accused coiners and clippers to their legally mandated punishment because they did not believe that the punishment was just.

The sorts of men who sat on Old Bailey juries were not, on the face of it, likely to be indifferent about the state of the coin. Qualified by the possession of assets of 100 marks (£66 13s. 4d.), London jurors were master craftsmen, shopkeepers, and wholesalers of every kind, whose cash and credit relationships were made much more difficult by the increasing monetary disorder.[65] Yet their views on the fitness of the punishment to currency crime diverged from those of the economic and political elite.

---

[63] Campbell, 'Burning', pp. 44–8. [64] Beattie, *Crime*, pp. 527–9.
[65] Beattie, 'Juries', p. 227.

Further down the social scale, the divergence was still sharper, with clippers themselves challenging official attitudes in ways that other criminals seldom did.[66] Many condemned clippers, while begging God's forgiveness for sins including Sabbath-breaking, swearing, excessive drinking, and lewdness, refused to confess to clipping even on the cart or at the stake on the grounds that it was 'no sin', even if, as one woman acknowledged, it was 'a Crime against the Nation'.[67] The Newgate Ordinary, whose task was to bring criminals to repentance, and was clearly keen to publish as many salutary examples as possible in his accounts, was often hard put to be able to say more of a clipper than 'he seemed penitent', or that 'he shew'd some signs of remorse'. In other cases even the Ordinary had to admit that the condemned were 'sullen' and that they refused outright to 'warn the people' with the appropriate dying speech. Clippers were thus less willing than other condemned criminals to play their allocated parts as 'central participants in a theatre of punishment, which offered not merely a spectacle, but also a reinforcement of certain values', presumably because—unlike many murderers and thieves—they did not endorse the scale of moral values on which they were condemned to die.[68]

Another gendered aspect of the criminal law offers further insight into attitudes to clipping further down the social scale than the respectable jurors. Of the thirty-six women condemned for currency offences during 1693–7, thirty-one 'pleaded the belly'—which is to say that they claimed to be pregnant in order to have the sentence respited. All but four of these pleas were successful, in marked contrast to the fewer than 30 per cent of women respited for pregnancy in other types of cases. Successfully pleading the belly following any conviction was usually tantamount to a pardon, as the authorities were very reluctant to throw the cost of caring for a baby onto the parish by executing its mother. It was a common complaint that women respited for pregnancy then did their best to fall pregnant to a turnkey while they waited in gaol.[69] Indeed, of the fifteen respited women in 1693–7 whose subsequent fates can be traced, all were eventually pardoned, despite going through the theatre of being 'called to their former judgement'.[70]

The belly plea was judged by a 'Jury of Matrons', empanelled on the spot from among women in the precinct of the court.[71] These six (or sometimes twelve) women were asked to determine whether the condemned woman was 'quick with quickchild'; that is, whether they could detect a moving foetus, as it was not before this stage of pregnancy that the law regarded life as having begun, and that carrying out the sentence would therefore take the life of an innocent party. It is

---

[66] Fleetwood, *Sermon*, pp. 25–6.
[67] POB, Ordinary's Account, 26 Jan. 1690/1; POB, Trial of Mary Walters, 11 July 1694.
[68] Sharpe, 'Dying Speeches', p. 156.   [69] Oldham, 'Pleading', pp. 22–3.
[70] See, for example, POB, Ordinary's Account, 18 Sept. 1695. Eleven were pardoned *en bloc*: 'Minute Book', 23 April 1697, *CSPD*, (1697–1697), p. 126.
[71] Oldham, 'Pleading', pp. 15–16; Thomas R. Forbes, 'Matrons'.

difficult to be certain about the social composition of these juries as there were no stable criteria to determine how they were selected, nor even what constituted a 'matron' beyond the requirement that they be 'discreet women'.[72] Their decisions therefore provide the best available clue to popular attitudes to the punishment of these crimes. Their far greater readiness to uphold the belly pleas of currency criminals than those of other types of criminals lends further weight to Fleetwood's fear that the common people did not share the elite's views on this question.

Fleetwood's account of why clipping constituted treason, and therefore why severe punishments were justified, reveals what had become the common sense of the day. Money arose when individuals decided to overcome the obvious shortcomings of barter by agreeing among themselves that some common thing could serve as a measure of all values. At first these had been exchanged by weight, which 'is men's security and the true intrinsic worth of money'. This still left the problem of the purity of the metal, and it was only now that the state got involved, for 'it was judged absolutely necessary [Fleetwood did not explain by whom] to intrust the Kings and Governors of Nations with the care and charge of coining all the publick money'.[73] As a result, 'we now have the Public Faith and Conscience, Interest and Honour, all engaged to secure to the receiver the weight and fineness of every single piece of money'. This was why any attempt to counterfeit the public stamp had always been a serious crime, 'because it takes away the trust and security men have in the Princes faithful and honest dealing with them'.

Such arguments were prominent in the intensifying debates over money throughout the later seventeenth century, advanced in a burgeoning number of broadsides, pamphlets, and books. By the time they were set out systematically by John Locke in 1691 in his influential *Some Considerations of the Consequences of the Lowering of Interest, and Raising the Value of Money,* they appear to have become the view of a large proportion of writers on the topic. These notions, as Desan has demonstrated compellingly, represented a radical departure from established monetary practice and theory.[74] The idea that the prince's only role in the monetary system was to guarantee the integrity of immutable monetary standards as agreed between ancestral subjects would have been staggering news to James VI and I, Elizabeth, or indeed any of their predecessors, for whom, as we have seen, the monetary standard was unquestionably part of their prerogative, to be modified from time to time as reasons of state might require.

While this radical reconceptualization of money was rapidly becoming mainstream among the elite, it is difficult to gauge its support or acceptance among other social strata. Fleetwood knew that he had work to do to bring his intended audience to monetary enlightenment when he went to some lengths to refute 'that

---

[72] Forbes, 'Matrons', pp. 26, 29; Oldham, 'Pleading', p. 15.   [73] Fleetwood, *Sermon*, pp. 5–7.
[74] Desan, *Making Money*, ch. 8, esp. 351.

impudent demand of *Who is wronged*' by clipping. He mocked the notion that value might lie anywhere other than in bullion. He asked rhetorically,

> Well, but the money passes still for good and current coin, and where then is the mischief? A little shilling buys as much as a great one, and the name and character of pieces are as good a standard measure of the price and worth of all things else, as if they were full weight, and answered to their name and character; and therefore where is the offence and injury? Who is thereby wronged? This indeed is the last resort of all the patrons of this practice; the refuge to which the guilty fly themselves, and the consideration that stirs the People's pity at their sufferings; they think that hereby none is injured, but this is a mistake, for everyone is injured more or less by clipping.[75]

The injury arose because the general circulation of such money constituted a *de facto* devaluation of the currency 'by making that to go for thirty pence which is indeed but worth twenty'. Like many who argued this way, Fleetwood explained the injury largely in terms of international trade. Clipped currency forces up the price of imports, which ultimately leads to a general rise in prices. It also led to foreigners insisting on the new, milled money in payments, which is why, according to Fleetwood, such money left the country so rapidly.[76]

Fleetwood was, of course, correct to point out that clipping had consequences well beyond the diminishing of the coins used for everyday domestic transactions. In fact, currency crime was the only point where the monetary actions of any of the common people impinged significantly upon the monetary world of the elite. As well as undermining the export value of the standard silver coin, clipping also helped to destabilize the relative and absolute values of the guineas and paper monetary instruments, such as bank notes and international bills of exchange, that were of greatest importance to those engaged in international and other high-value transactions.

While the silver coinage still just managed to serve its everyday domestic purposes throughout 1695, the monetary world of the elite had been seriously disrupted. As one put it privately, 'We are in great confusion about money. In all great bargains men generally contract whether to receive guineas or not, and whether they will take silver or goldsmiths or banknotes; for the most part notes are required.'[77] Private notes had thus become more stable signifiers of the units of account than the official coins they purported to represent.

In the face of these problems, the government's inability to secure popular cooperation for its judicial assault on clippers and coiners gave far greater urgency

---

[75] Fleetwood, *Sermon*, p. 11.   [76] Fleetwood, *Sermon*, p. 10.
[77] John Freke to Robert Harley, 5 Oct. 1695, *Portland MSS*, vol. 3, p. 570.

to the need for a recoinage. The silver coinage needed to be restored in order to stabilize the values of the various media of exchange and the terms of international remittances of every kind. But first it was essential to wrest back control from those who committed currency crime, and the unenlightened jurors and 'matrons' who declined to punish them. In fact, as Locke recognized, the task was beyond the power of the criminal law, no matter how draconian. The only answer was to 'make clipping unprofitable'.[78]

Monetary Revolution III: Coins

The failure of the judicial assault on clipping settled the ongoing debate about whether a recoinage should wait until after the war, although even as late as December 1695 there were a significant number of MPs who maintained that the currency should still be left alone in order that 'the people, on whose good affection the government so much depended, should not be provoked by fresh grievances, greater than any they had yet felt,... that must arise from the calling in the silver coin'. A recoinage would make 'trade stand still', producing 'such disorder and confusion' among the people as might 'drive them to a perfect despair... [and] the most terrible extremities'. The majority, however, were persuaded by arguments that were no less potent for their familiarity: 'by reason of the ill state of the coin, the change abroad was infinitely to the nations prejudice', which severely diminished supplies to the army; and was 'the unhappy cause that the Guineas advanced to thirty shillings'. If not remedied, 'this disease would every day take deeper root, infect the vitals of the nation; and... soon become incurable'.

Less familiar were the arguments about the positive benefits of a recoinage: '[O]ur enemies must be mightily intimidated by so great an action, and would sooner be induced to agree to honourable terms of peace, in case they saw us able to surmount this difficulty, by the retrieving the full state of the coin, on which their hopes of the nation's speedy ruin so much depended; and that it would justly create a mighty esteem abroad, of the greatness and wisdom of the Parliament of England, which was able to conquer such an obstinate and almost insuperable evil, in such a juncture of affairs.'[79] This was not the first time the nation's reputation had figured in monetary debates, but it was surely the first time it had been stated in such bellicose terms. It was no longer a question merely of maintaining honour but of using monetary policy as propaganda to build prestige and overawe enemies. Novel in 1695, this identification of England's national worth and power with the value and stability of its currency would recur through monetary debates across the centuries.

---

[78] Paper to Trumbull, in Kelly, *Locke*, p. 365.   [79] HPHC vol. 3, pp. 4–5 [10 Dec. 1695].

Only reminting at the old standard would achieve this great object. In the same debate Parliament therefore resolved that all clipped money be recoined 'according to the established standard of the mint'.[80] These resolutions marked the success of a lengthy political operation in which the ministerial supporters of a restoration of the currency, with the support of the king, progressively overcame devaluationist opinion within the government's own ranks and then in Parliament.[81] In the course of the struggle, debates that had been simmering in Parliament since 1689, initially in response to the rapid export of the milled silver coins, came to a head. Since then, a number of proposals had been made to devalue the currency, either by decreasing the weight of the existing denominations or by 'crying up' the value of existing pieces, as the Scottish government did more than once in this period. These proposals—some of which were plainly self-interested—came to nothing, defeated by interventions from no less self-interested individuals and groups.[82]

The growing acceptance that a recoinage was unavoidable crystallized arguments over the valuation of the currency that we have encountered in this and the previous chapter, giving rise, as Appleby puts it, to 'a flood of pamphlets which finally made explicit the political issue lurking behind the economic definitions.... For two years, contending pamphleteers addressed themselves to the question of whether money derived its principal value extrinsically from its being legal tender or strictly from its intrinsic, specie content.'[83] This is no exaggeration. Horsefield has identified no fewer than 250 extant items bearing on the controversy published in 1695-6 alone.[84] Many of these were based on manifestly incorrect assumptions, were self-contradictory, or both—occasionally to the point of making it difficult even to decipher what the writer was actually proposing.[85] While there is no need to review these works here, recognizing the confusion that often reigned in the debate can lessen the temptation to view it as a struggle between neatly defined and self-aware interests or between fundamental economic or political principles. In the seventeenth century the empirical and theoretical foundations hardly existed to develop anything so neatly or consistently defined. Moreover, as Li has shown, there was no available solution that did not carry significant costs and risks for almost everybody: the problem was that it was difficult to be sure what these might be, and therefore no obvious way to decide what to do.[86]

Sir Christopher Wren understood how clouded with uncertainty the whole question must be. In a passage that pointed to one of the structural problems of the old order of commodity money, he reflected on how deeply England had

---

[80] HPHC, vol. 3, p. 6 (10 Dec. 1695).   [81] Kelly, *Locke*, pp. 17–33.
[82] Kelly, *Locke*, p. 17; Kleer, 'Diana', provides an account of the self-interest of many devaluationists, although not of the restorationists.
[83] Appleby, *Economic Thought*, p. 220.   [84] Horsefield, *Experiments*, p. 37.
[85] Horsefield, *Experiments*, p. 53.   [86] Li, *Recoinage*, chs. 4–5.

become enmeshed in systems of international exchange, and how this could not but constrain its monetary choices: 'But here lies the difficulty. How shall the new money be fixed, when the value of bullion is so movable a thing? It depends manifestly upon the plenty or scarcity of it in Europe... yet if we do not humor it, our money runs from us, to the advantage, possibly, of some merchants, and the damage of the public.'[87]

To draw attention to such uncertainty, and the dogmatic incoherence that characterized much of the debate, is not to suggest that competing interests were unimportant to its outcome. There was a clear divide between those who were concerned mainly with the domestic economy, who advocated devaluation to bolster the domestic money supply, and those focussed on international transactions, who advocated restoration to stabilize the exchanges. In this form the whole controversy has often been presented as a debate between Locke, who argued for a restoration of the coin to its full weight, and William Lowndes, the Secretary to the Treasury whose report provided historical examples of previous devaluations to make a case for increasing the tale value of coins reminted to the current official weights, in order to set the mint price at a level that would remove any incentive to melt the coin, and to reflect some of the devaluation already brought about by clipping.[88] While this framing of the debate is an obvious oversimplification, it has the advantage of crystallizing the issues into the form that the government and Parliament understood them as they made their decisions.

For almost 250 years after the recoinage, it was widely agreed that Locke had 'crushed [Lowndes] to powder' in this debate.[89] Since the 1930s, however, writers have been more inclined to praise the historically informed and economically sophisticated arguments of Lowndes's report, blaming Locke for the economic and social misery that resulted from his alleged failure to foresee the drastically deflationary tendencies of his prescriptions.[90] From our point of view, however, the point is less to evaluate the positions than to understand why Locke's line of argument proved decisive in its specific context.

One of the greatest appeals of Locke's argument was that it offered a powerful antidote of immutable a priori truth to confusion and uncertainty. It was predicated on the claim that money was nothing other than pieces of silver whose weight was guaranteed by the state. It was therefore nonsensical to speak of the price of money rising or falling, as a given weight of silver can only be worth the same weight of silver. Locke thus swept away the underlying dilemmas

---

[87] 'Sir Christopher Wren's Proposal', reproduced in Li, *Recoinage*, p. 187, Appendix I.
[88] Caffentzis, *Clipped Coins*, pp. 33–8; Martin, *Money*, pp. 122–9; Feavearyear, *Pound*, pp. 132–6; Andreades, *Bank*, pp. 98–102; Lowndes, *Report*, pp. 80–2.
[89] Andreades, *Bank*, p. 100.
[90] Feavearyear, *Pound*; Appleby, 'Locke'. Among modern scholars, Caffentzis, *Clipped Coins*, and Kleer, 'Diana', are more sympathetic to Locke.

of the recoinage with a single tautology. It resonated with great force. We have seen it in Fleetwood's sermon, and it appeared in numerous texts of the period, including the responses of many of the thirteen experts whose views the government had sought in October 1695.[91] Tellingly, it was the first of only two arguments to refute the devaluationist case outlined in the report of the parliamentary debate of December 1695, when the final decision was taken. (The other was that only a favourable balance of trade could keep money in the country.) While it constituted a complete rejection of historical monetary practice and the theory that underpinned it, the argument nonetheless appeared to make sense in 1695. As Desan has argued, the identification of money with its bullion content 'was an intuition made easy by the evident value of the metal that coin contained and it gained particular strength when the government assumed the cost of making coin' and created a world in which for the first time it could appear that 'silver and money were literally interchangeable'.[92] In this context, especially among those who saw the coinage chiefly through the lens of international trade, it made sense to insist that 'the measure of commerce must be perpetually the same, invariable, and keeping the same proportion of value in all its parts', and to believe that the only underlying cause of monetary instability could be the illicit removal of bullion from the coins.[93]

While Locke's provision of a powerful intellectual and intuitive basis for restoration had a critical influence on the debate that was to resonate for centuries, it would not have been successful had it not harmonized with the interests of those who held monetary power. Despite the supposed opposition between landed and monied interests, that group included landholders in their capacity of legislators and leading members of the government. As many writers pointed out, landowners were mostly powerless to counter the inflationary effects of devaluation, as the money value of rents was normally set by long-term leases. This argument naturally carried additional force if one accepted Locke's equation of money with silver, of which landlords would receive less if the standard were to be reduced.

By the end of the seventeenth century, as we have seen, monetary power rested not only with the government, and the landlord class that still supplied its personnel and determined much of its ethos, but with the government's creditors, including those to whom it had ceded the power to create money. One of the major drivers of Locke's thinking, and of the recoinage, was the necessity to guarantee the coin that underpinned the new credit instruments, chiefly Bank of England notes.[94] Again, this was especially important for those who needed to exchange their notes for coin for use in international transactions. Locke and other supporters of maintaining the standard were also worried by the prospect of the government breaching faith with its creditors by reducing the amount of silver

[91] Goldsmiths MSS, 158. [92] Desan, *Making Money*, pp. 353–4.
[93] Locke, *Further Considerations*, p. 20. [94] Wennerlind, *Casualties*, pp. 122, 134.

represented by their claims. As Locke put it, the 20 per cent devaluation proposed by Lowndes 'will weaken, if not totally destroy the public faith, when all that have trusted the public, and assisted our present necessities, upon Acts of Parliament, in the Million Lottery, Bank Act, and other Loans, shall be defrauded of 20 per cent of what those Acts of Parliament were security for'.[95] This argument was repeated in many pamphlets advocating a recoinage at the existing standard. It was compelling in a way that it had never been before because the government's debts had reached staggering proportions, leaving it utterly dependent on its creditors' goodwill and solvency. The possibility that the government might lose its creditors' confidence was simply beyond contemplation.

In the event, the recoinage nearly destroyed the central institution of the monetary revolution. The scarcity of coin at the height of the recoinage drove noteholders to the Bank of England to get hold of what they could. By May 1696, the Bank's holding of coin was down to £36,000 to sustain an issue of £1,750,000, a ratio of just over 2 per cent, obliging it to stop payment. The fictionality of its notes' convertibility was exposed. As a result, the notes went to a discount of up to 20 per cent and did not return to par until the temporary return of peace in September 1697.[96]

The fright to the Bank notwithstanding, both the decision to recoin at the official standard and the process of recoining show clearly how monetary power was distributed, with the poor, the provincial, and those whose economic lives were largely domestic losing out most severely. Although Locke's proposal that the government instantaneously accept clipped silver only by weight was rejected, a very rapid schedule of demonetization was proclaimed, whereby all old coins would pass only by weight by the beginning of April 1696. The process would be progressive, with three or four weeks allowed in which the government would accept by tale a given denomination that had been demonetized for all other purposes. This clearly favoured those who had tax obligations to the government. The losers were the poor and the rural and provincial, who, unless they happened to live near one of only five provincial mints set up for the occasion, had no way of disposing of their coin.[97] Even the choice of locations for the mints reflects the government's focus on international trade. While many cities petitioned for mints, the five chosen were all heavily involved in overseas trade.[98] No thought appears to have been given to the general convenience of the provincial or rural population, for most of whom a mint remained impossibly far away. Nor did a desire to make the process as speedy as possible loom large in official thinking. The provincial mints contributed just over a quarter of the new coins between them and did not

---

[95] Locke, *Further Considerations*, pp. 12–13.
[96] Rogers, *First Nine Years*, p. xviii; Clapham, *Bank*, vol. 1, p. 51.
[97] Gaskill, *Crime*, p. 194.
[98] Caden, 'Mint Conditions', pp. 84–5.

even begin production until September 1696—eight months after the relevant legislation was passed and while demonetization was well under way.[99]

The fear of being stuck with coin whose value would shortly halve naturally made people, including tax gatherers, extremely reluctant to accept clipped coin in payment.[100] Even those who could access a mint laboured under the serious disadvantage of having to wait with no cash whatsoever until the new coins were actually produced. The results were catastrophic, leading to serious distress and anger amongst the people in many towns.[101] This was enough to force the government to slow its demonetization timetable marginally, but not to make any significant change to the process.[102] Rather, the government's response to 'the menaces of the rabble'[103] was to enjoin magistrates to use the relief provisions of the Elizabethan Poor Law, and to use their powers to disperse and suppress the 'unusual meetings of great numbers of persons in divers parts of this kingdom'.[104]

The bungling of the 1696 recoinage burned deep into the corporate memory of English politicians and civil servants. Eleven years later, the recoinage in Scotland attendant on the Act of Union would be managed carefully to create the least possible grievance. But as we shall see, even the architects of a silver recoinage in 1817 also sought, self-consciously and deliberately, to avoid any chance of a repeat of 1696.

The historian Ming-Hsun Li observed that the recoinage 'was a complete failure inasmuch as it did not achieve its purpose. The silver coinage was still at a low ebb after the recoinage. The new silver coins could not be kept in circulation. The silver standard, in fact, continued to lose ground to gold.'[105] This does not go far enough. The recoinage in fact achieved the opposite of what was intended by the chief advocates of maintaining the standard. The silver in the old, clipped coins was exported at a profit almost as soon as it was reminted into overweight coins. English silver coin therefore all but ceased to exist as circulating currency, and minting of silver went to even lower levels than it had been before. Instead, the currency of the ensuing century consisted of various kinds of tokens for very small sums, banknotes for large transactions, and guineas, half-guineas and quarter guineas, together with a mix of counterfeit guineas and genuine and counterfeit foreign coin in between. The price of asserting Locke's absolute certainty of an eternally stable system of commodity money in theory was to destroy forever the inherently unstable and uncertain silver coinage in practice.

---

[99] Caden, 'Mint Conditions', pp. 55, 61.
[100] The tax gatherers took the opportunity to profit by refusing to receive clipped money, while paying clipped money into the Exchequer. TNA SP 44/274 f. 275 (14 Aug. 1696).
[101] Gaskill, *Crime*, pp. 194–7.   [102] Li, *Recoinage*, p. 117.
[103] Minutes, 25 June 1696, TNA SP 44/274 f. 185.
[104] Lords Justices of England, *Whereas by reason of the Recoining...*, 2 July 1696, TNA SP 32/6 f. 219.
[105] Li, *Recoinage*, p. 179.

The recoinage did, however, achieve what many of its advocates regarded as the important purpose of stabilizing the price of the guinea, as a result of which gold would soon replace silver as the *de facto* monetary standard. One consequence was to reinforce the boundaries between the monetary worlds of the labouring poor—who were barely to use regal money at all until the nineteenth century—and the rest of society. The process that began with the introduction of gold coins in 1343 was now complete.

Together with the introduction of banknotes—which by 1697 were available only in denominations of £50 or more[106]—the recoinage completed a revolution that left the English monetary order more clearly stratified than it had ever been. The revolution also took to the heart of English monetary theory and practice two enduring ideological claims that were no less powerful for being incorrect: first, that the basis of its system of currency was the fixed relationship between the units of account and a given quantity of precious metal; and second, that the value of banknotes rested wholly on their capacity to represent that metal.

We shall see later how this system was to stabilize and how its central claims and assumptions were to be tested. In the meantime, however, we need to turn our attention to the very different monetary revolution under way in Scotland and how key elements of England's monetary revolution were extended there, even as the northern kingdom continued along its distinctive monetary trajectory.

---

[106] Byatt, *Promises*, p. 16.

4
Revolution, Union, and Divergence—from Scotland to North Britain

1689–1772

> I grow sensible how ridiculous I am in talking to your Lordship in this manner, when I am wholly ignorant of your customs and the nature of your Bank.
>
> Lord Halifax to the Duke of Montrose (1707)

To attempt to capture in a phrase the relationship between Scotland's monetary revolution and England's would be as fruitless and misleading as to attempt to capture almost any other aspect of the two countries' relationship. Scotland had its own distinctive monetary revolution, triggered by a crisis in its own monetary order, but the timing, severity, and form of that crisis was, inevitably, shaped in crucial ways by the almost contemporaneous revolution taking place in the much bigger and more powerful monetary order to the south. The interaction between the two countries' monetary revolutions was not, however, determined only by the obvious disparity in their size and wealth. Equally important were the two countries' very different places in the composite monarchy.

Political union in 1707 was a decisive episode in Scotland's monetary revolution. Triggered in part by an economic and monetary disaster almost entirely of the Scots' own making, it transformed but did not obliterate monetary difference between the two kingdoms. The complete union of the coinages which accompanied the political union created a British monetary order in which England was clearly hegemonic; and insofar as the state still retained power over the creation of money, the monetary union amounted to not much more than expanding the English monetary system northwards, along with most of its problems. But its effects on the new vehicles of money creation—especially Bank of Scotland and the Bank of England—were as complicated and distinct as those institutions' roles in the Scottish, English, and indeed British monetary orders, and their divergent relationships with sovereign power. Even as the two countries' banking systems became more thoroughly integrated in the decades after the Union, differences between them grew more pronounced. This chapter will trace Scotland's monetary revolution, including the process of monetary union and its long aftermath, in

Forging Nations: Currency, Power, and Nationality in Britain and Ireland since 1603. David Blaazer, Oxford University Press.
© David Blaazer 2023. DOI: 10.1093/oso/9780192887023.003.0005

order to tease out some of these paradoxical outcomes and contextualize future developments.

Storms from the South: Scotland's Money and England's Revolution

We saw in Chapter 2 that Scotland's monetary system had long been in disarray, that the scarcity of money—other than low-denomination coins—had been more serious there than in England, and that it had become even worse in the decades following the restoration of the monarchy. Minting resumed in the wake of the Haltoune scandal in 1688 just in time for the Williamite revolution and England's entry into war with France. As noted in the previous chapter, the war did not subject Scotland to the same colossal fiscal pressures as England. Nevertheless, the force field generated at the height of England's monetary revolution turned Scotland's disarray into chaos, as it violently pushed and pulled different kinds of money in and out of the country. In response, the Scottish government was obliged to take whatever countermeasures it could just to keep some sort of monetary system functioning. As we have seen, its capacity to take such steps rested on its decision, taken against the advice of its own commissioners, to operate a separate monetary standard from England.[1]

By the mid-1690s Scotland was so desperate for coin that even the despised token money produced by James II and VII in Ireland in 1689–90 found a market there, with the Privy Council banning its circulation and import in March 1695. In May, as the English clipping crisis worsened, the Council ordered that clipped English silver pass only by weight.[2] Although the English coin entering Scotland was getting lighter by the week, and although the demand in England for coins in almost any condition remained strong, the monetary vacuum in Scotland was still powerful enough to draw in the English coin, and for Scots to accept it by tale. Such coins were almost useless for foreign trade—except with England—and their circulation inevitably tended to keep higher-quality coins in hoards or reserved for export. Accordingly, the Council in July took steps to keep good money in circulation by raising its value by 10 per cent.[3] The passage of the English Recoinage Act in January 1696 added to the confusion, leading people to refuse even unclipped English hammered coins, which were due to be demonetized, and thus to leave holders out of pocket to the extent of seignorage and normal wear if they could not get their coins back to England or otherwise offload them in time.

---

[1] See Chapter 2, pp. 00–00, above.
[2] SPC, *Proclamation Discharging King James' Copper Coyne in Ireland*, 7 Mar. 1695; SPC, *Proclamation Discharging English Clipt Money*, 16 May 1695, RCS 2, pp. 245, 248.
[3] SPC, *Proclamation Cryeing up the Money*, 12 July 1695, RCS 2, p. 250.

In January 1696 the government had to threaten rigorous enforcement of acceptance by tale not only of these coins but also of its own unclipped merk denominations, emphasizing in a later decree that the merks were to be accepted, no matter how worn or thin.[4] The impending recoinage in England was, it seems, making people fear that the Scottish government would be forced to cry its own money down again, or perhaps even to recoin on similar terms as the English.

This proliferation of contradictory expedients shows a monetary system approaching complete breakdown. There were more to come. In May the government was obliged to act to stamp out a consequence of its earlier attempts to keep money in the country and encourage minting, when it had to close the mint to the acceptance of bullion, prohibit the melting down of English milled silver coins, and call their value back down to the English standard.[5] It appears that goldsmiths had been gathering up undervalued English coin and melting it to convert into overvalued Scottish coin at the mint. The introduction of 'free coinage' meant that this process came at no cost to the goldsmiths themselves. Such was the volume of bullion coming in that the mint could no longer cover its costs out of the allotted revenues. In June, the government attacked this problem another way by returning the Scots shilling-denominated coins to their original notional 12:1 exchange with their English counterparts and reopening the mint a week later.[6]

The completion of the English recoinage led to new problems. The temporary end of clipping in England as a result of the recoinage produced a spike in monetary crime in Scotland, leading Parliament to strengthen the laws against currency offences in October 1696.[7] When the English 'broad money' was finally demonetized, those English people furthest from a mint were the most likely to be stuck with it. The northernmost mint being in York, it was less difficult for people in places as far south as Newcastle to get it to Scotland, where it still went by tale. This was the last thing Scotland needed. The year 1696 was one in a string of the country's 'seven ill years' of intermittent famine, requiring the government to import large quantities of provisions from England to contain the death toll.[8] An insolvent treasury could not afford to collect its taxes by tale in coins that English merchants could now only accept at their bullion value. Moreover, the worn broad money naturally tended to push the heavier Scottish money out of circulation.

The government therefore had little alternative but to demonetize the English broad money in January 1697. At the same time, it tried to make the heavy money

---

[4] SPC, *Proclamation declareing old Unclipt Merk Peices and broad Unclipt English Money to be Currant*, 28 Jan. 1696; SPC, *Proclamation crying down English Milled Crowns...*, 21 May 1696, RCS 2, pp. 255, 258.
[5] SPC, *Proclamation crying down English Milled Crowns...*, 21 May 1696, RCS 2, pp. 257–8.
[6] SPC, *Proclamation crying down the Silver Scotts Crowne Peices...*, 2 June 1696; SPC, *Act for taking off the stop putt upon Bullion*, 9 June 1696, RCS 2, p. 259.
[7] *Act against False Coyning and Clipping of Money*, RPS 1696/9/175 (12 Oct. 1696).
[8] Whatley, *Scots and Union*, pp. 154–70; Saville, *Bank of Scotland*, p. 19.

circulate, and to bring usable English money into the country, by crying up the milled English silver again—this time by 8⅓ per cent.[9] This was probably beyond its powers, as there is no evidence that the king's permission had been formally sought. Five days later, however, the Scots were effectively indemnified for this decision when the English Privy Council authorized them 'to raise or diminish the value of the currency in that kingdom as they shall think proper, in consequence of the scarcity of money, to avoid inconveniences from the importation of foreign specie and English hammered money'.[10] This carte blanche was London's clearest recognition that Scotland's monetary system had become so unstable that the normal processes of governing the composite monarchy could no longer manage it.

In these circumstances the collection of taxes was near impossible, yet the need for revenue continued to grow. Bad harvests aggravated the difficulties, reducing revenues while forcing the export of coin to import grain on the other. Scotland was required to maintain large military forces at home to deal with the disturbances attendant on dearth, resistance to the new regime, and the related threat of a renewed Stewart incursion, but the state of the coin and the economy meant that there was never enough to pay the army.[11] And although the maintenance of the king's armies abroad was a charge on England's Treasury rather than Scotland's, the coinage crisis in England led the government there to demand help from Edinburgh on at least one occasion. In November 1696 the Scottish treasury was required to advance £2,000 sterling to fund recruitment of a Scottish regiment for Flanders, because 'the state of the coin in England' made it impossible for the English Paymaster General to find the cash.[12]

A Failed Revolution? Bank of Scotland and the Company of Scotland

This was the monetary environment in which Scots—mostly but not exclusively of the elite—took two initiatives intended, among other things, to bring strength and stability to Scotland's money. The first was to establish, in June 1695, the Company of Scotland Trading to Africa and the Indies; the second was to found Bank of Scotland the following month. The catastrophic failure of the first of these ventures was to add to the Scottish elite's reasons for seeking political and monetary union with England, which would culminate with the Treaty of Union in 1707. We will now consider both of these initiatives in order to tease

---

[9] SPC, *Proclamatione discharging English Unmillned Money to pass except by weight...*, 23 Jan. 1697, RCS 2, pp. 270–1.
[10] 28 Jan 1697, *CSPD*, (1697–1697), p. 24.   [11] Saville, *Bank of Scotland*, p. 5.
[12] 26 Nov. 1696, *CSPD*, (1697–1697), p. 446.

out their intertwined monetary implications, and to show how each helped to establish the terms on which Scotland would become part of a British monetary order.

Bank of Scotland was a very different institution from the Bank of England. Unlike the Bank of England, Bank of Scotland did not lend money to the government and was banned from doing so without specific parliamentary sanction. It therefore had no direct role in the management of the national debt, or the administration of the government's finances. Its banknotes were not issued on a foundation of state debt, but on the pledges of its proprietors. The Bank was founded on a capital of £1,200,000 Scots, or £100,000 sterling. So poor was Scotland, however, and so devoid of cash, that the founders had to look to England to raise even this sum: of the 172 initial subscribers, 36 were London-based. Most of these Londoners were Scots by birth, but under one of the provisions of the Act establishing the Bank any subscribers who were not Scottish-born would 'thereby be and become naturalized Scotsmen to all intents and purposes whatsoever'.[13] The Londoners, most of whom were merchants, subscribed one-third of the capital. Twenty-five Edinburgh merchants subscribed a quarter. But in contrast to the Bank of England, almost another quarter of the capital was supplied by sixty-three members of Scotland's landed classes, including twenty-four members of the titled nobility.[14] This basis in landed wealth gave Bank of Scotland a stronger family resemblance to the various land bank proposals than to the Bank of England.

Bank of Scotland therefore, unlike its southern counterpart, did not represent, or even appear to represent, some sort of arriviste challenge to the existing structures of power. Rather, it was 'an initiative of Scotland's established rulers', whose directors included senior judges and others of the politico-legal establishment, and who controlled vast tracts of Scotland's land, more than fifty castles, and large numbers of other fortifications.[15] Its leading merchants were not, like the Houblons or William Paterson, recent arrivals, or associates of a revolutionary regime, but the leading figures of old-established firms. And although the bulk of its titled subscribers were firm supporters of the Williamite regime, other aristocrats with substantial holdings, such as the Hamiltons and the Panmures, were not.[16] Unlike the Bank of England, Bank of Scotland enjoyed the active, self-interested support of virtually the entire ruling class.

It could not have survived otherwise, for it was a precarious enterprise launched in a perilous environment. The Act that brought it into being was passed in the middle of what was possibly the most turbulent year in Scottish monetary history to that point. By the time the Bank opened its doors for business in March 1696,

---

[13] *Act for Erecting a Public Bank*, RPS 1695/5/239 (17 July 1695).
[14] Saville, *Bank of Scotland*, p. 3.   [15] Saville, *Bank of Scotland*, p. 20.
[16] Saville, *Bank of Scotland*, Appendix 2, pp. 826–34.

conditions had only worsened and, as we have seen, would continue to do so throughout the year.

Unlike its London counterpart, Bank of Scotland made no secret of the fact that it intended to circulate notes. Indeed, its establishing Act specified that doing so would be one if its key activities, for unlike the English Parliament, the Scottish Parliament's main reason for establishing a bank was not to raise a loan for a government on the brink of bankruptcy but to increase the money supply for commerce and trade for a country on the brink of economic ruin.

This contrast was reflected in many aspects of the bank's early activities, which show another common element with the various schemes for land bank proposed in England. Although it lent on bills of exchange pledging non-landed assets, its main form of lending in its early days was on 'heritable bonds'—securities pledging land.[17] Moreover, while the Bank of England was exclusively a London operation, serving the government and the merchant elite of the City, and was not to establish provincial branches until the 1820s, Bank of Scotland established branches at Glasgow, Aberdeen, Dundee, and Montrose shortly after it commenced business, reflecting the non-metropolitan locations of many of the landowners who made up the largest single category of subscribers and borrowers, as well as the desperate need for currency of those towns. Despite this geographical spread, it is remarkable that the Bank's chosen monetary 'language' was English: the Bank's notes were denominated in sterling rather than in Scottish units of account, suggesting that the pledges securing them were denominated likewise, reflecting the extensive business relationships with England conducted by the landed and mercantile classes as well as what appears to be a complete lack of any nationalistic pride in the monetary sphere.

The bullion 'basis' of Bank of Scotland's notes was, if anything, even more fanciful than the Bank of England's. Only 10 per cent of the bank's capital was paid up. The security for its issues was simply the directors' right to call up as much of the remaining 90 per cent of the subscribed capital as it should require at any time. Bank of Scotland therefore began to make loans and issue notes on the basis of a capital stock of only £10,000 sterling. On this basis the directors seem to have been prepared at the Bank's foundation to issue notes on a ratio of nineteen pounds for every pound's worth of coin it held in its chest.[18] Given the illiquid nature of many of its subscribers' landed assets, as well as of the land pledged as security for loans, these were dubious foundations on which to weather the storms ahead.

The storms came quickly, and very nearly destroyed the bank. In July, the Bank stopped lending because too many of its borrowers—stricken by poor harvests, the scarcity of money, and the general stagnation of the economy—were unable to

---

[17] Checkland, *Scottish Banking*, p. 30.   [18] Saville, *Bank of Scotland*, p. 25.

repay loans. At the same time, the Bank faced a run on its notes engineered by its contemporary, the Company of Scotland. Founded by William Paterson, who was no longer associated with the Bank of England, the Company of Scotland Trading to Africa and the Indies, in typical Paterson style, apparently intended to go into the note-issuing business from the beginning, although according to one hostile contemporary its doing so caused 'universal surprise', as there were 'not six men among the whole subscribers that can say they had a thought of any such design when they subscribed'.[19] While banking was not expressly forbidden by the Company's charter, it was a clear breach of Bank of Scotland's, which had given it a monopoly on banking for twenty-one years. To help in its banking venture, the 'African Company', as it was commonly known, therefore set out to destroy its rival.

While the attempt failed, it had the incidental but highly consequential effect of largely severing Bank of Scotland's links to England, when the directors were obliged to make an emergency call of a further 20 per cent of capital subscribed. The London Scots were in no position, and perhaps no mood to oblige. To find the money in the midst of the English recoinage would doubtless have been very difficult, especially for those who might also have been subscribers to the Bank of England, which had also just called up capital to face a crisis.[20] Just as importantly perhaps, all bar one of the London subscribers were also involved in the Company of Scotland, which had rapidly raised £300,000 sterling from 200 subscribers in London when it was floated.[21] Almost all of the London subscribers therefore sold their shares to Scottish residents rather than comply with the call. This meant the beginning of the end also of the Bank's London committee, as well as its minor efforts to carry on business in England. Bank of Scotland was now an entirely Scottish affair. The stress of the crisis also soon made it an exclusively Edinburgh affair: in 1698 it closed the last of its four branches.[22]

Ironically, given the express purpose of Bank of Scotland's existence, its additional calls on its subscribers, together with the rush to subscribe to the Company of Scotland, worsened the scarcity of money. Between them, the two enterprises had amassed a total of £480,000 Scots (£40,000 sterling) of the country's meagre coin. The total amount pledged by residents of Scotland was around £4.4 million Scots (£366,600 sterling), more than twice the value of Scotland's annual exports.[23] As James Hamilton of Pencaitland wrote to his relative, the Earl of Arran, the little money that remained in Scotland after paying for imports of grain 'lies locked up in the bank, but more in the African affair, and so does not circulate'.[24] This can hardly have been news to Arran. He and his mother, the Duchess of Hamilton,

---

[19] Holland, *Short Discourse*, p. 19.   [20] Clapham, *Bank*, vol. 1, p. 42.
[21] Watt, *Price*, p. 36; Saville, *Bank of Scotland*, p. 14.
[22] Saville, *Bank of Scotland*, p. 38; Checkland, *Scottish Banking*, p. 36.
[23] Jones, 'Bold Adventurers', p. 37.   [24] 21 Nov. 1696, NRS, GD486/1/10848.

each had £8,000 'locked up' in the Bank, while the Duchess, as the African Company's first subscriber, had a further £3,000 in that concern.[25]

The collapse of the Bank had to be averted at almost any cost. In addition to the personal losses it would have meant to its wealthy and powerful subscribers, it would also have caused the collapse of Scotland's fiscal system, of which the Bank, despite not lending to the government, had quickly become an indispensable part. Apart from landowners and merchants, the Bank's other big customers were consortia of tax farmers, who borrowed the Bank's notes on the security of their anticipated collections to pay the government what was owing. The Bank also lent notes to government officials, albeit on personal security, to enable them to disburse money as required. Once again, we see wholly new monetary instruments rapidly acquiring the key features of 'moneyness': acceptance in payment by the government, and general acceptance in payments in society at large. But in seventeenth-century Scotland, as in England, this general acceptance could subsist only on a putative bullion basis. Richard Saville has recognized the collective acts of imagination this required: 'If the government and the tax-farmers could maintain the fiction that bank paper was really one step away from good coin of an intrinsic worth in silver or gold equal to the face value, then the economy would benefit along with the government.'[26] Conversely, though, if this fiction were to collapse, the country would collapse with it.

To suggest that Scotland might 'collapse' if Bank of Scotland were to fail is no mere hyperbole. Given the amount of capital tied up in it, the same claim might also be made about the Company of Scotland. And when that enterprise failed, Scotland really did collapse, in the sense that it was no longer capable of maintaining itself as a sovereign state and had little alternative but to seek political and monetary union with England.

The Company of Scotland was established on the model of trading companies founded by various European states between the sixteenth and eighteenth centuries, of which the British and Dutch East India Companies are the largest and best known. Founded as Scotland's first such company, it was destined to be its last. While its specific objectives evolved rapidly, its underlying, universally understood goal was to establish a Scottish empire in order to break free from the 'national sense of frustration, even of strangulation' arising from the mercantilist restrictions of its European neighbours, above all England.[27]

Despite its name, and its unexpected foray into the banking business, the eventual site selected for this venture—kept secret even from its ships' masters until they had put to sea—was Darien, on the isthmus of Panama, where the company aimed to establish an entrepôt colony.[28] Two expeditions of colonists in 1698 and 1699 ended in disaster, with the death through disease and starvation of

---

[25] Jones, 'Bold Adventurers', p. 31.
[26] Saville, *Bank of Scotland*, p. 28.
[27] Richards, 'Darién', pp. 31–2.
[28] Paul, *Anglophobia*, p. 8.

most of the colonists and the loss of supplies, ships, and other equipment. Much of this, including the ships, had been procured overseas, meaning that the loss of the company's capital was a dead loss to Scotland's economy.[29]

The company's lost assets eventually amounted to around a quarter of the liquid capital of Scotland. Scots from almost every class were directly affected, for the African Company had not only attracted investments large and small from a very wide cross section of society but also left unpaid bills and wages.[30] This distribution of loss would have enduring consequences for Scotland's monetary future.

One effect of the disaster was to deepen antagonisms between England and Scotland.[31] In January 1695, the English Parliament, following protests from the East India Company, resolved that the company's directors be impeached for high crimes and misdemeanours, the first of a series of actions culminating in the prohibiting of subscriptions by English residents and the working of the company's ships by seamen of 'England, Ireland or the plantations'.[32] While this led Scots to blame England for the company's eventual failure, it was less consequential than mismanagement of what was in the last analysis a scheme beyond Scotland's capacity to execute.[33] Despite the Anglophobia it generated, the Darien disaster made complete economic union with England much more attractive to many Scots, and helped to ensure that the economic arguments would overwhelmingly be on one side of the question.[34] With the Darien venture Scotland had tried one path out of the dilemma of being the small, poor, subordinate neighbour of a large, dynamic, commercially aggressive economy. It now had little choice but to try another by joining its own imperial ambitions with England's.[35]

The role of the failure of the Darien scheme in making the economic case for union overpowering is a commonplace of Scottish history.[36] The case was already strong. Access on equal terms to the markets and resources of England's growing empire were seen increasingly as a way out of Scotland's chronic poverty. Even as opposition to union became increasingly vocal, arguments against economic union remained muted.[37] This is not to suggest, of course, that the Union was driven solely or even primarily by economic factors. Rather, it needs to be understood broadly both 'as a response to a critical combination of problems—dynastic,

---

[29] Whatley, *Scots and Union*, p. 185.   [30] Jones, 'Bold Adventurers', pp. 33–7.
[31] Paul, *Anglophobia*, esp. pp. 11–13.
[32] JHC, vol. 11, p. 407 (21 Jan. 1695/6); JHL, vol. 15, pp. 618–19 (20 Dec. 1695). Watt, *Price*, pp. 39–45; Prebble, *Darien*, pp. 51–63; Paul, *Anglophobia*, pp. 9–10.
[33] Watt, *Price*, p. 253; Whatley, *Scots and Union*, p. 187.
[34] Smout, 'Economic Background', pp. 459, 466 n. 3. Whatley, *Scots and Union*, pp. 179–89.
[35] Richards, 'Darién', p. 42; Whatley, *Bought and Sold?*, p. 87.
[36] Whatley's section heading—'Darien: the Final Straw'—is representative of many historians' views: Whatley, *Scots and Union*, p. 79.
[37] Levack, *British State*, p. 156.

confessional, commercial', and within a European medieval and early modern context in which the union of nations within composite monarchies was a frequent occurrence.[38]

Exporting Revolution? The Union of the Coins

If opposition to economic union was weak, opposition to monetary union was non-existent. Not only was there no public debate about it but the negotiators settled the question quickly and easily. Unlike the other economic clauses of the treaty, there was not even any discussion of the terms on which monetary union would occur. As David Fox puts it, the monetary union 'did not seem to strike them as contentious'.[39] This complete lack of contemporary debate about monetary union, and the resulting absence of primary source documents, has meant that it has attracted next to no historical discussion.[40]

The monetary union nevertheless repays scrutiny. First, we need to consider why it was so uncontentious. For while we have already seen a strong inclination among many of the Scots elite in favour of assimilating Scotland's money to England's, we have also seen Scottish monetary authorities making use of their limited independence when it seemed necessary for Scotland's economic wellbeing. Why then, in the end, did Scotland's monetary independence have literally no defenders or even mourners? Second, we need to examine the specifics of the monetary union. Uncontroversial as it was, its implementation became the occasion of some sharp struggles between Scottish and English actors, and produced clear winners and losers. Third, the process of the recoinage necessitated by monetary union was crucial to the development of Bank of Scotland's role in Scotland's post-union monetary system. Finally, we need to consider the distribution of 'the Equivalent' paid to Scots from the English Treasury. The Equivalent not only was critical in securing support for the Union but also provided the funds necessary to cover the cost of assimilating the Scottish coinage to the English standard. Just as importantly, the process of its distribution was to have enduring consequences not only for the people of Scotland but also for the evolution of the relationships between the two countries' banking systems.

Monetary union was uncontentious because the Darien disaster entailed, first and foremost, the wreck of Scotland's already teetering coinage. The sudden dead loss of a quarter of a coinage that was already inadequate and chronically unstable, with the resulting crippling of the economic activity that was the only path to

---

[38] Robertson, 'Union', p. 226. The European context is elaborated in various ways by the essays in McKillop and Ó Siochrú, *Forging the State*.
[39] Fox, 'Monetary Union', p. 3.
[40] The exceptions are Fox, 'Monetary Union', and Murray, 'Scottish Recoinage'.

bringing bullion back into the country, put Scotland's already friendless currency into a death spiral.

The extreme scarcity of money inevitably drew enthusiasts for banking and currency schemes into Scottish debates, as it had already drawn Paterson. Hugh Chamberlen, having been frustrated in his schemes for a land bank in England, now saw an opening in Scotland, and published pamphlets in Edinburgh to that effect.[41] In opposition to Chamberlen, John Law proposed a land bank operated by a parliamentary commission issuing inconvertible, interest-bearing notes to landed men on the security of their land alone. He also proposed a recoinage and revaluation to place all circulating money in Scotland on the English standard. Another pamphleteer dismissed Chamberlen's scheme out of hand, proposing instead the creation of a token coinage solely for domestic use in order to free up gold and silver for international trade.[42]

Whatever their differences, all of these writers agreed that Scotland's 'general and raging Scarcity of Current Money' was growing steadily worse.[43] They mostly agreed also on the causes, as outlined by Chamberlen's anonymous opponent. The most important of these were ongoing famine and the consequent need to import grain; 'the great stock of money that was collected, exported, expended and lost upon the Darien project'; the indirect monetary effects of the long-running war with France; and the ongoing trade deficit, which was in large part due to the scarcity of money itself, by which 'all trade, all business, and all works private and public are stopped'.[44]

The problem did not just exercise pamphleteers. Bank of Scotland, after long deliberation, recognized a good business opportunity and reduced the lowest denomination of its notes from five pounds to one pound sterling in 1704, thus helping to get more notes into circulation to fill part of the monetary void. The unique nomenclature of the notes shines some light on the bank's expectations about who would use them. Its one-pound notes showed their value as 'Twelve Pounds Scots' as well as one pound sterling. While thus remaining within Bank of Scotland's sterling frame of reference, the notes were clearly intended chiefly for small traders to do everyday, domestic business using their familiar units of account. In this way, the central institution of Scotland's monetary revolution was able to mitigate the consequences of the ruin of the country's coinage—at least of its higher denominations.

The introduction of one-pound notes highlights another key difference between the banks of the northern and southern kingdoms. As we have seen, the Bank of England since 1697 had issued notes no smaller than fifty pounds, not

---

[41] [Chamberlen,] *Present Remedie*. For the specifics of the land bank scheme in Scotland, see Horsefield, *Experiments*, p. 177.
[42] Anon., *Overture*, p. 1.   [43] Anon., *Overture*, p. 1; [Chamberlen,] *Present Remedie*, p. 9.
[44] Anon., *Overture*, p. 1.

only underlining the very different roles the two banks played in their respective nations but also, as we will see, laying the basis of what was to become a defining monetary difference between England and Scotland that was to endure for two centuries and briefly to become the subject of sharp dispute within the Union.

The government, for its part, considered one expedient after another, but settled on none. Rumours inevitably circulated, with nearly fatal consequences for Bank of Scotland. In late 1704, a rumour 'industriously promoted and spread by some persons' that the value of the coin might be raised led to a run on its notes, as holders tried to exchange them for coin which might soon be exchangeable for notes to a higher value. This in turn sparked panic, leading the Bank to ask the Privy Council to audit it in order to show 'the sufficiency of the nation's security from the Bank'.[45] But however secure the bank was on paper, its cash ratios left it with no choice but to stop payment in December. Worse still, it could not resort to calling up any significant amount of capital to pay the notes, as there was so little specie in the country that to do so would have been to bankrupt the subscribers and demolish the Bank's own foundation. The 'fiction' underpinning its note issues was laid bare.[46] The Bank's declaration that it would pay interest on the notes for whatever period it would not be able to honour them provided enough of a fig leaf of respectability to allow the bank to survive until it resumed payments in May 1705, just as the Bank of England had survived the crisis of 1696.

That the rumours were not unfounded became clear in July, when Parliament did actively consider a proposal to raise the Scottish coin. This was rejected, but Parliament did agree to appoint a day to consider lowering the value of foreign coin. Nothing appears to have come of this proposal, but in February 1706 the Privy Council established a committee to try to find a way of keeping coin in the country and to 'set the mint house a coining', for as one of the committee's members put it privately, 'Our nation is in a most lamentable condition through the scarcity of money, which pinches to that degree that even the greatest in the nation find difficulties to get money to give to mercats.'[47]

The committee's initial task was quickly subsumed by deliberations over the Act of Union, the most radical change in Scotland's monetary history. Scotland's separate coinage would end, and, for the time being, a purely English coinage would serve as Britain's. It was not until the year after the Union that the designs of the coins changed to reflect their role in a British system, with the incorporation of Scottish and English devices onto a single shield, and the issue of a halfpenny (sixpence Scots) featuring a rose and thistle on a single stem surmounted by a crown.[48]

---

[45] Directors' Minute Book, 18 Dec. 1704, LBGA, BoS/1.
[46] Checkland, *Scottish Banking*, p. 38.
[47] John, Earl of Ruglen, to John, Duke of Hamilton, 5 Feb. 1705/6, NRS, GD406/1/6706.
[48] https://www.britishmuseum.org/collection/object/C_1919-0918-328-A; Grueber, *Handbook*, p. 142, plate 36.

Beyond this, union did not mean uniformity. To begin with, the relevant, sentence-length Article of the Act of Union did not define a new unit of account for Scotland, which continued to use both Scots pounds (and merks) and sterling, as it had done before the Union. As Fox points out, 'the provision was solely concerned with what was called in the eighteenth century "real" rather than "imaginary" money'.[49] That the drafters of the legislation appeared to think that to legislate for coin was to legislate for money is entirely in keeping with the prevailing contemporary views about money we explored in the previous chapter. Among other things, it meant that the framers of the Union saw no need to make any provisions concerning banks, not recognizing the critical roles that the Bank of England and Bank of Scotland now had in money creation. From the point of view of the Union project this was probably just as well; any attempt to unite or homogenize the banks would have posed formidable political and technical difficulties. Moreover, as we shall see shortly, Scots' faith in Bank of Scotland and the money it created were crucial to the success not just of the monetary union but also of key aspects of the whole union enterprise: the recoinage and the payment of the Equivalent.

The Equivalent was a sum of £398,085 10s. sterling to be paid to 'Scotland' under the terms of the Treaty of Union. Its ostensible rationale was to compensate Scotland for increased taxes and the share of responsibility that it would be required to take for England's national debt, which was now to become Britain's. The elaborate negotiations and arcane calculations required to arrive at this absurdly precise sum fooled very few, for, as Crawford Spence has shown, such a calculation was simply not possible.[50] In fact, as the process of its disbursement makes plain, the Equivalent was 'the price of Scotland', or rather, the amount required to appease 'Scotland's merchant and landowning class' for the surrender of the control of their country to foreigners.[51]

The notion that Scotland was 'bought and sold for English gold' became a popular refrain almost as soon as the Acts had passed.[52] Bolstered by Robert Burns's 'Parcel of Rogues in a Nation' in 1791 and subsequently by a succession of folk singers throughout the English-speaking world, it remains popular to the present day, especially among Scots nationalists. Insofar as it attributes the Union to the bribery of Scots parliamentarians it has generally enjoyed less favour among historians, who mostly see nothing in the passage of the Act beyond the standard contemporary tools of parliamentary management, and who, more recently, discern 'deeper roots and stronger principled support in Scotland' for union than have often been acknowledged.[53] Insofar as it refers to the payment of the

---

[49] Fox, 'Monetary Union', pp. 3–4.
[50] Spence, 'Accounting', esp. pp. 382–4. See also Watt, *Price*, pp. 227–30.
[51] Spence, 'Accounting', p. 381.   [52] Whatley, *Bought and Sold?*, p. 5.
[53] Whatley, *Scots and Union*, p. xiii, notes his own changed thinking on this question, along with a shift in the weight of scholarly opinion.

Equivalent as one of the terms of the Union, it has more weight. Even so, the reality is more complicated and, in some ways, more disturbing. For the mechanisms used for the recoinage and for the payment of the 'Equivalent' meant that Scotland was bought, sold, borrowed, and lent for a little gold, but, above all, for different kinds of paper including some that severely disadvantaged the recipients. As the modes of payment were the occasion of a complex struggle of competing monetary nationalisms and commercial interests in the short term, and as its longer-term effect was to extend Scotland's distinctive paper money system while simultaneously strengthening its links to London, it needs to be considered in some detail.

Although the Equivalent was, and often still is, described as being paid to 'Scotland', the Act of Union itself made this impossible, as Scotland thereby ceased to be a corporate entity to which payments could be made. The nearest attempts to provide money to 'Scotland' as a collective were the provisions that Scottish residents would be exempt from the increase in customs necessary to bring them to English levels, that £2000 annually should be spent on encouraging wool processing, and that any sums remaining after all other disbursements were to be spent on the development of fisheries or other economic infrastructure.[54] Neither of these sums was actually spent, the latter because the money ran out long before all the other commitments were paid; the former because, as it had nowhere been specified to whom the money should be paid, the commissioners for the Equivalent could not pay it.[55] The bulk of the money was to be paid, in order, to individuals to cover any losses they might suffer in the standardization of the coinage; to compensate subscribers to the Company of Scotland for the loss of their capital investment (with 5 per cent interest per annum added); and to pay any debts owed by the government. The payment (or, in the last case, non-payment) of each of these had significant lasting effects on the monetary order of Scotland and the monetary lives of large sections of the population.

The recoinage directly affected more people than any other aspect of the Equivalent. Although the valuation of the coin was not up for discussion, the process adopted showed clearly that lessons had been learnt from the debacle of 1696. Given that many Scots—especially outside the elite—were hostile to the Union, and that suspicions about English good faith regarding the Equivalent were widespread among 'the mob', this was elementary political sense. The elite, for reasons we will consider shortly, were deeply worried about how the Equivalent would be received on its arrival in Edinburgh, and their relief was clear when it turned out that there was 'but very small disturbance compared to what every body expected from our foolish folks', with a large gathering of

---

[54] Article XV, Articles of Union, RPS, 1706/10/257 (16 Jan. 1707).
[55] Equivalent Commissioners, 'Representation of the State of the Equivalent Paid to Scotland', 9 Jan. 1707/8, TNA, T17/1 ff. 225, 227–8.

spectators but only a few stones thrown.[56] It was well understood that the common people of Scotland were in no frame of mind to tolerate the inequity and hardship inflicted on their English counterparts eleven years earlier.

The authorities were therefore determined that the entire cost of bringing all the current money in Scotland—Scottish, English, and other—to the English standard would be borne by the state. As clipped coin of every description had long been demonetized in Scotland, this cost was proportionately smaller than it had been in the English recoinage. Nonetheless, the loss in weight through normal wear was significant, leaving the bullion content of the Scottish and foreign coins short by around 15 and 13 per cent, respectively, when recoined into English money, at a total cost of around £47,000 on the total collection of £371,117. The English coin posed a different problem. While it did not need to be recoined, the fact that it passed for 8⅓ per cent more in Scotland than in England required an elaborate scheme of issuing certificates to holders of English silver coin so that they could be compensated for the fact that their coins were now to circulate at their English ratings. These certificates—with a total value of £3,020 nationally—could be redeemed at Bank of Scotland for notes or coin at the bearer's option.[57]

People were also to be spared the hardship of being left with no money while waiting for their coin to be reminted, which had paralysed the English economy for months in 1696. It was Bank of Scotland, rather than the people at large, who were to do the waiting. While anybody could take sums of one hundred pounds or more of Scottish or foreign money to the mint to be recoined, virtually everybody with coins of sufficient value exercised the much more convenient option of exchanging their coins at Bank of Scotland for its notes or English coin (supplied by the Equivalent commissioners), as they preferred.[58] Holders of small sums of coin therefore simply exchanged their old coin for new, while many holders of larger amounts took the notes, which remained in circulation. The provision of a facility for people to instantly obtain new coin demonstrated an unprecedented solicitousness for the monetary needs of the poor. Even more remarkable, and in stark contrast to the approach in 1696, was the decision to show forbearance to people from the Highlands, who 'by reason of the distance and the badness of the weather' could not transmit their money to Edinburgh before the due date.[59]

For those with larger sums, the instant exchange of coins for Bank of Scotland notes was equally convenient, but the greatest beneficiary of the operation was the Bank itself, which was enabled to put a large number of notes into circulation, while acquiring a stock of good coin which it could lend at interest once the mint

[56] Sir James Erskine to the Earl of Mar, 5 Aug. 1707, NRS, GD124/15/616; Seafield to the Earl of Mar, 5 Aug. 1707, NRS, GD123/15/635.
[57] Equivalent Commissioners, 'Representation', 9 Jan. 1707/8, TNA, T17/1 ff. 224, 229.
[58] [Cope] to [Bank of England], [September 1707] BE M5/671. SPC, proclamations of 19 Sept. 1707, 12 Jan. 1708, 28 Apr. 1708, *RCS* 2, pp. 297–302.
[59] Equivalent Commissioners, 'Representation', 9 Jan. 1707/8, TNA, T17/1. f. 224.

had finished its work. The bank nonetheless saw itself as hard done by, especially when a promised ½ per cent commission on the entire coinage was never paid, despite years of lobbying and petitioning. It complained not only about its costs for 'constant and laborious attendance for more than seventeen months' but also of 'the burden of a real advance of sixty thousand pounds sterling for most of that time'.[60] The 'reality' of the advance might be questioned; the reality of the extension of the Bank's business cannot.

This increase in the quantity and reach of Bank of Scotland's notes, including its unique one-pound notes, eased Scotland's scarcity of money, and helped to make banknotes a regular and accepted feature of the monetary lives of large sections of the population. Thus, at the very moment of complete assimilation of the coinage, Scotland accelerated its progress down a monetary path divergent from England's. But the recoinage also had a contrary effect. As no provision was made either for minting copper in Edinburgh or for transporting it from London, Scots soon found themselves bereft of any official coin smaller than the high-value English—now British—silver sixpence, with a value of six shillings in the units of account that most Scots still spoke and thought in. But even this, being undervalued, disappeared as quickly from Scotland as it had from England, along with the other silver denominations.

An increased circulation of Bank of Scotland notes was not what the Bank of England and the English government had intended. Instead, the government hoped to establish a regular circulation of exchequer bills in Scotland, which the Bank supported as part of its strategy to maximize the profits on its role in the Equivalent. If successful, this would have integrated Scotland much more closely with England's system of paper credit. It could also have threatened the viability of Bank of Scotland. It was unsuccessful not only because Bank of Scotland and others resisted it for reasons of financial self-interest but also because many Scots opposed the government's plans out of hostility to the Union itself.

The Equivalent was initially remitted to Scotland in the form of £100,085 10s. in coin and £298,000 in exchequer bills. The inclusion of the latter was controversial from the beginning, as were many aspects of the manner of its payment. These were argued out between the Scots and English Equivalent commissioners. At first, the English plan was to make the Equivalent payable in London to the Scottish commissioners, who would then be required to acquit it before it left for Edinburgh, thus placing on them the considerable expense and risk of transporting any cash that might be needed by Scottish residents. Although this proposal was withdrawn, as was another to pay part of the sum in Bank of England notes, the English proposal to pay three-quarters of the Equivalent in exchequer bills proceeded against the protests of most of the Scottish

---

[60] Letter from J. Smith et al. to Lord High Treasurer of Great Britain, 13 Feb. 1714/15. LBGA, BoS, 2/6/1/1.

commissioners, who feared that they would 'be blamed most horribly by the nation if we take anything but clear cash'.[61]

The Earl of Mar, as Secretary of State and the key Scottish negotiator of the Union, worked hard to win the commissioners' acquiescence to the English plan. At that time very close to the leading English court politicians, and with some connections to the Bank of England, Mar argued that there would be no need for large amounts of cash for some time, as no payments of any kind were to be made until the losses on the coinage had been calculated. He recognized that the Scots negotiators were in a difficult position. On the one hand, 'any scruples or difficulties that were proposed in the method of the payment are thought here [in London] to be of our own making'. 'Then again in Scotland', he continued, 'tis but too probable we will be mistaken by people there'. Certain that more cash could be made available, Mar's strategy was to wait and see 'how the notes will be received', and for the Scottish commissioners to exchange some of the bills for cash in London if required. It was important, however, as he confided to Lord Seafield, the Scottish Chancellor, to keep the commissioners in the dark about the possibility of additional cash in order to make them accept the current English proposal. An inkling that more cash could be made available would only encourage them to demand it immediately, which 'might put such a stop to the affair that the Equivalent might be a long time of being paid'. In the meantime, 'all well wishers to the United Kingdom' should do their best to 'make this affair easy'.[62]

Although Mar hoped that 'people will be a little easy' once the Equivalent was on its way to Scotland, his own anxieties only increased.[63] It was still far from certain that the Scottish commissioners in Edinburgh would be willing to accept the bills as a full acquittal of the Equivalent. In his view people in England had an exaggerated view of the power of a few leading Scottish politicians, including himself, Seafield, and the Duke of Montrose, to influence events and attitudes. His position in British politics was therefore riding on what might happen in Edinburgh. As he wrote to Montrose, 'If the notes should be refused you cannot imagine what thoughts it would give people here of all sides almost of us.'[64]

Lord Halifax, who had done much to foster the Bank of England scheme in 1694, appears to have believed sincerely that objections to the exchequer bills could only have arisen because 'you [the Scots] either were resolved not to like any thing we can do or you had no right representation of the thing'. Insisting that there had never been any thought that the bills 'should be forced or imposed on any body', Halifax protested that he and his colleagues had thought that by giving the Scots the bills, 'which have the sanction of an Act of Parliament for their

---

[61] James Erskine (Lord Grange) to Earl of Mar, 21 June 1707, NRS, GD124/15/616.
[62] Earl of Mar to Earl of Seafield, 9 July 1707, NRS, GD124/15/635/2.
[63] Earl of Mar to Earl of Leven, 15 July 1707, NRS, GD124/15/643/1.
[64] Earl of Mar to Duke of Montrose, 9 July 1707, NRS, GD220/5/128.

currency, and repayment: and are as well secured as any Property in Great Britain and which have the obligation of the Bank of England to answer them on demand, wee had not dealt ill with you, and should rather have deserved your thanks, than your censure'.[65]

Halifax also suggested that the Scots could choose to make the bills current, as England had done. This was a common line of argument, demonstrating how the elite understood the nature of money during the monetary revolution. The Bank of England, for example, insisted that 'the Bills can be esteemed no otherwise than as money, being...current for all payments to and from Her Majesty', and because 'the Bank are at all times obliged by Act of Parliament to give the full value for them'.[66] If the Scots did not want to follow this path, Halifax suggested that Bank of Scotland could take them up in exchange, which would quadruple Scotland's 'running cash' and 'set up' Bank of Scotland, to the great benefit of the Scottish economy. In any case, if the Scots really felt they needed more cash, they could easily get it, for there was 'no other difference between [the bills] and money than the distance between London, and Edinburgh', so Scots could simply get them cashed 'according to the usual rates of exchange'.[67]

While Halifax acknowledged how 'ridiculous' he was to lecture Montrose while 'wholly ignorant of your customs and the nature of your Bank', he clearly had no idea just how ridiculous, for his suggestions and reassurances rubbed salt into every wound that Scots felt had been inflicted by the exchequer bills. From a Scottish point of view, to cite the bills' parliamentary sanction was pure arrogance, for, as one of the Scottish commissioners put it: 'nor can the law of England be any rule when its an agreement between the two nations'.[68] The suggestion that Bank of Scotland should take up the exchequer bills evinced a complete failure to understand its defining difference from the Bank of England. This ignorance later manifested itself as contempt. Reporting back to the Bank of England in September, the leading English commissioner, Sir John Cope, wrote that he had tried to get Bank of Scotland to take the bills, and had even offered a fund to underwrite their circulation, 'but they're of a narrow, nervous constitution, and not over well-affected, and refused us under pretence that by law they could lend nothing on public funds'.[69] This was, of course, no pretence at all, as Cope could have discovered had he read the Bank's charter. On the other hand, Cope was correct to feel that Bank of Scotland wanted to make it as difficult as possible for

---

[65] Halifax to Montrose, 26 July 1707, NRS, GD220/5/134.
[66] Court of Directors Minutes, 10 July 1707, BE, G4/6.
[67] Halifax to Montrose, 26 July 1707. NRS, GD220/5/134.
[68] Erskine to Mar, 21 June 1707, NRS, GD124/15/616.
[69] [Cope] to [Bank of England], [Sept. 1707] BE, M5/671. Despite Saville's passing claim that Bank of Scotland bought exchequer bills from 'mid-August' 1707 (Saville, *Bank of Scotland*, p. 77), I can find no evidence that the Directors changed their mind on this question during the disbursement of the Equivalent.

the commissioners to get the notes off their hands and was even keener to keep them out of circulation.

Halifax was right to say that the bills could not be forced, but the commissioners made no secret of their efforts to get them into circulation, most blatantly by paying first those who would take their whole sum in exchequer bills, forcing those who wanted cash to the back of the queue.[70] Unlike Halifax, the Bank of England directors were under no illusion that getting the notes to circulate would be easy. Indeed, they were clearly worried that the Scottish commissioners themselves would refuse them, and accordingly provided the English commissioners with meticulous instructions and encouragement, as well as contingency plans. The directors did, however, suffer (or affect to suffer) from a different delusion, which was that almost all the money owing on the Equivalent, including much of the compensation for the recoinage, would be due to people resident in London.[71] It was therefore determined that the commissioners would ensure that the Bank, rather than the Edinburgh money exchangers, would profit from the exchange.[72] To that end, it instructed the commissioners to issue their own Bills of Exchange, payable only at the Bank's office in Threadneedle Street, in exchange for the exchequer bills. Whether these found their way to London, or, as the directors also seemed to hope, might circulate in Scotland, the fact that the Bank of England was to monopolize the channel of remittance made it galling rather than reassuring that turning the bills into cash required Scots to pay only the usual rate of exchange.

The belief that most of the Equivalent was owed to people in London was extraordinary given that, as the Bank must have known, more than half— £232,884—was due to the stockholders and creditors of the Company of Scotland, almost all of whom lived in Scotland by virtue of the outlawing of the company by the English Parliament in 1695. These were the people, above all, whom the Equivalent was designed to pacify, as they included almost the entire leadership of Scottish society from national to local level, conveniently incorporated into one body.[73] As one opponent of the Union put it, 'this distribution... among the proprietors of the African Company, was the cleanliest way of bribing a nation'.[74] But the company's shareholders extended well beyond this group. Alongside the subscriptions of thousands of pounds from the titled nobility and wealthy merchants were many more of one hundred pounds or less from shoemakers, soap boilers, ministers of religion, and even servants and a labourer.[75]

---

[70] [Cope] to [Bank of England], [Sept. 1707] BE, M5/671. James Hamilton to the Duke of Hamilton, 27 August 1707, NRS, GD4061/1/5500.
[71] Court of Directors Minutes 10 July 1707, BE, G4/6.   [72] Saville, *Bank of Scotland*, p. 76.
[73] Spence, 'Accounting', p. 381.   [74] Lockhart, *Memoirs*, p. 272.
[75] A Perfect List Of the several Persons Residenters in Scotland Who have Subscribed as Adventurers in the Joynt-Stock of the Company of Scotland Trading to Africa and the Indies (1696), NatWest Group Archives D/4/1; Jones, 'Bold Adventurers', pp. 32–7.

Around 1,500 subscriptions represented perhaps twice that number of individuals, as many of the 'common good' subscriptions from towns and other incorporated bodies were made up of the contributions of individuals who put in as little as five pounds each.[76] By the time the Equivalent came to be paid, however, the number of shareholders was smaller. The prospect of payment had restored a market in the company's hitherto worthless shares, leading some—either because they were desperate for cash, or because they had no faith that the Equivalent would materialize—to sell them at a heavy discount, soon yielding handsome profits for the buyers. Around a quarter of the company's shares changed hands in this period.[77]

Supporters of the Union tended to see responses to the Equivalent in political terms, but the social composition of the African Company shareholders suggests that the matter was more complex. Seafield felt that the arrival of the Equivalent in Edinburgh 'was satisfying to all, excepting the Jacobites and such as are so foolish as to desire the Union to be overturned'.[78] Such feelings influenced at least some people's attitudes to the exchequer bills, although perhaps more among the elite than among those who simply needed the money. The Duchess of Hamilton, whose powerful and extensive family connection shared her hostility to the Union, and whose son, the fourth Duke, had been the erratic and ineffectual leader of parliamentary opposition, sent her agent to demand to be paid immediately in cash, well ahead of her place in the lists.[79] Despite 'great noise and grumblings' from those who should have been paid before her, the commissioners complied, out of 'deference to her grace'.[80] This was a shrewd political judgment. In the circumstances it would not have done to hand the Hamiltons a grievance on the issue of the Equivalent, in which so many Scots had a stake. Supporters of the Union, on the other hand, made it a point of conduct ('a punto') to take the bills. Unsurprisingly, most people seem to have lived between these extremes and were willing to take a mixture of bills and cash, no doubt relieved that they were being given anything at all for what had looked like a lost investment. It was nonetheless heavy going for the commissioners. To the chagrin of the Bank of England directors, the bills soon began to be sold at a 1 per cent discount, 'possibly by the silly, the necessitous or the malicious in order to discredit 'em'.[81] The more likely problem appears to be that while people were willing to take some bills from the commissioners, very few were willing to take them in the normal course of business, and even fewer were interested in losing money and time by following the Bank of England's tortuous proceedings for turning them into cash in London.

---

[76] Watt, *Price*, p. 234.   [77] Watt, *Price*, p. 232.
[78] Earl of Seafield to the Duke of Mar, 5 Aug. 1707, NRS, GD124/15/635/12.
[79] Von den Steinen, 'Antecedents'; Whatley, *Bought and Sold?*, pp. 40–2; Whatley, *Scots and Union*, p. 186.
[80] [David Crawford] to the Duchess of Hamilton, 29 Aug. 1707, NRS, GD406/1/5276.
[81] [Cope] to [Bank of England], [Sept. 1707] BE, M5/671.

This left 'the necessitous' with little choice but to realize the cash immediately by selling their bills at a discount.

The opportunity for profit this presented seems to have trumped commitment to the Union. Even people whom the commissioners knew to be in need of bills on London, including some they 'thought they could depend on', demanded cash from the Equivalent in order to buy discounted bills.[82] To alleviate this problem Cope procured a proclamation that receivers of revenue in 'North Britain' would accept the exchequer bills, followed by a further instruction to the receivers to exchange them for whatever cash they had on hand whenever requested.[83] This does not seem, as Cope had hoped, to have helped to 'introduce the credit of our Bills', but merely to have provided Scots with a convenient way of getting rid of them. The proclamation had conferred one of the key attributes of money (acceptance by the state), but, unusually, this failed to produce the other key attribute of acceptance by the community at large. This appears to have stemmed from a general resentment at the bills themselves on broadly 'national' grounds, underpinned by the fact that they could not –in theory or practice—be converted into coin anywhere else in Scotland.

The Bank of England's project to circulate paper in Scotland was therefore doomed. By late August, the treasury was obliged to replace £50,000 of exchequer bills with guineas, and in October the Bank waived the costs of exchange.[84] By December, there were no exchequer bills in circulation in Scotland.[85] The profitable business of circulating paper credit in Scotland would remain, for the time being, the exclusive preserve of Bank of Scotland.

Converging Diversity: Scottish and British Money after the Union

In the light of this episode, it is ironic that twenty years later, by a very indirect route, and initially against the wishes of the Bank of England, the Equivalent did provide the link between the Scottish monetary system and London-based paper credit. The reason was that the Equivalent was not sufficient to cover all the payments it specified. After meeting the costs of the recoinage, paying out the African Company shareholders, setting aside £14,000 to pay £2,000 a year to nobody for the benefit of the wool trade, and imposing their own fees and covering their costs (£30,500), the commissioners found themselves left with £70,681 to pay £223,098 under the different headings of public debts described

---

[82] Commissioners of the Equivalent [to the Treasury], 6 Sept. 1707, *CTP* (1702–1707), p. 533.
[83] Cope to Bank of England [extract], 12 Aug. 1707. TNA T17/1 f. 107.
[84] Cope to Bank of England, 8 Aug. 1707 (copy). *CTP* (1702–7), p. 524.
[85] Saville, *Bank of Scotland*, p. 77.

in the Equivalent Act. £24,736 of this was earmarked for people who had served as commissioners to the Crown under the Williamite regime. This left £45,945 to pay total debts of around £198,632 owing on the civil and military lists, as well as the unknowable cost of over one hundred lawsuits pending against the commissioners. The commissioners were almost as short on information as they were on money to deal with this problem, possessing neither accurate accounts of the claims nor any principles of priority or proportion on which to distribute the limited funds. They therefore distributed nothing.[86] The officers with salaries in arrears, or who were out of pocket after clothing their soldiers; the unpaid civil servants of every description; the tradesmen with outstanding bills; the chaplains and former bishops: all were to remain unpaid for at least seven years, when Scotland's customs and excise were due to be raised to the same rate as England's, and the debts paid off from the proceeds.

Even leaving aside 'the poor on Her Majesty's charity', who were left in a 'starving condition'[87] as a result of this process, these creditors were mostly people of modest means and little influence. Some claims were for under £10 and most were for less than £25; few were for more than £40.[88] Instead of money, the claimants were issued with unredeemable debentures, on which there was no possibility even of interest being paid before 1714. In fact, it was not until 1719 that the government legislated funds to pay the interest. This decision to pay was not out of concern for people of the lower and middling sort to whom most of the debentures had been issued, but for the benefit of the wealthy and powerful who had acquired them in the meantime. Inevitably, many of the original holders had sold to those who could afford to wait in order to realize some cash, often at substantial discount.[89] By 1719, when the first interest payments were made, almost 70 per cent, or £170,000 worth of the debentures, were in the hands of wealthy London Scots, who started to lobby to be incorporated to manage the £10,000 annual interest payment. This entailed a sharp struggle with the Bank of England, which was determined that the Company's activities be strictly limited to the management of the interest payments and could not—as the proponents clearly wished—transmogrify into a more general fund of credit. Despite these objections, a charter establishing the Equivalent Company was granted in 1724.[90]

Almost immediately, the company began to lobby for a charter for a Banking Company in Scotland. When this was granted in May 1727, Scotland had acquired not merely a second bank—the Royal Bank of Scotland—but a bank somewhat closer to the English model. In sharp contrast to Bank of Scotland, the entire

---

[86] Equivalent Commissioners, 'Representation', 1 Jan. 1707/8, TNA, T17/1, f. 225.
[87] Equivalent Commissioners, 'Representation', 1 Jan. 1707/8, TNA: T17/1, ff. 225-6.
[88] NRS, E302.
[89] John Clerk to Sir James Smallet, 18 Sept., [pre-1719] reported a 15 per cent discount. NRS, GD, 113/4/112.
[90] Checkland, *Scottish Banking*, pp. 49–51.

capital stock of the new bank consisted of perpetual government debt in the form of £110,000 of Equivalent debentures, owned by members of the Equivalent Company. Thus, almost thirty years after William Paterson's devious attempt to start a new bank in Scotland, the African Company had brought forth a bank from its grave, and twenty years after the Bank of England's attempt to exploit the Equivalent to muscle its way into Scotland, the Equivalent became the link between the Scottish monetary system and stocks of government debt held in London.

Bank of Scotland naturally did all in its power to prevent the advent of this competition, but it was in too weak a political position to do so. Its original charter had conferred a monopoly on banking in Scotland for only twenty-one years, and had not been renewed on its expiry in 1716. In general terms, Bank of Scotland appears to have had little influence in British political circles from the Union onwards, as demonstrated by its failure to get any traction for its repeated pleas to be paid the commission it had been promised for its role in the recoinage. This may have stemmed initially from its strained relationship with the Equivalent commissioners, especially regarding the exchequer bills, which, it will be recalled, the commissioners had taken as a sign of political disaffection.

Following the Jacobite rebellion of 1715, the imputation of disaffection stuck. This was based on nothing more than the fact that the Bank's treasurer, David Drummond, acted as treasurer of the fund to provide legal representation for some of those involved in the rebellion.[91] In fact, the Royal Bank of Scotland charter was a favour by the Whig government of Robert Walpole to the Duke of Argyll and his Whig associates, who had achieved political supremacy in Scotland under Walpole's patronage.[92] The Argyll connection, who were deeply involved in the Equivalent company, naturally did their best to propagate rumours of Jacobite sympathies against Bank of Scotland in order to win the government to their cause.[93] Their success may be measured not just in the grant of the charter but in the government's decision to favour it with key business from its inception. The Bank of England, despite its earlier opposition to the Equivalent Company, soon aligned its approach to the new dispensation. By March 1728 it extended the Royal Bank a £30,000 line of credit to help it manage the exchange between Edinburgh and London, and was ready to extend further credit for subsequent transactions.[94]

But while the Royal Bank assisted Scottish integration into British systems, the fact of its foundation established an important difference between the two countries. Bank of Scotland's inability to protect its monopoly meant that monopoly itself would not be countenanced in relation to Scottish banking. Attempts by the established banks to ban or limit the establishment of new banks in Scotland were

---

[91] Saville, *Bank of Scotland*, p. 91; Malcolm, *Bank of Scotland*, p. 41.
[92] Lenman, 'Client Society', pp. 82–8. [93] Checkland, *Scottish Banking*, pp. 57–9.
[94] Directors' Minute Books, 14 and 26 Mar. 1728, NatWest Group Archives RB/12/1, pp. 88, 93.

firmly rebuffed by the British government, on the basis that 'the Trade of Banking is a matter not of Public favour but of Right to every subject in common'.[95] This was completely inconsistent with repeated renewals of the monopoly provisions of the Bank of England charter, which prevented the establishment of other banks with more than six partners anywhere in England. The result was that, in marked contrast to Scotland, the English system of country banks that developed in the eighteenth and early nineteenth centuries was notoriously undercapitalized and unstable, leaving it prone to endemic failures, with catastrophic consequences for their customers.

Edinburgh's old and new banks—as the two concerns were soon generally known—immediately set out to crush each other, with potentially disastrous consequences not only for the customers of the vanquished but for Scotland's economy more generally. The new bank was in the stronger position and came closest to achieving its aim in March 1728, when Bank of Scotland was unable to pay its notes as a result of a run organized by the new bank's supporters.[96] When the old bank was forced to suspend payment, the Royal Bank kept up the attack in two ways. First, it offered holders of Bank of Scotland notes the facility to lodge their notes as security for loans of cash 'for the relief of such merchants as are to pay in money to the Revenue, and to prevent the revenues suffering on this occasion', thus not only winning those customers' business and goodwill but also underlining its own practical importance to the government. It also lent on similar terms for those with commercial debts, as well as 'to poor people that want specie to go to mercat'.[97] The new bank took all possible steps to ensure that the latter were not acting as fronts for the wealthy, who might be regarded as the old bank's supporters. People who borrowed in this way were allowed to repay the loans with the same Bank of Scotland notes they had used as security once the old bank resumed payments. This, of course, would furnish the new bank with a good stock of notes with which to launch another run. The second line of attack was to take legal action against Bank of Scotland as a holder of its notes for non-payment. This was thrown out by the Court of Session in Edinburgh, where Bank of Scotland still had many influential friends, but was later upheld in the House of Lords, where it did not.[98] The centre of decision-making about Scottish banking, including the right of money creation, had shifted decisively southwards.

Despite this, some aspects of the monetary divergence between the countries continued to grow, especially regarding the use of paper money. In order to compete with its established rival, the Royal Bank not only rapidly developed its own branch structure but also began to issue one-pound notes on its foundation, thus helping to relieve the scarcity of money problem for small traders. In order to

[95] Quoted in Goodspeed, *Instability*, p. 70.   [96] Saville, *Bank of Scotland*, p. 103.
[97] Directors' Minute Books, 28 Mar. 1728, NatWest Group Archives RB/12/1, p. 96.
[98] Checkland, *Scottish Banking*, p. 62.

expand its note circulation and its profits, it also invented the 'cash credit' system, or what later came to be called the overdraft. This was crucially important to Scotland's monetary history, and would be one of the main bases of Scots' later opposition to government attempts to impose uniformity with England on Scottish banking. These credits, for amounts up to one hundred pounds, were issued in banknotes to provide working capital to people who could offer no personal security, but for whom any two people of good credit were prepared to act as guarantors. Interest was calculated daily only on the amount outstanding rather than the maximum sum available. The availability of one-pound notes helped borrowers ensure that they incurred no more interest than they absolutely needed to at any given time. These facilities, which Bank of Scotland emulated within a year, enabled countless small traders of every description to establish and sustain themselves in business, and reduced their dependence on coin, which remained very scarce. Thus the 'bank war', once it had subsided to a grudging coexistence between the two chartered banks, eased the monetary lives of many Scots and aided the development of their country's domestic economy in ways that the Bank of England, with its focus on financing wars and large-scale mercantile transactions centred on London, did not.

Another bank war in the mid-1740s accentuated this difference while strengthening the Scottish banking system's integration into a London-centric, British system. Beginning with the foundation in 1746 in Glasgow of the British Linen Company (with the active support of the Royal Bank), this saw the appearance of a further two banks in Glasgow and a short-lived venture in Aberdeen that was crushed by the united efforts of the Edinburgh banks. All of these issued business loans in the form of notes as their core business, to which the Edinburgh banks responded by organizing runs against their notes. As a defence against this tactic, banks made the convertibility of their notes into specie increasingly difficult, including by the crude expedient of counting out sums as slowly as possible in sixpences.[99] As the Edinburgh banks had done since the 1730s, many inserted an optional clause into their notes allowing the bank to choose whether to redeem at face value on demand or at a premium six months later. They would also offer to redeem their notes with long-dated bills of exchange drawn on London.[100] These practices became more common as additional banks were established in the following decades. Scotland thus developed an increasingly paper-based system, with little or no expectation of convertibility in the English sense, but did so in part on the basis of paper credit in the London money market.

The optional clauses came in for severe attack from both contemporary commentators (including Adam Smith) and later historians, who regarded them as an illegitimate way for banks to prevent the obligation of convertibility on demand,

---

[99] Goodspeed, *Instability*, p. 38.   [100] Checkland, *Scottish Banking*, p. 135.

which for most was the only basis on which banknotes could claim legitimacy. In practice, however, the clauses were not used against customers, nor even rival banks, but against interest rate arbitrageurs when trade deficits and/or speculation caused large-scale specie outflows from Scotland. These actors 'sold bills on London at high premiums for Scottish banknotes, which they then immediately unloaded onto the Edinburgh banks for redemption in specie', which they then sent back to London to repeat the cycle.[101] As monetary union had removed the possibility of devaluation against sterling, this use of the optional clause was the banks' (and Scotland's) only protection against such operations.

Optional clauses were outlawed in 1765. Although the ban was not especially congenial to the established Scottish banks, they accepted it as part of an Act they had sought to prevent the proliferation of new banks and other issuers of low-sum notes, which posed an obvious threat to their profits, and which, they maintained, destabilized the banking system as a whole.[102] Despite the banks' claims—echoed by many later writers—there is little evidence of a small note 'mania' or of frauds by their issuers.[103] Rather, the emergence of such small notes met a real need in an economy where, despite Scotland's much-vaunted one-pound notes, small money had become desperately short—in the short term because of the specie flows just discussed, but in the longer term as a direct result of the Union, which denuded Scotland of the silver and copper money required by the great mass of the people, for whom even one-pound notes were rarely if ever of any use.

The monetary problems arising for such people as a result of union with England quickly became apparent. Only a decade later, the estate journal of Malcolm MacNeill, Laird of Carskey, in Kintyre, shines some light on how severe it was for a remote Scottish community, and how the people managed with a mixture of monetary transactions conducted in British or foreign coin, or settled in whole or in part by barter mediated by monetary values, as well as transactions in which monetary values were simply not used.[104] Rents were usually, but not always, reckoned as cash values, but were paid almost entirely in labour and crops. MacNeill was also a merchant who sold imported footwear ('pumps') to sell mostly to servants and tenants. These incurred monetary debts, but there is no evidence that they were settled in cash. A shoemaker who owed £1 16s. Scots (three shillings sterling) for a cow seems to have settled at least part of this debt by selling the laird's imported shoes in his own shop. 'Entress' paid on the commencement of a lease, which was always reckoned in money, was mostly paid in cash, but the means and terms of payment could vary. In May 1717 a tenant agreed to pay entress of 'fifty mrks Scots', thus incurring a debt that appeared as 33*l* 06s. 8*d*. in the invariable pounds, shillings, and pence Scots of the ledger column. In November 1719 he paid £21 Scots 'in money' and agreed to deliver a

---

[101] Goodspeed, *Instability*, p. 23. [102] Goodspeed, *Instability*, pp. 61–75.
[103] Goodspeed, *Instability*, ch. 2, esp. pp. 30, 46–8, 58–9. [104] *MacNeill Journal*, p. 48.

cow worth £14 the following May. This implies a credit of £1 13s. 4d. in the new tenant's favour, which appears to have been settled by his delayed settlement of an exchange of horses, for which no monetary value was calculated.[105] The payment of labour could be equally complex and protracted. In 1720–1 Malcolm McGibbon received payment for digging ditches in the form of a share of a cow, with no monetary value ascribed; the retirement of a loan of two shillings Scots; a coffin board with a Scots monetary value; and a sterling half-crown also valued in Scots units of account. The transaction took some time, with the first labour performed in the summer of 1720, and final settlement the following February.[106]

Copper coin is conspicuously absent from these transactions, as it was for the whole of the eighteenth century. In 1729 there were complaints about the scarcity of copper coin and the 'quantities of halfpence of very base stuff' being imported from Ireland.[107] Ten years later Edinburgh's *Caledonian Mercury* even offered a prize of four guineas for the best poem on the topic.[108] And at the end of the century the same paper complained that 'the best halfpence are totally excluded from circulation while those not half the value are the only currency'.[109] The latter were counterfeits, which, as we will see in the following chapter, proliferated throughout Britain and Ireland.

MacNeill's transactions suggest that pound notes as well as coin could be hard to come by, a problem that does not appear to have been remedied by the proliferation of notes in the bank war. In 1742, Forbes of Culloden bemoaned a scarcity of money, which he claimed was worse 'than ever was at any time within memory known, even in this poor country'. Using a turn of phrase indicative of the status paper money had acquired in Scotland, he added that 'paper is the only coin one sees, and even it is far from being in any tolerable quantity'.[110]

The problem persisted. In the 1780s in Fife—a relatively monetized part of the Scottish economy—annual labourers had as little as 40 per cent of their wages even calculated in money terms, with the remainder consisting of an unpriced (and therefore fixed) measure of oats. Of the money sum, more than half might be deducted for the rent of land, housing, and food, leaving at least one labourer with only 13 per cent of his total annual income in cash calculated to the value of £10 12s.10d., expressed—more than sixty years after the Union—in Scots units of account.[111] As this was £1 7s. 2d. Scots short of the value of the smallest notes then permitted, it could only have been paid with the nearest equivalent sterling value (17s. 8¾d.) in British or foreign coins. Given their perennial scarcity, this might not have been easy to manage. At the margins of the official monetary order, where the mass of Scots lived, the presence or absence of notes for one pound

---

[105] *MacNeill Journal*, pp. 50–2.   [106] *MacNeill Journal*, p. 61.
[107] Areskine to Secretary of State, 6 Sept. 1729. TNA SP 54/19 f. 329.
[108] Leslie, *Scarcity*, 'Advertisement'.   [109] *Caledonian Mercury*, 25 June 1796.
[110] Quoted in Lang, *History of Scotland*, vol. 4, p. 416.   [111] Gibson and Smout, *Prices*, p. 263.

sterling was actually of little or no importance and did nothing to narrow the monetary gulf between rich and poor that had been widened to English proportions by monetary union. By seeking a ban on smaller notes, the established banks had demonstrated their indifference to this problem.

The 1765 legislation helped to reshape Scottish banking in unforeseen ways, giving rise to a major monetary crisis that demonstrated Scotland's increasing integration into a British monetary system. The crisis was the failure in 1772 of Douglas, Heron and Company, better known as the Ayr Bank, arguably the greatest financial disaster to befall Scotland between Darien and 2008. The firm was established in 1769 during a liquidity squeeze: the 1765 Act had not only driven out smaller banks and note issuers; its ban on the optional clause had made the major banks far more cautious in issuing notes, fearful of the consequences of any possible sudden demand for specie.[112] Coming during a long boom, this contraction of credit threatened the viability of many enterprises, both under way and projected.[113] The Ayr was not the only bank to exploit the commercial possibilities of this situation, but it was by far the largest, with a nominal capital of £150,000, of which £96,000 was subscribed immediately. Rather like Bank of Scotland before it, Douglas, Heron included many members of the establishment among its partners, including dukes, earls, and other major landowners, as well as leading business- and professional men of Scotland's south-west.[114] Like Bank of Scotland, the bank's solvency was ultimately underwritten by the unlimited liability of its wealthy proprietors.

Bank of Scotland and the Royal Bank accepted the newcomer into the 'circle of exchange' established after the bank wars, by which banks accepted each other's notes, used them as reserves, and regularly exchanged notes and cleared balances. As the Edinburgh banks retreated, the Ayr Bank's issues expanded rapidly, reaching 25 per cent of Scotland's circulation in only a few years.[115] As first described by Smith, much of the bank's lending was financed by chains of 'fictitious' bills of exchange drawn and redrawn on London, leaving the bank paying an effective annual interest rate of 8 per cent for funds from this source while lending at 5 per cent—the maximum allowed by the usury laws.[116] By 1772, 'a third of its assets and almost half of its liabilities' were in the London bill market.[117] The vulnerability of the bank to any crisis in the London money market—and vice versa—is obvious.[118]

The crisis began on 9 June 1772 when Alexander Fordyce, a partner in the predominantly Scottish London banking firm of Neale, James, Fordyce and Down

---

[112] Recent accounts of the Ayr Bank by Kosmetatos, *Crisis*, esp. pp. 26–36 and Conclusion, and Goodspeed, *Instability*, esp. ch. 1 and pp. 124–8, challenge different aspects of the 'standard' accounts. See Smith, *Wealth*, vol. 2, pp. 298–300; Hamilton, 'Failure'; Checkland, *Scottish Banking*, pp. 124–33.
[113] Hamilton, 'Failure', pp. 407–8.   [114] Checkland, *Scottish Banking*, p. 124.
[115] Goodspeed, *Instability*, p. 4.   [116] Smith, *Wealth*, vol. 2, p. 298.
[117] Kosmetatos, *Crisis*, p. 240.   [118] Hamilton, 'Failure', pp. 411–12.

absconded to Europe after his speculations in East India Company stock came undone, leaving his firm with debts of £243,000.[119] The crisis immediately engulfed London, beginning with the many firms that had extensive dealings in Scottish bills of exchange. It reached Scotland within two days—as long as it took the news to travel. Despite desperate attempts to salvage its position, the Ayr Bank closed its doors the following week, triggering a series of failures of banking and other firms throughout Scotland and precipitating a severe economic depression.[120]

The crisis shows much more than links between Scottish banking and money creation and the London money market, for by 1772 the latter was central to an increasingly integrated national—and indeed quasi-global—system, meaning that a crisis in London, however caused, would spread rapidly throughout the British Isles, to many countries on the Continent and to Britain's colonies in North America and the Caribbean.[121] The system connected not just places but economic sectors. As Julian Hoppit points out, unlike earlier crises, which were generally limited to the sector in which they began, 'the crisis of 1772 was general, as the causes were all too effectively communicated throughout the prospering economy'.[122]

In England, the dependence of the rapidly growing system of provincial or 'country' banking on London was critical to these linkages. Like the Scottish banks, all such banks had a London 'correspondent' in the form of a private bank on which they drew bills.[123] These in turn redeemed the bills drawn on them with Bank of England notes, which circulated as cash in London among those who dealt in sums of fifty pounds or more, or could be cashed at the Bank of England for guineas. As early as 1750, the most important business of London private banks was acting as agents for country banks and proto-banks. As country banking evolved, the London private banks became 'indispensable linchpins in the system, connecting the country banks not only with the London money market but also with one another'.[124]

In the panic triggered by Fordyce's flight a number of London bankers suspended payment, with dire consequences for their corresponding country banks, many of which also stopped payment and one of which failed completely, leaving noteholders with nothing more than pieces of paper with broken promises on them.[125] Thus the unravelling of systems of credit and paper money in Ayrshire and London precipitated the sudden annihilation of money across England as well as Scotland.

---

[119] Kosmetatos, *Crisis*, pp. 2–8. Goodspeed, *Instability*, pp. 1–3.
[120] Hamilton, 'Failure', pp. 413–16.   [121] Kosmetatos, *Crisis*, pp. 3–8.
[122] Hoppit, 'Financial Crises', p. 54.   [123] Pressnell, *Country Banking*, ch. 4, esp. pp. 116–20.
[124] Cameron, *Banking*, p. 23.   [125] Pressnell, *Country Banking*, Appendix 20, p. 595.

This interconnection had an additional aspect. It is now clear that the Bank of England in this crisis attempted, with some success, to operate on the system in order to contain its consequences. Although the notion of a 'lender of last resort' would not be given theoretical expression for another thirty years,[126] Paul Kosmetatos has shown that the Bank deliberately took that role during this crisis. The Bank 'not only injected liquidity to the market as a whole by allowing a "liberal discount" [of bills of exchange] of unprecedented levels but also targeted specific firms through substantial direct lending.... Intended beneficiaries included firms...who were systemically important for their role in their bills of exchange network.' By supporting the London money markets, the Bank of England therefore acted 'as the backstop of Scottish credit'.[127] Important as Scotland's distinctive monetary practices would remain, the banking system that animated them was already thoroughly integrated into webs of interdependence spun around the City of London and the Bank of England.

In this and other ways the Union was thus the formative moment of Scotland's monetary revolution. It locked Scotland into a single currency area, which was dominated by the English fixation on maintaining an eternally fixed standard at any cost. It handed legislative authority over Scottish banking to a Parliament dominated by English members. It paved the way for Scotland's enmeshment in London-based systems of paper credit, including, via the Equivalent debentures, those based on government debt. But pre-Union Scottish developments had an ongoing role in determining the terms of Scotland's participation in the British monetary order. The existence of Bank of Scotland ensured that Scottish rather than English paper would play a key role in the process and aftermath of monetary union. The antipathies created by that process helped to ensure that, unlike the Bank of England, Bank of Scotland would get no protection from competition, thus setting Scottish banking on a distinctive path of development within an increasingly British monetary and banking system.

While Scotland's monetary relationship conferred significant advantages on Scotland, it came at a cost, particularly to those at the bottom of the monetary hierarchy. Ireland, by contrast, gleaned few such advantages and many more costs, as it remained in an unequivocally subordinate position on the margins of the British monetary system throughout the eighteenth century. This peculiar situation, in the context of British developments, will be the focus of the following chapter.

---

[126] Thornton, *Paper Credit*, ch. 4.
[127] Kosmetatos, *Crisis*, p. 246. See also James, 'Panics', p. 306.

5
Engines of State, Emblems of Nation, Tokens of Trust
1695–1796

> Is Ireland the only ground, where no grass will grow?
> Francis Hutchinson, Bishop of Down and Connor (1721)

During the eighteenth century, Britain and Ireland saw ongoing struggles between factions, interests, and nations over the distribution and operation of monetary power in the context of chronic shortages of coin and the growing importance of paper money and other forms of credit. But the overall tendency was clear: a widening of the gulf between the monetary worlds of the elite and the common people and a strengthening elite consensus around the architecture and key principles of the monetary system. These processes unfolded differently in each country and produced different results.

Focussing mainly on Ireland's monetary evolution, and how it was framed by the kingdom's relationship with Britain, this chapter will explore these struggles, convergences, and differences across the three nations, and trace the differing attitudes to monetary issues they reflected and engendered until the suspension of cash payments at the Bank of England and the Bank of Ireland in 1797 shook the system to its foundations.

Monetary Standards, New and Non-Existent

We have already seen that the undervaluation of silver at the London mint caused silver coin to disappear from England and Ireland following the recoinage of 1696, and from Scotland when its silver was recoined to the English standard in 1707. The problem only got worse. In the ninety years between the Anglo-Scottish Union and the suspension of cash payments at the Bank of England, a total of only £788,791 of silver was minted, at an average of £8,688 yearly, compared to an average of £896,645 worth of gold.[1] This low average figure was inflated by a few

---

[1] Abstracted from Challis, *Mint*, pp. 691–3.

years of abnormally high production owing to exceptional events or efforts on the part of the government, including the offer of a premium payment of 2½–3*d*. per ounce on silver brought to the mint—a remarkable reversal of the centuries-long tradition of mint charges.[2]

The relentless loss of silver and massive imports of gold (mostly from Brazil) moved the government repeatedly to seek advice from Newton as Master of the Mint. His report of September 1717 showed that the price ratio of gold to silver in English coins was out of line with that of other European countries, making the guinea worth somewhere between 20*s*. 5*d*. and 20*s*. 8½*d*. in European terms, rather than the 21*s*. 6*d*. at which it circulated and was accepted in taxes in Britain. The government could solve the problem instantly by reducing the value of the guinea by 10 or 12 pence. Alternatively, the scarcity of silver would, Newton thought, eventually put a premium on payments in that metal, thus correcting the ratio. Newton's recommendation, adopted by Parliament in December, was to reduce the guinea by only 6*d*. This would lessen the incentive to export sufficiently to allow the market to disclose 'what further reduction would be most convenient for the publick'. This approach might have worked if the European ratio had been the main problem and the government had been willing to make further changes to the rating of the coins. Neither condition applied. As Newton noted, the far deeper problem was the very large discrepancy in the gold to silver ratio between Europe and Asia, which 'carries away the silver from all Europe'.[3] In these circumstances, the government's solution was like applying a Band-Aid to a flesh wound while ignoring a severed artery.

Despite one MP placing the blame on 'the Dutch, Hamburghers, and other Foreigners, in concert with the Jews and other traders here',[4] the main exporter had long been the East India Company, whose silver operations dwarfed those of the mint. In the forty years following Newton's report its exports reached an average of two million ounces—enough to coin £500,000 of silver annually, which was more than the total coined in the whole of that period.[5] Britain was now so thoroughly enmeshed in global networks of trade that the time had long passed when only European conditions needed to be considered in framing monetary policy.

The logic of Newton's report, together with the disappearance of the silver, have led some writers to conclude that Britain accidentally adopted a *de facto* gold standard when the government adopted his recommendation.[6] Newton saw it differently. According to the French-Irish political economist Richard Cantillon, Newton, when questioned why he adopted what was 'the least natural and the most disadvantageous policy' of reducing the price of gold coins rather than

---

[2] Craig, *Mint*, p. 213.
[3] Sir Isaac Newton's State of the Gold and Silver Coin, 25 Sept. 1717, TNA, T1/208, ff. 209–10.
[4] HPHC, vol. 6, p. 174 (20 Dec. 1717). [5] Craig, *Mint*, p. 219. Dalrymple, *Anarchy*, p. 70.
[6] Feaveayear, *Pound*, p. 155.

raising the value of the silver, responded that, 'according to the fundamental laws of the Kingdom, silver was the true and only monetary standard, and that as such, it could not be altered'.[7] Given that Newton had supported changing that standard during the recoinage debate, this can be read as his acceptance of the new political reality: preservation of a working currency of silver had become secondary to the notion that silver coins must constitute an eternally fixed weight of metal.

The situation was even stranger than the mere 'accidental' adoption of a new standard.[8] Weeks after adopting Newton's recommendation, the House of Lords resolved never to change the value of either gold or silver coin again.[9] This was to repeat the similar resolution of 1696. But the new promise carried far more weight. Mint indentures following 1696 left the official rating of the guinea at twenty shillings—the notional value specified in every indenture since its first appearance. This meant that the practical rating of the guinea could still be seen as floating independently of the indenture and therefore tangential to the standard, as Newton thought. But the indenture of 6 May 1718 valued the guinea for the first time at its declared rating of twenty-one shillings, giving it a reality that made any subsequent change as unthinkable as a change to the silver standard.

The fact that this made nonsense of the silver standard was partially obscured by the fact that there was hardly any silver in circulation, leading some to argue that Britain was on a bimetallic standard during this period.[10] But the government made no effort to maintain an effective circulation of silver. As in the period of the classical gold standard, the silver coins in practice functioned as tokens, albeit very defective ones.[11] By the middle of the century they were so old and worn that it was impossible even to make out the impressions on them, and thus whether they were of foreign origin, counterfeits, or demonetized coins that had survived the 1696 recoinage. As early as 1729, trials had shown that a £100 bag of sixpences in Ireland was more than 10 per cent short in weight. Larger denominations had fared better because they circulated less rapidly, but even crowns had lost close to 3 per cent of their silver. In England in 1742, Peter Vallavine found more serious deficiencies: many of the sixpences were reduced to 'about two thirds of their just weight' and shillings were 'not much better'. Higher denomination silver coins were 'rarely to be met with'.[12]

For those who exercised monetary power the deterioration of the silver coinage was at most a second-order problem. The priority was to maintain the standard, and the government's actions during the eighteenth century show that the standard was gold. In 1774 it limited silver coins' legal tender status by tale to a maximum of £25, and in 1797, when the market price of silver at last fell below the mint price, the government closed the mint to silver to prevent people

---

[7] Cantillon, *Economic Theory*, pp. 214–15.   [8] Sargent and Velde, *Small Change*, pp. 292–3.
[9] JHL, vol. 20, pp. 585–6 (25 and 27 Jan. 1717/18).   [10] Redish, *Bimetallism*, ch. 3.
[11] Sargent and Velde, *Small Change*, pp. 291–302.   [12] Vallavine, *Observations*, pp. 27–8.

bringing it there and taking away coin of a higher value than the bullion. Silver had long since ceased to matter. Importantly, the government had first begun to use gold for its overseas remittances in the latter part of the first decade of the new century and had completely abandoned silver for that purpose in 1717—the year it revalued the guinea.[13]

Gold did not take the place that silver had previously occupied. Thanks to the monetary revolution that place no longer existed. As I have argued, the root cause of that revolution was that the endlessly growing monetary needs of the state and commerce had rendered *any* system of commodity money inadequate. This remained true even after the value and availability of the standard money commodity was dramatically increased by the *de facto* change from silver to gold. Desan has argued that 'parliament's intransigence on the question of recalibrating coin effectively destroyed commodity money as a working proposition', but the fact that this was the opposite of what most of the members were trying to achieve suggests that the destruction of commodity money happened independently of their will and was beyond the command of parliamentary resolutions.[14] Their intransigence did, however, rescue gold as a commodity to perform a new role in the new order: to legitimate and help regulate the officially sanctioned systems of credit and international exchange that could grow elastically, in line with the needs of the commercial and political elite.[15] As Desan also argues, the guinea, 'wrapped...in a plethora of token moneys, both large and small', acted as the 'pivot' of a new monetary system that in practice was far more consistent with the ideas of credit theorists of money than with Lockean dogma.[16] Paradoxically, adherence to the latter remained essential to the system, which for another two centuries subsisted on the claim that it was 'based' on metal of a legally fixed monetary value compatible with the needs of the mercantile elite and the government's creditors, including those overseas.

In Ireland, any such claim was barely tenable for the first third of the century. It was not merely that coin of every kind was even scarcer there than in almost every part of Britain and that there was no bank whose paper could anchor the relationship between commodity money and commercial credit. Ireland's problem was more fundamental. Put simply, a combination of factors meant that until 1737 the country lacked an effective monetary standard of any description.

This was due to monetary anomalies and disadvantages that had long beset Ireland. The units of account remained Irish pounds, shillings, and pence, whose value had settled at $12/13$ of their English counterparts by 1701. Ireland still had no mint, and the only coins struck specifically for Ireland before 1797 were copper pennies and halfpence rated at thirteen pence to the English shilling, which together with English gold and silver coins were the only coins that could pass

---

[13] Jones, *War and Economy*, p. 76. [14] Desan, *Making Money*, p. 376.
[15] Wennerlind, *Casualties*, pp. 134–5. [16] Desan, *Making Money*, p. 360.

by tale. All three types were desperately scarce. The minting of copper for Ireland not only was intermittent (as it was for Britain) but—as we will see—could be uniquely problematic. Not only was English/British silver scarce for the same reasons as it was in Britain, but the legislative prohibition on the export of sterling money to Ireland was actively enforced, adding to Ireland's difficulties.[17] In any case, Ireland's chronic balance of payments deficit—fuelled in part by rents due to absentee landlords—ensured that the flow of money across the Irish Sea was overwhelmingly eastwards.

To these established problems were added anomalies surrounding the rating of the guinea and foreign coins that made up the bulk of the circulation. Like Scotland, Ireland had been subject to the powerful monetary turbulence emanating from England near the end of the previous century. In 1695, the soaring price of guineas in England, coupled with the significant undervaluation of foreign coins in Ireland as compared with England and other places, had caused a huge drain of coin out of Ireland, leaving insufficient revenue to pay the army. The concomitant unfavourable exchanges had 'shutt up all forreigne trade', reducing many families 'to beggery'. The English government's decision the previous month to allow the Lord-Lieutenant to authorize collectors of the revenue privately to accept guineas at whatever rate was necessary to prevent their export had failed; people continued to hoard guineas ('the general cash of the kingdom') in the hope that the official rating would be raised.[18] In April, the Lords Justices sought permission to raise the value of foreign gold coin consistently with a guinea valuation of twenty-five shillings.[19] In response they received permission 'to act as the present exigency requires', resulting in a proclamation significantly raising the values of all circulating foreign coins a few weeks later.[20] The proclamation was silent on the values of English coins, but it appears that English coins were raised to their highest values ever at around this time.[21]

The Irish government came under pressure from London to reduce the foreign coins as early as 1697. On that occasion the objections of the Irish House of Commons, although resented by some in the English government, succeeded in maintaining the status quo until 1701, when, after some procedural wrangling between Dublin and London, the 1695 values were restored, apparently without controversy.[22] Both governments took care to ensure that as much of the collected revenue as possible was expended before the values were reduced, thus ensuring

---

[17] 17 June 1701, *CTP* (1696–1702), p. 51.
[18] Capell to Shrewsbury, 25 Apr. 1695, TNA, SP63/357 ff. 42–6 (and enclosed report by 'Mr Robison' [Sir Leonard Robinson], Deputy Receiver-General).
[19] LJI et al. to Duke of Shrewsbury, 23 Apr. 1695, TNA, SP 63/357 f. 38.
[20] Shrewsbury to LJI, 4 May 1695, TNA, SP 67/2 f. 18.   [21] Magennis, 'Whither?', p. 191.
[22] LJI to Shrewsbury, 2 Sept. 1697 (enclosed address of the Irish House of Commons), TNA, SP 63/359 f. 218; James Vernon to Lord Ambassador Williamson, 14 Sept. 1697, TNA, SP 32/8 f. 29; LJI to Vernon, 6 May and 16 May 1701, TNA, SP 63/361 f. 186, 190.

that the governments' employees and creditors, rather than the Exchequer, bore the financial burden.[23]

While there is nothing in the sources to show directly that the ratings of British coins were changed at this time, it is clear enough that guineas in Ireland passed for 23 shillings Irish from 1701.[24] At the 12:13 parity this was just under 21s. 3d. sterling when the guinea circulated in England at 22 shillings. In 1717, When Britain revalued the guinea to 21 shillings, its value in Ireland remained unchanged. So while Britain moved to an effective gold standard, Ireland was left with a purely notional standard of silver at 108.3 per cent of the British standard, and a value for the *de facto* British standard coin that was consistent with neither that coin's value in Britain nor the Irish value of the largely absent British silver.

Irish governments appealed unsuccessfully in 1698 and 1701 to stabilize the currency by establishing a temporary mint to convert foreign coin into English. These appeals failed on the grounds that they might draw coin out of England, and that their staff, once the mints were closed, might deploy their skills as counterfeiters.[25] Underlying all was Newton's argument that Ireland, although nominally a kingdom, 'is one of the English plantations...and like the other plantations, is and ought to be inferior to this kingdom and subservient to its interests'. Given that, as we have seen, mints were repeatedly denied to England's other 'plantations', this was enough to clinch the argument.[26] Moreover, to allow a mint might be to pave the way for Ireland 'to separate from this Crown'.[27] Such questions of 'dependency' would frame much Irish monetary debate for the rest of the century.

In these circumstances the most important currency regulations concerned the valuation of foreign coins. Following a brief period in which Ireland, together with the other 'plantations', had been permitted a degree of autonomy over this question, Queen Anne's government reclaimed central imperial authority during the first decade of the eighteenth century.[28] This made it far more difficult for Irish or colonial governments to remedy what had become wildly inconsistent valuations of the bullion in different foreign coins, which had created complete monetary dysfunction. To give some Irish examples, the rating of the Spanish silver crusado at 3s. 3d. equated to a silver price of 76d. per ounce, compared to a price per ounce of 70½d. for the silver in an English shilling at 1s. 1d. The value of the silver in other coins fell somewhere between these two. More importantly, the valuation of the Portuguese gold moidore at 30 shillings Irish from its appearance in 1712 equated to a price of 94s. 4d. per ounce, higher than the gold in any other

---

[23] Vernon to Lords Justices of Ireland, [1701], *CSPD* (1700–2), p. 323.
[24] Simon, *Irish Coins*, p. 65; Johnston, 'Irish Currency', p. 16.
[25] Vernon to Lord Lieutenant, 19 July 1701 (enclosures), TNA, SP 44/102 ff. 191–2.
[26] See Chapter 2, pp. 61–62, above.
[27] Newton to Lords Commissioners of the Treasury, 18 Aug. 1698, TNA MINT 19/2.
[28] Caden, *Mint Conditions*, pp. 178–85, 204, Valenze, *Social Life*, p. 45.

coin and higher than the moidore's relative valuation in Britain.[29] The advent of a new gold coin from Portugal in 1725 made matters worse. Rated at four pounds Irish, implying a bullion price of 95s. 2d. per ounce, these coins began to take the place even of the moidore and led to the export of still more silver coin.[30] The scarcity of official coin for everyday transactions was thus even more severe in Ireland than in England or Scotland.

These disparities were important because all foreign coins were legally required to be taken by weight, with specified deductions made to the value of each individual coin to compensate for various degrees of lightness. In other words, the currency actually obtainable in Ireland had been reduced to bullion in accordance with Lockean dogma, but without Locke's first premise that the price of a given quantity of bullion will always be equal to the price of the same quantity of bullion. This left Ireland with a 'monometallic bullion standard', determined in practice, as at least one contemporary recognized, by the moidore as the coin with the highest gold price.[31]

Even by early modern standards this was a chaotic state of affairs, attributable in large measure to Ireland's almost complete monetary subordination to Britain and the ability of various Irish interests to exploit a widespread popular mistrust of English monetary intentions. But before we examine how Irish people managed this problem, and the difficulties that faced various attempts to change it, we need to look a little more closely at some developments in Britain in order to understand the course of Irish debates.

Struggles over Credit I: the South Sea Bubble

In England and Scotland as well as Ireland a persistently inadequate supply of coins ensured that credit of all sorts and sizes remained central to monetary practice at every social and economic level, from transactions reckoned in pennies in the countryside and small towns to those worth hundreds of pounds transacted in or through major cities. Struggles over credit—who could issue it, on what terms, and to whom—were therefore central to eighteenth-century monetary debates. Despite important overlaps, the content and course of these struggles differed markedly between the three kingdoms, depending on their differing economic priorities, monetary architecture, and respective places in the composite monarchy. The most conspicuous such struggles—in contemporary public discourse as well as subsequent historiography—were over paper money and the management of public debt.

---

[29] Johnston, 'Irish Currency'.
[30] Johnston, 'Irish Currency', p. 18; Simon, *Irish Coins*, p. 72 amd Appendix CVI.
[31] Johnston, 'Irish Currency', p. 19; Prior, *Observations*, p. 55.

The most notorious of these was the rise and fall of the South Sea Company. Despite a growing consensus among historians that the bursting of the South Sea Bubble in 1720 was far less economically consequential than was previously thought, it remains an important episode in the British financial revolution, if only for the influential myths it engendered after the fact.[32] It is less significant in Britain's monetary history. From our point of view its importance is threefold. First, it shows that whatever differences of principle of political economy might have been at stake in the debates over the foundation of the Bank of England and the National Land Bank, they had dissipated quite quickly. Secondly, its the Bubble's outcome cemented the role and increased the power of the Bank of England. Finally, but most importantly for the present chapter, the crash helped to sink the plans of those who had been trying to set up a national bank in Ireland.

The company was established in 1711 under the auspices of the Tory government of Robert Harley to provide a Tory counterweight to the Whig-dominated Bank of England and East India Companies.[33] The aim was to loosen the Bank's grip on the national finances and consequently the dependence of governments on its goodwill. Simultaneously, it would demonstrate to the sovereign and the investing public that effective management of the nation's increasingly complex finances was not the exclusive preserve of the Whigs.

The company's immediate purpose was to convert unsustainable, unfunded short-term debt into long-term debt. Owing to a crisis in the government's credit precipitated by the advent of a Tory ministry, the government's short-term debt instruments were once again trading at crippling rates of discount.[34] The plan was to offer holders of these debts the opportunity to exchange them for shares in the South Sea Company, which would receive 6 per cent per annum for the debt it thereby acquired. The company also had excellent prospects as a profitable trading company owing to the government's award of the 'Asiento'—a monopoly of the slave trade to Spain's colonies in the Americas, conceded to Britain in 1711 after the War of the Spanish Succession.[35]

This was a Tory venture purely in a party-political sense. It offered not even the flimsiest claim to differ from the 'Whig' companies in any way but in its associations and its willingness to work cordially with Tory ministers. Indeed, the Tories had moved so far from whatever principled or ideological objections they had asserted against the Bank of England that they tried, unsuccessfully, to take over its Court of Directors in its 1711 elections.[36]

Although the South Sea Company was not a bank, its founders were all former directors of the Hollow Sword Blade Company, which despite its name tried to

---

[32] Hoppit, 'Myths'; Paul, *Bubble*, p. 111.   [33] Paul, *Bubble*, p. 36; Hoppit, 'Myths', p. 142.
[34] For this crisis—known to contemporaries as the 'Loss of the City'—see Wennerlind, *Casualties*, pp. 161–89; De Krey, *Fractured Society*, pp. 223–30.
[35] Paul, *Bubble*, p. 1; Wennerlind, *Casualties*, pp. 217–34.   [36] Carruthers, *City*, pp. 144–5.

compete with the Bank of England by issuing banknotes and discounting bills of exchange, in clear breach of the Bank of England's charter and supporting legislation.[37] It had also gained a stake in government debt in 1702, when it offered shares in exchange for £200,000 of discounted army debentures.[38] It duly became the South Sea Company's banker. Harley kept a tight rein over the latter, determined not to let it fall under the control of Whigs, who still constituted a sizeable majority of the monied men of the City of London. Harley himself was governor and filled its board with political appointees. But such a naked exercise of partisan control was a double-edged sword. When Tory loyalty was in question following the Hanoverian succession in 1714, the shareholders unceremoniously removed the Tory politicians from the company's court.[39]

The company was therefore well placed to work with Walpole's Whig administration, and in 1719 it offered to take over the whole of the government's unfunded debt in another debt-for-equity swap. After some negotiations this was reduced to exclude all debt held by the Bank of England and the East India Company, leaving a sum of thirty million pounds. The company offered attractive terms to the holders of these debts and also put additional shares up for sale. Remarkably, it also lent its shareholders money on the security of their shares, enabling those who wanted to do so to buy more. These operations helped to fuel a speculative boom in South Sea and other stocks, including in the similarly doomed French Mississippi scheme. The Bubble burst in September, taking the share price rapidly from an extraordinary 1,000 to 124 in December. The Hollow Sword Blade went bankrupt, although the South Sea lived on as a profitable concern in the slave trade, responsible for the delivery of more than 60,000 captive human beings as property into lives of subjection and exploitation.[40]

In England, economic activity was barely affected, even in the short term. And while Scotland experienced a sharp credit crunch, the crash appears to have had little lasting effect on Scots' appetite for investment.[41] Although it is clear that many individuals suffered serious real losses (and greater paper losses), these were overwhelmingly people who were born rich and died rich.[42] Compared proportionally to the losses suffered in the Darien venture, it was a trivial affair that affected a small slice of society.

The political aftermath was also trivial given the level of malpractice. The Committee of Secrecy of the House of Commons found evidence of bribery, deception, and insider trading. Directors of the company were punished (although some later had confiscated assets quietly restored), but thanks to Walpole's careful political management the corruption in the higher reaches of the government and

---

[37] TNA, T 29/16 f. 95.   [38] Wennerlind, *Casualties*, p. 190.   [39] Carruthers, *City*, p. 155.
[40] Paul, *Bubble*, p. 62. For the company's post-crash life, see Paul, *Bubble*, ch. 9. On the South Sea Company and slavery, see Wennerlind, *Casualties*, ch. 6.
[41] Walsh, 'Periphery', pp. 121, 124.   [42] Hoppit, 'Myths', pp. 148–52.

aristocracy was kept from public view. Nevertheless, Walpole's nickname at the time of 'Screen-master General' suggests a widespread understanding that such corruption had been rife.[43]

Walpole also reconstructed the public finances, in which a major element was the Bank of England augmenting its own capital by taking four million pounds of public debt off the Sword Blade's hands. More importantly, the ignominious failure of a novel entrant into the field of government financing, and the Bank of England's role in helping to stabilize the situation, left the Bank unassailable as the British government's financier, keeper of the public credit, and issuer of uniquely venerated paper money. Already, the Bank was acting in some degree as the 'great engine of state' that Adam Smith was to call it half a century later.[44]

It was clearly understood as such. In 1745, when Jacobite successes precipitated a run on the Bank, Henry Fielding described those who came for their cash as 'the most flagitious and profligate enemies of their country'.[45] To stem the run, 'upwards of 1100 of the most eminent traders of the City and suburbs of London, and afterwards many more' publicly signed a declaration that they would not only accept the Bank's notes but do all in their power to use them in all payments. According to *The Westminster Journal*, the declaration would make it impossible 'to create either diffidence or confusion upon this head, which cannot but give the highest satisfaction to all who wish well to the present constitution in church and state, and to the maintenance of public faith and private property'.[46] The declaration and names of the signatories duly filled the first four pages of the next issue of *The London Gazette*.[47] For the first time, although not the last, use of the bank's notes became a test and a sign of British patriotism.

Struggles over Credit II: Banking in Ireland 1721–82

The Bubble's most serious lasting effects were felt in Ireland, where it ensured that there would be no such engine of state for decades to come.[48] Initially, the departure of large amounts of money from Ireland to invest in the stock market boom acted as a major spur to a fresh attempt to establish a national or public bank, following an unsuccessful petition to Parliament in 1695 and an ephemeral prospectus for an Irish joint stock bank circulated by a Londoner the following year.[49] According to the initial proposer of the scheme eventually considered by

---

[43] Paul, *Bubble*, pp. 51–2.   [44] Smith, *Wealth of Nations*, vol. 1, p. 303.
[45] Fielding, *The True Patriot and Related Writings*, p. 72, cited in Shin, 'Paper Money', p. 432.
[46] *Westminster Journal*, 5 Oct. 1745.
[47] *London Gazette*, 14–28 Sept. 1745. Later signatories were listed in the next issue.
[48] Walsh, *Bubble and Ireland*, chs 6–8. See also Ryder, 'Bank of Ireland', esp. pp. 570–2.
[49] Hall, *Bank of Ireland*, p. 15; Holt, *Seasonable Proposals*.

the Irish Parliament, the country's shortage of specie was part of a vicious circle in which a chronic balance of payments deficit was in turn aggravated by the lack of specie to drive economic activity, including export industries. But recent circumstances had made matters much worse, because as the 'expectation of extravagant gain has prevailed on many persons, to send over all the mony they had credit for, to purchase Mississippi and South Sea stocks... this Kingdom is exhausted of the greatest part of its current cash'. A public bank would solve the problem by issuing as much paper money 'as shall be requisite to employ our people to carry on our trade and manufactures'.[50]

This was early in 1720; by the time a proposal was being considered by Parliament in September 1721 both bubbles had long burst, providing powerful ammunition for those who argued that establishment of a bank was fraught with danger, and leading many to change their minds, including some MPs who moved from commitments to subscribe to active hostility.[51] The House of Commons nevertheless agreed to refer the proposal to a committee on 25 September, but peremptorily threw out the relevant bill a few weeks later.[52] In December, both houses of the Irish Parliament crushed efforts to keep the proposal alive by resolving that anyone who tried to procure a charter to set up a public bank would be deemed 'to act in contempt of this House, and an enemy to his country', as the Commons put it.[53]

There is no disputing the historian Patrick Walsh's argument that 'the influence of the bubble was central to the framing of the debates around the bank'.[54] But as Walsh points out, the debates rested on misreadings of both the Bubble and the bank, which allowed them to be seen as fundamentally similar, despite the best efforts of the bank's supporters to point out the obvious differences between them.[55] The causes for the bank's ultimate failure were complex, and raised a number of issues that went well beyond the fear of bubbles, including, as Michael Ryder has shown, many of the 'court versus country' arguments that had been prominent twenty-five years earlier in debates over the founding of the Bank of England.[56]

Opponents of the proposal argued that it posed various threats to Ireland's political institutions and social fabric. MPs who were directors of the bank would be open to undue influence by the government as the bank would depend on it for renewal of its charter. Alternatively, the bank could use its money and influence as a creditor to secure the election of MPs to do its will. In an obvious reference to the South Sea Company, an indebted government, or indebted ministers, could be obliged to do the bank favours, even to the extent of covering up illegality and peculation.

---

[50] Irwin, *To the Nobility*.   [51] Walsh, *Bubble and Ireland*, p. 169.   [52] JHCI, vol. 3, p. 256.
[53] JHCI, vol. 3, p. 289 (9 Dec. 1721); JHLI, vol. 2, p. 720.   [54] Walsh, *Bubble and Ireland*, p. 164.
[55] Walsh, *Bubble and Ireland*, pp. 163, 72–4. Hutchinson, *Letter*, pp. 18–23.
[56] Walsh, *Bubble and Ireland*, pp. 163, 172–4.

Other objections went deeper into the threat the bank posed to the nation's constitutional, religious, and social fabric. By issuing paper money, the bank would denude the country of the little specie it had left and export it for profit, leaving the country without the means to raise armies, thereby giving 'as fair an opportunity as could be given to the Pretender or any Popish prince that is prepared to espouse him'.[57] Because it would be allowed to lend money on landed security, it could potentially destroy the landed interest by acquiring the whole landed property of Ireland through foreclosures. This was doubly dangerous because Roman Catholics might attain a controlling interest in the Bank of Ireland.[58] In another argument arising from the South Sea Company, the bank, if allowed to lend money to the government, could neutralize Parliament's power over supply, regarded as the most important bulwark against arbitrary government. In short, the bank would amass too much power for any other social force or institution to resist it, leaving it free to impose what policies it saw fit, including, as some feared, a land tax.[59]

It was futile for supporters of the bank to point out that some of these fears were mutually contradictory: the prospect of a public bank had conjured up a dystopian picture of state and monetary power fused into a leviathan capable of using any means—including the manufacture of war scares and accusations of Jacobitism—to sustain itself and crush resistance.[60] Thus the bank 'may, and probably will end in our destruction, and the razure of our little remains of liberty'.[61]

The bank's supporters pointed out that many of these fears were 'chimerical', being utterly inconsistent with other nations' experience of actually-existing banks.[62] The bank's opponents did not engage with this argument; their image of the bank was a hybrid of the South Sea Company and the hypothetical banks that their English predecessors had feared in the mid-1690s. Even their references Scotland considered not the highly relevant and encouraging case of Bank of Scotland but the Darien enterprise, which was held up as an object lesson for what might go wrong if the Bank of Ireland were to incur England's displeasure.[63]

The fact that such arguments prevailed in Ireland, unlike England and Scotland, points to contrasts between the three countries that suggest that the conditions for monetary revolution were lacking in Ireland in this period. In England, the dichotomy between trade and land was always less salient in practice than many critics of the Bank of England liked to imagine. While merchants dominated the early subscriptions to the Bank of England, the leading Whig politicians who secured the Bank's charter and steered the necessary legislation through Parliament were all large landholders, as of course were the peers and almost all

---

[57] Anon., *Late Intended Bank*, p. 6.
[58] Rowley, *Answer to a Book*, pp. 39–40.
[59] Rowley, *Answer to a Book*, pp. 38–9.
[60] Misolestes, *Objections*, pp. 3–4.
[61] Rowley, *Answer to a Book*, p. 5.
[62] Hutchinson, *Letter*.
[63] Rowley, *Answer to a Book*, p. 6.

of the MPs who voted for it. It was because the boundaries between trade and land in England were blurred in multiple ways that, as Ryder says, 'the insistence that the interests of land and trade were identical was a staple of Augustan political argument'.[64]

Such arguments made little headway in Ireland, where the economic and social division between land and trade would remain far clearer for far longer than in England.[65] Despite genuine economic achievements and developments in Ireland that have been energetically rehearsed by some scholars, the fact remains that England in this period had become a wealthy commercial country while Ireland remained 'a largely undeveloped agricultural economy supporting a generally under-capitalized landlord class, significant numbers of the more prosperous of whom resided permanently, or much of the time, outside the country'.[66] Above all, there was nothing in Ireland that could compare with London, where the aristocracy and gentry came to socialize, marry off their children (increasingly, although not typically, to members of merchant families), and transact all kinds of business with members of the merchant classes. This was the milieu in which the class of 'gentlemanly capitalists' described by Cain and Hopkins began to coalesce.[67]

One point at which 'trade' and 'land' did intermingle in Ireland was in the business of banking itself, but in a way inimical to the proposed bank's political prospects. Not only was the main business of Irish banks the remittance of rents from the countryside to Dublin and from Dublin to London, rather than the provision of credit to the state or the commercial world, but many of the bankers themselves were sons of the landed elite.[68] Those who sat in Parliament were unanimous against the bank in the critical vote:[69] the bank's offer to lend at 5 per cent rather than the usual 8 was a clear threat to their profits. But it is telling that critics of a public bank did not extend their arguments to critiques of banking in general. Instead, some made a virtue of the puniness and transience of the private banks that served the needs of the landed classes without ever threatening their power.[70] Arguments that the size, constitution, and broad financial base of public banks ensured their stability and longevity merely stoked the opponents' fears; the proposed bank's immortality heightened the risks involved in establishing it.

Finally, for all of the serious consequences of Ireland's shortage of specie, there was in Ireland in 1721 no state, and no political elite, that collectively saw the immediate raising of money by almost any available means as indispensable to the survival of their regime, their property, their religion, and their nation's place in

---

[64] Ryder, 'Bank of Ireland', p. 574.   [65] Hoppit, 'Landed Interest', p. 94.
[66] Kelly, 'Political Economy', p. 109. For a positive view of the Irish economy, see Cullen, 'Irish Economy'.
[67] Cain and Hopkins, *British Imperialism 1688–1914*, vol. 1, pp. 66–7.
[68] Cullen, 'Landlords, Bankers', p. 32.   [69] Walsh, *Bubble and Ireland*, p. 177.
[70] Misolestes, *Objections*, p. 4.

the world. In Ireland, it was the bank proposal itself that appeared to present such existential threats.

The specifically 'national' aspects of opposition to the bank proposal highlight the contrasts that enabled Scotland to establish a bank while Ireland could not. Scotland in 1695 was a poor, predominantly agricultural, country, prone to recurring famine and desperately short of coin: far more like Ireland in 1721 than England in 1694. But two distinguishing circumstances ensured that its plan for a bank did not meet the same fate as Ireland's.

Bank of Scotland, as we have seen, was from the beginning an enterprise of the Scottish establishment that rested heavily on its landed proprietors' pledges of land as security. Critics of the Irish bank proposal made much of the fact that although the consortium of mostly landed men who led it initially undertook to 'charge their estates' to secure the bank, the nature of that pledge turned out to be very limited in the regulations of the bank by the time they reached Parliament.[71] Moreover, the preponderance of landed men among the subscribers reduced significantly between the initial proposal and the height of the debate, making the bank even more vulnerable to critiques based on its lack of a landed foundation.[72] When the projectors set out to prove the strength of the enterprise by opening a fresh subscription book in the face of Parliament's rejection of the bill in October 1721, the resulting list was immediately lampooned by Jonathan Swift. As well as undermining its national credentials by highlighting the number of 'French' subscribers, Swift twice itemized the presence of people such as a 'Popish Vintner', a bricklayer, and a pewterer, among other plebeians, in order to query how much land such a list of people could own, given the relative paucity of aristocrats, baronets, and knights among them. The subscription list of Bank of Scotland had been open to no such question.

Another question that did not arise in Scotland was where political control over the bank would lie. This was a central concern of William King, Archbishop of Dublin, strong supporter of the Williamite cause, intermittent Lord Justice, leading thinker of the 'Irish interest', and one of the bank's most influential and strenuous opponents.[73] King argued that it was not safe for a dependent kingdom to establish something as powerful as a bank over which it did not have legislative control. This view was framed by the British Parliament's harsh restatement and extension of the Irish Parliament's subjugation in the Declaratory Act of April 1720, which had dashed King's hopes of legislative autonomy and meant that 'the Protestant interest in Ireland began to consider and debate all questions, whether

---

[71] Anon., *Late Intended Bank*, p. 13.
[72] See Swift, *Eyes of Ireland*. Walsh, 'Periphery', p. 160, Table 7.4, shows a decrease in MPs (36.4 to 21.5 per cent) and an increase in merchants (5.3 to 12.4 per cent) from the original list in May 1720 to the list of October 1721; Ryder, 'Bank of Ireland', p. 572.
[73] O'Regan, 'King'.

political or economic, in the light of their subordination to Westminster'.[74] For some, this was a reason to support the bank, but for King and many others Ireland's dependency multiplied the bank's dangers.[75] Hercules Rowley spelt this out:

> As Ireland is a dependant Kingdom, and can neither make laws nor repeal them, when it pleases, ... we ought (in my humble opinion) to be very cautious, how we pin anything down upon our selves, the consequences whereof are at least very doubtful ... For it is certain, that if the intended bank prove advantageous to us, by increasing our trade, and encouraging our manufacturers ... and should in the least interfere with, or injure the trade of England, then we may expect, they will procure a repeal of the charter ... On the contrary, if it happens to impoverish us, and drain our little substance into Great Britain, then indeed, we may be sure of a continuation.[76]

Such 'secret fears' of England's power and underlying malevolence were prominent in much of the rhetoric against the bank.[77]

Scots in 1695 entertained no such fears, at least in relation to banking. With no equivalents of Poynings' Law or the Declaratory Act, Scots saw their Parliament as the equal of England's, and were blithely confident that it would exercise ultimate power over its bank. Remarkably, they seem to have remained unconcerned even as the end of their Parliament came into view. To my knowledge no concerns about the loss of legislative control over Bank of Scotland were raised in the course of debates about the Treaty of Union, although, as we have seen, Scots resisted the Bank of England's attempt to establish a circulation there in 1707.

In his critique of the opposition to the Irish bank proposal, Francis Hutchinson cited Edinburgh along with other places where banks had been beneficial. He demanded that the critics give 'a plain reason, why a bank may not thrive in Dublin, as well as in these places. Is Ireland the only ground, where no grass will grow?'[78] For the reasons just discussed, the answer would remain 'yes' until the dependent status of Ireland's Parliament had been radically revised.

That took sixty years. Even as late as February 1780, Parliament's resolution that 'the erecting of a public Bank upon a solid foundation, under proper regulations and restrictions, is at this time highly necessary' led to nothing.[79] Two years later, however, the government introduced the heads of a bill which produced an Act within six weeks. The required £600,000 of subscriptions were paid by March 1783, and a charter—deliberately modelled on the Bank of England's—was granted in May. The Bank of Ireland was born.

---

[74] Hutton, 'Archbishop King', pp. 81, 86. On the politics of the passage of the Declaratory Act see Hayton, 'Stanhope/Sunderland'.
[75] Hutton, 'Archbishop King', p. 89.   [76] Rowley, *Answer to a Book*, pp. 4–6.
[77] Hutchinson, *Letter*, p. 28.   [78] Hutchinson, *Letter*, p. 7.
[79] JHCI vol. 10, p. 78 (25 Feb. 1780).

At no time after February 1782 was the success of the proposal in doubt. Debates were relatively brief and the parliamentary majorities were overwhelming. The proposal nevertheless attracted vehement criticism inside and outside Parliament. The arguments of critics and supporters carried echoes of the debates of 1721, but they also demonstrated how dramatically Ireland's economic and political context had changed and how thinking on this issue had developed during the six decades that the idea of a public bank in Ireland had appeared to languish.

One pamphleteer against the bank tried to revive 1721 quite deliberately when he referred to the bank as a 'ministerial' bubble and cautioned against repeating the disasters of the Mississippi scheme and the South Sea Bubble.[80] In this he appears to have been alone, but he was not alone when he referred to the much more recent Ayr Bank failure. This was deployed as part of an argument against the increased size and reach of circulating paper that for many was one of the national bank's main attractions.[81] According to the authors who cited this episode, the size of a country's circulation must be proportioned to its level of economic activity.[82] Repeating Smith's analysis, they argued that the Ayr Bank's extensive note issues to support fictitious bills of exchange for the use of 'projectors' demonstrated that any attempt to increase the circulation to stimulate the economy must end in disaster. Only Ireland's private bankers, with unique insights into the state of commerce, and (thanks to Ireland's 'most perfect code of bankrupt laws') exposed to the risk of ruin if they issued more notes than they could support, could be trusted to exercise the caution required to keep note issue safe.[83]

Ireland's experience of private banking limited the appeal of this kind of argument. The examples of failures and frauds that critics of private banking had advanced in 1721 had multiplied in the interim. Indeed, each major wave of failures had rekindled interest in the idea of a public bank. Thus George Berkeley's ideas for a national bank developed in the wake of the failure of Burton's Bank for £94,000 in 1733.[84] Similarly, the long-running crisis of 1754–9, which saw five of Dublin's eight banks fail along with two more in Galway, provoked—along with some legislative locking of the stable door—a number of pamphlets that ranged from outright hostility to all forms of bank paper through to a proposal for a bank on the model of the Bank of England.[85] These failures, and legislation in 1756 to prohibit merchants from carrying on business as bankers, appear to have arrested the growth of Irish banking and thus the number of failures, although the general

---

[80] Secundus, *Letters*, p. 48.
[81] The Provost (John Hely Hutchinson), HPHCI, vol. I, p. 301 (27 Feb. 1782).
[82] Secundus, *Letters*, pp. 34–8; Jebb, *Considerations*, p. 14.   [83] Secundus, *Letters*, p. 13.
[84] Dudley, 'Burton's', p. 11. Some of Burton's creditors had still not been paid by 1817 (p. 29). For the influence of Burton's failure on Berkeley see Magennis, 'Whither?', pp. 196–200; Kelly, 'Berkeley', pp. 105–6.
[85] Hall, *Bank of Ireland*, pp. 8–12; Johnston-Liik, *Irish Parliament*, p. 393; A Gentleman in Trade, *Observations*, pp. 37–40; Anon., *Present Calamities*, pp. 14–15; T—w, *Paper-Credit*.

Anglo-Scottish crisis of 1772 precipitated the failure of Colebrooke's bank the following year as a result of the failed speculations of its London-based chief.[86]

Despite this dismal record and the misery left in its wake, opponents of the national bank revived an argument of 1721 when they claimed that the failures of private banks were of necessity limited, while the scope and power of a national bank ensured that it would affect everybody.[87] This was an aspect of the familiar argument that a national bank would simply amass too much power or, alternatively, confer too much power on the state. According to 'Junius Secundus', the Bank of England had already produced great evil to the state and was bound ultimately to destroy it.[88]

The bank's resemblance to the Bank of England aroused further concerns. Henry Flood argued that the Bank of England 'is not a national bank, because the nation is not security for a shilling' beyond what the nation had borrowed from it. John Gray—an Englishman who may have never visited Ireland, but who had first gone into print to support an Irish national bank in the wake of the 1772 crisis—had made a different point in response to the 'narrow, impolitic and selfish plan of the Dublin monied men' in 1780. They, he argued, had asked the 'government to give them gratis, the public credit, to enable them to lend that credit at second hand to others, and even to lend at a high interest to government itself'.[89] Instead of this 'corporation bank', Gray proposed a bank that would borrow £200,000 on the security of Parliament to issue £1 m of notes under strict parliamentary oversight. Any additional issues would have to be backed fully by stocks of bullion coin.[90]

Such concerns were far from baseless. The Bank of Ireland was largely the creature of the biggest Dublin mercantile houses and banks, in particular La Touche, which was Ireland's largest and oldest, having survived every crisis since its foundation in 1713. Its chairman, David La Touche MP, had been a strong supporter of the bank from the beginning and became its first governor. By March 1785 La Touche and four of his family collectively owned £48,800 of the bank's £600,000 stock.[91] Reflecting these origins, it resembled the Bank of England in that its purpose was to serve the needs of the government and the mercantile elite of the capital—a purpose it affirmed with its decision to lend money only by discounting bills and not on the cash credit basis of the Scottish banks. Its notes—whose form was virtually identical to those of the Bank of England, but with Hibernia in place of Britannia—were further evidence of its place in Irish life. Initially they were issued in denominations between ten pounds and five hundred pounds Irish, although in 1784 the bank began to issue notes in multiples of five or

---

[86] Kosmetatos, *Crisis*, pp. 3–8; Johnston-Liik, *Irish Parliament*, p. 394. Cullen, 'Landlords, Bankers', p. 37, notes the irony that the 1756 legislation came 'at the nadir point of the banking fortunes of the banking gentry'.
[87] Jebb, *Considerations*, p. 29. [88] Secundus, *Letters*, p. 12. [89] Gray, *Letter*, pp. 22–3.
[90] Gray, *Essay*, pp. 35–6. [91] Dickson and English, 'La Touche', p. 22.

more guineas, with their awkward Irish value printed in full.[92] Thus a five-guinea note promised to pay £5 13s. 9d. Finally, like the Bank of England, it had almost no presence beyond its own environs, but was protected from serious competition anywhere by a monopoly of joint-stock banking, ensuring that all the weaknesses of private banking cited in support of its establishment would remain in place, at least until 1824, when joint stocks were permitted outside a 50-mile radius of Dublin.

For the bank's supporters, however, its resemblance to the Bank of England was one of its chief attractions. This was more than a matter of outward forms. Unlike any previous proposal for an Irish bank, the stock of the Bank of Ireland consisted entirely of government debt, not as a subscribed loan as in the Bank of England, but, on the model of the Royal Bank of Scotland, in the form of existing debentures on an Irish national debt that had first come into being when the Irish government had to borrow to fund additional regiments to send to England to defeat the 1715 Jacobite rebellion.[93] Holders of these debentures, then trading at a discount of 20 per cent, could exchange them at par for bank stock, thus absorbing a proportion of the national debt and raising the value of the remaining debentures. This was an attractive proposition for the holders, many of whom, we might note, were MPs.[94]

Arguments against the bank carried little weight because Ireland's constitutional relationship with Britain was changing rapidly. The initial parliamentary debate on the bank took place at the height of the Irish protestant elite's struggle to end the status of 'dependency' which had been so important in sinking the 1721 proposal. In 1779, as a result of 'patriot' agitation, which included the marching of volunteer militias, the British government had conceded 'free trade' to Ireland, by which was meant participation in the British mercantile system on the same terms as Britain. Only a few weeks before the vote on the bank, the Dungannon Convention had assembled to demand full legislative independence in the form of the repeal of the Declaratory Act and Poynings' Law. This was largely achieved by July. For many, a national bank and an increased circulation of money were essential if Ireland was to capitalize on 'free trade'.[95] Others looked further ahead, suggesting that a national bank 'leads to all the marks of a great and independent nation' and hoping that it would lead to a mint.[96]

Not all 'patriots' were so optimistic in their assessment of the bank's effects or the British government's intentions. Beauchamp Bagenal argued that Ireland still lacked both civil and commercial liberty and that the bank would 'give the finishing stroke to all our hopes, for by adding to the influence of government,

---

[92] Hall, *Bank of Ireland*, p. 53. [93] McGrath, 'Public Wealth', p. 178.
[94] McGrath, 'Public Wealth', p. 185.
[95] Sir Lucius O'Brien, HPHCI, vol. 1, p. 298 (27 Feb. 1782); Gray, *Letter*, p. 14.
[96] J. Foster, HPHCI, vol. 1, p. 299 (27 Feb. 1782).

it will turn the city of Dublin, which... ought to be the bulwark of national liberty, into a ministerial borough'.[97] Writing after the bank legislation had been passed, 'Junius Secundus' went further. In echoes of earlier fears about Catholics purchasing stock, he claimed that English merchants would gain a controlling interest and use it 'to destroy every extension of your trade, every infant manufacture of this country'.[98] The reforming Lord-Lieutenant and Chief Secretary had been 'sent here to peculate, to plunder the kingdom at discretion, provided they increased the influence of the crown'.[99] For Bagenal and Secundus, England's malignity appeared as bottomless and formidable as it had to their forebears in 1721.

Ireland: Struggles over Coin

The defeat of the bank proposal in 1721 left Ireland with an increasingly anachronistic system of commodity money for another six decades. Irish monetary debates in the period were therefore confined almost entirely to questions of coinage, which remained the medium in which taxes were paid and commercial transactions settled. The first such debate began in July 1722, when William Wood, a Wolverhampton ironmaster connected to Whig governing circles, bought a patent from the king's mistress, the Duchess of Kendal, to coin 360 tons of copper into £108,000 worth of Irish halfpence and farthings. With the British government's agreement, Wood decided to mint the coins in Bristol. Opposition in Ireland began at the most senior levels of government immediately the patent was granted and spread rapidly as the news became more widely known.[100]

The immediate objections concerned the coins' quality and quantity. As one of the more measured pamphleteers demonstrated, the intrinsic value of a pound of copper was twelve pence, as against the thirty pence tale value Wood was contracted to mint, representing '60l loss in 100l'.[101] This was a much smaller intrinsic value than current English copper coinage, although greater than that of the most recent Irish patent. But as the coins began to reach Ireland, claims that they were far under the stipulated weight abounded. An assay of the coins at the London mint under the supervision of its chief officers did nothing to allay this fear. Wood had sent up the specimens from Bristol and it was taken as given in Ireland that they were not a representative sample.[102]

The quality of the coins mattered all the more because of their quantity. While it was understood that copper coinage always worked on a token basis, this was acceptable for as long as their quantity was no more 'than what is absolutely

---

[97] B. Bagenal, HPHCI, vol. 1, p. 321 (5 Mar. 1782).   [98] Secundus, *Letters*, pp. 29–30.
[99] Secundus, *Letters*, p. 39.   [100] Caden, 'Mint Conditions', p. 209.
[101] Bindon, *Some Reasons*, p. 6.   [102] Caden, 'Mint Conditions', p. 239.

necessary for small payments'.[103] The Irish experience of the steady loss of silver and gold coin through inconsistent valuations led to a reasonable assumption that Wood's £108,000 of copper would replace an equal amount of gold and silver. Ireland's total coin circulation at the time was commonly estimated at about £500,000, although far lower estimates were also given. As Wood's coins would therefore amount to one-fifth of the circulation, it was inevitable that they would be used for payments beyond small change, and even be needed for payments overseas, where only their bullion value would count.[104] The problem would be aggravated further by the import of the large quantities of counterfeits which coins of such low intrinsic value would inevitably inspire. Moreover, Wood himself was not to be trusted to confine his quantity within the limits of his patent, given the difficulty of enforcing laws against exporting coin.[105]

Trouble began immediately. In July 1722, Archbishop King, one of the Lords Justices, wrote to the Lord-Lieutenant warning that the coins would 'drain the Kingdom of the little gold and silver that is left in it, and complete the general misery which is already intolerable'.[106] The following month the Irish revenue commissioners wrote, enclosing a paper outlining the problems created in the 1690s, when copper coins minted by a Colonel Roger Moore had 'insensibly' become such a large part of the circulation that many people had used them to pay their excise while soldiers had refused them as wages.[107] They added that 'such a patent will be highly prejudicial to the trade and welfare of this Kingdom, & more particularly to his Majesty's Revenue which we have formerly found by experience to have suffered very much by too great a quantity of the like small base coin'. The following month they repeated these points, adding that 'many persons of rank and fortune, and the merchants & traders here' were imploring them to do their best to prevent it.[108]

This complaint from this source went to the heart of these objects' 'moneyness', which, as I have argued, derives from a combination of the state's decree of its value and acceptability in all payments, its capacity to acquit taxes, and the broad social acceptance that these attributes usually confer. Owing to the government's commitment to making only precious metal coins legal tender, it was explicitly stated in Wood's patent that nobody would be obliged to accept his coins.[109] The first condition was thus absent, leaving the coins dependent on the last two. The commissioners of the revenue had made it clear that these were unlikely to apply.

---

[103] Bindon, *Some Reasons*, p. 6.   [104] Caden, 'Mint Conditions', p. 255.
[105] Commissioners of the Revenue, Ireland to Edward Hopkins (Copy to the Lords of the Treasury), 29 Aug. 1724, SP/63/380 f. 110.
[106] McNally, 'Carteret', p. 355.
[107] 10 Apr. 1690, *CTP* (1556–1696). Moore had apparently taken over the Armstrong patent issued in 1680 (see Chapter 2, p. 63, above). On this occasion execution of the patent was suspended 'till Ireland is reduced'.
[108] TNA, SP/63/380 f. 110.   [109] Goodwin, 'Wood's Halfpence', p. 651.

The acceptance of the coin as taxes remained a central element of what became a struggle between a mobilized Irish people and all the institutions of Irish government on one side and the British government on the other.[110] Popular opposition was expressed not only through a flood of petitions but from disturbances, including one in Cork that prevented a cargo of coins from being landed and included a threat to burn the ship.[111] Associations were established and public declarations made to boycott the coins, which was the obvious strategy to defeat the patent.[112] One such declaration signed by the High Sheriff, Justices of the Peace, Grand Jury, nobility, clergy, gentlemen, and freeholders of the City of Dublin included the names of nine Privy Councillors among about 170 other signatories.[113]

Such commitments would be more difficult to maintain if the coins could be tendered for taxes, especially on the lower rungs of the social ladder. In December 1723, the Irish House of Commons therefore resolved unanimously to request that the king direct the revenue officers to refuse them. In August the following year, as the strength of the resistance became clearer, the British government directed the Lords Justices to order the commissioners of the revenue and all other officers in Ireland to revoke any 'orders, directions, significations or intimations whatsoever' they may have given against accepting the coins. The Commissioners replied that they had never given any such order.[114] To a direction that they order their officers not to receive more than fivepence halfpenny in any one payment (presumably intended to mollify the opposition) they replied that even that order would be taken as 'a strong intimation' that they should receive sums under that amount. Explaining somewhat disingenuously that people had been schooled to believe that taxes could only be paid in sterling money, and therefore that 'such orders would be thought arbitrary', the commissioners effectively refused to comply out of 'a regard to the publick quiet of this Kingdom, & our apprehension of the ill consequences to the revenue'.[115]

The British government rejected the economic case against the coins. This was in part because of the Irish Parliament's principled refusal to send witnesses to an inquiry in July 1724 by the English Privy Council into the findings of the inquiry conducted by the Irish House of Commons which had condemned the patent. But it was also due to repeated assertions by Irish bodies and pamphleteers that Ireland had no need for small change, which appeared to contradict earlier protestations that a shortage of small coin was one of Ireland's most troublesome economic problems.

---

[110] McNally, 'Carteret'.   [111] Goodwin, 'Wood's Halfpence', pp. 664–5.
[112] Goodwin, 'Wood's Halfpence', p. 661; Hutton, 'Archbishop King', pp. 97–8.
[113] 'At a General Session of the Peace…', 3 Sept. 1724, TNA, SP 63/384 f. 139.
[114] Goodwin, 'Wood's Halfpence', p. 662.   [115] 29 Aug. 1724, TNA T1/248 f. 17.

This increasingly assertive non-cooperation of the whole apparatus of Irish government could not but make the dispute constitutional, at least in the eyes of a British government that found itself completely powerless to enforce its will in a country whose constitutional status was designed to ensure that it could. British ministers became convinced that economic objections were a cloak for a push for legislative independence.[116] Yet apart from a couple of rather ambiguous lines of Archbishop King's correspondence there is only one clear indication that this was the aim of any of the Irish protagonists.[117] This was the fourth of Swift's famous *Drapier's Letters*, whose mordant questioning of the British government's rights over Irish affairs resulted in the arrest of its publisher and an unsuccessful attempt to bring Swift to trial for seditious libel.[118] But as the new Primate and Lord Justice, Archbishop Boulter, made clear in January 1724/5, Swift's view was far from typical of the patent's opponents. While acknowledging that 'some foolish and other ill-meaning people have taken this opportunity of propagating a notion of the independency of this kingdom', he stressed that 'those of the best sense and estates here...abhor any such notion', understanding as they did that the security of their property depended on 'the kingdom as well as King of England'.[119] When Carteret arrived near the end of 1724 to take up the Lord-Lieutenancy, he portrayed the attitude of the Irish Privy Council in similar terms, explaining the members' 'extreme abhorrence' of both the coins and 'independency'.[120] In the following months Carteret and Boulter managed to persuade the ministry in London that the struggle was lost.[121] Accordingly, the government withdrew the patent in September 1725.

While the crisis did not give rise to any widespread desire to change Ireland's constitutional status, it did incite demands for one specific type of autonomy for Ireland—the monetary autonomy that comes with the possession of a mint. As Mara Caden shows, demands for a mint had not disappeared but 'moved underground' since the Lords Justices had tried to secure one in 1701. It quickly became a central theme of many pamphlets against the patent, some pointing to pre-union Scotland as an example.[122] Despite their fierce and effective resistance to the halfpence, however, no part of the Irish establishment ever raised this point publicly, suggesting that it was well understood that to do so was to challenge Ireland's dependent status, a step for which they had no appetite.

---

[116] Goodwin, 'Wood's Halfpence', p. 667.

[117] Both Hutton, 'Archbishop King', esp. pp. 95–7, and Goodwin, 'Wood's Halfpence', pp. 667–8, use this evidence to claim that King's aims were 'constitutional'.

[118] The letters were collected in Jonathan Swift, *Drapier's Letters*. Historians have long recognized that a focus on Swift produces a misleading impression of the issues at stake. See Goodwin, 'Wood's Halfpence', pp. 647–8.

[119] Boulter to Newcastle, 19 Jan. 1724, Boulter, *Letters*, 1, p. 8.

[120] Carteret to Newcastle, 20 Oct. 1724, TNA, SP 63/384 ff. 159–65.

[121] Hutton, 'Archbishop King', p. 367.   [122] Caden, 'Mint Conditions', pp. 218, 261–79.

One of the oddest aspects of the Wood's halfpence episode was the repeated insistence that Ireland had no shortage of small money. While this was manifestly untrue, and obviously contradicted previous claims by Irish writers and politicians, it did not follow that a very large supply of severely underweight copper coins would help.[123] To begin with, Ireland appears to have been overstocked with base metal currency in the form of counterfeit halfpence and farthings known as 'raps'. These were allegedly imported in large quantity and sold in bulk for gold or silver. According to Wood's critics, however, his coins would only make this problem worse, as most of the raps had appeared 'during our late coinages of copper' as it was impossible to distinguish them from those of the patentees.[124] Wood's copper would have caused exactly the same problem.

Despite Swift's best efforts, the next minting of copper coins for Ireland was almost completely uncontroversial.[125] Boulter, its leading advocate, had clearly absorbed the lessons of the Wood's halfpence fiasco and was determined to avoid a repeat. The contrasts are stark. The process originated visibly in Ireland, beginning formally with an address of the Irish House of Lords, and subject to consideration by the Lords Justices and the Privy Council. There was no private patentee and the profits were to accrue to the Irish revenue. Moreover, the proportion between the coins' weight and tale value was to be the same as English copper coins at the 12:13 parity. Finally, only 50 tons was to be produced at first, with future minting to be determined by the perceived need.

Only one of the objections against Wood's halfpence remained: the new coins were not to be minted in Ireland. They were, however, like previous regal coinages for Ireland, to be minted at the Tower of London, as the Lords had requested.[126] This did not silence all criticism. The following day the Commons resolved, *nem. con.*, 'that a mint... for a coinage of copper half pence and farthings... will be of great advantage to this Kingdom'.[127] Boulter later explained that the 'warm men' who had moved the resolution, being 'very zealous for a mint here', were worried that coining copper at the Tower would 'mark out a way for coining gold and silver for us' and thus spoil the chances of a mint ever being established in Ireland.[128] While demands for a mint persisted, the coinage of coppers for Ireland at the Tower appears to have remained uncontentious and continued fairly regularly from 1737 until 1782, after which it ceased altogether.[129]

Copper coin nevertheless remained chronically scarce throughout the century not only in Ireland but in England and—as we have seen—Scotland. Helpful as it could be to the common people, the regular minting of copper was unattractive to the authorities. Not only was it expensive and time-consuming for the mint

---

[123] Caden, 'Mint Conditions', p. 251.   [124] Anon., *Defence*, p. 11.
[125] Caden, 'Mint Conditions', pp. 278–9.   [126] JHLI, vol. 3, p. 144 (14 Apr. 1730).
[127] JHCI, vol. 3, p. 650 (15 Apr. 1730).
[128] Boulter to Duke of Dorset, 21 Apr. 1731, Boulter, *Letters*, vol. 2, p. 53.
[129] Challis, *Mint*, pp. 437–8.

(noting that it required 504 English halfpence to make as much money as a single guinea), but the coins were readily counterfeited by being melted and remade lighter, or adulterated with lead. Despite being made a felony in 1771, counterfeiting copper became big business.[130] A 1783 petition of Newcastle merchants, manufacturers, and traders pointed out numerous loopholes in the law and called for an adequate supply of good halfpence from the mint, claiming that 'large quantities of base copper money are frequently conveyed by land and water carriage to all places of trade in the Kingdom'.[131] A Wolverhampton petition in 1786 complained that it was not an offence in Britain to counterfeit Irish money, resulting in 'great quantities' being circulated there, while in Dublin large quantities of counterfeits of both British and Irish halfpence appeared periodically.[132] By 1796, Patrick Colquhoun, a leading London magistrate, described highly organized national distribution networks for light halfpence and farthings manufactured in London, Birmingham, and other cities, and estimated that three-quarters of the circulating copper was fraudulent.[133] The Newcastle traders had put it at 90 per cent.

For their users, counterfeits were only a problem when other people refused to take them. Small dealers, who had little choice but to accept them from their customers, lost badly if their suppliers, who had to make payments further afield, rejected them. For the poor, whose monetary lives might be conducted almost entirely in copper, the counterfeits only became a problem during periodic crackdowns, such as when merchants collectively resolved not to take them in any payment worth sixpence or more and to scrutinize all copper coins closely.[134] Such resolutions make it clear that the underlying problem was the shortage of silver. As the Newcastle traders put it, 'very few payments in country trade are any where to be obtained without large portions of copper coin'.[135] It was only because people tendered coppers for payments worth sixpences, shillings, and more that the business of counterfeiting them was worthwhile or even feasible: careful scrutiny of the number of halfpence and farthings required even for relatively small payments was time-consuming, and—if there was little good coin to be had—fairly pointless anyway.

Ireland: towards a Sterling Standard

Boulter's success in getting good copper coin minted for Ireland in 1737 was accompanied by success in his longer and more controversial campaign to have all

---

[130] Styles, 'Money Makers', p. 177.   [131] JHC, vol. 39, p. 319 (26 Mar. 1783).
[132] *Ipswich Journal*, 28 Oct. 1786 (BNA); *Saunders's News-letter*, 19 June 1779 (BNA).
[133] Colquhoun, *Police*, pp. 120–4.   [134] *Caledonian Mercury*, 23 Oct. 1784 (BNA).
[135] JHC, vol. 39, p. 319 (26 Mar. 1783).

gold coins, together with British silver, put 'on the current bottom they pass for in England'.[136] This, he believed, would stop the outflow of silver and small gold coins and end the predominance of high-value Portuguese coin, which, according to one estimate in 1736, made up about 90 per cent of the circulation.[137] Boulter had to overcome significant hurdles in the eleven years it took to achieve this reform. In Ireland he faced vocal opposition, including within the Privy Council and Parliament. In England he faced indifference from a government for whom Ireland's monetary problems were always a long way down the list of priorities. As in his campaign for a copper coinage, he had to beseech the Lord-Lieutenant and English politicians repeatedly to give the issue their attention, explaining to them the 'inconceivable' distress caused by the shortage of money, not to mention the emigration of Protestants from the north, where the shortage was most severe.[138]

As with his campaign for the copper, Boulter's difficulties were increased by the fact that many Irish supporters of such a reform of the gold also advocated changes that were as unacceptable to him as to the British authorities. His report to the Lord-Lieutenant that 'It has been with some difficulty that we have been able to manage things so well, and to keep off meddling with the English silver, and trying to get the advantage of England; as likewise to prevent the addressing for a mint to be established here' indicated problems he had to manage throughout his campaign.[139]

Boulter thus walked a narrow monetary path, and saw the grasping hands of 'the bankers and remitters' in any deviation.[140] David Bindon, who was one of the most insightful writers on Ireland's currency problems during this period, he dismissed as 'a broken merchant', apparently identifying him with a self-interested proposal of which Bindon was actually sharply critical.[141] Bindon's own proposals amounted to nothing less than establishing the monetary standard that Ireland lacked. In Bindon's view, only coins ordered 'by the authority of the state' to be accepted in payments by certain denominations could be 'properly called money'. Ireland, where almost all coin had to be weighed, was unique in having no 'national coin'. The only remedy was to establish a mint, 'in order to regulate all the jarring pieces of different nations and bring them into a proper mass of money'—that is, to recoin the foreign money on an Irish standard.[142] This standard should be determined by conditions in England as Ireland's main trading partner, but at the market rate of silver and gold rather than the British mint

---

[136] Boulter to Carteret, 21 Dec. 1726, Boulter, *Letters*, vol. 1, p. 112.
[137] Anon., *Letter from a Gentleman*, p. 3.
[138] Boulter to Duke of Dorset, 3 Aug. 1736, Boulter, *Letters*, vol. 2, p. 172.; Boulter to Duke of Newcastle, 16 July 1728, Boulter, *Letters*, vol. 1, p. 251.
[139] Boulter to Carteret, 21 Dec. 1726, Boulter, *Letters*, vol. 1, p. 113.
[140] Boulter to Newcastle, 2 May 1730, Boulter, *Letters*, vol. 2, p. 8.
[141] Bindon, *Essay*, pp. 11-15. [142] Bindon, *Essay*, pp. 3, 18, 21.

price.[143] Broadly similar arguments were advanced by other writers.[144] These were radical proposals on two fronts. Not only did they depart from the slavish adherence to Locke that was only slightly less universal in Ireland than England, but they once again proposed a level of monetary autonomy that Ireland had not enjoyed since the fifteenth century.[145]

Despite these and other calls for a mint, 'national' feeling was muted in this debate.[146] Thomas Prior, for example, believed that the king would grant Ireland its own money 'out of his affection for his faithful people of Ireland' and was actually indifferent about where it should be minted.[147] Like Bindon, one reason he gave for reform was that it would also benefit Britain by making Ireland less likely to import its coin.[148] Swift was almost alone among advocates of reform when he claimed that Ireland's coinage problem stemmed from the 'Hatred, and Contempt, born us by our Neighbours, and Brethren, without the least grounds of Provocation, who rejoice at our Sufferings'.[149] According to Boulter, such attempts to revive 'the whole game of Wood's half-pence' came from the opponents of change: bankers and merchants who had 'bestirred themselves to the utmost' to organize petitions against the change and had 'universally possessed the people that the scheme is an English project, formed in England... with a design to drain this kingdom of their gold, as they are already drained of their silver'.[150]

Swift swapped sides late in the debate. When the reform was proclaimed in August 1737, he famously raised a black flag above St Patrick's Cathedral to mourn the Irish currency, and publicly threatened Boulter with the violence of the mob. This was not altogether idle: Boulter received so many threatening letters at this time that his house was placed under military guard.[151] The fact that Swift's stance was wildly inconsistent with his earlier position did not go unnoticed. Writing in support of the change, an anonymous author quoted Swift's words back at him at length, suggesting that he was motivated not by patriotism but purely by 'private spleen'.[152]

Boulter's opponents organized a surge of petitions claiming that the country would be drained of all its gold without any increase in its silver.[153] MPs from Cork came under pressure from constituents to deny supply until the

---

[143] Notwithstanding Kelly's claim to the contrary, several writers in this debate recognized the undervaluation of silver at the English mint, and even the disproportion of the European and Asian gold to silver ratios, as significant to Ireland's problems. See Kelly, 'Political Economy', p. 112; J.R., *Short Reasons*; Prior, *Observations*, pp. 11, 13, 46; Broadloom, *Hue and Cry*, p. 5.

[144] Prior, *Observations*; Broadloom, *Hue and Cry*; *Relief of Ireland*.

[145] Kelly, 'Political Economy', p. 117.   [146] Magennis, 'Whither?', p. 194.

[147] Prior, *Observations*, p. 61.   [148] Prior, *Observations*, p. 61.

[149] Swift, *The Intelligencer*, XIX (1728), ed. Woolley (1990), 208; *Relief of Ireland*, p. 16, made a similar claim.

[150] Boulter to Carteret, 13 May 1729, in Boulter, *Letters*, 1, pp. 300, 306–7.

[151] Lord George Sackville to Duke of Dorset, 6 Oct. 1737, *Stopford-Sackville MSS*, p. 166.

[152] Anon., *Reflections*, p. 16.   [153] JHCI, vol. 4, pp. 235–8 (18 and 24 Oct. 1737).

proclamation was withdrawn,[154] a threat reflected in some of the petitions' suggestions that the change would make it impossible to pay taxes. The reduction also increased the burden of debt and would bring losses to exporters. Instead, the value of silver coin should have been raised to its 'intrinsic' (that is, market) value. But the fate of the petitions revealed the strength of the government's support on an initiative that increased the bullion value of rents and appeared to harm only bankers. Resolutions to consider the petitions or endorse their claims were defeated by large majorities, although the House did agree to agree to consider them in twelve months' time, presumably in an effort to calm the situation and in the correct belief that the storm would blow over.[155] By the time it did, Parliament had been prorogued, meaning the petitions were never considered.

Boulter's revaluation of the gold removed much of the confusion about Ireland's monetary standard. Insofar as silver at 62 shillings per pound could still be said to be the British standard, then silver at 67s. 2d. was now the Irish standard, even though no silver coin would ever be minted at that rate. This clarification may have, as one historian suggests, 'finally ended two decades of enormously disruptive monetary conditions',[156] but it did not solve Ireland's problems with either gold or silver any more than the minting of copper in 1736 solved its problems with small change. Silver drained out of the country just as the opponents of the reform had predicted.[157] The shortage of small money continued to plague the Hanoverians' Irish subjects even more severely than those of Great Britain for the remainder of the century and beyond.

Credit and Counterfeits: Managing the Scarcity of Money

The guinea also remained subject to the vagaries of commodity money with an immutable standard. While the British government supplied guineas to Ireland, the latter's chronic balance of payments deficit ensured that these were steadily repatriated. The ban on the private export of British coin to Ireland, insofar as it was enforceable, cannot have made the situation any easier.[158] The Bank of England, which successfully opposed the Irish government's appeals to lift the ban in 1751, presumably thought it was effective in preventing the loss of guineas.[159] Scarcity of guineas was therefore a recurring problem in Ireland, and the use of foreign coin remained widespread. This triggered some debate on whether the Irish valuation of circulating gold should once again depart from

---

[154] Sackville to Dorset, 6 Oct. 1737, *Stopford-Sackville MSS*, vol. 1, p. 166.
[155] JHCI, vol. 4, p. 238 (26 Oct. 1737).   [156] Kelly, 'Political Economy', p. 119.
[157] Simon, *Irish Coins*, pp. 75–6.
[158] The ban was lifted as one of several liberalizations of Irish trade passed unanimously by the British House of Commons in 1780.
[159] Sackville to Thomas Waits, 24 May 1751, *Stopford-Sackville MSS*, vol. 1, p. 172.

the British standard, a suggestion that was strongly repudiated on Lockean principles.[160]

This aspect of the debate effectively came to an end in 1775, when all foreign coins were demonetized. According to the Lord-Lieutenant and Council's urgent request to the British government, Irish people had followed the example of their British fellow subjects and refused 'by common consent' to accept any but British coin in 'ordinary payments'. Given that foreign coins were still current, however, receivers of revenue had no choice but to take them. As a result there was eleven thousand pounds' worth of foreign gold coin in the treasury, with another seventeen thousand expected. As the coins would not circulate, they could not be used to pay the army.[161] The episode illustrates yet another way that the relationship between state endorsement and general acceptance of a means of payment could unravel, forcing the state to protect the revenue by demonetizing the object in question. A similar process and similar complaints had led to the demonetization of Spanish pistoles twenty-five years earlier. While this had been generally welcomed at first, no adequate provision had been made to replace what had become by far the largest component of the silver coinage, triggering deflation and recession.[162]

Guineas were also scarce in Britain for most of the century. The gold price in London was above the mint price every year from 1717 to 1772 by an average of eightpence per ounce of fine gold. For the last fifteen years of that period the average disparity was nineteen pence.[163] The result was extensive melting and export of guineas and increased imports of foreign coin, especially moidores, which were overvalued in relation to guineas, leading one observer to claim in 1742 that they had become 'in great measure the current coin of the kingdom'.[164]

As in the 1690s, the scarcity created opportunities for counterfeiters, as people were willing to use any plausible substitute for regal coin. The most successful and productive such efforts were centred on Halifax, Yorkshire, the victim of a slump in its established textile industries from the 1760s. The main activity was the remanufacture of coin clippings, or even whole full-weight coins into underweight coin—usually moidores, as counterfeiting foreign coin was not a capital offence. The use of clippings was enabled by the fact that the circulating coins had become so worn that clippers were able to reproduce a version of their milled edges by the use of a file. Full-weight coins were obtained through local business networks. The remanufactured light coin would be used to purchase local bills of exchange,

---

[160] For both sides of this debate, see Citizen of Dublin, *Question*, and Anon., *Proposals Humbly Offered*.
[161] Lord-Lieutenant and Council to the King, 21 Feb. 1775. TNA PC 1/10/77 f. 4.
[162] Magennis, 'Whither?', p. 203.
[163] Figures abstracted from Officer and Williamson, 'Price of Gold'. See also the discussion in Smith, *Wealth of Nations*, 1, p. 52.
[164] Quoted in Styles, 'Money Makers', p. 176. The following discussion of the Yorkshire coiners is based on Styles's work.

which were sold in London for Bank of England notes, which would then be cashed at the Bank for full-weight coin. The Bank itself regularly took worn coin it received in the course of business to the mint. As the mint would only take the coin at its bullion value, this entailed a loss which the Bank was willing to bear in order to sustain the credit of its notes. This is perhaps the most striking example of the absurdities generated by the intersection of a system of coinage based on Lockean principles with a working system of credit-based money creation.

In echoes of the attitudes of London jurors in the clipping crisis of the previous century, John Styles has shown that Yorkshire's so-called 'yellow trade' enjoyed 'massive and active popular support' at the local level.[165] This was partly because the fresh product of the secretive local 'mints' often contained as much gold as the badly worn official counterparts, but also because the trade itself involved many participants at almost every social level, including respectable local manufacturers and merchants. In London, the counterfeiting of guineas appears to have been far more sporadic and far less organized.[166] Typically it involved the production of guineas from metals of lesser value, including silver and copper, which, as Styles has shown, enjoyed no popular sympathy anywhere.[167] The small number tried for such offences at the Old Bailey were less likely than other criminals to be acquitted by juries, reflecting the selective nature of such prosecutions on the one hand, but also a general intolerance of this form of currency crime.[168]

As in 1696, the activities of the Yorkshire coiners were only brought to an end by a recoinage following the failure of a concerted judicial assault in 1769–70.[169] In July 1773 the government legislated for all receivers of revenue to refuse and to cut all excessively light guineas. These were then accepted only by weight, at a cost to their holders of around £300,000 on the £3.8 m withdrawn. This destroyed Yorkshire's yellow trade 'within days'.[170] It also bore most heavily on those who had the least discretion about which coins they could accept. Subsequent withdrawals of less diminished coins over the next two years were conducted at the government's expense.[171]

Shortages of circulating guineas and half-guineas created inconvenience for many and opportunities for some, but they did not create the same systemic problems as coin shortages in previous centuries owing to the extensive use of formalized paper credit. The diaries of Thomas Turner of East Hoathly, Sussex, show that in the 1760s even a shopkeeper from a small village was enmeshed in networks of London-based paper credit that allowed him and those he dealt with to economize heavily on the use of coin. At the local level, Turner and his customers minimized the need for silver through the use of shop credit, which could be accumulated until payable in sums that required gold, with which Turner

---

[165] Styles, 'Money Makers', p. 187.   [166] POB.   [167] Styles, 'Money Makers', p. 178.
[168] POB.   [169] Styles, 'Money Makers', pp. 220–30.
[170] Styles, 'Money Makers', pp. 236–7.   [171] Alborn, Glittered, pp. 85–6.

could clear his own debts. British gold coin was the mainstay, although foreign coins of various denominations were always present and on occasion might make up more than half the value of a substantial payment. When parcelling coins to make payments, Turner always included some spares to cover the rare contingency that some coins he tendered might be rejected as 'light'.

Turner made many of his wholesale payments with bills of exchange, drawn mostly on Margesson and Collison, a firm of Southwark haberdashers with whom he had extensive dealings. A journey to London in 1759 saw him draw over £180 on Margesson and Collison to pay various London suppliers. He in turn paid Margesson and Collison a bill for £130 drawn on a private London bank which he had received expressly for this purpose from Sam Durrant, a haberdasher in Lewes, and 'a bank bill value £20'.[172]

This use of a banknote was unusual for Turner despite his living within 80 kilometres of London. The growth of country or provincial banks in England was still in its early stages while Turner kept his diary, and Sussex was not one of the places where they developed early. Scholars generally agree with Edmund Burke's observation that in 1750 there were not a dozen 'banker's shops' outside London. This grew to 119 by 1781 and much faster thereafter.[173] These country banks tended to be well away from London, concentrated in the most rapidly growing economic regions, or in the richest agricultural counties with surplus funds to invest.[174] The few banknotes Turner mentions were therefore almost certainly those of the Bank of England, which thus appear to have had a very limited circulation outside the immediate environs of the capital.

Although Durrant was not a banker, his role in furnishing Turner with his London bill indicates one of the ways that provincial banking could evolve in England, when a business heavily involved in the distribution of goods from the metropolis also managed the flows of cash and credit that made that commerce possible. Other pathways to banking were the management of remittances to London arising from the collection of government revenue; the manufacture of local means of payment such as tokens and small notes, especially in industrial districts; and (for lawyers) acting as a 'money scrivener'—in effect an investment manager—for people with surplus funds. Eventually, some of these gave up their original businesses to become fully fledged bankers by taking deposits, making loans, and issuing notes, in addition to handling the remittance of money.[175] As we saw in the previous chapter, all of these—even proto-bankers like Durrant— required a London 'correspondent' upon whom to draw bills.[176] These banks typically redeemed the bills drawn on them with Bank of England notes, which circulated as cash in London among those who dealt in sums of ten pounds or

---

[172] Turner, *Diary*, pp. 177–9.   [173] Pressnell, *Country Banking*, pp. 4–6.
[174] Cameron, *Banking*, p. 23.   [175] Pressnell, *Country Banking*, ch. 3; Cameron, *Banking*, p. 24.
[176] Pressnell, *Country Banking*, ch. 4, esp. pp. 116–20.

more, or could be cashed at the Bank of England for guineas. Although living at a fairly early stage in this process and barely using banknotes himself, Thomas Turner was, through the normal conduct of his village business, enmeshed in an elaborate web of paper credit and paper money spun around the Bank of England's promise to redeem its notes at par for gold coin minted to an unchanging standard.

By the end of the eighteenth century that web, mediated by different kinds of banks, stretched across Ireland as well as Britain. While it allowed a far greater volume of economic activity than could possibly have been sustained by any system of 'pure' commodity money, it remained vulnerable to its inherent tensions and instability. For many, especially in Ireland, the absolute shortage of coin remained the most pressing problem. For those further up the monetary ladder, the commodity 'basis' of the credit money they needed for their day-to-day business rendered the system permanently liable to crises that were increasingly likely to be systemic. That system would soon be put to the test once again by the supreme crisis of war, forcing a searching examination of its fundamental economic, political, and moral foundations.

6
The Only True, Intelligible Standard
1793–1822

> HONOUR and INTEGRITY, the prominent characteristics of Englishmen, are more current than coin.
>
> Simeon Pope (1797)

Britain's wars around the turn of the nineteenth century subjected the country's finances to greater strain than ever before. The mere declaration of war by France in February 1793 triggered a financial crisis whose extent and severity reflected the ever-strengthening geographical and sectoral linkages created by a financial system even 'more systematized' than it had been in 1772.[1] But this was just a foretaste of the monetary effects of the ensuing decades of war, which shaped all that was to follow in Britain's and Ireland's monetary history for the whole period covered in this chapter and beyond. As in the 1690s, and again in the First World War, the situation could only be met through radical innovation. This chapter outlines these innovations and examines the discourse surrounding them with a focus on three main issues: first, the different effects of monetary crises and innovation in England, Ireland, and Scotland, and how they reflected and refashioned the monetary relationships between them; second, the mobilization of patriotism to win acceptance and active support for innovation, including among the common people; and finally, the role of the ideological and institutional legacies of the 1690s in shaping attitudes to currency during the wars and the eventual resolution of the long crisis of the United Kingdom's monetary order in the years following.

The Suspension of Cash Payments

The next major crisis triggered by the war was a pivot point akin to that of the 1690s. It differs from that crisis, however, in that it did not mark the irrevocable end of one system and its permanent replacement with the elements of another. Rather, it offered a preview of a monetary system whose key elements would not

---

[1] Hoppit, 'Financial Crises', p. 56.

reappear until 1914, and not be normalized until after 1931. And while the debates it prompted fashioned much of the monetary theory and management of the next 130 years, the principles that were to prevail were, in their essentials, little different from those enunciated in the 1690s.

The crisis was systemic from the start. It originated in a panic whose origins lay not in a loss of confidence in any particular bank but in the nation's capacity to maintain the whole monetary system in the event of military defeat. It was begun by fears of invasion triggered by the appearance of a French fleet in Bantry Bay in the south-west of Ireland in December 1796. In Cork, 85 kilometres away, confidence in local banknotes was shaken, leading the banks to suspend payment and prompting an agreement among the city's merchants to accept and pay the notes in the meantime. Although there was also anxiety in Dublin, a similar resolution at a meeting a few days later was abandoned when one of the city's leading bankers declared that it was unnecessary and would only spread the panic it was intended to prevent.[2] Demand for coin in Ireland, which was already heavy, increased significantly, placing further strain on the Bank of Ireland.[3]

This episode created the preconditions for the decisive crisis of February 1797. Rumours of invasion multiplied, intensified by the government's highly visible precautions against an attack on Britain's east coast.[4] At the same time, the drain of gold to Ireland, coupled with the British government's request early in February for a loan of £1,500,000 for the Irish government, pushed the Bank of England's concerns about its gold reserves to breaking point.[5] These were already at a low ebb owing to the ongoing financial exigencies of the war, which stimulated economic activity and entailed a great deal of government spending abroad on both British and allied armies. At the same time the French government abandoned the issue of paper *assignats* and returned to a metallic currency, thus creating enormous demand for gold in France.[6]

Alarmed by the government's precautions, farmers at the Newcastle market on 18 February sold their livestock at knock-down prices and immediately cashed the notes they received at their issuing banks, leading them to suspend payment by mutual agreement while they waited for gold to arrive from their London correspondents. Similar events on a smaller scale occurred in a number of towns across Britain without leading to any suspensions. In Newcastle, a meeting of the city's leading tradesmen on the 20th agreed that they would receive the notes of all the local banks in the usual manner.[7]

---

[2] *Dublin Evening Post*, 31 Dec. 1796 (BNA); Foster, 'Report', pp. 20–1.
[3] Hall, *Bank of Ireland*, p. 63.   [4] Shin, 'Paper Money', p. 421.
[5] Committee of Treasury minutes, 8, 9, and 10 Feb. 1797, BE, G8/6.
[6] For a heterodox account of the end of the *assignats*, see Spang, *Stuff and Money*, ch. 6; Feavearyear, *Pound*, pp. 179–81, 185–6. Fetter, *Orthodoxy*, pp. 17–18, disputes the importance of Bank advances and foreign loans in precipitating the crisis. See also Alborn, *Glittered*, ch. 3, esp. pp. 51–6.
[7] Shin, 'Paper Money', p. 424.

When the orders from the provincial banks reached London on the 22nd, the London correspondent banks in turn called on the reserves they kept in the Bank of England. The following day, news of the Newcastle crisis was published in the London papers. Unease grew rapidly, and people in London began taking their notes to the Bank of England. This was a stake in the heart of the entire system, which threatened, as in 1745, to expose the fictionality of the metallic 'basis' of the notes. To make matters still worse, news of the landing in Wales of a militarily useless French force reached London on the 25th, dramatically increasing the sense of panic.

Throughout February, the Bank had warned the government of the strain on its reserves with ever-increasing urgency. Until the invasion scare, the most significant immediate cause of strain had been the government's demands for loans to be spent abroad and in Ireland. While the Prime Minister, William Pitt, had ignored the Bank's entreaties to quell his demands for cash, it was clear by the last week of February, when the Bank was left with just over one million pounds' worth of gold coin, that if drastic action were not taken the Bank would simply have nothing left with which to honour the promise of convertibility on its notes.[8]

On 26 February the government took the extraordinary step of summoning the king to London on the Sabbath for a meeting of the Privy Council. An Order in Council was immediately published prohibiting the Bank of England from paying coin for its notes. In other words, the Bank of England was ordered to suspend payment. While many sought solace in the belief that this state of affairs would last only days or weeks, it is clear that the whole of the political and commercial classes of England were horrified at the government's measure. By detaching the Bank of England's notes from their ostensible 'backing' the government had crossed a Rubicon. And despite the best efforts of the political and commercial elite, the end of the suspension, which did not come for 24 years, proved only that it is impossible to cross the same river twice.

Even the words people would use to describe Britain's currency changed irrevocably during the restriction. At the same time as the Order in Council was given, the Bank of England was authorized to prepare banknotes of £1 and £2 for immediate issue, thereby overturning the 1777 ban on small notes in England and Wales. For the first time, the pound became a stable means of exchange as well as a unit of account for everyday life outside the commercial world. No coin of that value had actually circulated since the unites and laurels of the early Stuarts, at which time they had been of use only for large transactions.

On the eve of the Bank suspension, pounds did not circulate in England except in the multiples of five or more represented on banknotes. Even there they were by no means universal. Many country banks denominated their notes in guineas, and

---

[8] Committee of Treasury minutes, 21 Feb. 1797, BE G8/6.

Bank of England notes had only the number of units printed: whether the units were guineas or pounds was written in a blank space by the teller when the note was issued. And as we have seen, the Bank of Ireland had issued series of fully printed notes in multiples of both pounds and guineas almost since its inception.[9] The choice of denomination for the small notes therefore caught many by surprise.[10] Most newspapers anticipated the issue of notes worth one guinea and two guineas, and so far was 'the pound' from their consciousness that when the new denominations were announced some newspapers described them at first as notes for twenty shillings and forty shillings, although 'one pound' and 'two pounds' very quickly became by far the most common usage.

By the time the Bank of England first tried to resume payments in gold in 1817, this situation was completely transformed. Notes of one and two pounds had been circulating in every part of the country and across a broad social spectrum for two decades, and it now seemed natural that the basic coin in circulation should be worth one pound. Moreover, the rest of the currency was now calculated in terms of its relationship to the pound, whose value had come to be understood, as we shall see, purely from its representation of a fixed amount of gold. Henceforward, 'the pound' was the synecdoche of the British currency.

On 2 March the Irish Lord-Lieutenant, acting on instructions from Westminster, ordered the Bank of Ireland to suspend payment. Despite the ire of some MPs, the suspension was duly ratified by the Irish Parliament on 13 May, with the inclusion of a clause specifying that cash payments would resume in Ireland three months after they did in England.[11] The decision to suspend the Bank of Ireland's cash payments had its origins in the need to protect the Bank of England from further drains of gold in that direction. As a committee of the UK House of Commons was to declare bluntly in 1804, the restriction 'did not arise in Ireland from any consideration of the circumstances of that country'.[12]

Despite the request of the two Scottish chartered banks 'to be put on the like footing with the Bank of England, in making their notes a legal tender', no suspension was ordered for Scotland. Indeed, despite the important differences between England's and Scotland's banking systems, Scottish banks were routinely lumped with English country banks in discourse on the banking system for the duration of the bank restriction.[13] As such, the government was content to allow the Scottish banks to respond to the crisis by adopting the same technically illegal practice as the English and Irish country banks, which was to pay their notes—on the rare occasions that payment was demanded—only with the now inconvertible notes of the Bank of England.[14]

---

[9] See Chapter 5, pp. 151–2, above.   [10] Byatt, *Promises*, p. 31.
[11] House of Commons of Ireland Debates, vol. 17, pp. 452–3 (13 May 1797); Hall, *Bank of Ireland*, p. 82.
[12] Commons, *Irish Pound*, p. 6.   [13] 11 March 1797, NRS, GD51/5/235/3.
[14] Shin, 'Paper Money', p. 429.

Unlike in London and Dublin, the suspension at first created genuine panic in Edinburgh. A Scottish banker described the scene:

> The instant this resolution of paying no more specie was known in the street, a scene of confusion and uproar took place, of which it is utterly impossible for those who did not witness it to form an idea. Our counting-house, and indeed the offices of all the banks, were instantly crowded to the door with people clamorously demanding payment in gold of their interest-receipts, and vociferating for silver in change of our circulating paper.... They were deaf to every argument and although no symptom, nor indeed threatening of violence appeared, their noise, and the bustle they made, was intolerable; which may be readily believed when it is considered that they were mostly of the lowest and most ignorant classes, such as fish-women, carmen, street porters and butcher's men, all bawling out at once for change, and jostling one another in their endeavours who should get nearest to the table, behind which were cashiers and ourselves endeavouring to pacify them as well as we could.[15]

This passage has had an interesting life in subsequent historical accounts of the suspension, which exemplifies a tendency to ignore important national differences on currency questions and a readiness to impute to the lower orders a general, irrational terror of paper money. While some have used Forbes's account to add colour and movement to descriptions of events in London in otherwise Anglocentric accounts, others, such as Edwin Cannan, have conscripted the Edinburgh crowd for transparently ideological purposes.[16] In 1919, Cannan edited an edition of the 1810 report of the House of Commons Committee on the high price of gold bullion—one of the key documents of the major debate triggered by the restriction. It was a tract for the times. As we shall see in Chapter 8, the United Kingdom operated a *de facto* suspension throughout the First World War, and theorists, bankers, and other creditors now clamoured, as they would in the 1810s, for a return to gold at the previous parity. As a high priest of monetary orthodoxy, Cannan saw the 'moral' of the earlier episode for his own day very clearly: 'When the scales at last fall from the eyes of the people of Europe, groaning under the rise of prices, they will no longer cry to their Governments "Hang the profiteers !" but "Burn your paper money, and go on burning it till it will buy as much gold as it used to do!"' Cautioning that 'it must not be supposed that the transition of 1797 from a metallic to a paper standard was effected with a total absence of disturbance and confusion',[17] Cannan devoted two pages of his forty-two-page

---

[15] Forbes, *Memoirs*, pp. 83–4.
[16] For an example of colour and movement, see Mayhew, *Sterling*, p. 136. Clapham, *Bank*, 1, pp. 4–5, describes the same events, but makes a clear distinction between Scottish and English circumstances.
[17] Cannan, *Paper*, pp. xli, xiv–xv.

introduction to the report to a verbatim quotation of Forbes's description of events in Edinburgh as indicative of what had happened generally. Other historians, largely sharing Cannan's views on the sanctity of the gold standard, and perhaps misled by their own readings of Forbes, have also imputed general dismay and panic to the 'less instructed portion of the community'.[18]

According to Cannan, the value of Forbes's account lay in the fact that, 'being published long after the need for professing a confidence which was not felt had passed away, [it] provide[d] a useful supplement to the dry bones of official notices and brief newspaper reports of meetings'.[19] If Cannan is to be believed, the only reason events in London were not described in terms similar to Forbes's was because the literate classes had unanimously exercised a public-spirited self-censorship.

There is no reason to accept Cannan's view, or to allow Edinburgh to serve as a proxy for London. We have one contemporary account of the events in London, which tells a very different story. On 28 February, the 'Fashion' column of the *Telegraph* noted that 'The unusual circumstance of the Bank yesterday stopping the payment of cash, drew a great number of people to the place, among whom were several known pickpockets.'[20] The placement of this titbit in a column filled with the royal family's leisure activities and other society gossip, together with the presence of the pickpockets, leaves us to infer that the anxious people outside the Bank of England, far from representing the 'less instructed portion of the community', were relatively well-to-do. This is to be expected. These were the people who were likely to own stock in the Bank, to have cash deposited there, or to be in possession of the Bank's notes. The Bank's fortunes—including the status of its notes—affected them directly. Given that the notes were available in denominations no smaller than five pounds, this crowd inevitably had a different composition to that in Edinburgh, where one-pound notes had been in everyday circulation for almost a century. Equally, it is no surprise that there also appears to have been complete calm in Dublin, where the Bank of Ireland issued notes no smaller than five guineas.[21] Moreover, none of the contemporaries with an interest in showing events in the worst possible light ever claimed that any disorderly scenes of popular panic took place. The Foxite Whigs, who castigated the government throughout the ensuing parliamentary sittings, made no references to disturbances or agitated crowds outside the Bank. Indeed, one radical critic of the suspension expressed his disappointment at the *lack* of disturbance: 'That the government of a country should have made a law to make the paper of a particular corporation equal to gold, or that the people of a country should have submitted to

---

[18] Francis, *Bank*, 1, p. 240. See also Giuseppi, *Bank*, p. 76.
[19] Cannan, *Paper*, p. xv.
[20] *Telegraph*, 28 Feb. 1797 (Burney Newspaper Collection).
[21] Hall, *Bank of Ireland*, p. 81.

such a law without a single remonstrance, are circumstances that never would have been thought possible, if they had not taken place.'[22]

While there was clearly panic among the common people of Edinburgh over their banks' response to the restriction, for most wage earners anywhere in Britain or Ireland it must have been a matter of almost complete indifference. Only the best-paid craftsmen would have earned enough to find even a half-guinea coin in their weekly wages in 1797.[23] In any case, the problem presented by a pound note for an artisan was exactly the same as the familiar problem presented by a golden guinea: how to get change in silver and copper to enable the week's purchases. Unskilled male labourers, many of whom were paid daily, would be unlikely ever to have owned either a guinea or a pound at any time before, during, or even long after the restriction period.[24] Female wage earners, and domestic servants of either sex, would have been still less likely to have any use for paper money. The chief concern of most people in 1797, as at other times, was with the state of the money they actually used: low-denomination coins, whether silver, copper, or brass, and whether issued by the government or by private traders. From this point of view their overall experience of the restriction period was perhaps more positive than negative, as both temporary expedients and carefully considered reforms had the effect of making such everyday currency more readily available and eventually, as we shall see in the next chapter, far more reliable than ever before.

The first such expedient was adopted almost immediately. In all the hours of debate focused on national dishonour and the trampling on the rights of the government's creditors, William Wilberforce Bird, the Member for Coventry, managed to get the House of Commons to consider the question of the effects of the restriction on specie payments on employers, who would have nothing with which to pay wages at the end of the week. With surprisingly little debate, the House agreed to his proposal to allow businesses to issue paper promissory notes for any amount, payable three days after demand. This permission was to last for one month, by which time coin had returned to circulation after being hoarded in the immediate aftermath of the restriction.[25]

Although the introduction of one- and two-pound notes can have had little lasting effect on transactions of less than a pound, the authorities gave the problem of small payments more serious attention during the restriction than they had at any time since the restoration of the monarchy. In the first month of the restriction the Bank of England issued Spanish dollars at 4s. 9d., overstamped with a small bust of George III. These were soon counterfeited in large numbers and recalled in a somewhat chaotic process that disadvantaged people holding

---

[22] Anderson, *Iniquity*, vol. 1, pp. 20-1.
[23] Quarter-guineas had been struck only in 1718 and 1762 and must have been extremely rare.
[24] Clark, *Prices and Wages*, http://gpih.ucdavis.edu/Datafilelist.htm.
[25] *Parliamentary Register*, vol. 1, pp. 694-7 (1 Mar. 1797). Feavearyear, *Pound*, p. 190.

fewer than twenty of them.[26] Their place was taken in September by gold seven-shilling pieces, or one-third guineas, in weight proportionate to that of the guinea. In 1804, the Bank began to issue five-shilling token 'dollars', apparently in order to provide the government with some means to pay seamen and workers at the naval dockyards.[27] These were issued by the Bank rather than the mint, as—containing significantly less silver than their face value—they were regarded as credit instruments, repayable in standard coin. They neatly symbolized the Bank's status as a private institution at the centre of state power: on the obverse they looked like ordinary regal coinage, with a classical bust of the king, and the circumscription 'GEORGIVS III DEI GRATIA REX'; the reverse featured a large, crowned lozenge bearing an image of Britannia resembling that on the regal copper coinage (rather than the Britannia on the Bank's notes). A ring around the lozenge read 'FIVE SHILLING DOLLAR' and was in turn circumscribed 'BANK OF ENGLAND'. Despite the fact that the Bank of Ireland by 1804 had a far less significant place in the state than its English counterpart, the tokens it began to issue the following year looked even more like regal coins. They did away with the lozenge on the reverse, and surrounding a seated Hibernia had the single circumscription, 'BANK OF IRELAND TOKEN • SIX SHILLINGS'.[28]

Both banks' tokens were counterfeited in large numbers, but at least managed to remain in circulation, in the English case partly as a result of a decision to call up their value by 10 per cent in 1811. In the intellectual frame of reference established at the great recoinage, which was to be forcefully repeated by many voices across the course of the bank restriction, this flexibility regarding the rating was only possible because the coins were produced as tokens, and because silver was *de facto* no longer the standard. On 9 July of the same year the Bank also began to use tokens of three shillings in payment of fractional sums, with tokens of half that value following shortly afterwards.[29] These also bore a bust of the monarch on the obverse.

Further down the monetary hierarchy, the government began to issue significant quantities of copper pennies and halfpennies in England in July 1797, using Matthew Boulton's steam presses for the first time. When the price of copper rose shortly afterwards and these coins were rapidly melted for their bullion, the government responded by ordering proportionately lighter halfpennies and farthings, which remained in circulation.[30] The government also tolerated an enormous increase of tradesmen's tokens, which began to appear in denominations as high as one shilling in 1811, and whose suppression the government repeatedly postponed.[31]

---

[26] Kelly, *Dollars and Tokens*, pp. 32–3.
[27] Liverpool, *Treatise*, p. 194; Kelly, *Dollars and Tokens*, pp. 57–60.
[28] Kelly, *Dollars and Tokens*, plates iv and v.   [29] 6 July 1811, BE M5/2 f. 22.
[30] Redish, *Bimetallism*, pp. 153–61; Feavearyear, *Pound*, p. 187.
[31] Feavearyear, *Pound*, p. 207; Mathias, 'Official and Unofficial', p. 73.

Remarkably, a request to make some provision for low-value currency for Scotland was subverted on the day it was made by the man who officially made it. A little over a week after the restriction, James Frazer, Treasurer of Bank of Scotland, wrote to Henry Dundas in London on behalf of the Scottish banks asking for a suspension of the ban on notes in Scotland of less than twenty shillings. On the same day, Frazer wrote privately to Dundas explaining that his 'duty to you [Dundas], the Banks, and the Country' required him to set out the reasons that he had advised that day's meeting of the directors of the banks against making the request. According to Frazer, there was no less silver in Scotland than there had been before the restriction; the problem was that some people were holding it in the hope of exporting it at a profit 'into the North of England and to Ireland'. The coins' apparent scarcity would soon force them back into circulation, whereas the production of notes as substitutes would make export easier.[32] The Scottish banks' request was denied.

Outside Scotland, evidence of popular alarm about the restriction in 1797 is slim and indistinct. Almost as a matter of form, radical bodies added 'the ruin of public credit, the stoppage of the Bank, and other consequent evils'[33] to their grievances against the government. In this they echoed the Foxite Whigs in the House of Commons, who reserved their strongest outrage for the terrible wrong which they alleged Pitt had done to the Bank and its proprietors. Of all the people in society whom they claimed had been defrauded or otherwise injured by the suspension, it was towards the proprietors of bank stock and the holders of government debt—the people who most likely made up the crowd outside the Bank on 27 February—that the Opposition displayed the most tender concern. As Fox put it, these people were now to be paid 'not in money but in something else, which would virtually imply an act of national bankruptcy' that could 'put an end altogether to Britain's existence as a powerful nation'.[34]

These concerns were echoed in speeches, pamphlets, and cartoons over the weeks following the suspension. Many shared Fox's view that the damage was irreparable. The radical writer William Morgan, for example, claimed that the restriction had reduced 'the dignity of British credit... from its lofty pre-eminence to a state of the most humiliating degradation'. It was a 'wound' which, even if it did not prove fatal, could certainly never be 'perfectly healed'.[35] Another pamphleteer likewise doubted that it would be 'possible to repair so great a misfortune, to give it no other name'.[36]

More conspicuous and numerous than those who assailed the government were those who tried to make the suspension of payments work. Crucially, this required

---

[32] 11 Mar. 1797, NRS, GD51/5/235/4–5.
[33] London Corresponding Society, *Proceedings*, 31 July 1797.
[34] *Parliamentary Register*, vol. 1, pp. 644, 650 (27 Feb. 1797). [35] Morgan, *Appeal*, pp. 64, 66.
[36] Fortune, *Bank*, p. 102.

general acceptance of the new, low-denomination notes as money. Two days after the suspension, *The Times* urged that 'great precaution must be taken to render them as current as possible, so as not to be objected to by any one. Some step must also be taken to procure an exchange of these Notes among the lower orders of the people. There is some difficulty in this respect, which we shall be glad to see removed.'[37] The key, as in the case of the provincial farmers, was to convince people that others would accept the notes in their turn.

Hiroki Shin has shown that this was achieved by what amounted to a 'declaration movement' of which the meeting at Newcastle was only the first of around 150 meetings and declarations 'organised around local political leaders' throughout England, Scotland, and Ireland in February–April.[38] The declarations consisted of a pledge signed by the landowners and the political and commercial leadership of the locality that they would accept the notes of their local banks and, often, Bank of England notes as well.[39] They were then reported approvingly by the local and national press, often with praise for the patriotism of the signatories, and in some cases, comparison with the similar declarations of 1745.[40] Reporting the large London meeting of 27 February, whose declaration attracted more than 4,000 signatures, one newspaper went so far as to suggest that the name of anybody refusing to take banknotes at their face value 'ought to be published for the abhorrence of Englishmen', for to do so was 'worse than perjury, and equivalent in conscience to treason'.[41]

Such strictures were important. As Shin notes, 'the banks' customers were not the only people the banks needed to persuade'.[42] Not only did they need to reassure those currently in possession of notes, for example by declaring that they would be accepted as rent payments, but also, as *The Times* editorialist understood, those who would soon be using notes for the first time needed to be reassured that they would have value. This was the first time that the circulation of banknotes among the lower orders was held by the English or Irish elite to be desirable. It was also the first time that a major campaign was mounted to teach the common people what constituted positive patriotic financial behaviour. No longer were judicial terror and the stigma of treason enough.

Some pamphleteers were at pains to turn opposition interpretations of the crisis on their head. Simeon Pope, a stockbroker and lottery office keeper, dismissed 'croakings of dread of national bankruptcy'. He condemned the Opposition, who were attempting unscrupulously to stir up discontent by preying on the monetary ignorance of the 'subordinate classes of society'. He emphasized the duty of

---

[37] *The Times*, 1 Mar. 1797.   [38] Shin, 'Paper Money', pp. 425, 426.
[39] Shin, 'Paper Money', p. 428.
[40] Shin, 'Paper Money', p. 432; *The Times*, 28 Feb. 1797; *General Evening Post*, 28 Feb.–2 Mar. 1797 (BNA); *Whitehall Evening Post*, 25–8 Feb. 1797 (BNA); *Lloyd's Evening Post*, 27 Feb.–1 Mar. 1797 (Burney Newspaper Collection); *Morning Chronicle*, 6 Mar. 1797 (BNA).
[41] *Whitehall Evening Post*, 7–9 Mar. 1797 (BNA).   [42] Shin, 'Paper Money', p. 429.

patriots to encourage the circulation of the notes of 'our national bank'. The fact that many had chosen to accept them should be a cause for national rejoicing, as it had shown the French that they could make no impression on public confidence. Far from demonstrating weakness, the whole episode had shown that the credit of the country sat on the 'rock of real property'. The restriction and its aftermath had shown that the Bank could 'refuse to issue gold on its notes, and yet retain the firm confidence of the people'. This was because 'HONOUR and INTEGRITY, the prominent characteristics of Englishmen, are more current than coin'.[43]

This patriotic theme was echoed in William Combe's *Plain Thoughts of a Plain Man, Addressed to the Common Sense of the People of Great Britain* (1797). Unlike Pope, Combe acknowledged that Britain was in the midst of 'a very awful crisis', that the restriction was a 'very strong measure', and even that a 'temporary panic, to which Englishmen are not subject', had had 'a strong though transient effect on the public mind'.[44] But he agreed with Pope not only that the Opposition's sole concern was to 'propagate mischief' but also that the crisis would prove beneficial in the longer term:

> The suspension of paying cash at the bank in exchange for notes, is an event which, six months ago, I should have considered as the Passing-Bell of Old England; and yet it has been grounded on such circumstances, managed with such skill, and supplied with such remedies, as to encourage the nation instead of depressing it. For, as the quelling an insurrection always strengthens the arm of government; I know not whether, by a temporary suspension, credit itself may not be sometimes advanced.[45]

This happy outcome was rendered certain by the inherent patriotic virtues of the British people. Combe concluded by addressing his readers directly, trusting that, 'possessing a name which has surpassed that of every rival nation, and securing that freedom with which no other people are blessed, you will continue to shew yourselves worthy of the character you have so long maintained...I have the firmest confidence, that the present period of difficulty and danger will, by your characteristic patriotism and courage, increase the honours of the British name, and secure the prosperity of the British people.'[46]

The Foxites were unusual in talking up the extent of the problem at the height of the crisis, but it is clear that while most members of the political and mercantile classes understood that it was necessary to support the restriction on patriotic grounds, the suspension of cash payments was a profound shock. The introduction of inconvertible paper money created an almost unbearable tension in the minds and hearts of politicians, merchants, bankers, and public commentators,

---

[43] Pope, *Scarcity*, pp. 8, 25, 35, 40.
[44] Combe, *Plain Thoughts*, pp. 66–7.
[45] Combe, *Plain Thoughts*, p. 65.
[46] Combe, *Plain Thoughts*, pp. 67–8.

most of whom believed fervently in both the necessity and the actuality of a currency system based on bullion, but who now had to work and hope for the success of a system overtly based on paper credit sustained by fiat.

This tension was clear in the cartoons of James Gillray. In his first on this topic, published on 1 March 1797, Gillray urged the common people and the nation, personified as usual by John Bull, to cooperate with Pitt, ignore the blandishments

Figure 6.1 William Pitt reinvents Midas by suspending cash payments at the Bank of England: James Gillray, March 1797.

© The Trustees of the British Museum

of the Opposition—personified by Fox and R. B. Sheridan—and to accept the Bank of England's paper unconditionally in exchange for gold in order to save the country from the French. But Gillray was fierce in his satire on Pitt's measure and the policies which allegedly led to it. The following week he produced a bitter lampoon of Pitt as a latter-day Midas transmuting gold into paper. (See Figure 6.1.) As in one version of the Midas legend, Pitt has been given the ears of an ass as a sign of his shame. Like Midas, he tries to cover them, in this case with one- and two-pound notes. While his distended abdomen consists of gold coins, banknotes spew from his mouth, and the gold coins coming from his anus become notes as they fall into a structure marked 'Bank of England', where the proprietors have come to collect their dividends. At the centre of the chamber, being deluged with Pitt's magical paper shit, stands a domed gazebo—the traditional symbol of the constitution. While ministerial cherubim ascend heavenwards with news of the country's prosperous financial state and evidence of Pitt's prudent financial management, Fox and his supporters—inspired by imminent French invasion—proclaim Pitt's shame by chanting incessantly, 'Midas has ears'.

Gillray impugned the Opposition's patriotism, but there is no doubt that he shared their horror at the Bank of England's suspension of cash payments. It is also clear that he endorsed their claims that Pitt's financial policies had created the crisis. In a famous cartoon published two months later, he depicted Pitt in the act of despoiling the Bank in every possible sense of that word.[47] Represented as 'the old lady of Threadneedle Street' for the first time, the Bank had nothing but a flimsy garment of £1 and £2 notes to cover her nakedness and protect her honour, symbolized by a chest of coins, which Pitt is now demanding for the latest loan.

Paper against Gold: the Push for Resumption

Once the immediate crisis had passed and the new small notes were circulating as readily in England, Wales, and much of Ireland as they had long done in Scotland, a growing body of English commentators began to yearn for a return to the prelapsarian ideal of a currency based upon circulating gold coins minted 'at the ancient standard rate of 3.l. 17s. 10 ½ d' per troy ounce.[48]

The desire to return to that ideal began to take coherent shape as early as 1803, when a brief period of sharply rising prices led Lord Peter King, a Whig peer, to argue that the Bank's pursuit of profit had led it to produce too many notes, thus depreciating the currency.[49] While he was obliged to concede that the depreciation was 'not sufficient to produce an actual difference in value between gold coin and banknotes in the ordinary transaction of commerce', he insisted that the effect of

---

[47] See https://www.bankofengland.co.uk/explainers/who-is-the-old-lady-of-threadneedle-street
[48] Peel, 'Resumption Report', p. 15.   [49] King, 'Restriction', p. 212.

the depreciation was 'not the less real or certain' and that it 'must have contributed' to the general rise in prices.[50] For King—who would later write an admiring biography of Locke—this monetary disorder stemmed from failure to adhere to the fundamental moral principle that 'the establishment of a medium of exchange, either not really possessing, or not truly representing intrinsic value, is contrary to the first principles of justice'.[51]

The lack of empirical support for King's case in England led him to turn his attention to Ireland, where the Bank of Ireland's note issues since the restriction had increased by 300 per cent as opposed to the Bank of England's 70 per cent increase.[52] There was little disputing that the Bank of Ireland's notes had lost value in terms of gold and British banknotes, given that premium prices were being offered for guineas in Dublin, and, interestingly, payment in 'guineas or Scotch Bank notes' was required for the purchase of items in Belfast.[53]

Ireland's peculiar situation supported the belief that the removal of the restraint on overissue of paper money brought about by the suspension of cash payments must necessarily result in depreciation of the currency both in terms of foreign exchange and domestic prices. Ireland was therefore pressed into service to advance the views of advocates of the earliest possible end to the bank restriction. Spurred by allegations of peculation on the part of senior officials in Ireland, who customarily received their salaries in British rather than Irish money, the House of Commons established a committee to investigate.[54]

The committee focussed overwhelmingly on questions of exchange. It based much of its argument on a conceptual distinction between what it termed the 'real' and the 'nominal' exchange. The 'real' exchange was the rate of exchange between Bank of England notes (then still at par with gold on European exchanges) and the guineas which dominated commerce in Belfast, while the 'nominal' exchange was between the paper of the Bank of Ireland and the Bank of England. This provided experimental elegance, as the real exchange could be said to stem from 'real' factors such as the balance of payments, while any difference between it and the 'nominal' exchange could be attributed to purely monetary factors.[55] On the basis of this evidence, and with the help of some cherry-picking of the data series, the committee concluded that the sharp depreciation of the Irish pound in relation to the British was entirely due to excessive issues of notes by the Bank of Ireland.[56]

While exchange was the focus of the committee's work, it was of little concern to all but a small minority of Ireland's people, specifically the 'absentee landlords

---

[50] King, 'Thoughts on the Effects of the Bank Restrictions', p. 127.
[51] King, 'Bank Restrictions', p. 124. [52] Hall, *Bank of Ireland*, pp. 83–4.
[53] See for example *Dublin Journal*, 15 Oct. 1803 (INA); *Belfast News-letter*, 10 July 1804 (INA).
[54] Fetter, *Irish Pound*, pp. 27–8. [55] Foster, 'Report', pp. 3–4.
[56] Foster, 'Report', pp. 3, 7, 46. See also Ó Gráda, 'Reassessing', for a discussion of the committee's rejection of 'real' factors.

and merchants dealing between Dublin and London'.[57] For the rest of the population, the state of the silver coin, and of the numerous other low-value monetary instruments in circulation, was a much more pressing problem. The committee did acknowledge what all witnesses agreed was 'the miserable situation of the Silver Coinage, or rather of the base metal and notes and I.O.U.'s substituted in its place'.[58] But, like true zealots, the members were certain that this problem too must have its roots in the unfavourable exchange, which should be remedied by contracting the issues of the Bank of Ireland. Admitting that the current circumstances must give rise to a 'temptation to increase the nominal value of the current coin', the committee reiterated the sanctity of the currency settlement of 1696 by insisting that 'no depreciation, either of the chief or even of the inferior coins of these kingdoms, ought to be looked forward to as the means of remedying the evils resulting from a too extensive issue of paper'.[59]

It is true that the bank restriction period saw a proliferation of 'unofficial' monetary instruments, including low-value 'silver notes' issued by banks and other businesses, base metal tokens, and, above all, counterfeit silver.[60] This was merely an extreme form of Ireland's typical status quo, and enabled economic activity to go on in a context where the government had failed to establish a functioning monetary order. The Irish government's role, in fact, had largely been to permit people to fill the void that it had left, not only by winking at unlicensed issue of paper money and circulating IOUs but by accepting and giving counterfeits and severely light coins in payments, much as the British government was obliged to do.[61] But the latter provoked a crisis in March—while the committee was sitting—when it ordered the Post Office in Ireland to stop accepting counterfeits. This caused immediate panic, which temporarily made all small currency worthless, causing real hardship to the common people, and leading the Irish government to fear riots.[62] The situation was only alleviated when the British government softened its stance on the counterfeits and authorized the Bank of Ireland to issue token silver coins of six shillings, ten pence, and five pence.[63] In April 1805 it also commissioned Boulton to mint new copper pennies and their fractions for Ireland as well as Britain.[64]

The fact that the House of Commons established a committee to inquire into the state of the Irish currency was only possible because the Act of Union had abolished the Irish Parliament and brought the United Kingdom of Great Britain and Ireland into being on 1 January 1801. But the fact that there was still a distinct Irish currency to inquire into reflects a major difference between the Irish and the Scottish unions. For while the unification of the currencies had been the least controversial aspect of the earlier Union, it was equally uncontroversial that no

---

[57] Fetter, *Irish Pound*, p. 26.   [58] Commons, *Irish Pound*, pp. 16, 72–85.
[59] Commons, *Irish Pound*, p. 17.   [60] Carr, *Stranger*.   [61] Kelly, *Dollars and Tokens*, p. 64.
[62] Commons, *Irish Pound*, p. 49; Carr, *Stranger*, pp. 63–4.
[63] Kelly, *Dollars and Tokens*, pp. 65–6.   [64] Challis, *Mint*, pp. 755–6.

change to the relationship between the two nations' currencies was even proposed during the debates over the later one.

The lack of contemporary discussion leaves us with little direct evidence for the reasons for this consensus, but they are not difficult to surmise: quite simply, the abnormal monetary conditions in both countries at the time of the Union made any such idea inconceivable. Britain's general financial weakness at the time of the union with Ireland was also reflected in the fact that—again unlike 1707—the two countries' exchequers and national debts remained separate for the time being, which made full monetary union both more difficult and less necessary than it had been when England had, in a fiscal sense, swallowed Scotland whole.[65] The financial pressures of the war obviously ruled out a device like the Equivalent to facilitate the amalgamation of Britain's' and Ireland's respective national debts.

Moreover, the question of a recoinage hardly arose as there was no separate Irish coin other than copper minted in London. Of the coinage already notionally in use on both sides of the Irish Sea, no silver coin was then being struck, and precious little gold. Some one-third- and half-guineas were struck on the day the union came into effect, on which the king's title was changed simply to 'BRITANNIARUM', dropping the separate designations of Great Britain and Ireland, while incidentally also dropping the English monarchy's claim to France and the House of Hanover's German titles. All of this was purely symbolic. It would take another quarter-century, the amalgamation of the exchequers, and the resumption of cash payments by the Bank of England and the Bank of Ireland before a full monetary union could take place.

No action followed the Irish Pound Committee's report. For reasons that had nothing to do with the Bank of Ireland's note issues, the exchange fell sharply soon after the committee reported, reducing Ireland's value for advocates of immediate resumption equally quickly, along with their level of interest in Ireland.[66] In fact the committee's report would not even be discussed by the Parliament for another five years, and even then was overshadowed by a new committee focussed on England.

That committee, established in 1810, essentially repeated the conclusions of its predecessor, on which six of its members had also served. Its arguments were bolstered by the crystallization of a powerfully argued 'bullionist' position, especially under the influence of David Ricardo's ideas, which first appeared in *The Morning Chronicle* in August–November 1809. The report triggered a lengthy parliamentary and public debate which attracted enormous attention in pamphlets and the press, and extensive scholarly discussion since.[67]

---

[65] Jackson, *Two Unions*, p. 112; Hall, *Bank of Ireland*, pp. 112–14; Ó Gráda, *Ireland*, pp. 44–6.
[66] Fetter, *Orthodoxy*, p. 39.
[67] In a stimulating discussion of the controversy within a literary frame of reference, Dick, *Romanticism*, p. 36, calculates that 800 pamphlets on the currency question appeared during the twenty-four years of the restriction. Classic scholarly accounts can be found in Fetter, *Orthodoxy*, chs 1–3; Hilton, *Corn, Cash*, ch. 2; Feavearyear, *Pound*, chs 8–9.

The observable facts were domestic inflation and an increase in the price of gold in terms of Bank of England notes, marked by a discount of Bank of England notes in international payments.[68] The key theoretical issue at stake, as in the Irish case, was whether these phenomena were due, in part or in whole, to an excessive issue of notes by the Bank of England. In short, had the value of the Bank's notes depreciated because the Bank was issuing too many of them? This raised moral issues that revolved largely around what Mary Poovey has called the 'problematic of representation' in the monetary sphere.[69] Starting from Lord King's widely shared premise that a just medium of exchange must either contain or represent intrinsic value, the disjunction between the value of banknotes and the gold coin they purported to represent raised difficult questions about the fictionality of the notes as against the reality of the coin, which in turn raised questions about where responsibility lay for bringing the situation about and how it could be ended.[70]

In May 1811 the Commons rejected, by a four to one majority, the committee's key resolution that convertibility should be resumed in two years. There is no doubt that many members were unpersuaded, especially as the Bank of England directors insisted that the volume of their note issues could have no effect on the exchange rate. Like the Bank of Ireland seven years earlier, they argued that, provided all the bills of exchange which they took as security for their note issues represented real transactions, then their increased issues of banknotes could only be reflecting and facilitating economic growth. More important than these theoretical considerations, however, was the fact that the country was still at war, and the majority accepted, with Lord Liverpool, that the continuation of bank restriction was 'indispensably necessary to the salvation of the country'.[71] For the time being patriotism still required that paper money—however unrepresentative of gold—continue to be supported.

The demands of patriotism would soon take the government still further down the path of monetary heresy, from which there was no return until military victory was secured, when monetary patriotism took a different shape and demanded different sacrifices. Almost immediately after the defeat of the Bullion Committee, Lord King attempted to bring matters to a head by notifying his leasehold tenants that, as they had contracted in 1807 'to pay the annual rent of 100*l* in good and lawful money of Great Britain', and as banknotes had depreciated, he would no longer accept £100 in banknotes as payment. Instead, he would accept payment only in guinea coins or, if they were unobtainable (as they mostly were), in Portugal gold coin of equivalent weight. Alternatively, tenants could pay £114

---

[68] Ricardo, *Price*. [69] Poovey, *Genres*, p. 251.
[70] King, 'Bank Restrictions', p. 124; Dick, *Romanticism*. ch. 3, esp. p. 83; Poovey, *Genres*, pp. 5–6, 17, 179.
[71] Parl. Deb. (series 1), vol. 19, c. 1076 (8 May 1811).

12s. 8d. in notes, this being the amount required to purchase the weight of gold that would be contained in the requisite number of guineas.[72]

The result was precisely the opposite of what King had hoped. Within days, Parliament legislated to make any claim he might make against a tenant who offered to pay him £100 in Bank of England notes unenforceable. Relying on a motion of Earl Stanhope, one of its radical opponents, and performing all kinds of legal and linguistic contortions to deny that it had done so, the Tory government of Spencer Perceval, by supporting the passage of the Gold Coin and Bank Note Bill, had in effect made Bank of England notes legal tender for the first time, meaning that they could not be refused at face value in payment of a debt.

For King's supporters, his willingness to risk 'odium and unpopularity' in order to force the government's hand stemmed from 'motives of pure patriotism'.[73] Perceval, on the other hand, professed surprise that King had not grasped that previously only 'pedlars, and Jews, and smugglers' had behaved in similar ways. This sneer fitted comfortably into standard tropes about the perpetrators of socially unacceptable monetary behaviour, which were often generously spiced with anti-Semitism. By framing his criticism this way, Perceval reinforced that the real problem was not King's motivation, nor even the personal justness of his claims, but the broader social consequences of his actions. Perceval 'could conceive of no act whatever, that in proportion to the limited sphere of an individual, was calculated to produce such formidable effects against the interests of society'.[74] Alexander Baring implicitly endorsed King's hostility to the bill when considered 'merely in the light of an abstract question', but insisted that the real issue was 'whether the situation of the country was such as to render such a measure necessary'. Failure to understand this was a failure of patriotism: 'The circulation of the country rested on no other security but a combination of wealthy individuals in the country; and the general good faith among individuals held the place of compulsion.... [N]othing could be more honourable to the country at large than that no person, under any temptation, had yet ventured to refuse the notes of the Bank of England. This, indeed, shewed a high spirit of patriotism in the country at large.'[75] Stanhope's Act was necessary because King's demand on his tenants had blown apart the elite patriotic consensus established in 1797.

Baring's notions of patriotism might be predictable coming from a director of the Bank, but Stanhope, a landed proprietor, took an even stronger view, declaring that, 'To speak figuratively, he regarded the Bank of England as one of the bottom planks of the ship of England; if we permitted it to be bored through, we risked the whole vessel.'[76] For opponents of the bill, this increasingly symbiotic relationship

---

[72] King, 'Stanhope's Bill', p. 7.
[73] Lauderdale, Parl. Deb. (series 1), vol. 20, c. 768 (27 June 1811).
[74] Parl. Deb. (series 1), vol. 20, c. 885 (9 July 1811).
[75] Parl. Deb. (series 1), vol. 20, c. 894–5 (9 July 1811).
[76] Parl. Deb. (series 1), vol. 20, c. 763 (27 June 1811).

between the state and the Bank was precisely the problem. For King, the alleged benefits of the restriction to the nation were either unimportant or morally dubious: on the one hand the government received some financial accommodation, but this was at the price of a Faustian bargain, as the Bank's overissues, and the attendant 'defalcation of three shillings and five pence in the pound on all fixed incomes', enabled the government to receive 'the shameful profit of defrauding the public creditor, by compelling him to receive payment in depreciated paper money'.[77]

King and his supporters countered attacks on their patriotism by raising the bogey of Jacobinism, accusing supporters of the Act of 'conversion to the code of Robespierre'.[78] King compared his situation to that of individuals in France who had been accused of 'incivism' for preferring 'good metallic money to worthless assignats'. Britain was now heading down that awful path: 'to judge from the language of his Majesty's servants, who are endeavouring to inculcate the acceptance of paper money as a moral and political duty, we are here also to be governed according to the true Jacobin doctrine, which required individuals to regulate their conduct not by their own proper interest and convenience, but according to some speculative principles'.[79] Remarkably, Henry Brougham judged that this 'establishment of a compulsory currency, and the denunciations of vengeance against those who refused to accept it' was of all the crimes of the French revolution the most 'revolting to English justice and English feeling'.[80]

Both sides of the debate thus staked strong claims to monetary patriotism, but on radically divergent grounds. For King and his supporters, it consisted in adherence to a pure set of political principles resting solidly on the rights of private property untrammelled by government, based on what they regarded as natural law, and recognizable as the antithesis of the principles of the French Revolution—by then, as Linda Colley has shown, a marker of 'British' national identity, just as opposition to 'Catholic' France had been.[81] Adherence to metallic money as a mainstay of indefeasible property rights thus became another way for some Britons to imagine 'the French as their vile opposites, as Hyde to their Jekyll'.[82] For King 'to make a stand in defence of [his] property' was therefore patriotic, because it rested on the principle that in a 'well-regulated state [as opposed to France], the proper interest of individuals is inseparable from that of the government'.[83] For the government, on the other hand, true monetary patriotism consisted in supporting the existing expedients to ensure the nation's ultimate

---

[77] Parl. Deb. (series 1), vol. 20, c. 799 (2 July 1811).
[78] Abercromby, Parl. Deb. (series 1) ,vol. 20, c. 889 (9 July 1811).
[79] Parl. Deb. (series 1), vol. 20, c. 798 (2 July 1811).
[80] Brougham, Parl. Deb. (series 1), vol. 20, c. 927 (15 July 1811). For a comparison of UK and French war finance, see Bordo and White, 'Tale'.
[81] Colley, *Britons*, pp. 328–30.   [82] Colley, *Britons*, p. 387.
[83] Parl. Deb. (series 1), vol. 20, c. 798 (2 July 1811).

victory in its existential struggle with France, 'whatever might be the inconveniences attendant on the present state of the currency'.[84]

Stanhope's Act explicitly excluded Ireland from its operations, leaving landlords there free to insist on the payment of rents in coin. The government's justification was that this was merely to maintain the status quo in both countries. In much of Ulster, nothing but coin had ever been paid for rent, before or since 1797, whereas in England, Scotland, and the rest of Ireland, it was most common for rents to be paid in paper.[85] Other legislators had a more jaundiced view of Irish practice. Lauderdale thought it strange to argue, 'because the practice of extortion among landlords had long prevailed in Ireland, that therefore it should be suffered to continue'. He described a scenario where tenants had been advised by the steward that they could buy guineas at a premium at a nearby chandler's shop. One hundred guineas had been cycled through this process seventy times to pay a total rent of £7,000.[86] That this was no isolated incident is suggested by the fact that Maria Edgeworth depicted a similar episode in her 1812 novel *The Absentee*, with an emphasis on the vulnerability of the tenants and the corruption of the agent.[87]

The government's decision the following year to extend the Act to Ireland outraged Irish Whigs and radicals including Henry Parnell, Sir John Newport, and George Ponsonby, who all, as well as rehearsing the familiar arguments against the principle of legal tender, stressed Ireland's differences from England. As well as the different monetary customs in the north, Parnell pointed to the fact that leases in Ireland were generally much longer than those in England, meaning that landlords would have to endure a much longer period of depreciation of the paper before they could raise their rents. The effect of the bill would simply be to 'take the money out of the pockets of the landlords and other creditors and put it in that of tenants and debtors'.[88]

The government took its stand on both the distress of Irish tenants and the need for uniformity across the United Kingdom when it insisted on the injustice of continuing 'to permit the Irish landlord to drag his tenant to prison for non-payment in coin, while the landlord enjoyed no such power in this part of the empire'.[89] Aside from the relief it brought to tenants, the extension of the Act to Ireland was thus another small step towards uniformity of the monetary orders of the three kingdoms.

No one was more outraged by Stanhope's Act than the political journalist and campaigner William Cobbett. Indeed, the episode could be argued to be a critical factor in Cobbett's evolution from a plebeian anti-Jacobin propagandist broadly

---

[84] Liverpool, Parl. Deb. (series 1), vol. 20, c. 879 (8 July 1811).
[85] Ó Gráda, *Ireland*, pp. 60-2; Cullen, 'Landlords, Bankers', pp. 39-41.
[86] Parl. Deb. (series 1), vol. 20, c. 877 (8 July 1811).   [87] Barry, 'Edgeworth's', pp. 262-3.
[88] Parl. Deb. (series 1), vol. 21, c. 283 (10 Apr. 1812).
[89] Perceval, Parl. Deb. (series 1), vol. 21, c. 292 (10 Apr. 1812).

congenial to the government to its most widely read radical opponent. Cobbett regarded King's actions as nothing more than a just attempt to preserve what was rightfully due to him as a landowner.[90] According to Cobbett, the tenants had been able to increase the price of their corn and cattle to compensate themselves for the depreciation of the paper: 'consequently, it will require only *four loads* of wheat to pay £100 now, but it must have required *five loads* to pay £100 in 1802'.[91] This could only end with rents having virtually no real value at all, resulting in the destruction of the landlord class. The ultimate tendency of the paper system, especially as enshrined by Stanhope's Bill, would be to distribute 'the lands and houses of the rich amongst those who are not rich', a prospect that left Cobbett aghast.[92]

Cobbett's importance in this study rests on the fact that he was the earliest and most influential opponent of paper money to address himself to the common people, or to claim that he spoke for their interests. Historians have broadly endorsed this claim, regardless of whatever reservations they might have about many aspects of his career and thought. Taking their cue from G. D. H. Cole's conclusion that Cobbett was 'the last great tribune of the agrarians [who] was, by force of circumstances, also the first great tribune of the industrial proletariat', historians have generally accepted that he was, in some way or another, a 'tribune of the people'.[93] Certainly, his *Political Register* was the most influential organ of radical opinion until his death in 1835.[94] As we shall see in the remaining chapters, Cobbett's views on paper money had an enduring influence on later radical movements, including Chartism, many of whose leaders learnt much of their politics in the pages of Cobbett's work. Their later denunciations of paper clearly bear his mark.

The paucity of evidence about what the common people of England actually thought and felt about paper money during the restriction makes it tempting to take Cobbett's views as a proxy for the views of his audience or, even more dubiously, for those of the labouring poor. Both temptations should be resisted. Before examining the scanty contemporary evidence available concerning the views of Cobbett's intended audience, it will be helpful to scrutinize his arguments and prejudices on paper money in order to clarify whose interests they might be regarded as representing, and thus to decide who that audience may have been.

Cobbett's interest in paper money appears to have been sparked by King's speeches and pamphlet of 1803, which he immediately quoted with approval.[95] But while King typically argued in the abstract, Cobbett's natural mode was to personalize, casting individuals and groups as villains or victims. One group of

---

[90] Cobbett, *Paper against Gold*, p. 354. [91] Cobbett, *Paper against Gold*, p. 372.
[92] Cobbett, *Paper against Gold*, p. 356.
[93] Cole, *Cobbett*, p. 291; Stevenson, 'Cobbett', p. 123. For commentaries on changing views of Cobbett, see also Wiener, 'Image'; Dyck, 'Rabble'; Griffiths, 'Cole and Cobbett'.
[94] Williams, *Culture*, p. 23. [95] *Cobbett's Annual Register*, 26 Nov. 1803.

victims for whom Cobbett exhibited a tender concern were the fundholders—owners of government debt of various kinds. On this point we find Cobbett at his most incoherent and self-contradictory. His ideas nonetheless repay analysis, for they provide valuable clues to help us discover who his intended readers were, and who were 'the people' of his imagination in this context.

Like other popular radicals, Cobbett was deeply influenced by Thomas Paine's *Decline & Fall of the English System of Finance*, a savage critique of the system of government finance established in the 1690s which predicted the imminent bankruptcy of the Bank and hence the government.[96] According to Cobbett, who first read Paine in the same year as he read King, the system had been established to serve 'sinecure placemen and pensioners', whose insatiable greed necessitated large government expenditure, and who lent their support to a government whose wars placed still further burdens on the taxpayers by mortgaging future taxes and providing Cobbett's other favourite hate figures—the Bank of England, 'the Jews', and stockjobbers like 'Messrs Muckworm and Company'—with opportunities to profit at the public expense.[97] Only the removal of these people's claims on the public purse could make possible the eradication of paper money and a return to the ideal state of a purely metallic currency.[98] Unfortunately the proliferation of wars and sinecures had had the opposite effect. As the system had grown, the monetary system had progressively worsened, leading to the production of notes of ever-smaller denominations, culminating in 1797 with the suspension of cash payments and the circulation of £1 and £2 notes.[99]

The funding system was a monstrous injustice also because the owners of the debt had already been paid far more in interest than the sum they had originally lent. Yet the owners of that debt, in the guise of the unfortunate fundholder defrauded by payment in paper, figure repeatedly as helpless victims in Cobbett's polemics. In *Paper against Gold*, Cobbett illustrated the dangers of the system through the plight of 'poor Grizzle Greenhorn', for whom her father, 'farmer Greenhorn', has put £2,000 in the funds. Instead of gold, all Grizzle now has in return for her father's money is '*her name written in a book*, at the Bank Company's house in Threadneedle Street, London, in consequence of which she is entitled to receive the interest of the two thousand pounds'.[100] Later we are invited to sympathize with her on the grounds that she can now receive only bank paper instead of 'good gold and silver' in payment of her half-yearly dividend.[101]

A few years later, correctly predicting a major financial crisis, Cobbett urged all '*holders of Funds, Scrip, Shares and all sorts of Paper-Money*' to get rid of them as

---

[96] Paine, *Decline*.
[97] Poovey, *Genres*, p. 182; Cobbett, *Paper against Gold*, pp. 20, 459. For Cobbett's anti-Semitism, see Osborne, *Cobbett*, pp. 222–3.
[98] Cobbett, *Paper against Gold*, p. 320.
[99] Cobbett, *Paper against Gold*, pp. 137–40.
[100] Cobbett, *Paper against Gold*, p. 20.
[101] Cobbett, *Paper against Gold*, p. 289.

soon as possible on the grounds that 'perhaps, in less than a year, *a hundred pounds of stock* will not yield enough of interest to pay one single week's wages of a labourer'.[102] The 'people' in Cobbett's mind's eye when he wrote about paper money are now clearly visible: substantial farmers who worried about how to pay their labourers, or who invested savings for their daughters, even to the tune of £2,000. As we shall see, he was largely indifferent to the monetary trials of the labourers themselves.

There is little evidence, however, to suggest that even his intended audience shared Cobbett's hostility and distrust of paper money during the bank restriction. Indeed, the Bank's initial steps towards the resumption of cash payments present compelling evidence that they preferred paper to gold coin. As one country banker told the Commons committee appointed to investigate the expediency of the resumption of cash payments, 'In the year 1816, when Guineas were easily obtained from the Bank of England, the public showed no disposition to take them. I have, as a banker, directed my clerk to offer bright new Guineas to individuals who came to my banking house, and, in the greater number of instances, they were refused.'[103] The following year the Bank of England made the new gold 'sovereigns' available in exchange for notes. Consignments were sent out to country banks, which stood ready to issue them at their customers' pleasure.[104] The country banks returned them to the Bank of England, there being 'little or no demand for cash'.[105] The Bank of Ireland also had few takers for gold coins when it made them available.[106] Despite the chorus of propaganda from the Parliament, and in the pages of the respectable journals and the radical press of every stripe, nobody had wanted the new coins. Notwithstanding the views of their tribune, 'the people' were, for the time being, content to keep their 'rotten rags'.

These attempts to issue guineas and sovereigns mark the government's and the Bank's first, unsuccessful attempts towards resuming cash payments. With final victory over Napoleon achieved in 1815, pressure to end the suspension grew. This was not a simple matter. A resumption at the former rate would require a contraction of the currency, which would increase the already severe economic distress which accompanied the peace. Moreover, the Bank directors, upon whose goodwill and cooperation the government still relied for the management of its highly problematic finances, remained unconvinced of bullionist doctrine and unwilling to change what was, as their critics pointed out repeatedly, a highly profitable arrangement.

The government's repeated postponements created impatience among bullionists and others—not least Cobbett, who believed it affirmed his view that

---

[102] Cobbett, *Gold for Ever*, p. 11.
[104] Feavearyear, *Pound*, p. 216.
[106] Hall, *Bank of Ireland*, p. 104.
[103] Harrowby, 'Resumption Reports', p. 149.
[105] Harrowby, 'Resumption Reports', p. 3.

resumption had become impossible. The Coinage Act of 1816 was in part an attempt to placate the critics. It made gold the official monetary standard for the first time and affirmed the government's commitment to return to the path of monetary righteousness by specifying that gold would be rated according to the existing mint indenture.[107] The Act gave rise to the minting, for the first time since the reign of Charles I, of a gold coin of twenty shillings value, tellingly named the 'sovereign'. The coin's reverse featured Benedetto Pistrucci's image of St George at the point of slaying the dragon.[108] Its triumphalism may have been appropriate for a nation emerging victorious from decades of war, but the choice of the patron saint of England for the flagship coin of the United Kingdom provides a striking illustration of where the centre of monetary power lay and how much thought monetary decision-makers gave to Scottish or Irish sensibilities. The fact that this appears to have been completely uncontroversial suggests that at this moment English hegemony over currency matters was generally accepted.

The People's Money

Despite the focus of many contemporaries and subsequent commentators, the most important consequence of the Act for most people's lives was not the pledge to a monetary standard that was already preordained and was still five years away from implementation. Rather, it was the decision to produce, for the first time in centuries, reliable and stable silver coin which would remain in circulation for the conduct of the everyday transactions of the great mass of the population.

We have seen that the government's expedients to try to meet the desperate need for small coins during the restriction had met with mixed success and that enormous quantities of unofficial tokens and other promissory instruments of varying reliability had filled at least some of the gap. The government, although initially inclined to postpone any reform of the silver until after the resumption of convertibility, appears to have been convinced that a sudden influx of overvalued French silver coins was laying up serious problems for the future.[109]

The solution adopted had first been proposed in 1805 by the Prime Minister's father, the first Earl of Liverpool, in *A Treatise on the Coins of the Realm; in a Letter to the King*, a work remarkable for its attention to the need of the common people for a plentiful supply of reliable, low-denomination coins for everyday transactions. In Liverpool's assessment, the silver coin was scarcer, lighter, and in worse condition than it had been at the time of the great recoinage, having

---

[107] 56 Geo. III c. 68, *Statutes*, p. 437.
[108] See https://www.britishmuseum.org/collection/object/C_1994-0915-758. Pistrucci's image, as it appeared on a 1979 commemorative coin, appears on the cover of this book.
[109] Baring, Parl. Deb. (series 1), vol. 30, c. 89 (9 Mar. 1815).

degenerated to 'mere counters, without any impression on the face or reverse, or any graining on the edges, or indeed any exterior mark, by which they can be distinguished as coins'.[110] He estimated the total value of the legal silver in circulation at no more than £3,960,435 and 'probably very much less',[111] or less than eight shillings per head for a population of over ten million people. His proposed remedy was to make gold alone the 'standard measure of property', leaving silver to play a purely subsidiary role. This did not mean that he saw the silver as less important: indeed, having proposed it as a purely domestic currency, he urged that it was more important to keep silver in the country than gold, which should be allowed to be freely exported as required in the course of international trade.[112]

The challenge was to value the silver coins so that there would be no profit in either melting or counterfeiting them. Liverpool's formula to avoid melting was to value the coin at a rate equal to the best available estimate of the average foreseeable price of the bullion it contained plus the cost of minting it.[113] His solution to the counterfeiting problem was to use Matthew Boulton's steam-powered presses at the royal mint, 'for machines, which act with a given force, can work with more truth and accuracy than the arm of man', a point later reinforced by Boulton himself.[114]

Liverpool's recommendations only became politically acceptable when gold became the legal standard, at which point they became largely uncontentious. Apart from a couple of MPs who would have preferred a return to a silver standard, the only objections concerned the timing, with Francis Horner questioning 'whether, in the present temper and circumstances of the lower orders, this was a favourable period for a new experiment on their peace, or for imposing an additional hardship on them'. This concern was echoed by another MP, who worried about the consequences of spreading 'panic and alarm'.[115]

These were valid concerns in the economically difficult and socially tumultuous post-war years, and the authorities, led by William Wellesley Pole, the Master of the Mint, clearly did their best to minimize potential problems and avoid any repetition of the 'extremely distressing' process of 1696.[116] Rather than requiring people to bring in their own coin and wait for new coin to be returned from the mint, the exchange was to be made instantaneous by distributing £2 million of new coins throughout England and Scotland. Crucially, the expense was to be borne by the public purse, with old coins being exchanged for new at par, no matter how worn or smooth. Places to exchange the coins were to be established

---

[110] Liverpool, *Treatise*, p. 168. [111] Liverpool, *Treatise*, p. 186.
[112] Liverpool, *Treatise*, p. 166. [113] Sargent and Velde, *Small Change*, pp. 302–5.
[114] Liverpool, *Treatise*, p. 202; Redish, *Bimetallism*, pp. 144–6; Selgin, 'Steam', p. 491, argues that the crucial improvement was in engraving techniques rather than the introduction of steam power.
[115] Parl. Deb. (series 1), vol. 34, c. 965 (30 May 1816).
[116] Pole, Parl. Deb. (series 1), vol. 34, c. 952 (30 May 1816).

all over Britain so that nobody would have to travel more than 15 to 20 miles in order to exchange them during the fortnight allowed. Inspectors were to be appointed for each place of exchange, usually from among the ranks of local bankers, to ensure that no foreign coins or counterfeits were accepted. This was indeed a possible source of unrest, for as Lord Archibald Hamilton put it, 'a great portion of [the coin] was in such a state, that he did not know how it was possible to determine whether or not it had ever been issued by the Mint'.[117] To ameliorate this potential problem the inspectors were instructed to carry out their work in a 'liberal' spirit, and to give the public the benefit of any possible doubt.[118]

Ireland, not yet in a formal monetary union with Britain, was excluded from the process, despite the Committee on Coin's recommendation that it be included and that an additional £500,000 be minted for that purpose. In the only dedicated study of the recoinage, Kevin Clancy argues that a range of factors was at work in this decision. First, Ireland's need for silver was seen as being largely met by Bank of Ireland silver tokens, which, unlike their English counterparts, were legal tender and accepted in taxes. Secondly, including Ireland in the process would add time and expense, delaying the work in Britain by some months. Finally, the decision was consistent with the 'selective amnesia which afflicted Westminster politicians on the subject of Irish currency'.[119]

The newspaper notices and reports suggest that the exchange of old coins for new went smoothly in most places. Considerable pains were taken to make it as easy as possible for the labouring poor. The exchange took place mostly in local banks, although in some towns it was conducted in public venues such as town halls because bankers feared 'that their property would be endangered' by opening their doors to 'all ranks of the community'.[120] Some of the larger towns had more than one place of exchange; London had twenty, including the Bank of England and sixteen 'subsidiary stations' located in convenient everyday venues such as inns, apothecaries, and a theatre.[121] In Oxford, only small sums were to be exchanged during the first two days, 'for the accommodation and convenience of the labouring classes'.[122] Authorities in Leeds sought the same end by asking shopkeepers to bring their coin in at ten o'clock each morning counted and labelled, while everybody else was asked to come an hour later.[123] The bailiffs of Eye, 'in order that the industrious poor may not lose their time', charged church wardens with the task of collecting parishioners' small sums to bring for immediate exchange.[124]

---

[117] Parl. Deb. (series 1), vol. 34, c. 1018–20 (7 June 1816).
[118] Parl. Deb. (series 1), vol. 34, c. 1021 (7 June 1816). [119] Clancy, 'Recoinage', pp. 90–4.
[120] Clancy, 'Recoinage', p. 120; TNA M1-54; 6th head, p. 418, quoted in Redish, 'Evolution', p. 802 n. 27.
[121] *The Times*, 1 Feb. 1817.   [122] *Jackson's Oxford Journal*, 8 Feb. 1817 (BLN).
[123] *Leeds Mercury*, 22 Feb. 1817 (BNA).   [124] *Ipswich Journal*, 1 Feb. 1817 (BNA).

Even so, there were hitches. In Scotland, people in Selkirk were still complaining a year later of losses they had suffered as a result of missing the exchange period,[125] despite the fact that Selkirk had one of Scotland's ninety exchange stations. While the exchange was in progress, many papers reported rumours that large numbers of new counterfeits had already been identified.[126] The rumours were possibly exaggerated, reflecting people's uncertainty about unfamiliar coins.[127] But most of the problems arose before the exchange took place, when people became uncertain about what coin would be accepted, leading to sporadic disturbances when tradesmen began to refuse current silver.[128] In some places, rumours circulated that sixpences would not be accepted, leading to some of the poor 'selling their sixpences for fourpence to Jews'.[129]

On the whole, however, the introduction of the new silver coin was a success, which radically and permanently improved the monetary lives of everybody in England and Scotland, and especially those who only ever used money of small denominations, for whom a centuries-old affliction largely disappeared in the space of a fortnight. For its part, the Bank of England quickly followed up the exchange of the old silver by exchanging new silver for its tokens in December 1817, and with an active, well-publicized programme of exchanging its small notes for new silver in the years leading up to the resumption of payments in gold.[130] This departure from the principles of commodity money, combined with careful management, thus enabled a major step in creating a unified and reliable currency throughout the United Kingdom, with stable relationships between the small currency and the other elements of the system. This reform was critical in making money unproblematic for most people's daily lives, and thus providing it with a taken-for-granted quantity that put it beyond the need or possibility of critique.

In a remarkable sign of his priorities, Cobbett's only reference to the reform of the silver coinage very rapidly transitioned into a harangue about paper money's perversion of the natural order of things. The ministers were to be thanked for introducing the reform because it would ultimately 'drive out of circulation that fictitious trash, of those despicable and dirty rags, which have long been an eyesore to me. We shall now, to a limited extent at any rate, hear our tills once again rattle, our pockets chink with the sound of something real; and, if men are brought to the gallows for counterfeiting hereafter, it will be, as in good old times, for counterfeiting the King's coin.' But although he praised the measure, and although he had commented favourably elsewhere on other aspects of Liverpool's *Treatise*, it appears that he had not taken much trouble over Liverpool's proposals for

---

[125] Curwen, Parl. Deb. (series 1), vol. 37, c. 332 (11 Feb. 1818).
[126] For example, *Morning Post*, 20 Feb. 1817 (BNA); *Leeds Mercury*, 22 Feb. 1817 (BNA); *Ipswich Journal*, 22 Feb. 1817 (BNA).
[127] Clancy, 'Recoinage', p. 133.   [128] Clancy, 'Recoinage', pp. 83–8.
[129] *The Times*, 3 Feb. 1817; *Liverpool Mercury*, 10 Jan. 1817 (BNA).
[130] BE M5/2. ff 120, 125, 133, 163.

reforming the silver, or the government's outline of its scheme, being unclear about whether, as he hoped, the new silver coins were to be 'of their former real value'.[131]

Cobbett's treatment of this important reform shows the strong similarities between his views and those of parliamentary advocates of early resumption, which were rapidly coalescing into a powerful consensus. The operation of the consensus over the ensuing hundred years will be explored in later chapters, but its key elements as it burgeoned into an irresistible force in favour of the creation of a monetary order based on circulating gold coin can be seen in Cobbett's remarks. First, there is considerable indifference to the monetary needs of the wage earners who made up the bulk of the population. Second, there is a fetishistic obsession with metallic currency, and in particular with gold, based on the belief that the value of money can derive only from the 'real' value of precious metals and that any other basis of monetary value is therefore 'fictitious'. Finally, there is a growing concern that the punishment of paper money forgery has usurped royal prerogatives in the enforcement of the monetary order.

Disquiet at the punishment of forgery gained force as the pressure for resumption grew. Radicals had long protested at the large number of forgers and utterers of banknotes subjected to punishments of death or fourteen years' transportation, respectively, and had particularly criticized the Bank of England for producing notes that were significantly less difficult to forge than those of many other banks. Cobbett portrayed these 'victims' of the restriction in pitiful terms. In order to keep its small notes in circulation, the Bank 'kept the hangman in almost constant employ' dispatching the Bank's 'human sacrifices', simply because they were 'not proof against the temptation to imitate' the Bank's notes.[132]

This vision of forgery and forgers was powerfully reinforced by George Cruikshank's 'Bank Restriction Note', which created a considerable stir when it first appeared in the window of the radical publisher William Hone in January 1819.[133] A clever parody of a Bank of England note, its dominant feature is a sketch of eight men and three women hanging from a gibbet. The usual Britannia vignette is depicted eating her children; the distinctive wavy line watermark has become an ocean dotted with convict transports; the cashier's signature has been replaced by that of Jack Ketch, the emblematically awful public executioner; while the £ symbol has been formed out of the looped rope of a noose. The note made several political points by claiming to be valid 'During the Issue of Bank Notes easily imitated, and until the Resumption of Cash Payments, or the Abolition of the Punishment of Death'.

The ease with which the Bank's notes could be imitated was a significant topic of public discussion and deliberation by the Bank's management throughout the

---

[131] *Cobbett's Weekly Political Register*, 1 Feb. 1817.   [132] Cobbett, *Rotten Rag*, pp. 5, 8.
[133] Byatt, *Promises*, p. 52.

restriction period, as it was believed greatly to increase the likelihood of forgery.[134] Despite these concerns, and despite Cobbett's and Cruikshank's implicit picture of ordinary men and women casually tempted into forgery, it is clear that most forgery was carried out by organized criminal gangs, many of whom had switched over from counterfeiting coin during the suspension of cash payments.[135] Even allowing that the Bank's notes were not especially difficult to imitate, the process of forging still required specialized skills as well as capital investment in engraving plates and a printing press. Moreover, as the prosecution depositions show, the typical modus operandi of the utterer of forged notes was to use them to get change by making reasonably expensive purchases, such as silk handkerchiefs and expensive shoes, which were not such as would ever be made by an ordinary wage earner. Court records suggest that—apart from the professional criminals—they had occupations such as shopkeeper, skilled craftsman, and horse dealer. These people appear to have operated as wholesale purchasers of notes from the organized forgers.[136] Unlike the labouring poor, all of these people would have routinely handled genuine banknotes. While this does not make the historical spectacle of frequent executions for forgery any less repulsive, nor the fate of those killed or torn from their homes by transportation any less dreadful (not to mention the miseries of the families they left behind), it is important for analytical purposes to bear in mind that many of these 'victims' of forgery, like those investors in stocks whose fate so worried Cobbett, came from narrow and reasonably elevated strata of the 'common people'.[137]

Implicit in Cruikshank's note (as in Cobbett's comments on the silver coinage) was the important political argument that the Bank's role in the prosecution of banknote forgery usurped the traditional prerogatives of the state. This argument has been fully vindicated by Randall McGowen, who has shown that the Bank and its lawyers made all of the important decisions about who was to be prosecuted and for what crime.[138] It also provided critics with further examples of the directors' obtuseness, helping to bring radical criticisms of the Bank further into the mainstream. Asked by the government to provide statistics concerning forgery prosecutions, the Bank protested against what it saw as an 'incroachment on the rights and privileges of the Bank'.[139] The Bank's persistent failure to make its notes harder to forge added grist to the mill. For its part, the Bank claimed to have applied itself assiduously to the problem, but as none of the plans and proposals it considered could promise a truly inimitable note, it chose to do nothing.[140]

---

[134] Hewitt, 'Beware'.   [135] McGowen, 'Gallows', pp. 83–5.   [136] POB.
[137] Palk, *Prisoners' Letters*, Introduction, provides an excellent brief account of the situation of men and women prosecuted by the Bank. The letters themselves provide an immediate sense of the horrors of their situation. See also Palk, 'Mercy'.
[138] McGowen, 'Gallows'.   [139] 23 Apr. 1818, BE G8/7.
[140] Hewitt, 'Beware'; Hewitt, 'Applegarth's Answers'.

By 1819 concerns about forgery had coalesced with the general critique of the bank restriction. This was shown in Cruikshank's 'Restriction Barometer', which was displayed in Hone's window alongside the 'Restriction Note'.[141] The vertical barometer was arranged symmetrically from the middle, with stormy weather, desolation, a gibbet, and a despairing Britannia at the bottom, and clear skies and general prosperity at the top. Each of the woes listed as the result of the restriction in the bottom half was mirrored by a corresponding benefit at the top. Thus 'Frequent and useless inflictions of the barbarous punishment of death' was at the bottom, while 'The number of useless Public Executions diminished' was at the top. Remarkably, in the light of the disastrous deflation that was to accompany the resumption, contraction of the currency and a fall in prices were each listed in the top half, corresponding to the profusion of currency and inflation caused by inconvertibility. Resumption had become a panacea.

The Price of Gold

As the moral authority of the Bank directors weakened, so the case for resumption gained strength. Following further bouts of exchange rate instability, inflation, and rises in the price of bullion the directors' continuing adherence to the 'real bills' doctrine, and their blank refusal to consider that the extent of their note issues could have any effect on either inflation or the exchanges, appeared increasingly obtuse and self-interested. As a result, by 1819 an expeditious return to cash payments largely ceased to be a party or sectional issue.[142] Support embraced a clear majority of Tories and Whigs and every sectional interest represented in Parliament: metropolitan, rural, and provincial; landed, moneyed, and mercantile. And while the miniscule number who took up heterodox views were mostly bankers of one kind or another, many more bankers in Parliament supported the resumption.

The consensus also transcended national boundaries. There was no distinct body of Irish or Scottish opinion raised in debates over resumption in Parliament or elsewhere. Indeed, insofar as there was a Scottish voice on the currency question, it was *The Edinburgh Review*, which was the most important single organ in the development and popularization of political economy and of the principles of bullionism among the educated classes throughout and even beyond the United Kingdom.[143] While Sir John Sinclair, one of the few writers anywhere in favour of an inconvertible paper currency, was Scottish, his compatriots

---

[141] Dick, *Romanticism*, pp. 119–20.   [142] Hilton, *Corn, Cash*, pp. 37–40, 56–66.
[143] See Fetter, 'Authorship', on *The Review*'s economic opinions and influence. Dick, *Romanticism*, pp. 59–73, provides a nuanced account of *The Review* during the bullion debate.

ignored him even more completely than did the English press.[144] For their part, Scottish bankers regarded the issue as outside their remit, as 'they had no problem of depreciation of bank paper in terms of gold, and they left concern over the foreign exchanges to London'.[145] In Ireland the tiny smattering of press comment on currency questions supported resumption, and the Bank of Ireland was content to follow the government's assumption that it would, with minor variations, shadow the Bank of England throughout the process.[146]

Parliament shared the assumption that there was nothing specifically Scottish or Irish to say about the currency. In March 1819 each House appointed a committee to determine—as the Lords committee put it—the 'mode and period which may be most advantageously adopted for ultimately bringing back the Currency of the Country to its ancient standard'.[147] Only the Lords committee called representatives from the Bank of Ireland, who confirmed that they would be able to resume cash payments six months after the Bank of England, as required by the current legislation.[148] The only witness from Scotland was Ebenezer Gilchrist, manager of the British Linen Company, who had only lived in Scotland since after the restriction began. The chief interest of both committees was whether the resumption would create a demand for gold coin in Scotland, which Gilchrist assured them it would not.[149] Beyond a bald statement of the Bank of Ireland's ability to resume cash payments, neither committee made any comment on Scotland or Ireland, or about how the resumption might affect those countries' monetary arrangements or economic well-being.

Ironically, almost the first act of the committees was to recommend another suspension of cash payments. We have seen that nobody had wanted gold coins for their own use, but when the foreign exchanges moved in July 1817 so as to make it profitable to export them, the demand was intense. Approximately £6,756,000 had left the Bank since that date, none of which had gone into circulation.[150] As this was obviously counterproductive, the government stopped it while the Parliament worked out how to return to cash payments on a sustainable basis.

Consistent with bullionist theory, the plan was to remove the gap between the values of notes and gold by reducing the volume of notes in circulation. Following a proposal put forward by Ricardo, the gold price would be reduced in stages without the need to put gold into circulation.[151] From 1 February 1820 the Bank

---

[144] *Morning Chronicle*, 18 Sept. 1810; 5 Oct. 1810 (BNA). *The Morning Post* carried a debate between Sinclair and the arch-bullionist William Huskisson across three issues: 13, 14, and 22 Dec. 1810 (BNA).
[145] Checkland, *Scottish Banking*, p. 435. [146] Hall, *Bank of Ireland*, pp. 103–8.
[147] Harrowby, 'Resumption Reports' (First Report, n.p.).
[148] Harrowby, 'Resumption Reports', p. 261. [149] Peel, 'Resumption Report', pp. 215–16.
[150] Peel, 'Resumption Report', pp. 4–5.
[151] Ricardo, *Proposals*, pp. 24–37; Bonar, 'Ingot Plan', describes the evolution of Ricardo's plan and his conversion of the Resumption Committee.

would be required to sell gold for £4 1s. 0d. of its notes, reducing by stages to the mint price on 1 May 1821. Being available only in ingots of 60 ounces, gold could only be obtained in payment of sums well over £200 and thus be useful only for mercantile transactions. This would prevent any sudden panic causing a demand for gold, which would require a new restriction. The bank would have gold available on this basis for a further two years, before returning to full convertibility in coin on 1 May 1823. The committee also hoped that making the contraction of the money supply gradual would minimize any distress that might ensue.[152] In reality, the witnesses and members of the committee could only trade guesses at how much distress might ensue. Of one thing they were certain: whatever 'difficulties' might arise would be 'outweighed by the important and permanent benefits of restoring the standard'.[153]

A significant theme of the committee reports and subsequent parliamentary debate was the need to impose a clear and definite sequence of actions to ensure that the Bank could no longer delay resumption.[154] But the directors' actions during the committee hearings, and a sharp protest they sent to the government in response to the committee reports, raised the older and more fundamental issue of the Bank's power over a state prerogative. In his opening speech in the Commons debate on resumption, Peel quoted the most offensive passage of the memorandum:

> it is incumbent on them [the Directors] to bear in mind not less their duties to the establishment over which they preside, than their duties to the community at large, whose interests in a pecuniary and commercial relation have, in a great degree, been confided to their discretion.[155]

This was the Bank—as in its approach to forgery prosecutions—simultaneously claiming the prerogatives of a public body while insisting on its rights as a private one. For Peel, this showed the urgent necessity for the Parliament to 're-trace its steps', and to 'recover the authority which it had so long abdicated'.[156] Liverpool summed up what that authority consisted of, and why the Bank directors should not exercise it: 'would parliament consent to commit to their hands what they certainly would refuse to the sovereign on the throne, controlled by parliament itself—the power of making money, without any other check or influence to direct them, than their own notions of profit and interest?'[157] The fact was, however, that

---

[152] Peel, 'Resumption Report', pp. 15, 20. Fetter, *Orthodoxy*, p. 93, suggests that the committees thought little about distress. My reading of the report and evidence suggests that the desire to minimize distress was important to their deliberations and was a major attraction of Ricardo's plan.
[153] Peel, 'Resumption Report', p. 14.
[154] Hilton, *Corn, Cash*, pp. 51–2; Harrowby, 'Resumption Reports', pp. 197–8.
[155] Quoted by Peel, Parl. Deb. (series 1), vol. 40, c. 688 (24 May 1819).
[156] Parl. Deb. (series 1), vol. 40, c. 689 (24 May 1819).
[157] Parl. Deb. (series 1), vol. 40, c. 612 (21 May 1819).

the Parliament had given the Bank that power not in 1797, but in 1694. The Resumption Act was the beginning of a series of attempts to put the genie back in the bottle with the magical power of gold.

No one would play a more important role in those attempts than Peel, who was converted to bullionism during the 1819 committee hearings. He began his speech in the debate by citing Locke and Newton to justify his new conviction 'that a certain weight of gold bullion, with an impression on it, denoting it to be of that certain weight, and of a certain fineness, constituted the only true, intelligible, and adequate standard of value'.[158] He looked back to previous 'restorations' of the value of the currency, which he claimed to have occurred in the reigns of Edward VI, Elizabeth, and William III, as 'periods to which every man must look with feelings of admiration and delight'.[159]

Hudson Gurney pointed out the critical historical difference between those episodes and the current situation by arguing that the distribution of monetary power had changed radically in the interim. Previously, there had been no national debt, which meant that 'the subject was tributary to the crown, not the crown to the subject'. As a result, any improvement in the coin had previously meant an improvement in the Crown's revenues, whereas now it would merely increase the burden of taxation to service the debt. It was absurd 'that an ounce of gold should, under the taxation of a debt of 800 millions, pass for no more than 3l. 17s. 10½d. happen what might'.[160] Lord Folkestone referred to the common argument that returning to cash payments at any lower standard would defraud the creditor, but pointed out that most existing debts and contracts—public and private alike—had been made since 1797 in the depreciated currency of the restriction period. In an echo of the 1696 recoinage debate, which would echo again after the First World War, Folkestone argued that returning to the 'ancient standard' would therefore be a greater injustice than acknowledging the depreciation.

Such warnings were ignored. The resolutions implementing the committees' recommendations were passed without a single dissentient in either House. The only evidence of any kind of opposition to the resumption appeared in a petition 'signed by between 4 and 500 of the most respectable merchants in the city of London' at a meeting which was seriously disrupted by radical supporters of immediate resumption.[161] Unlike the merchants' meeting of 1797, to which

---

[158] Parl. Deb. (series 1), vol. 40, c. 680 (24 May 1819). Peel returned later in the speech to mock the notion of an abstract pound at some length.
[159] Parl. Deb. (series 1), vol. 40, c. 762 (25 May 1819).
[160] Parl. Deb. (series 1), vol. 40, c. 766-7 (25 May 1819).
[161] Lauderdale, Parl. Deb. (series 1), vol. 40, c. 597-600 (21 May 1819). This single petition against implementation of the committees' resolutions should not be confused with some earlier petitions made against resumption taking place before the Bank's notes had been brought to par. The Resumption Committee grilled a number of witnesses to try to prove that these were the result of an organized campaign.

many comparisons were made on this occasion, the meeting appears to have had no counterpart outside London. The gist of the petition was that 'a forced, precipitate, and highly injurious contraction of the circulating medium' could only increase the burden of the public debt and taxation, and cause depression and unemployment in every sector of the economy.

The Bank's resistance to Parliament's assertion of monetary sovereignty ensured that such predictions came true to the fullest possible extent. Forced into a resumption it did not want, the Bank was determined, at the very least, to defy the aspects of the resumption that encroached most directly upon its own commercial prerogatives. It duly set out to defeat the phased return to convertibility and bring about resumption on its own terms by contracting its note issues as quickly as possible.[162] It also quickly withdrew its own low-denomination notes, although the Act did not require it do so.

This sharp contraction of the money supply aggravated the severe post-war depression. Despite the protection afforded by the 1815 Corn Law, falling agricultural prices meant that many farmers who had borrowed depreciated currency to purchase land or to make capital improvements, or who had signed leases at inflated rents, found that they could not earn enough in the revalued currency to meet their commitments. Widespread bankruptcies followed, as well as unemployment, underemployment, and sharp wage reductions. Meetings—mostly but not all peaceful—were held all over the country to protest, and to frame petitions to Parliament. In the twenty-seven months to March 1822, 475 such petitions had been received from all parts of England together with two from Ireland and five from Scotland.[163] The small number from Ireland indicates merely that the effects of the contraction of the currency there were less obvious than the crop failures that produced famine in 1822.[164]

In response to pressure from a handful of MPs, the Commons established a select committee to investigate the causes of the distress and propose remedies. While there could be no disputing the extent or severity of the distress, the bullionists on the committee ensured that the currency issue was heavily downplayed in its final report.[165] The committee thus became one of the battlegrounds where supporters of the gold standard strove to 'subordinate trade policy to the sway of international gold supply'.[166] Following Ricardo—whose argument rested in turn on David Hume's price-specie flow mechanism—the bullionists believed that the free interchange of the currency commodity—gold—was an essential condition for the free interchange of all commodities that would ultimately ensure optimal production and pricing of commodities.[167] As Karl Polanyi argues, free

---

[162] Hilton, *Corn, Cash*, pp. 50-3, 87-91.
[163] Great Britain, Parliament, 'Petitions Complaining of Agricultural Distress'.
[164] Cullen, *Economic History*, p. 104.   [165] Gooch, 'Report', pp. 5-6, 35.
[166] Alborn, *Glittered*, p. 68.   [167] Hume, 'Balance', pp. 137-40.

trade and the gold standard, together with a free market in labour, were the indivisible elements of the self-regulating market system of their utopian vision.[168]

Other than the originators of the committee, very few were willing to attribute the problems to the return to the pre-war gold standard, and fewer were prepared to criticize that decision. Fewer still could countenance reversing it. Edward Ellice, for example, condemned what he saw as the anodyne and futile conclusions of the committee and argued that 'unless the country was prepared to submit to a total revolution of property, it was in vain to expect contracts entered into in a depreciated currency could be fulfilled at the ancient standard, or the same amount of taxation borne on the diminished profits of a reduced capital'. Even so, he accepted reluctantly that 'it was almost impossible to reconsider or retrace our steps'.[169]

The most radical advocate of a revision of the standard was Matthias Attwood, who with his brother Thomas was one of the developing 'Birmingham School' of currency reformers, who were to propose various alternatives to the gold standard for four decades inside and outside Parliament.[170] In the debate on the distress report, Matthias emphasized the radical destructiveness of the resumption, arguing that 'what is called the restoration of the ancient standard of value... has been in truth, and in fact, and in law, the substitution of another standard for the then existing legal standard of value, in which... all the debts, and taxes, and salaries, and leases, and monied contracts of the country had been founded'. He pleaded with the house:

> How much longer shall we, instead of boldly applying ourselves to the nature of these evils and their removal, endeavour to amuse ourselves and the people by a succession of contradictory and contemptible theories—irreconcilable with facts, with experience, or with sound principles, in the vain hope and expectation that time or accident, or the industry or resources of the people, will surmount at length the calamities we have occasioned, and save the legislature the mortification of acknowledging and repairing its errors.[171]

For most MPs, though, there was much more at stake than the mortification of the Parliament, or even future prosperity. Supporting Gooch's motion to establish the committee to investigate the distress petitions, the ultra-Tory Sir Edward Knatchbull was confident that both his constituents and his class would oppose any meddling with the standard, because 'he was persuaded that he might confidently declare on the part of the agriculturists, that they were ready to

---

[168] Polanyi, *Transformation*, pp. 135, 138. See also Ingham, *Capitalism Divided*, pp. 104, 113.
[169] Parl. Deb. (series 2), vol. 6, c. 1440 (3 Apr. 1822); vol. 4, c. 1334 (19 Mar. 1821).
[170] Miller, 'Monomaniacs?'; Moss, 'Banknotes', pp. 20–1; Moss, *Attwood*, pp. 79–83.
[171] Parl. Deb. (series 2), vol. 5, c. 112 (9 Apr. 1821).

make any sacrifices for the preservation of the national honour'.[172] For Lord Londonderry the relationship between national honour and prosperity was not a matter of mere expediency, but of morality. The 'foundation of national honour' was a 'religious respect for public credit... without which no nation can be, or ought to be prosperous'.[173]

These ideas carried all before them. Charles Western's motion to review the standard was defeated 194 to 30.[174] The overwhelming majority of the landed and moneyed men who sat in the Parliament were committed—as the overwhelming majority of their successors of every political persuasion and sectional interest were to remain for more than another century of recurrent crises and structural change—to Peel's and Locke's dogma that a fixed weight of metal remained the only just and meaningful monetary standard and that any alteration was incompatible with the nation's honour.

---

[172] Parl. Deb. (series 2), vol. 5, c. 1143 (7 Mar. 1821).
[173] Parl. Deb. (series 2), vol. 5, c. 361. (15 Feb. 1821).
[174] Parl. Deb. (series 2), vol. 5, c. 896, 1027 (11–12 June 1821).

7

The Limits of Perfection

1825–1914

> The great body of the people have no precise idea of what is meant by the term 'money', nor do they ever reason upon the cause or the nature of its power.
>
> John Bray, *Labour's Wrongs and Labour's Remedy* (1839)

While the resumption of cash payments emphatically reiterated the principles of the 1696 recoinage and cemented in law the *de facto* gold standard established in its wake, the tensions between a commodity standard and proliferating credit money retained instability at the heart of the system. Moreover, although three separate kingdoms had been replaced by a unitary state governed from England, differences in their respective monetary orders persisted. This chapter examines the growth of the intellectual and cultural hegemony of the gold standard through repeated crises, and the concomitant increase in monetary uniformity across England, Ireland, and Scotland in the period between the resumption and the First World War.

Uniformity and Its Discontents: the 1825 Crisis and Its Aftermath

The government's sole concession to the critics of the deflationary effects of the resumption was to extend the period for which country banks might continue to issue small notes from 1823 to 1833. Uncontroversial at the time, this 'partial repeal' of the Resumption Act (as Cobbett called it)[1] was reversed at the next convulsion in the monetary system, which would see not only the reinstatement of the principles of a 'pure' metallic currency in England but an attempt to impose them on the entire United Kingdom.

The financial crisis of 1825 marked the end of a boom that had for the first time included large-scale investment in foreign loans, specifically to South American states. In retrospect it is easy to see many signs of an imminent crash in the course

---

[1] *Cobbett's Political Register*, 29 June 1822, p. 769.

of 1825.[2] But these were aggravated by the House of Commons' declaration that country banks must pay their notes in coin rather than Bank of England notes, as many had continued to do after the resumption. That option had long gone for the individual small notes that made up about half of the country bank circulation, as the corresponding Bank of England notes had already been withdrawn from circulation, but statements by ministers made it clear that banks could make no difficulty or delay about paying their notes of any denomination in gold.[3] This led some banks to contract their issues, aggravating a general contraction of credit, which in turn led to the failure of a number of country banks.[4]

The decisive event came on 13 December, when Pole, Thornton & Co., correspondent to forty-three country banks, collapsed despite being secretly advanced £300,000 by the Bank of England six days earlier.[5] When Pole's correspondents failed, their noteholders and depositors suffered catastrophic losses.[6] Customers of other country banks naturally panicked, creating a run in which many of England's 770 banks temporarily closed their doors and 60 did not survive.[7] The remaining country banks contracted their circulation as quickly as they could, thereby aggravating the slump.

By December 1825 many feared that the entire monetary and financial structure might collapse. On the 17th, according to Harriet Arbuthnot, there was 'no circulating medium, no means of getting money or of paying for any thing'.[8] The week was also characterized by bitter disputes between key ministers and the Bank, and among the government's supporters.[9] Critically, at the insistence of President of the Board of Trade William Huskisson, the government ruled out any suspension of cash payments. For Huskisson, who regarded 1797 as 'a kind of original sin from which we have never recovered',[10] this decision would force the Bank to pay closer attention to the foreign exchanges in future by teaching it that a restriction could not be seen as the 'natural remedy to a drain of specie'.[11] At the same time, the government insisted the Bank lend money on any reasonable security, including property.

With such assistance to the financial sector, cataclysm was averted; but disaster remained, for which culprits had to be found. Publicly, the Bank and the government joined in placing the blame on the country banks, and in particular their issues of low-denomination notes. The government's own analysis was deeply

---

[2] Capie, 'Crises', p. 11.
[3] Parl. Deb. (Series 2), vol. 13, c. 1272–5 (22 June 1825); c. 1382–1400 (27 June 1825).
[4] Pressnell, *Country Banking*, pp. 483–4.
[5] Kynaston, *City*, vol. 1, p. 68; Forster, *Marianne Thornton*, pp. 113–29, reproduces Marianne Thornton's letters to Hannah More as the crisis unfolded.
[6] Feavearyear, *Pound*, pp. 235–8.   [7] Pressnell, *Country Banking*, p. 490.
[8] Arbuthnot, *Journal*, p. 428.
[9] Hilton, *Corn, Cash*, pp. 215–20; Arbuthnot, *Journal*, pp. 426–8.
[10] Huskisson to Herries, 20 Dec. 1829, BL Add. MSS 38758 ff. 64–71.
[11] Huskisson to Abercrombie, 16 May 1826, BL Add. MSS 38748 f. 34.

contradictory. In a long memorandum to the Bank directors (later tabled in Parliament) Liverpool and the Chancellor, Frederick Robinson (later Viscount Goderich), began by claiming that there could be 'no doubt that the Principal Source of [the crisis] is to be found in the rash spirit of speculation... supported, fostered and encouraged by the Country Banks'. The remedy was a 'recurrence to a Gold Circulation' through an immediate ban on the issue of small notes. This would dampen speculation by transmitting the 'pressure' produced by an external drain more strongly to both the Bank of England and the country banks, thus making the operation of the gold standard more automatic by reducing the artificial buffer of paper.[12] Strangely, although banning small notes was so urgent that, rather than wait for legislation, the government summarily directed the Commissioners of the Stamps to stop stamping them, such a ban 'would by no means go to the root of the evil'. In phrases that would be thrown back at them from north of the Tweed a couple of months later, the ministers pointed out that small notes could not be 'the sole, or even the main cause of the evil in England', because Scotland, although it had had small notes continuously in widespread use, had 'escaped all the convulsions which have occurred in the Money Market of England for the last thirty-five years'. Moreover, England had experienced similar convulsions in 1793, when it had no small notes at all.[13]

According to the memorandum, one aspect of Scotland's banking system provided an exemplar for England. Scotland's banks were mostly large, well-capitalized, joint-stock concerns with multiple branches, which had stood firm in the recent crash. The effect of the Bank of England's monopoly on joint-stock banking in England, however, was 'to permit every description of banking except that which is solid and secure'. The nub of the memorandum was to ask the Bank of England to concede this element of its charter and to warn that that there was no prospect that it would be extended when the charter was next due for renewal in 1833. 'Such privileges', the authors warned, 'are out of fashion.'[14] This was part threat, part statement of fact: as free trade doctrines gained ever greater traction, the era of monopolistic charters designed to secure mercantile ends was clearly nearing its end.[15] After an initially churlish reply, the Bank eventually agreed to follow the model of the Bank of Ireland legislation of 1811, which had limited its monopoly on joint-stock banking to an area within 50 miles of its head office in Dublin.[16] In England this *cordon sanitaire* was to be 65 miles from Threadneedle Street.

---

[12] Court of Directors Minutes, 20 Jan. 1826, BE G4/48 f. 202.
[13] Treasury Minute Book, 27 Feb. 1926, TNA, T29/254 f. 21; Court of Directors Minutes, 20 Jan. 1826, BE G4/48 ff. 203–4.
[14] Court of Directors Minutes, 20 Jan. 1826, BE G4/48 ff. 203–14. (Emphasis original.)
[15] Alborn, *Conceiving Companies*, pp. 27–31, 63–70.
[16] Court of Directors Minutes, 26 Jan. 1826, BE G4/48 ff. 221–6.

In England, outside the dwindling ranks of the supporters of a system of inconvertible paper, the government's measures won almost universal acclaim.[17] The Bank's monopoly on joint-stock banking had long been seen as destabilizing, and hostility to small notes in the wake of the crisis was almost universal. But the government's plan to extend the ban to Scotland produced a wildly different response, in what is often presented as the strongest manifestation of Scots nationalist feeling of the nineteenth century.[18] Contrary to some accounts, agitation against the change was well under way before Sir Walter Scott (under the transparent pseudonym of Malachi Malagrowther) published the first of his long letters on the question in the *Edinburgh Weekly Journal* on 22 February. Even in December, before the government had given any indication that it intended to ban small notes in Scotland, newspapers were lecturing their readers on the general inferiority of the English system.[19]

The government was well aware of the kinds of objections their plan would meet well before they announced it. On 18 January, Viscount Melville (then minister with effective responsibility for the political management of Scotland, and a director of Bank of Scotland) wrote to Gilbert Innes, deputy governor of the Royal Bank of Scotland, asking him to sound out other senior Edinburgh bankers on the possibility that Parliament might move to ban small notes. Given that the government would probably soon eliminate a major difference between the two countries by allowing joint-stock banks in England, thus making English banks as solid as Scottish, the onus would be on the Scottish banks to show how the continuation of the one remaining difference between the systems would be in the public interest.[20] Innes's reply—strongly supported by his colleagues—set out the bones of arguments that would develop in the course of the campaign against the ban.[21] There had been virtually no Scottish bank failures since banking began there; the system worked because of the capacity and willingness of Bank of Scotland and the Royal Bank to assist other banks when necessary; the obligation to deal in gold for small sums would make banking less profitable and thus make it impossible for banks to give interest on deposits or to discount small bills. Most importantly, the ban would mean the end of the system of small cash credits, with consequent losses to merchants and manufacturers. For these reasons, 'every description of the public would prefer our present small notes to gold'.[22] As many others were to do, Innes pointed out that the mere existence of joint-stock banking could not in itself be the reason for the stability of Scotland's paper money, as most of Scotland's banks had no more than six partners in any case.

---

[17] A minor exception was the *Yorkshire Post and Leeds Intelligencer*, 25 Feb. 1826 (BNA).
[18] See the discussion in Harvie, *Scotland and Nationalism*, pp. 29–42.
[19] *Scotsman*, 17 Dec. 1825 (BNA).   [20] 18 Jan. 1826, NRS, GD51/5/346/1.
[21] Cadell to Melville, 30 Jan. 1826, NRS, GD51/5/347/2.
[22] Innes to Melville, 30 Jan. 1826, NRS, GD51/5/346/2.

Melville was disappointed that this reply did not provide enough 'arguments exclusively Scotch' that would be required 'to persuade any persons at present that a gold circulation was not preferable to a paper one'.[23] Melville's correspondents shared his thoughts with their colleagues, who undertook to develop the necessary arguments. In the meantime, they urged that the government, 'by abrogating the law and practice of Scotland for above 120 years', would 'spread bankruptcy and ruin' across the country owing to the revoking of cash credits that bankers would be obliged to inflict in order to fund the withdrawal of their notes. The positive economic benefits of these credits had been pointed out by no less an authority than Adam Smith. The practice of paying interest on deposits had been similarly beneficial, as it made the banks 'act almost as savings banks to the poor as well as to the rich'.[24]

Public mobilization to save the small notes began a few days later. *The Caledonian Mercury* editorialized against it on 13 February. Two days later, a meeting of the Society of the Writers to the Signet in Edinburgh passed a series of resolutions denouncing the measure, which they organized to transmit to 'the Convenor of every county and the Chief Magistrate of every Royal Burgh to urge them to stage public protest meetings'.[25] Meetings accordingly took place across the country in the ensuing weeks. In one such meeting in Edinburgh, Gibson Craig—a director of numerous banks, a prominent liberal Whig and former Foxite, who appears to have been the driving force behind the initial meeting of the Writers to the Signet, after extolling the benefits of the Union and his unwavering support for it, argued that to impose the change in the face of the people's 'unanimous' opposition 'merely to assimilate her operations to those of England' would be to treat Scotland 'as a conquered province, deprived of her independence, and obliged to submit to the will of her conqueror'.[26]

Whether or not Craig had read the first of Scott's Malachi Malagrowther letters that day in *The Edinburgh Review*, his speech shared one of its key characteristics. In addition to the economic arguments we have already seen, Craig and Scott each framed the issue in terms of Scotland's national rights. To Scott, the whole episode was an example of a pathological English desire for uniformity, and a growing contempt for Scotland's ancient rights and usages.[27] Scott and Craig were unusual in making these points so explicitly, yet the frequent claims that the issue transcended class, region, and sector imply that it was seen as a national issue. The universal Scottish identity of the pronouns in the following resolution of a

---

[23] Melville to Innes, 3 Feb. 1826, NRS, GD51/5/346/3.
[24] Cadell to Melville, 11 Feb. 1826, NRS, GD51/5/347/4.
[25] *Caledonian Mercury*, 16 Feb. 1826 (BNA).
[26] *Fife Herald, and Kinross, Strathearn and Clackmannan Advertiser*, 2 Mar. 1826 (BNA).
[27] Scott, *Change*, p. 39. For a discussion of Scott's position see Colella, 'Monetary Patriotism'. See also Scott, *Scott and Scotland*, pp. 78–85; Dick, *Romanticism*, pp. 177–81.

meeting of the 'merchants, shipowners, agriculturalists, tradesman and other inhabitants' of Kirkcaldy is crystal clear:

> That we implore the legislature to pause before it deprives us of the benefit of our ancient habits and institutions, under which our wealth and prosperity have increased with a rapidity and to an extent almost unexampled within the last half century; and that our comforts, security, and best interests, may not be wantonly sacrificed to a misapplied principle of uniformity, when it is not pretended that any practical inconvenience has ever at any time arisen out of our system of banking or the nature of our currency, that could be prejudicial to ourselves or to the people of England.[28]

The lack of a single utterance against the Union in the course of the campaign should not be allowed to obscure its national significance. Indeed, the fact that the struggle embraced the Whig Craig and the Conservative Scott, who had nearly duelled over a bitter political dispute only a few years earlier, gives some indication of how powerfully it united Scots.[29] Like Craig, Scott reiterated his support for the Union whatever the outcome of the dispute. Disparaging the tendency of the Irish to violent rebellion, he wrote: 'God forbid Scotland should retrograde towards such a state.... We had better remain in union with England, even at the risk of becoming a subordinate species of Northumberland, as far as national consequence is concerned, than remedy ourselves by even hinting at the possibility of a rupture.'[30] Scott's point, like Craig's, was that the imposition of the ban against Scotland's interests and wishes was contrary to the spirit of a union between equals.

Irish responses to the small notes ban differed from the Scottish campaign in revealing ways. Ireland in 1826 had ten issuing banks, of which three, including the Bank of Ireland, were well-capitalized, effectively run joint-stocks with branch structures, and the remainder either private or small partnerships. In the panic of 1825, only two small Irish banks failed, neither of which issued notes.[31] Irish bankers were accordingly no less hostile to a ban on their small notes than their Scottish counterparts, and put forward practically identical arguments against it. In Ireland, however, the populace at large declined to mobilize, despite the best urgings of *The Dublin Evening Mail*, which pointed to the beneficial effects of small notes for Scotland's economic development, and argued that only the continuation of small notes would allow Ireland to follow a similar path. The alternative was to condemn Ireland to 'at least another century of barbarism'.[32]

The response was discouraging. There were few meetings and fewer petitions. A meeting in Belfast, following a lengthy and somewhat acrimonious debate on

---

[28] *Fife Herald*, 9 Mar. 1826 (BNA).   [29] Macleod, 'Craig'.   [30] Scott, *Change*, p. 17.
[31] Kenny and Turner, 'Wildcat Bankers', p. 55.   [32] *Dublin Evening Mail*, 20 Feb. 1826 (BNA).

the general merits of paper and gold; the probity and public spirit of bankers in general and Belfast bankers in particular; the government's economic policies; and the differences between the monetary needs of the north and south of Ireland could agree only to adjourn, without, as one speaker put it, endeavouring 'to annoy Ministers in their attempt to restore to us the decided advantages of sound and stable currency of metallic and paper money'.[33] By the end of March, *The Dublin Evening Mail* was ready to despair at 'supineness and apathy' in the face of a measure 'calculated to sink this country to the very lowest depths of misery and degradation'. By contrast, Scotland, 'which has arisen as one man against the meditated enactment...—wise, calculating, improving Scotland—will be saved, while grovelling, thoughtless, unfortunate Ireland will be lost'.[34]

In a decade when Irish political life was dominated by sustained mass agitation for Catholic Emancipation, the *Mail*'s suggestion that the Irish people's failure to mobilize was due to apathy about their own interests was laughable. The problem lay elsewhere. On the one hand, Ireland's paper circulation was proportionately much smaller than Scotland's, of much more recent origin, and attended with at least its fair share of stoppages and failures. Of the banks in existence in 1826, the Bank of Ireland was only four decades old, the Provincial was founded in 1825, and the Northern had only become a joint-stock in 1824 after fifteen years as a partnership, and did no business outside Ulster. Moreover, as we have seen, that province had only begun to use paper money at all during the bank restriction. In short, issuing banks had much shallower roots and narrower canopies than their Scottish counterparts.

Moreover, despite *The Dublin Evening Mail*'s protestations that the small notes dispute was 'one in which the members of different creeds...all should unite', it was clear to at least one Dublin merchant that religious difference did play a significant role in the establishment and patronage of Irish banks.[35] Ireland's banks were overwhelmingly owned and led by Anglo-Irish Protestants. The Provincial Bank was an exception only in that its capital was entirely English, its Board of Directors met in London, and most of its senior officers had been sent from England. The vignette on the bank's notes, depicting a garland-headed Hibernia bowed to a taller, helmeted Britannia, provides a representation of how the bank's management saw its role in Ireland, and provides a clue about why the Irish masses failed to identify the Provincial Bank's commercial interests with their own national aspirations. (See Figure 7.1.)

In the face of the Scottish campaign the government retreated by the well-trodden path of a select committee. The committee heard from only bankers and

---

[33] *Belfast Commercial Chronicle*, 15 Mar. 1826 (BNA).
[34] *Dublin Evening Mail*, 29 Mar. 1826, reprinted in *Waterford Mail*, 1 Apr. 1826 (INA).
[35] *Dublin Evening Mail*, 20 Feb. 1826 and 10 Apr. 1826 (BNA); Peel, 'Promissory Notes Report', pp. 83–4.

Figure 7.1 Hibernia shows her subordination to Britannia: Provincial Bank of Ireland note, 1825.
© The Trustees of the British Museum

substantial merchants, which on the one hand avoided any expressions of Scottish national feeling by putting the whole matter purely on a 'business' footing, and on the other ensured that the only Irish witnesses were keen supporters of small notes. The committee's evidence therefore made Irish and Scottish attitudes look much more closely aligned than they actually were.

Despite being led by committed bullionists (Peel and Huskisson), the committee did not grill the witnesses, and its report largely retailed their arguments in favour of the continuation of small notes. In the committee's interesting formulation, there were 'sufficient grounds... for permitting another trial to be made of the compatibility of a Paper Circulation in Scotland with a circulation of Specie in *this* country'.[36] Part of Huskisson's thinking equated the habit of using one-pound notes with alcoholism. It was proving difficult enough to 'reclaim' the English from it, but the Scots had 'indulged more continuously, and in their ruder climate they stood more in need of this paper dram'.[37]

The committee's acquiescence was due to something more than fear of the possible political cost of persisting with the ban. While they were privately and publicly sceptical of the claim that the system of cash credits depended on the availability of small notes, they were nonetheless unwilling to risk any damage to 'a system admirably calculated... to excite and cherish a spirit of useful enterprize,

---

[36] Peel, 'Promissory Notes Report', pp. 11–12. Italics added.
[37] Huskisson to Abercrombie, 16 May 1826, BL Add. MSS 38748 f. 34.

and even to promote the moral habits of the people, by the direct inducements which it holds out to the maintenance of a character for industry, integrity and prudence'.[38] Huskisson—perhaps bitten by the experience of the Bank of England's rush to resumption—feared that the Scottish banks, if thwarted on the small notes, would collude to make their own prophecy true and ensure that the cash credit system would indeed collapse. Believing himself thus forced to choose between the end of the small notes and the survival of the cash credits, he consciously chose the latter, whose 'economical, moral and political' advantages outweighed the 'inconveniences' of the small notes. This was only tolerable, however, because the Scottish banks would now be at least 'incidentally liable' to the control of an English system that had at last been rendered 'sound' by the government's changes.[39]

For the time being, the limits of monetary convergence between England and the rest of the United Kingdom had been reached. The committee was determined, however, to ensure that further convergence would not happen in the wrong direction. This was a particular bugbear of Huskisson's, who believed that excessive discounting by Scottish banks of English bills of exchange that could not find accommodation anywhere else had contributed significantly to the crisis of 1825.[40] He feared that Scottish banks that continued to enjoy the commercial advantage of circulating small notes would rapidly replace the metallic currency in the north of England with their own paper. This was one topic which actually produced searching questions from the committee and a recommendation for legislation to confine the circulation of Scottish notes to Scotland. If an effective law could not be framed, there would be 'no alternative' but to ban small notes in Scotland itself.[41]

The fear that the Scottish system might contaminate England found its most extreme expression in the verse of Thomas Love Peacock, for whom the Scots' campaign against the ban on small notes revealed their fundamental dishonesty and aggressive intentions. Peacock's 'Chorus of Scotch Economists on a Prospect of Scotch Banks in England' argued that the Scots were bent on controlling England by exporting their system of paper money:

> The English we'll saddle—Oho! Oho!
> We'll ride them a-straddle—Oho! Oho!
> They beat us in battle,
> When Money would rattle,
> But now they're our cattle—Oho! Oho!
> In parley metallic—Oho! Oho!

---

[38] Peel, 'Promissory Notes Report', p. 12.
[39] Huskisson to Abercrombie, 16 May 1826, BL Add. MSS 38748 f. 34.
[40] Huskisson, Memorandum, 8 Feb. 1826, BL Add MSS 38755 ff. 229–55.
[41] Peel, 'Promissory Notes Report', p. 12.

> They bothered our Gaelic—Oho! Oho!
> But with sly disputation,
> And rag circulation,
> We've mastered their nation—Oho! Oho![42]

When the government banned Scots and Irish notes in England, Peacock celebrated in 'Chorus of Northumbrians on the Prohibition of Scotch One-Pound Notes in England':

> Vainly you snarl anent
> New Act of Parliament
> Bidding you vanish from dairy and 'laurder';
> Dogs, you have had your day,
> Down tail and slink away;
> You'll pick no more bones this side of the border.[43]

This absurd piece of paranoid chauvinism had no basis in fact. While Scottish notes had circulated in English border regions, the committee was unable to find any evidence that this had been promoted by Scottish banks, nor did it find evidence of any but the most marginal discounting of English bills by Scottish banks. The ban was therefore a very small price to pay for the continuation of small notes in their own country. For Cobbett, however, such professions were mere pretence.[44] He insisted that 'the curse of paper money, that false and fraudulent thing' (which he usually blamed on Jews, Quakers, sinecurists, and Scots in more or less equal measure) 'was introduced by the Scotch: it is the SCOTCH CURSE'. He warned:

> Let all Englishmen bear in mind, that this horrible system is the SCOTCH SYSTEM. The whole of the tribe stand pledged to it; their power, their influence, the very victuals and drink that go down their throats, depend upon the continuance of the Scotch system; that system once blown up, the whole tribe must get out of England.[45]

Uniformity Bungled: the Assimilation of the Irish Coinage

1826 also saw a far less controversial move towards monetary uniformity. The assimilation of the Irish coinage came into effect on 6 January 1826 following

---

[42] Peacock, *Works*, vol. 7, p. 136.
[43] Peacock, *Works*, vol. 7, p. 139. For Peacock's Scotophobia and anti-Semitism, see Grampp, 'Scots, Jews', pp. 545–50.
[44] *Weekly Political Register*, 28 June 1828.   [45] *Weekly Political Register*, 26 Apr. 1828.

legislation that appeared simply to be tidying up unfinished business. Its prime mover, Henry Parnell, had argued as early as 1809 that 'the difference which now exists between the currencies of Great Britain and Ireland contributes to keep alive a feeling of separation and distinction between the inhabitants of these countries, very inconsistent with their mutual prosperity: that it gives a character to the respective parts of the United Kingdom that belongs rather to countries foreign to each other than to members of the same community, a character by no means belonging to the spirit of real union and the true interests of the people'.[46] In particular, a separate coinage maintained the existence of an exchange, which was a significant barrier to trade, thus limiting a major potential benefit of the Union. Parnell's proposal was rejected in 1809 and again in 1821 only because the general state of currency matters and the exchange between the two countries made it untimely.[47] There was no dispute over the principle.

The Master of the Mint, Thomas Wallace, introduced legislation four years after the resumption, by which time the exchange had stabilized. In material terms the assimilation required simply the replacement of the Irish copper coins with the slightly heavier British coins. This should have been a relatively trivial matter—certainly much easier than the British silver recoinage of 1817. The more complicated task was to change the units of account. As Wallace pointed out, the coinage remained a royal prerogative, so it was only the need to revise all existing contracts currently specified in Irish units of account by multiplying them by twelve-thirteenths (converting a debt for thirteen pounds Irish to twelve pounds sterling) that required legislation at all. This, of course, included rents.

Like Parnell, Wallace cited the harmful effects of the current exchange regime on trade as a reason for the change. More importantly, assimilation of the currencies 'would remove a great subsisting distinction, and by doing so tend to draw closer the bonds of union and encourage a diffusion of British capital throughout Ireland', which would increase employment and alleviate 'the distress and poverty which had been the parent of all the crimes and disorders by which Ireland has been so long disgraced and afflicted'. He admitted that the change to the value of the copper coins would be significant to the lower orders but stressed that it could do them 'no real injury'. Problems could arise only from 'the ignorance of one of the parties' to a transaction, but this could be prevented if the change was publicized sufficiently.[48]

Writing in the *Dublin Morning Register* the day before the assimilation, 'A Tradesman' doubted that the transition would be so benign, as businesses of every kind, including landlords, would charge in British pence what they had previously charged in Irish—an increase in real prices of over 8 per cent. The

---

[46] Parl. Deb. (series 1), vol. 14, c. 75 (18 Apr. 1809).
[47] Parl. Deb. (series 2), vol. 8, c. 459–64 (19 Apr. 1821).
[48] Parl. Deb. (series 2), vol. 13, c. 576 (12 May 1825).

newspaper's editorialists disagreed, providing examples of many businesses that had advertised the anticipated adjustments to their prices.[49] 'A Tradesman' was closer to the mark. Within days the newspapers were complaining of frauds 'committed upon the humbler classes', which in their view stemmed largely from mismanagement by the authorities, whose publicity concerning the change had been both too late and hopelessly inadequate.[50] As a result many shopkeepers, residential landlords, and employers either misunderstood the meaning of the change or tried to turn the situation to their advantage, even, in some cases, before the change officially took place.[51] The problems were not confined to petty transactions. Prices on the Dublin Corn Exchange were demanded in sterling 'at nearly the late Irish currency', with the increase in the real price no doubt being reflected in the price of bread.[52] As a result there was significant confusion and hardship, as shopkeepers and others attempted to charge the same prices in the new money as they had in the old, or refused, from 6 January, to give thirteen of the still-circulating Irish pence for an English shilling, as they were required to do.

Such problems were aggravated by the dilatory approach of the British monetary authorities, which failed to arrange an adequate supply of copper coin to replace the Irish coin. This was immediately apparent. The day after the assimilation, *The Dublin Evening Post* complained of the government's failure to furnish a supply of the 'British copper coin' in time.[53] More than a fortnight later, *The Belfast News-Letter* was outraged to learn that only £500 in pennies and farthings had been delivered to the Custom House for exchange: '£500 for the trade of Belfast! *Prodigious!*—a pinch of snuff in a brewing pan...would cut as great a figure as this petty importation of pence and farthings, when compared with the current trade of this town.' To avoid the 'very great perplexities' that must follow from having the two currencies circulating simultaneously, the *News-Letter* advised traders to hold onto the new coins until there was an adequate supply, which it estimated at £7,000–8,000 for the city alone.[54] The paper was not mollified a few days later when the whole of Ulster received that amount, noting that it represented 'something better than three farthings to each inhabitant'.[55] The same consignment included £5,000 for Dublin, prompting *The Freeman's Journal* also to urge that traders not put it into circulation.[56]

By the middle of the year there was 'still not half what would be requisite to carry on the retail trade of the poor', leaving Ireland 'for six months without any standard by which the price of a single commodity can be known with certainty', but creating many opportunities for the unscrupulous to defraud the poor.[57] To solve the problem the British government issued a royal proclamation to raise the

---

[49] *Dublin Morning Register*, 5 Jan. 1826 (BNA).
[50] *Dublin Evening Mail*, 9 Jan. 1826 (BNA).
[51] *Saunders's News-Letter*, 6 Jan. 1826 (BNA); *Freeman's Journal*, 5 Jan. 1826 (INA).
[52] *Dublin Evening Mail*, 6 Jan. 1826 (BNA).
[53] *Dublin Evening Post*, 7 Jan. 1826 (BNA).
[54] *Belfast News-Letter*, 24 Jan. 1826 (INA).
[55] *Belfast News-Letter*, 27 Jan. 1826 (INA).
[56] *Freeman's Journal*, 1 Feb. 1826 (INA).
[57] *Freeman's Journal*, 14 July 1826 (INA).

nominal value of Irish copper coin to parity with English.[58] This came as a complete surprise in Ireland, with some uncertainty about its consequences, and even its meaning. *The Limerick Chronicle*, for example, observed that some people supposed that the British silver shilling had been lessened in value. *The Freeman's Journal* was outraged 'that those who took British shillings a week back, for thirteen pence each must now pay them away for twelve pence'. The paper correctly pointed out the sheer anachronism of this measure: 'We had thought that the practice of raising money above its standard had been altogether abandoned: we were deceived, and are sorry to find that the measure has been resorted to in Ireland.'[59]

Many wage earners, who by now had six months' experience of manipulation of prices that left them worse off, understood the change as a cut in their real wages, which would be precisely its effect if traders were to raise prices on the claim that the shilling had been devalued. They responded by demanding to be paid on the same terms as they were now being charged. A large, peaceful meeting of workers in Phoenix Park resolved unanimously 'to turn out for the payment of their wages in British money', by which they meant payment of the same sum in sterling as they had previously received in Irish money. According to *The Dublin Evening Post*,

> The carelessness, or ignorant bungling, with which the government proceeded on the act of assimilation of the currency, could not have failed to cause the greatest confusion; and that it has produced a positive and serious loss to those least able to bear it, is equally certain, from the ignorance or peculation of the small provisions dealers, and others with whom the poorer classes must deal in copper. We are, therefore, not much surprised that the operatives are seeking to throw the burden off their own shoulders upon their employers.[60]

Employers dug in. On the same day as the Phoenix Park meeting, the master boot and shoemakers resolved to resist their striking workers' demands to be paid in British currency, convinced that 'those men will see their error, and return to their employment, glad that they are not like other poor men, starving for want of it'.[61] The employers' confidence that the workers would be disciplined by the spectre of unemployment was well founded. One effect of the change had been a mild revaluation of the Bank of Ireland's notes to bring them to parity with those of the Bank of England. Its steps to achieve this had been generally deflationary, with the usual negative consequences for employment.[62] By the time of the meetings in July, however, that was the least of the Irish economy's troubles, for in common

---

[58] By the King, *A Proclamation*, 12 July 1826, TNA MINT 12/12.
[59] *Freeman's Journal*, 24 July 1826 (INA).
[60] *Dublin Evening Post*, 25 July 1826 (BNA).
[61] *Dublin Evening Post*, 25 July 1826 (BNA).
[62] Cullen, *Economic History*, p. 107.

with the rest of the United Kingdom the country was in the grip of the economic depression triggered by the 1825 crisis.

Orthodoxy and Heterodoxy: the Unequal Struggle over Gold

While the crisis of 1825–6 reaffirmed Scots' commitment to paper money of all denominations, it had the opposite effect in England. The English elite's suspicion of paper money and corresponding commitment to a metallic currency now extended to all social strata. What decades of polemics against banknotes (and particularly low-denomination banknotes) by elite theorists and 'plebeian' radicals like Cobbett could not achieve, was wrought in a few weeks by the failure of scores of country banks and the disasters it brought to those unfortunate enough to hold their notes.

One of the ideological successes of bullionism has been to conflate the historical differences between the hostility to convertible paper money of the mass of the English population following 1825 with their apathy about inconvertible paper in 1797 and their general preference for paper during the bank restriction period. This is not to argue that popular attitudes to money were not informed by ideas, as opposed to stolid reaction to the direct experience of financial loss. Rather, it suggests that the common people's reception of ideas about money was framed by their own practical understanding of it. To borrow from E. P. Thompson's ways of thinking about popular political and social belief in this period, people responded to ideas that made sense of their experience, which ideas in turn helped to shape their reading of that experience.[63] From this perspective it becomes possible to understand English working-class hostility to paper money as the overdetermined result of bank failures, the polemics of Cobbett and other popular radicals—especially as these were transmitted through the leadership of working-class movements—and the strikingly similar opinions of elite monetary theorists and politicians like King, Ricardo, and Peel, echoed in almost the whole of the 'respectable' press.

Neither the suppression of the element of 'Scotch Banking' of which the bullionists disapproved (small notes) nor the adoption of the element they believed to constitute its great strength (joint-stock banking) did much to stabilize the English banking system. As Scots writers tried to show during the controversy of 1826, it was not the mere fact of joint-stock banking but the frequent exchange of notes between the banks and the settlement of outstanding balances by means of drafts on London that was crucial to the relative stability of the system. For English bullionists, this last point merely demonstrated the ultimate dependence

---

[63] Thompson, *Poverty*, pp. 199–201.

of the Scottish system on the English gold standard, which from their point of view was the only thing that could make its continuation tolerable.[64]

The removal of small notes from circulation in England obviously restricted the use of paper money to higher social strata. Given that banknotes were in fewer hands, this possibly did help to prevent local bank failures and stoppages of payment from becoming systemic crises, as the government hoped. It also limited their total note issues. But neither the ban on small notes nor the introduction of joint-stock banking reduced the average numbers of failures in any given decade. English joint-stock banking soon became a mania of its own. After a fairly slow start following the legislation of 1826, more than 110 new banks had been founded only a decade later—more than half of them in 1839 alone.[65] Many of these were run by people with little knowledge of banking and few scruples about how they might seize the opportunity to make large amounts of money by the business of making money. Between 1839 and 1843 alone no fewer than eighty-two of these went bankrupt, including twenty-nine banks of issue.

While these local failures did not threaten to topple the whole system like the London-originated crisis of 1825, they still exacted a high toll on those who held deposits, notes, or shares. Some of the directions this could take were captured in fictionalized form in Elizabeth Gaskell's *Cranford* when the failure of the 'Town and County Bank'—set in the late 1830s—brought heartbreak to the hard-working tradesman who had put his savings in the bank to surprise his wife and children with Christmas gifts, only to find that he could not spend the note he had withdrawn for the purpose. It also brought ruin to the ageing, unworldly Miss Matty Jenkins, whose tiny fortune was invested entirely in its shares.[66]

Following the crisis of 1825–6, the number of commentators who placed blame for any of the United Kingdom's monetary disorders on a metallic currency itself, rather than on deviations from it, became vanishingly small. As Fetter has observed, 'among economists from the 1820s on, the gold standard was a matter of economic theology rather than economic analysis'.[67] Fetter explained this departure from the political economists' general commitment to rationalism in terms of their distrust of the Bank of England arising from the bank restriction, their hostility to any monetary arrangement that allowed 'discretion' in the issue of money, and their disbelief that the price level had any effect on the level of real economic activity, which prevented them from considering possible negative consequences of the downward pressure on prices that followed from tethering the money supply to a finite resource.

The first of these concerns might well have been met simply by placing the Bank under closer government supervision and public scrutiny, as the 1844 Bank

---

[64] Huskisson to Abercrombie, 16 May 1826, BL Add. MSS 38748 f. 34.
[65] Fetter, *Orthodoxy*, p. 165; Alborn, 'Moral'; Alborn, *Conceiving Companies*, pp. 99–115.
[66] Gaskell, *Cranford*, ch. 13.   [67] Fetter, *Orthodoxy*, p. 142.

Charter Act would later do. The others were more directly linked with a commitment to gold. The economists' disregard of domestic prices arose from the fact that their attention was focussed strongly on foreign exchange—the same place as the attention of the victors in the 1696 recoinage debate. As in 1696, that focus demanded a commitment to an unchanging metallic standard. This commitment enabled strict control of the creation of money to be reconciled to the political economists' more general commitment to the principles of laissez-faire by making it 'automatic'.[68]

The respectable monetary discourse of the 1830s and beyond was thus conducted almost entirely within the paradigm of a fixed metallic standard, and revolved largely around how to make that as secure and effective as possible. Even the decision in 1833 to make Bank of England notes legal tender in England—although on the face of it inimical to a metallic standard and therefore opposed by some bullionists—was seen by many of its supporters as a way to protect the metallic standard from runs on the Bank.[69] This concern had gained additional salience the previous year, when supporters of the Great Reform Act had plastered London with posters reading 'To Stop the Duke Go For Gold' in an attempt to engineer a run on the Bank of England that would deter the king from appointing an anti-reform government under the Duke of Wellington.[70] Although the number of people who responded directly to this appeal (as opposed to those who cashed their notes out of fear) remains unclear, Wellington was not appointed and there is little doubt that the tactic helped the cause of reform.[71] This revealed a monetary vulnerability in the political order that strengthened support for making the notes legal tender.[72]

The other main themes of the debates around money and banking between 1826 and the passage of Peel's Banking Acts of 1844 and 1845 were: on what basis should the currency be expanded and contracted (or, to put it another way, when and how should money be created and destroyed)? Should private enterprise be allowed to create money, and if so, on what terms and to what extent? Finally, what was and was not money, and what activities constituted its creation?

One striking feature of these debates is that, apart from Cobbett's relentless drumbeat of hostility to paper money in all its forms, which ended only with his death in 1835, they were conducted overwhelmingly among the elite. The monetary broadsides and shorter pamphlets of the 1690s that appeared alongside the works of writers like Locke and Lowndes, or during the bank restriction period, are far less conspicuous in these later debates. The difference, as Mary Poovey argues, is largely due to the emergence of political economy as a coherent and

---

[68] Knafo, *Modern Finance*, pp. 128–9. [69] Fetter, *Orthodoxy*, p. 159.
[70] 'Papers: 1832 (2 of 3)', in Rowe, *London Radicalism*, pp. 86–101.
[71] Brock, *Reform Act*, pp. 297–9; Flick, 'Attwood', pp. 364–5. [72] Fetter, *Orthodoxy*, pp. 135–6.

increasingly specialized system of thought. It was during this period that 'establishment writers were refining the definition of what counted as authoritative financial—or economic—writing'. For this reason, she argues, Cobbett's ideas were ultimately uninfluential: by the middle of the century a canon had been defined in which he could hold no place.[73] This is persuasive insofar as it refers to 'respectable' opinion on financial or monetary questions. But beyond that sphere Cobbett's writings had an enduring major influence on radical and working-class movements, which would severely limit their capacity to generate or entertain critiques of the monetary system that did not start from the premise that all non-metallic currency was simply a fraud.

Such critiques were available. We have already encountered the Birmingham School. Thomas Attwood, its leading light, usually advocated a system of managed, inconvertible paper money, although he and his colleagues variously advocated a silver standard or a standard that could vary with the market price of gold.[74] Thomas was first spurred to action by the deflation immediately attendant on the peace, which, as he explained to the Committee on Distress, bore especially heavily on Birmingham's large munitions industries.[75] While he echoed the comments of other critics (and the anti-Semitism of many) concerning the injustice done to debtors by the deflation of the currency and the corresponding increase in the burden of the national debt, his main focus was on the reduced purchasing power resulting from a contraction of the money supply, which he believed reduced the level of economic activity and hence of employment.[76] A century before Keynes, the Attwoods would argue that the purpose of monetary policy should be price stability, 'the full employment of labour' and 'the full development of productive power'.[77] On these grounds Thomas argued—in marked contrast to bullionists and almost everybody else—that wartime inflation had been beneficial.[78]

Other notable heresies originated with Robert Owen and John Taylor, who each advocated a circulating medium with no intrinsic value. Beyond that, however, they had little common ground. Owen's writings on money were brief and sketchy. They centred on 'a paper representative of the value of labour'.[79] This was a system of 'labour notes' issued to workers in exchange for the labour time required to produce commodities they deposited in a central store, which could in turn be purchased with the notes. An attempt by the Cooperative Movement to establish a version of such a system in the 1830s enjoyed some initial success, but

---

[73] Poovey, *Genres*, p. 195.
[74] Moss, 'Banknotes'; Henry Miller, 'Monomaniacs?', pp. 360, 365–6; Fetter, *Attwood Writings*, p. xviii.
[75] Gooch, *Report*, p. 261.   [76] Attwood, *Scotch Banker*, pp. 23–5, 56; Attwood, *Letter*, p. 9.
[77] Attwood, *Letter*, p. 12. See Fetter, *Attwood Writings*, xiv; Miller, 'Monomaniacs?', p. 359.
[78] Attwood, *Scotch Banker*, pp. 23–5, 56.   [79] Owen, *Lanark*, p. 52.

foundered fairly quickly on the rocks of fraud, competing schemes of local note issues, and the notes' inability to circulate outside a narrow circle.[80]

Owenite ideas were developed further by John Bray, for whom money creation and lending by banks originated in the exploitation of labour and was a mainspring of power 'sufficient, in defiance alike of trades' combinations and political changes, to keep the working class the slaves of the capitalists until doomsday'.[81] For Bray, neither paper nor precious metals possessed any value other than that conferred by 'conventional usage'. The scarcity of money created by the existing gold-based system was responsible for most existing inequality. Instead, money 'should be in sufficient quantity to represent the whole of the nation's fixed capital'.[82] Versions of the notion that money should be created in proportion to some factor in the real economy (rather than simply on the basis of labour time) were central to subsequent monetary thinking in the Owenite tradition, including that of the Chartist leader Bronterre O'Brien, whose monetary heresies were prominent among the reasons for his ultimate marginalization in the movement.[83] Equally important was the idea that nothing worthwhile could arise from changes to the monetary system alone. Important as money was as a tool of exploitation, it could be 'broken asunder only by a power which at the same time overthrows the present system'.[84] This revolutionary viewpoint put Bray in marked contrast with almost all monetary reformers then and since, including his contemporary John Taylor.

Like the Attwoods, Taylor was spurred to think about currency by the resumption of cash payments. He identified three kinds of money: real money, by which he meant anything that could be exchanged, including capital, labour, and commodities; symbolic money, by which he meant any form of token of exchange including paper; and coin, which, as the precious metals are commodities, combined the characteristics of real and symbolic money. Coins had originated in the state's need to levy taxes and make payments, superseding payments in kind for that purpose. Their value therefore derived from their stamp rather than the market value of their bullion.[85] Coin, however, has two inherent disadvantages: its supply is inelastic, making it unable to expand with the economy, and in times of panic it cannot represent the total of existing 'real money'.[86] Symbolic money suffered from neither of these disadvantages and was therefore the 'perfect' form of money.

On the basis of this theoretical viewpoint, Taylor evolved two remedies for the United Kingdom's monetary and financial problems. First, gold and silver should be treated like all other commodities whose prices change according to supply and

---

[80] Poovey, *Genres*, p. 211.
[81] Bray, *Labour's Wrongs*, p. 150. See the discussion of Bray in Poovey, *Genres*, pp. 206–9.
[82] Bray, *Labour's Wrongs*, pp. 142–3.   [83] Turner, *O'Brien*, ch. 4.
[84] Bray, *Labour's Wrongs*, p. 154.   [85] Taylor, *Essay*, p. 3.   [86] Taylor, *Essay*, p. 111.

demand. Acknowledging that precious metals were necessary for settling balances in foreign trade, Taylor argued that the Bank of England should keep a reserve of gold to buy and sell at the prevailing market price expressed in terms of units of account. Payments would be made in legal tender exchequer notes issued in denominations as low as one pound. These notes would be issued annually by the government to an amount equal to the anticipated revenue for the year and would be cancelled as soon as received as taxes. This was crucial to the whole scheme. It would prevent the irresponsible overissue of paper which he believed had ruined the *assignats*, while at the same time ensuring there were sufficient funds in the community to allow taxes to be paid.[87] Any shortfall in the quantity of notes for day-to-day transactions could be filled by banks, including the Bank of England, issuing their own non-legal tender paper money exchangeable for gold at the market price.

Unlike the Birmingham reformers, Taylor did not advocate inconvertibility. Rather, he argued that notes should be convertible at the current market price of gold. Unlike the Birmingham School, he also believed that only the state should issue legal tender money, although private banks, subject to some prudential regulation, should be free to issue whatever paper credit people were willing to accept.[88]

Notwithstanding their obvious diversity, these non-metallist approaches to money were all doubly marginalized: ignored or ridiculed by middle-class and aristocratic political economists and execrated by almost all plebeian radicals. Deprived of the discipline of meaningful contention with rival views, too small to develop thorough internal debate, and rarely if ever exposed to the searching test of practical application, such approaches—whatever their initial insights or potential value—never developed into viable traditions, but repeatedly degenerated into utopianism or crankery.[89]

English popular radicals' deep-rooted hostility to paper money was demonstrated emphatically by Thomas Attwood's political destruction in 1839.[90] Attwood by then was closely allied with the Chartist movement, having formed the unfounded view that enfranchisement of the working class was the key to achieving currency reform.[91] This belief had led to his leadership of the Birmingham Political Union of the Lower and Middle Classes of the People, and his effective championship of the 1832 Reform Act, which had helped attract support for his monetary ideas from working-class reformers in his home town. His tragedy was his failure to understand that he had risen to national

---

[87] Taylor, *Essay*, pp. 111–12. [88] *Douglas Jerrold's Weekly Newspaper*, 2 Jan. 1847 (BNA).
[89] Fetter, *Orthodoxy*, pp. 235–6, makes similar points about the post-1844 period.
[90] Fetter, *Orthodoxy*, p. 164, suggests that the Birmingham School's ideas had lost all traction outside Birmingham by 1837.
[91] Moss, *Attwood*, p. 14 and ch. 11.

leadership—first of bourgeois and then of proletarian movements—despite his ideas about currency rather than because of them.

In 1839 it fell to Attwood to introduce the Chartist Great Petition in the House of Commons. Inevitably, he raised the currency question. He asked:

> But what did the working classes say?... they said the house gave them the Corn Laws to make scarce the corn; they gave them the money laws to make scarce the money.... The petitioners said the house had the power to repeal the Corn Law; it had the power to repeal the poor law; it had the power to repeal the money law![92]

The Chancellor, Lord John Russell, gleefully seized the opportunity to enlighten Attwood on the real state of working-class opinion by reading out a declaration by the Chartist leadership that asserted that 'amongst the number of measures by which you have been enslaved, there is not one more oppressive than the corrupting influence of paper money' which defrauded industry, was the great support of despotism and depression, and was 'sapping the moral foundations of the nation'.[93] To reinforce the point, the next issue of the Chartists' *Northern Star* condemned not only Attwood's theories but Attwood himself for raising them in the context of his speech on the petition.[94] The episode marked the end of Attwood's illusions, and of his political career.[95]

The only surprising aspect of this episode is Attwood's surprise. The Chartist press makes it perfectly clear that by 1839 the organized working class was overwhelmingly committed to monetary views derived from Cobbett's version of the ideas which had prevailed in the bullion debate and were promoted not only in Cobbett's own writings but also in many of the journals of popular radicalism under his influence or that of his supporters. Among these were *The Yellow Dwarf*, and *The Gorgon*, which was partly funded by Jeremy Bentham and the veteran radical campaigner Sir Francis Burdett, who had strongly supported King in the debate over Stanhope's Act in 1811.[96]

Attwood believed that the similarity between Cobbett's views and those of the elite bullionists was due largely to Cobbett's own efforts: 'the Bank of England note might still have retained its moral power for a long period, if the doctrines of Mr Cobbett had not been adopted in the heart of the government and if such influential statesman as Lord Goderich and Grenville had not been so far infatuated as to lend themselves to *his* views, and in open parliament to stigmatise paper money as *"worthless rags!"*'.[97] Attwood was wrong about causation: as we have seen, the proponents of bullionism had arrived at their conclusions quite

---

[92] Parl. Deb. (series 3), vol. 39, c. 242 (12 July 1839).
[93] Parl. Deb. (series 3), vol. 39, c. 242 (12 July 1839).   [94] *Northern Star*, 20 July 1839 (BLN).
[95] Moss, *Attwood*, p. 287.   [96] Parl. Deb. (series 1), vol. 20, c. 903–5 (9 July 1811).
[97] Attwood, *Scotch Banker*, p. 56.

independently of Cobbett, and on the basis of different reasoning. But Attwood's insistence on the similarity of their views goes a long way to accounting for the completeness of his own marginalization. It also goes a long way to accounting for the quiescence of plebeian movements and writers on monetary questions during and after the passage of Peel's banking legislation of 1844 and 1845 and the numerous monetary and financial crises that followed.

No Failure Like Success: the Banking Acts of 1844 and 1845

The Bank Charter Act of 1844 and the Acts of the following year that extended its principles to Ireland and Scotland attempted to resolve debates that had been running since early in the bank restriction period on the basis of the principles of 1696. Introducing the Act, Peel began as he had in 1819, with quotations from Locke and other authorities, to prove yet again that a pound could 'mean nothing else' but 'a certain definite quantity of gold with a mark upon it to determine its weight and fineness'.[98]

The central aim of the Act was to achieve finally what the Resumption Act and the legislation of 1826 had attempted, which was to 'ensure the uniform equivalency of Bank notes to coin'. Its first set of provisions related to the Bank of England's issue of paper money. Central to it—and underpinning the Act in its entirety—was the separation of the Bank of England into a banking department and an issue department. This created a distinction between private and public that secured the government's right to legislate on the issue and thus reclaim the sovereign prerogative ceded to the Bank at its foundation. As Peel explained, 'We think that the privilege of issue is one which may be fairly and justly controlled by the state and that the banking business, as distinguished from issue is a matter in respect to which there cannot be too unlimited and restricted a competition.'[99] Claiming that historical experience had taught that unregulated issue led bankers to behave against the public interest in the pursuit of profit, he also argued that the benefit of free competition in the production of any item was that it ensured an abundant, cheap supply, which, in money's unique case, was highly undesirable. Against these arguments was the fear that governments entrusted with issue would inevitably give in to the pressure to 'relax the screw' in times of economic depression and produce paper that was not truly representative of coin.[100] But if neither private enterprise nor the state could be trusted to maintain monetary purity, who should be? The answer the Act purported to provide was, in effect, 'nobody'.

---

[98] Parl. Deb. (series 3), vol. 74, c. 723 (6 May 1844).
[99] Parl. Deb. (series 3), vol. 74, c. 743 (6 May 1844).
[100] Ripon, Parl. Deb. (series 3), vol. 76, c. 705 (12 July 1844).

The provisions designed to achieve this, and thus to reconcile laissez-faire principles with regulation of a crucial economic function, constituted the centrepiece of the Act. It required the Bank to hold a fixed amount of fourteen million pounds' worth of government securities on which it could issue banknotes. All additional issues would be backed entirely by the Bank's holding of bullion. This approach largely reflected the Bank's current practice, which in turn was underpinned by David Hume's 1752 argument concerning the specie flow mechanism.[101] On the basis of a rule first set out by the Bank's governor, J. Horsley Palmer, in 1832, the Bank aimed to hold a constant fourteen million pounds of securities and, at any moment that the foreign exchanges were 'full' and poised to turn against the United Kingdom, to hold half that amount of bullion as the basis of a total circulation of twenty-one million pounds. As soon as the exchanges turned and merchants came to exchange their notes for gold for export, the Bank would restrict its discounting of bills to ensure that the volume of paper in circulation did not increase. Thus the amount of the Bank's money in circulation would respond 'automatically' to changes in the foreign exchange, slowing the economy and the volume of imports until the exchanges returned to equilibrium.[102] This would ensure the stability of the standard. The Act made the Palmer rule law, thereby simultaneously ensuring the primacy of foreign exchange in determining the supply of money, while supposedly removing discretion altogether from the operation of monetary policy—the twin priorities of English politicians and many monetary theorists since the Restoration.

Foreign exchange was as central to the 1844 Act as it had been to the resumption and the 1696 recoinage. The minor concession made to advocates of bimetallism registered this priority clearly. Although insisting that there could only be one standard, the Act permitted the Bank to hold up to one-fifth of the bullion backing for its notes in silver. Peel's justification was that silver remained the standard in other countries, and thus merchants' calls on the bank for bullion could often be more conveniently met by silver than by gold.

The Act was both an acknowledgement of and an attempt to regulate the sharp deviation from the principles of commodity money that took place at the Bank's foundation, when it began to issue paper money on the basis of its holdings of government debt, rather than of bullion. This change in both the nature of money and the distribution of monetary power had reached its zenith during the restriction, and was powerfully demonstrated by the way the restriction ended. It could not be completely reversed except by the withdrawal of close to half the circulating currency of England—a contraction beyond even Peel's contemplation. Instead, the Palmer rule accepted this £14 m as the base level of England's circulation,

---

[101] Hume, 'Balance', pp. 137–40.   [102] Horsefield, 'Origins', p. 183.

and used the bullion-backed holdings to create the simulacrum of an entirely metallic system.

The remaining provisions were designed to ensure that other banks of issue were as subject to the new system, and hence to the foreign exchanges, as the Bank of England itself. Ideally, Peel would have banned private banknotes outright and replaced them with those of the Bank of England. While his widely accepted argument that issuing money was a sovereign prerogative would have provided sufficient justification, he concluded that it was necessary 'to deal considerately with private interests'.[103] Instead, he froze the private banks' issues at their existing levels, banned the establishment of new banks of issue, and mandated that existing rights would lapse permanently as soon as they stopped being exercised for any reason. The aim, achieved in 1921, was gradually to extinguish all note issue in England other than the Bank of England's.

What the Act did not do was as consequential as what it did. While it closely regulated the issue of banknotes, it made no attempt to regulate other forms of credit. Bank lending in the form of deposit creation, and the circulation of cheques and other financial instruments to transfer that credit from hand to hand, did not, in Peel's view, constitute the creation of money. It thus fell entirely into the realm of banking activity, where no such regulation could be justified. While any attempt to regulate credit creation and circulation on the same narrow, self-acting basis on which the Act regulated note issue was almost certainly impossible, Peel's approach ensured that what were soon to become the most economically and financially significant activities of banking—and the most destabilizing forms of increased liquidity—developed largely beyond reach of the state. Exponents of the so-called 'banking school' of theorists criticized the Act on these grounds, leading to increasingly arcane debates in the pages of the political economy journals among writers who all, it is important to note, saw themselves as 'uncompromising defenders of the gold standard'.[104]

The only provision of the Act to apply to Scotland and Ireland was the ban on new banks of issue. This was a cause of some complaint in the newspapers, although the Scottish banks, now protected from additional competition, had little to say about it. But Peel's statement that he intended to legislate specifically for those countries after 'the fullest consideration' roused Scots to action. As early as 14 June, the *Dundee, Perth and Cupar Advertiser* was predicting that Peel's principles guaranteed the 'entire annihilation' of Scotland's small notes. In December, a long article appeared in *Blackwood's Edinburgh Magazine*, rehearsing the events and arguments of 1826, and urging Scots to 'COMPROMISE NOTHING' in their opposition to any change.[105] By the end of the year a campaign of meetings and petitions on the 1826 model was under way. While many of these passed

---

[103] Parl. Deb. (series 3), vol. 74, c. 740 (6 May 1844). [104] Fetter, *Orthodoxy*, p. 192.
[105] 'The Scottish Banking System', *Blackwood's Edinburgh Magazine*, vol. 56, no. 345, p. 686.

resolutions against 'any interference' with Scotland's banking system on the grounds that it could not be improved, the burning issue was the potential loss of the small notes and the consequent loss of the cash credits system. The widespread belief that Peel 'has got a pet notion that the money circulation of Scotland must be assimilated to that of England' gave the campaign its bite. As a Mr Cadell put it at the Edinburgh Merchant Company meeting, 'If Sir Robert will let alone the one pound notes, he may do anything else he likes, provided always that he gives us equal security for our circulation.'[106]

In the absence of any definite threat to the small notes, the campaign never reached the pitch of 1826, to the evident disappointment of some writers and speakers.[107] A meeting of the county of Edinburgh—a body of the elite—highlighted the lack of unanimity when an amendment to take no action until Peel's intentions were clear was only defeated on the casting vote of the chair. The key supporters of the amendment, Lords Melville and Dunfermline, were to incur the wrath of the campaign's supporters. Melville, Governor of Bank of Scotland, who had had a long career as a Tory politician, was accused of putting party above nation, while Dunfermline stood condemned as a staunch bullionist and supporter of the Bank resumption, which for many in Scotland, as in some English agricultural districts, had become a byword for the disastrous application of bullionist theory.[108] Most meetings, however, were much closer to unanimity in supporting action of some kind.

The campaign began to fizzle out in March, as it emerged in the course of Peel's consultations with Scottish bankers that he did not intend to touch the small notes. The London correspondent of *The Inverness Courier* expressed the mood when Peel announced this publicly: 'Your well-beloved banks will not be swamped. Your well-thumbed one-pounders will still flutter from pocket to pocket. Even Malachi Malagrowther would hardly grumble at the premier.'[109] Late in their negotiations with Peel, the bankers had attempted to dig their heels in on the principle that any change to the Scottish system must be for the worse. Some papers persisted in this line after Peel had introduced the Acts, but really the campaign was over.

Although there was absolutely no campaign on the issue in Ireland, Peel treated Ireland and Scotland almost identically as he took significant steps towards bringing both countries' monetary systems into alignment with England's metallic system, even offering the banks an incentive—not available to English and Welsh banks—to rest the issue of their notes more firmly on a metallic basis. Unlike English banks, whose circulation was now frozen permanently at the 1844 level, the banks of Scotland and Ireland would be allowed to increase their circulation

---

[106] *Dundee, Perth, and Cupar Advertiser*, 29 Nov. 1844 (BNA).
[107] *Elgin Courant, and Morayshire Advertiser* 22 Nov. 1844 (BNA); Miller, *Warning*, pp. 9–11.
[108] Miller, *Warning*, p. 42.   [109] *Inverness Courier*, 30 Apr. 1845 (BNA).

provided that any additional amount over the 1845 level was backed pound for pound by holdings of gold. Although deposit banking rather than note issue was becoming the more important part of banking business, Scottish and, to a smaller extent, Irish banks took advantage of this provision to increase their circulation, with the corollary that an increasing proportion of their notes rested on a bullion basis.[110]

This was the last legislative act before the First World War to reduce Scottish and Irish difference from England. The only further attempt was a bill introduced in 1864 by Sir John Hay, a Scottish member with apparently no interest and little knowledge of banking, to make Bank of England notes legal tender in Scotland and to establish branches of the Bank in Glasgow and Edinburgh.[111] His stated aims were to remove the demand for bullion in Scotland in times of panic, and to counter the 'monopoly' of the shrinking number of Scottish banks. Objections to the bill immediately went to fears that it signalled an English attempt to assimilate the two countries' systems on the basis of the Act of 1844, and that the small notes were therefore again in danger. Hay's extolling of 'the benefits of a uniform currency' was hardly calculated to ease Scots' fears. The bill was withdrawn at its second reading in June after Scottish members raised objections. In the course of this short-lived controversy, old grievances inevitably resurfaced, including the ban on new banks of issue in the 1844 Act.[112]

The 1844 Act did not prevent recurring financial crises of varying degrees of severity over the next half-century. Even worse, as some critics had foretold, it made it harder for the Bank of England to manage them—at least at first. Only three years after the Act, a crisis originating in excessive speculation in railway shares and corn bills could only be contained by the government 'suspending' the provisions of the Act that limited the fiduciary issue.[113] As the crisis had deepened, the Bank had refused to allow the banking department to provide extra credit for fear that it would produce demand for additional notes or gold from the issue department, which the Bank might not be able to meet under the terms of the Act. Instead, the directors waited in vain for the automatic reflux of gold envisaged in the Act to do its work, only seeking the suspension when it was almost too late.[114]

This and subsequent crises in 1857 and 1866 disabused most observers of any notion that Peel's system would run automatically, or that the banking department could behave like a normal bank, competing in the market with others. In these crises the Bank was much quicker to ask for a suspension. This recognized the fundamental problem: the hallmark of a serious crisis was a rush to obtain

---

[110] Checkland, *Scottish Banking*, pp. 384–5; Capie and Webber, *Monetary History*, 1, pp. 327, Table III (1).
[111] Parl. Deb. (series 3), vol. 176, c. 109–11 (22 June 1864).
[112] *Dundee Courier*, 28 May 1864 (BNA). Parl. Deb. (series 3), vol. 176, c. 111–26 (22 June 1864).
[113] Clapham, *Bank*, 2, pp. 208–10.
[114] Feavearyear, *Pound*, pp. 282–4. Capie, 'Crises', p. 12; Kynaston, *City*, vol. 2, pp. 151–64.

'high-powered money'—gold coins or Bank of England notes—as even normally impeccable forms of credit became suspect or unavailable.[115] But the Act had deliberately tied the Bank's hands to make this money scarce, meaning that it would not be able to fulfil its role of lender of last resort. It would literally run out of money, not merely ruining the money market but threatening the entire system of payments.

In the wake of the 1866 crisis, triggered by the shock failure of Overend, Gurney and Co., the largest discount house in the world, much of the accumulated understanding of crisis management was systematized by the editor of *The Economist*, Walter Bagehot, in *Lombard Street: a Description of the Money Market* (1873). Bagehot argued that the crisis showed the system working largely as it should despite the 'folly' of Overend, Gurney and the Bank's failure to properly understand its responsibilities.[116] The Bank was the holder of the nation's banking reserve, and, as it should, had used a range of tools, including very high interest rates, to ensure that its reserve was used to best effect to contain the economic consequences. But the system would work better if the Bank understood and acknowledged its responsibility to support the money market in difficult times. This would reduce panic by creating certainty that credit would always be extended—at a price—to any solvent business.[117]

The Golden Age

The Overend, Gurney crisis was the last time before the First World War that the Bank sought a suspension of the Act. The Bank had absorbed the lessons of each crisis and near crisis, realizing that it had to use the enormous market power of the banking department almost continuously to pilot the money market away from the rocks.[118] The tools the Bank used, including very frequent adjustments to its rates of interest and restriction of the quantity or type of securities it would lend on, came at significant cost to the economy far beyond the City of London, including slumps in demand that brought waves of bankruptcies and increased unemployment.[119] Despite the misery and uncertainty this created, there was very little critique of the fundamentals of the system. While each crisis inspired the foundation of organizations dedicated to some kind of radical monetary reform,

---

[115] Capie, 'Crises', pp. 1–2.   [116] Bagehot, *Lombard Street*, p. 273.
[117] Bagehot, *Lombard Street*, ch. 8.
[118] Capie, 'Crises', p. 11; Feavearyear, *Pound*, pp. 287–305, 322–30, 334–6, outlines the Bank's experimental and often reluctant steps towards more effective control. See also Knafo, *Modern Finance*, pp. 152–64, for a useful challenge to conventional interpretations of the Bank's role in this period.
[119] Ford, 'International Financial Policy', pp. 219–26. For a graphical representation of the frequent, sometimes wild, fluctuations of interest rates in the decades following the act, see Dimsdale and Hotson, 'Crises', p. 28, Fig. 3.1.

these attracted miniscule support, and were generally ignored by orthodox academics and financial journalists.[120]

Between 1844 and the bimetallist agitation of the late 1880s, the nearest thing to an exception came in the wake of the crisis of 1847—before the passage of the Act had faded into historical memory. That crisis saw a brief rekindling of activity by the Birmingham School and the establishment of various (apparently unrelated) Currency Reform Associations in Liverpool, Manchester, and Glasgow. It also produced the London-based Anti-Gold-Law League, devoted to the propagation of ideas derived from John Taylor. Although the League generated enough publicity to attract refutation from *The Economist* and repeated mockery in *The Times*, its public meetings dwindled steadily until it folded in 1849.[121] Its successor, the National Currency Reform Association (unrelated to its provincial namesakes), produced some pamphlets before it too folded by the end of 1850.[122] But this was a record of success compared with the products of later crises. Only one has left enough in the historical record even for its aims to be clear: in the wake of the 1857 crisis, an ultra-bullionist British Currency Reform Association briefly advocated abolition of the Bank of England fiduciary issue.[123]

This is not to say that money market crises and their consequences, or even the failure of individual firms, did not cause widespread anger and disquiet, but these rarely went to institutional questions, least of all the gold standard or the terms on which the Bank issued notes. On the rare occasions that questions moved beyond the personal culpability of individuals, they focussed on the proliferation of paper credit and the activities of the money market.[124] In the clichéd metaphor, deployed with varying proportions of wonder or disapproval, the system was an inverted pyramid, with gold at the bottom supporting a middle layer of Bank of England notes, which in turn supported a much wider, thicker layer of credit instruments, principally bills of exchange and cheques. The latter grew rapidly after the middle of the nineteenth century and became a part of the money supply, although not of the currency. As Bagehot observed in 1873, the amount of bullion was 'so exceedingly small that a bystander almost trembles when he compares its minuteness with the immensity of the credit which rests upon it'.[125] Crises brought to the fore suspicions—never altogether absent—that this credit was not merely groundless but fraudulent, the product of the arcane manipulations of swindlers.

There were certainly enough swindlers for this to be persuasive. The frauds and failures of bankers, railway tycoons, and others, sometimes ending with the disappearance, suicide, or criminal conviction of those directly responsible, were

---

[120] Fetter, *Orthodoxy*, pp. 235-6.
[121] *Times*, 1 Oct. 1847, 24 Dec. 1847; *Economist*, 20 Nov. 1847.
[122] National Currency Reform Association, *Tracts*.
[123] *Cheshire Observer*, 25 Dec. 1858 (BNA).   [124] Alborn, 'Money's Worth', p. 214.
[125] Bagehot, *Lombard Street*, p. 18.

not only reported widely in the press but became models for bestselling literary characters such as Dickens's Mr Merdle (*Little Dorrit*, 1855-7), Trollope's Augustus Melmotte (*The Way We Live Now*, 1875), and Gissing's Bennet Frothingham (*The Whirlpool*, 1897).[126] While the details of these characters' dealings were left mysterious, it was always clear that their frauds had ruined innocent investors and avaricious speculators alike.

After the 1860s, as the City's business began to focus increasingly on the provision and management of credit around the globe, such anxieties settled not just on the increasingly arcane nature of the money market, where many people had relatively modest sums invested, but on the supposed 'cosmopolitanism' and allegedly questionable national identity of many of its operators.[127] Such anxieties could appear as outright anti-Semitism directed towards Rothschild and other Jewish firms, or—as in the Boer War—unnamed, sinister conspirators who exercised an unwholesome influence on the government.[128] Alternatively, as in the near failure in 1890 of the world's largest merchant bank, Baring Brothers, it could appear as xenophobia towards unworthy foreigners to whom City firms had advanced investors' money, or even, bizarrely, towards the Rothschilds and the Bank of France, whose decisive assistance in the crisis was worrisome evidence of their power.[129]

Such concerns did not undermine faith and pride in the unequivocally 'British' components of the system. The Bank of England was admired as a stabilizing influence, preventing the worst consequences of financiers' misdeeds. The gold standard itself became a symbol and agent of the UK's global hegemony as a rapidly growing list of countries adopted it and as the vast bulk of all international transactions came to be conducted in sterling-denominated instruments drawn on London and ultimately redeemable in gold. The reappearance of Pistrucci's triumphal St George on the sovereign in 1871 after almost fifty years' absence, and the addition, at Queen Victoria's insistence, of the monarch's title as Empress of India to the entire coinage from 1893, provided everyday reinforcement of money's place in the nation's global reach and power.[130]

Support for the gold standard and the Acts of 1844-5 had broader and deeper roots than the entrenchment of orthodoxy among the erudite or even the international prestige of the gold standard. More important than either of these was the lack of any clear or obvious connection between what might go wrong in the remote world of finance and the gold, silver, and copper coins of everyday life. For

---

[126] For discussion of Victorian fictional treatments of real-life swindlers see Alborn, 'Moral'; Russell, *Mammon*, esp. chs 6-7.
[127] Blaazer, 'Sharks', pp. 142-9.
[128] Hirshfield, '"Jewish Conspiracy"'; Colbenson, 'Anti-Semitism'; Hobson, *War*, pp. 189-97.
[129] Blaazer, 'Sharks', pp. 149-51.
[130] Alborn, 'Coin and Country', pp. 252-3, 275-6; Roselli, 'Money', pp. 319-22; de Cecco, *Money and Empire*, p. 43.

the first time in centuries these had become uncomplicated for everyday use: unlikely to be counterfeit or clipped, and, at least in England and Scotland, adequately supplied in the denominations required for wages and everyday purchases.

Remarkably, the bulk of banknotes were similarly benign. Bank of England notes, whose circulation became steadily more geographically widespread in the decades after 1844, had now—in Mary Poovey's arresting phrase—fallen 'beneath the horizon of cultural visibility—in which they could pass without scrutiny or question'.[131] Losses to noteholders from bank failures also became far less frequent. Progressive mergers and takeovers reduced the number of banks and increased the average size and capital base of those remaining. They also reduced the number of issuing banks, as Peel had intended. Of the 170 bankrupt banks recorded in England in the thirty years after 1844, only eight issued notes, none of them joint-stocks.[132] Other provisions of the Act helped the process along. The Liverpool Borough bank, whose failure in 1857 was a major vector of transmission of the collapse in American railroad stocks to the UK, was one of forty-three banks to have made arrangements to circulate Bank of England notes instead of its own shortly after the Act was passed.[133]

Ireland presents a similar picture. John and James Sadleir's Tipperary Bank had agreed to circulate Bank of Ireland notes well before its collapse in 1856.[134] The Munster Bank failed in 1885 but, having been established in 1864, was never entitled to issue. Scotland alone saw major failures of issuing joint-stock banks: the Western Bank of Scotland, also early in the 1857 crisis, and the City of Glasgow Bank in 1878, whose failure was arguably more serious than the Ayr Bank 106 years earlier.[135] On both occasions, the Scottish banks' long-established practice of accepting the notes of their failed competitors saved the noteholders from loss, although their hesitation in doing so when the Western collapsed fuelled great anxiety and resentment in Glasgow against the Edinburgh banks. The failure of the Western also rekindled English hostility to 'Scotch' banking.[136]

All of these failures were disastrous: in the short term for depositors whose funds became inaccessible; in the long term for their shareholders, whose unlimited liability to the depositors left many ruined.[137] Their consequences locally were thus even more severe than they were nationally. But unlike previous banking failures and crises, none of these episodes resulted in money in people's purses

[131] Poovey, *Genres*, p. 219.
[132] Great Britain, Parliament, House of Commons, 'Return'. On the political and ideological ramifications of the transition of banking from issuing notes to taking deposits see Alborn, *Conceiving Companies*, part II, esp. ch. 5.
[133] Feavearyear, *Pound*, pp. 292–3; McCulloch, *Supplement*, p. 10.
[134] Ó Gráda, 'Failure', p. 201.
[135] Checkland, *Scottish Banking*, pp. 466–73. On the City of Glasgow Bank, see Alborn, *Conceiving Companies*, pp. 133–5; Alborn, 'Moral', esp. pp. 217–20.
[136] Checkland, *Scottish Banking*, p. 468.   [137] Acheson and Turner, 'Death Blow', p. 239.

becoming valueless. Banking remained problematic, and as larger numbers of people of modest means became depositors, it became newly dangerous, at least until the development of the Post Office Savings Bank in the 1860s.[138] Money itself, however, had become safe and reliable as never before.

It was reliable in another important sense. Not only did the gold standard provide the exchange rate stability that had been the elite's monetary holy grail for centuries, but the unique circumstances of the period also produced remarkable price stability. This confounded much of the critique of the Act, which had argued that by making money artificially scarce it would place relentless downward pressure on prices, which in turn would depress the economy. That things did not work out this way had little to do with the Act. Instead, a complex and contradictory set of monetary factors, largely unforeseen by supporters or critics, operated to ensure a reasonable level of price stability for much of the period between 1844 and the First World War. The rapid growth of cheques as a circulating form of near-money provided the additional liquidity required by a rapidly growing economy, reducing deflationary pressure. To this was added the discovery of large deposits of gold in California and Australia in 1849 and 1850, respectively, much of which found its way to the Bank of England and the mint. Later in the century, further discoveries in South Africa and the Yukon, combined with improved mining and refining techniques, increased the global supply still more dramatically. That these discoveries were not inflationary, as some critics of Peel's Acts hoped, was due to countervailing global demand for gold as most major economies adopted the gold standard.[139] As Keynes would later observe, as a result of such 'half-accidental' factors, the post-1844 gold standard provided not only a stable exchange but a stable price level.[140]

The only significant challenge to the gold standard since the aftermath of the resumption emerged as soon as this accidental equilibrium began to break down in the 1880s.[141] The fixed exchange of the gold standard ensured that the whole effect of the increase in the global price of gold and the even more dramatic fall in the global price of silver as more countries adopted the gold standard would be felt in prices.[142] This chiefly took the form of an increase in the value of money, but also a disturbance of the relativities of prices between gold standard countries and silver standard countries, above all India, which was both a source of raw materials and a major market for Britain's cotton industry.[143] The prolonged bimetallist agitation, which reached its peak as the price level hit its trough in the mid-1890s, was a direct result of this disruption. For its advocates, the global remonetization of silver at an internationally agreed price would not only raise falling prices,

---

[138] Alborn, *Conceiving Companies*, pp. 131–40.
[139] Alborn, *Glittered*, pp. 186–9; Eichengreen, *Globalizing*, pp. 15–19.
[140] Keynes, *Monetary Reform*, p. 158. [141] Keynes, *Monetary Reform*, p. 158.
[142] de Cecco, *Money and Empire*, pp. 47–52. [143] Green, 'Rentiers', p. 597.

especially of agricultural products, but restore the competitiveness of UK exports in silver standard markets.

The partial solution adopted took the opposite direction, when the UK authorities put India on a gold-exchange standard from 1896.[144] First forced onto a silver standard in 1816 (thus making Indian gold available for the new gold coinage in the UK), India suffered grievously from the decline of the global silver price later in the nineteenth century, being obliged to use its depreciating silver currency to fund growing sterling remittances for the so-called 'home charges' which included interest payments, maintenance of the army, London's administrative expenses, and pensions for civil servants retired to the UK.[145] The depreciation was nonetheless beneficial to the City, ensuring that India's highly competitive export prices would sustain a massive trade surplus with the rest of the world, allowing the UK to balance its own deficits with the USA, Germany, and its own colonies of white settlement, while leaving the City's earnings free for further international transactions.[146] It was only abandoned when the fiscal burden in India threatened to become so great as to raise fears of nationalist revolt.[147] This was merely the most conspicuous of many examples of the use of imperial policy to serve the monetary ends of the UK's elite in the nineteenth century, continuing the practices we have seen in relation to Ireland and the American colonies in the seventeenth and eighteenth centuries.

Although support for bimetallism was complex and came from a number of different interests and sections of opinion, its main sources of support were the great centres of the cotton industry in Lancashire and some other manufacturing areas, and among agriculturalists.[148] Despite support from some individuals in the City, the money market was overwhelmingly and implacably hostile, lobbying against any interference with the gold standard, and, at the peak of the bimetallic campaign, organizing a well-supported Gold Standard Defence Association.[149] Throughout the campaign 'the British State demonstrated a consistent bias towards City opinion'. This was unquestionably in large part, as E. H. H. Green contends, because of the power of the 'Treasury-Bank-City' nexus and the importance of the structural relationship between the government and its creditors.[150] But the City was far from the only source of opposition to bimetallism. By the late nineteenth century, the gold standard remained sacrosanct for

---

[144] Cain and Hopkins, *British Imperialism*, vol. 1, p. 345.
[145] de Cecco, *Money and Empire*, p. 63; Davies, *Holocausts*, p. 303.
[146] Davies, *Holocausts*, p. 297; Ingham, *Capitalism Divided*, pp. 123–4.
[147] de Cecco, *Money and Empire*, pp. 66–7.
[148] The complexities and fragmentation of support for and opposition to bimetallism are debated in a stimulating exchange between E. H. H. Green and A. C. Howe. See Green, 'Rentiers'; Green, 'Empiricism Belimed'; and Howe, 'Controversy Re-Opened'.
[149] Green, 'Rentiers', p. 605; Gold Standard Defence Association, *General Statement*.
[150] Green, 'Rentiers', p. 612.

the great mass of people in every class and sector, even as its benefits became less obvious.

The nascent labour movement reflected this general opinion, as well as the legacy bestowed upon it by Cobbett (via Chartism) and the principles of liberal political economy in which many of its early leaders were steeped. Despite some local support for bimetallism among trade unionists in the cotton districts and elsewhere, at a national level every sector of the movement was hostile to any alteration to the gold standard. Keir Hardie, addressing the annual conference of the Independent Labour Party (ILP) at the peak of the agitation, expressed 'astonishment' that bimetallism could 'find favour with some workers'. It was a 'side issue' that could bring no benefit to workers, whose condition would not improve 'so long as production and distribution were for profit-making'.[151]

The ILP, founded in 1893 to elect working men to Parliament independently of the existing parties, was one of four bodies that would later federate to form the Labour Party.[152] It persistently refused even to discuss currency proposals at any time before the First World War, even when (unlike bimetallism) such ideas originated in its own ranks with an avowedly socialist purpose.[153] Instead, it was content with occasional outbursts against 'Jewish financiers', not only during the Boer war but in gratuitous statements from its conference platforms.[154]

Other future constituents of the Labour Party were equally hostile. Harry Quelch, Marxist editor of the Social Democratic Federation's weekly, *Justice*, denounced bimetallism, arguing that it was only another form of protection, designed to prevent the inexorable loss of British commercial supremacy in the face of growing international competition.[155] Money circulates as a commodity, not 'a mere token', and an attempt to put an artificial value on any commodity, including silver, was certain to fail.[156] Even if bimetallism could benefit manufacturers, it could bring no improvement to workers under a capitalist system.[157] The pages of *Justice* were closed to any questioning of the working of the gold standard. So while the paper gave favourable notice to works of social criticism by the veteran Owenite John Sketchley, it urged readers to skip his monetary ideas.[158] The Fabian Society, whose economics derived largely from Ricardo, left currency questions severely alone. The stockbroker author of its sole pre-war departure from this practice—a speculation on the potentially 'socialistic' consequences of the growth of banking monopolies—even felt constrained to begin by

---

[151] *York Herald*, 17 Apr. 1895 (BNA).
[152] The Labour Representation Committee was formed in 1900 and changed its name to the Labour Party in 1906.
[153] See the unsuccessful efforts of John McLachlan and his Levenshulme ILP branch to have monetary questions discussed at ILP conferences: ILP, Report of the Annual Conference, 1907, p. 67; 1908, p. 12.
[154] ILP, Report of the Annual Conference, 1908, p. 35 (J. R. MacDonald, Chairman's Address).
[155] Quelch, *Bubble*, pp. 7, 12–13.   [156] Quelch, *Bubble*, p. 10.   [157] Quelch, *Bubble*, p. 14.
[158] *Justice*, 20 Dec. 1884 (BLN).

disavowing any association with 'currency cranks', whom he denounced as 'the most foolish of theorists'.[159]

The early labour movement's support for the gold standard was even more unequivocal than its often-remarked support for free trade—the other great shibboleth of liberal political economy. As Frank Trentmann has shown, although the movement was unanimously hostile to Joseph Chamberlain's campaign for tariff reform early in the twentieth century, the movement's support for free trade was more nuanced and provisional than this might suggest.[160] While its leaders adhered to the ideals of liberal internationalism that were prominent in contemporary free trade discourse, writers and speakers from every section of the movement questioned it on various grounds, not least its tendency to undercut wages through the free importation of 'sweated goods'.[161] These observations challenge Trentmann's own argument that free trade 'was the closest Britain ever came to a national ideology'.[162] That honour surely belongs to the gold standard—the 'faith of the age', to use Polanyi's term.[163]

The late nineteenth century was the most barren possible ground for any attempt to canvass, much less effect, change to the monetary order. Just how hopeless is shown by the attempts of successive Chancellors of the Exchequer to win support for even the most modest reforms. A proposal in 1869 to reduce the weight of the sovereign by 1 per cent in order to fund an overdue reminting of the large number of gold coins made light through wear was stymied by the predictable groups—bankers and the financial press—for the predictable Lockean reason that foreign creditors would be paid 'a part only of the commodity agreed upon'.[164] This would destroy trust in the coin and make it less acceptable internationally. A proposal fifteen years later to solve the same problem by putting the half-sovereign on a token basis in the manner of the silver coinage and using the gold saved to 'rehabilitate' the sovereigns was withdrawn in the face of opposition stemming from the belief that, as Alborn puts it, 'any coin with gold in it needed to be preserved, owing to the metal's strong identification with commercial morality and national pride'.[165]

Proposals in 1886 and 1891 to introduce one-pound notes in England met the same fate. The first, proposed largely to solve the problem of wear of the coins, never reached the point of public discussion. It was rejected by the Governor and Deputy Governor of the Bank on the basis of anachronistic myths. Such notes would be in the hands of the 'ignorant' labouring classes, who were 'easily moved by panic'. The notes would therefore require a proportionately higher reserve in order to prevent any threat to the convertibility of the Bank's entire issue. On the

---

[159] Pease, *State Banking*, p. 2.   [160] Trentmann, *Free Trade*, pp. 177–8.
[161] Trentmann, *Free Trade*, pp. 178–85.   [162] Trentmann, *Free Trade*, p. 2.
[163] Polanyi, *Transformation*, p. 25.
[164] Alborn, 'Coin and Country', p. 261, quoting Bonamy Price.
[165] Alborn, 'Coin and Country', p. 268.

basis of figures from the restriction period, they argued that the cost to the Bank and the 'ignorant class', who were unable to discriminate between forged and genuine notes, would be too high.[166] The second such proposal was floated early in 1891 by George Goschen, the Chancellor, who eventually agreed to recoin the gold at a final cost to the taxpayer of £650,000. The purpose of his proposal was not to economize on the use of gold but to increase the size of the Bank's reserve in the wake of the Baring crisis. A year of desultory private and public discussion followed in which opinion among bankers and in the press went from lukewarm to outright hostile.[167] The argument that it 'runs counter to the Act of 1844' was the clincher for many.[168] The Act had become holy writ.

As for the standard itself, it had moved beyond the reach of reason or the ken of history. As a writer in *The Illustrated London News*—apparently without irony—had explained as early as 1847, anyone with a 'grain of common sense' who asked why gold should be 'fixed at £3 17s 10½d' would see immediately that it was 'for no other reason than because an ounce of gold cuts up, or coins, into that quantity, and no more or less, and will do so till the end of the world'.[169] The end of the world is the subject of the next chapter.

---

[166] Currie and Collet to Chancellor of the Exchequer, 17 Dec. 1886, BE C12/4.
[167] Kynaston, *City*, vol. 2, pp. 39–43, 52–6.
[168] Grenfell to Governor, Oct. 1891, BE C12/4. Kynaston, *City*, vol. 2, p. 56.
[169] *Illustrated London News*, 4 Dec. 1847, p. 9.

8
Things Fall Apart
1914–1931

> It is time that we took control of currency ourselves. It is time that the State controlled it.
>
> R. C. Wallhead (1928)

Between July 1914 and September 1931 the monetary order of the United Kingdom was radically and irrevocably transformed. During seventeen years of relentless monetary crisis, circulating bullion coin disappeared from England forever to be replaced by low-denomination paper money, and the United Kingdom went off the gold standard twice—the second time permanently. London's status as a global financial centre became highly ambiguous. While remaining the largest and in many ways the most important centre in the international monetary system, it lost its unquestioned hegemony, becoming reliant as never before on the support of Paris, and more especially New York, the financial centre of the world's new great creditor nation, whose currency eventually took the place of gold as the United Kingdom's monetary standard.[1] The monetary relationships between England, Ireland, and Scotland were also reconfigured. While the newly founded Saorstát Éireann (Irish Free State) established its own currency in 1928, the remaining parts of the United Kingdom developed greater monetary uniformity than ever before.

The long crisis highlights themes that have recurred throughout this book. It demonstrates yet again the absolute priority that those with monetary power gave to the preservation of a constant sterling exchange rate in all circumstances save the most catastrophic wars. It shows a strong tendency to identify that preservation with the honour, prestige, and worth of the nation, and hence to enlist patriotism in its support. It exposes the undeveloped state of alternative ideas that could present a cogent challenge to the priorities of those who wielded monetary power. Finally, it provides an example of the complex ways that many of these issues could be refracted through the UK's history as a monetary union.

---

[1] Ingham, *Capitalism Divided*, pp. 187–8.

The First World War: Remaking the Monetary Order

The approach of the First World War triggered the most serious financial crisis in the history of the world, rivalled for its severity and reach only by the Global Financial Crisis of 2007–8.[2] It began as a crisis in international money markets. Inevitably, London was at its centre. Unlike any crisis since 1825–6, it posed an imminent threat to the money that people used every day, which was averted only by unprecedented innovation. As in the slower-moving and more localized crises of the 1690s and 1790s, radical monetary expedients became essential to Britain's capacity to fight the war.

The crisis had its roots in panic in stock exchanges around the world triggered by the diplomatic crisis. On 27 July—as Austria–Hungary presented its ultimatum to Serbia—the markets in Vienna and Budapest both closed. This created a domino effect as operators on other exchanges who also held securities on the closed exchanges desperately sought liquidity that was rapidly drying up. To prevent wholesale ruin, other exchanges therefore closed, culminating with the closure of the London exchange on 31 July. New York and other exchanges around the world followed soon afterwards. Numerous commodity exchanges in London and elsewhere also closed.

The closures created severe liquidity problems for banks, as the stocks they held as collateral against loans to the money market became unsaleable. There is also evidence that they faced unusually high demands for gold, driven at least in part by an impulse to hoard. The joint-stock banks therefore began to refuse to pay out gold coin to their depositors beyond their usual demands, insisting, as they were legally entitled to do, on paying with Bank of England notes instead.[3]

People who wanted gold were therefore obliged to make their way to the Bank of England to enact that exchange of notes for gold on demand which constituted the central covenant of the entire system and the key to its legitimation. This led to a rapid loss of gold from the Bank, whose gold coin holdings almost halved in five days.[4] Even in the midst of the European diplomatic crisis this pushed the financial crisis from the City pages to the front pages of the newspapers on the evening of 31 July and the following morning. The crowds demanding gold at the Bank of England on 1 August were therefore large, and there were isolated reports of Bank of England notes being refused.[5] For the first time since 1825, the Bank's notes became suspect. For a few days, hoarding of both gold and silver coin produced severe shortages that made it impossible to get change for a five-pound note.[6]

---

[2] See Roberts, *Saving City*, pp. 5, 231–2. This book is the indispensable guide to what was previously a strangely neglected episode.
[3] Roberts, *Saving City*, pp. 45–50.   [4] Roberts, *Saving City*, p. 53.
[5] Roberts, *Saving City*, pp. 58–9. Charles Price, Hansard HC, vol. 63, c. 1998 (5 Aug. 1914).
[6] Hansard HC, vol. 63, c. 1993 (5 Aug. 1914); Roberts, *Saving City*, p. 119.

The following day being a Saturday, business closed at 1 p.m. On the bank holiday Monday that followed, the government announced that the City and banks throughout the UK would remain closed until Friday. The response worked out in that time included a series of ever-expanding moratoria on payments, which eventually embraced all commercial debts, including bank deposits, contracted before 4 August. Through these and a series of other measures the Bank of England, underwritten by the government, freed financial institutions from their liabilities and enabled them to liquefy their assets.[7] As the Chancellor, Lloyd George, would boast in his memoirs, the government had 'saved the City'.[8]

These measures were hammered out in a series of conferences over 4–6 August involving the Chancellor and his Conservative predecessor, Austen Chamberlain, leading figures in the Treasury, the Governor of the Bank of England, and the heads of major merchant banks. The heads of the largest joint-stock banks participated, but were excluded from proceedings at critical moments and overruled when their priorities were in conflict with the others.[9] Representatives of the Scottish and Irish banks were called in together to discuss arrangements for their countries. As John Peters has observed, the crisis is 'an exemplar of the power of the City-Bank-Treasury nexus in the British state'. For this inner circle of monetary decision-makers 'saving the City' was the absolute priority, indistinguishable in their minds from saving the nation. In the process they overturned almost every principle of the existing system, with the exception of the sanctity of the pursuit of profit.[10]

Only slightly less fundamental was sanctity of contracts, which the moratorium rendered meaningless. As *The Economist* conceded, this obliterated 'the pride and the boast of English banking that anyone who can present a claim on an English bank will get it immediately and unquestionably turned into gold'.[11] It was a boast that would never again have quite the same certainty.

It helped the Liberal government's efforts to win support for these extreme measures that the Conservative opposition was equally committed to 'saving the City'. Public perceptions and responses could thus be managed by emphasizing national unity even more readily than in 1797. Chamberlain provided one such emphasis by congratulating Lloyd George in Parliament and reporting the 'common desire on all sides to meet the present emergency with the least possible disturbance, and the least inconvenience possible to all the different interests concerned', which he claimed to have seen demonstrated in the conference.[12] This was fanciful. There was considerable acrimony between the joint-stock

---

[7] Keynes, 'War', p. 460.   [8] Lloyd George, *War Memoirs*, vol. 1, ch. 4.
[9] Keynes, 'War'; Cecco, *Money and Empire*, ch. 7; Peters, 'Divide', p. 128; Roberts, *Saving City*, pp. 63–5, 230.
[10] Peters, 'Divide', pp. 127, 129–30, 135.   [11] Withers, *War*, p. 40.
[12] Hansard HC, vol. 63, c. 1996–7 (5 Aug. 1914).

banks and the inner circle throughout the crisis, both inside and outside the conference.[13]

Any notion of panic was also suppressed despite plentiful evidence from private sources that it was widespread.[14] Thus the *Financial News* headed its story with 'STOCK EXCHANGE MEETS THE CRISIS WITH COMMENDABLE CALM AND DIGNITY', explaining that 'there is only reflected crisis in London, and no panic at all'.[15] Panic was for foreigners, as the *Financial World* explained: 'Admittedly, the European situation is serious, and with characteristic excitability the continent is panic-stricken. At such a time we British people must keep cool heads and wise counsels.'[16]

Despite separate, panicked requests from the Bank of England and the joint-stocks for a suspension of cash payments, the Treasury, armed with an emphatic memorandum from Keynes, galvanized Lloyd George to resist.[17] But convertibility became purely a matter of form, which could only be maintained for as long as almost nobody chose to exercise it. The government's need for gold for overseas transactions was such that it resolved to get it out of circulation as quickly as possible and replace it with paper. On 6 August the government therefore took the unprecedented step of printing its own 'currency notes' in denominations of one pound and ten shillings.

The need to enlist the public's support for these notes' notional convertibility was both more imperative and more challenging than enlisting popular support for the suspension had been in 1797, as it involved a much larger proportion of the population. Unlike guineas and half-guineas in 1797, sovereigns and half-sovereigns were money that all wage earners handled regularly. Also unlike 1797, the notes were not only unfamiliar to their new and much larger group of users, they were also something that people had long been schooled to execrate. It was therefore essential to use the spurs of patriotism to encourage people of every class not only to accept the notes but to exchange whatever gold they had for them. Only then would the government be able to sustain the fiction that it had been 'able to meet the emergency without in the slightest degree interfering with our present basis'.[18]

The efforts began even before the notes appeared. Lloyd George spelt out what was required when he made 'an appeal to the patriotism of every citizen in this land' to 'assist to carry the country through this terrible emergency'. Addressing hoarders directly, he equated failure to follow his precepts with treason: 'anyone who...withdraws sums of gold and appropriates them to his own use...is assisting the enemies of his native land, and he is assisting them more effectively

---

[13] TNA T170/14; de Cecco, *Money and Empire*, ch. 7. See also Roberts, *Saving City*, ch. 6.
[14] Kynaston, *City*, vol. 3, pp. 4–6. [15] *Financial News*, 30 July 1914.
[16] *Financial World*, 1 Aug. 1914. [17] Roberts, *Saving City*, pp. 118–19, 125–8.
[18] Lloyd George, Hansard HC, vol. 63, c. 1992 (5 Aug. 1914).

probably than if he were to take up arms'.[19] As requested by Lloyd George and others, the newspapers reported this statement widely and some dug in the spurs from different angles.[20] The *Daily Mail* warned that 'to have gold instead of letting the banks have it will be a disgrace'.[21] One can only imagine how Lord King might have responded. Here, without apology, was enforcement of the 'Jacobin' idea that to regulate one's monetary conduct without regard to the government's requirements or the public good, was incivism.[22]

Compliance was general, but not complete. Early in the war some tradesmen refused the currency notes.[23] There were also intermittent alarms about gold hoarding, and some sarcastic commentary on the amount of gold people found to buy war bonds in the latter stages of the war, even in Scotland,[24] where the circulation of gold coin had become 'a noticeable feature' of the pre-war years.[25] Remarkably, given Scots' long history of using paper money, Sir George Anderson, Treasurer of Bank of Scotland, believed that Scots held onto their gold far more tightly than English people in the early months of the war.[26] A year into the war the government thought that gold hoarding was enough of a problem throughout the UK to warrant posting an appeal to the public in banks and post offices for people to pay in any gold they still had.[27]

The biggest problem for most people was an ongoing, sometimes severe, shortage of silver coin, despite unprecedentedly high levels of minting throughout the war.[28] Various explanations were advanced, including the expatriation of silver coins in soldiers' pockets and increased prices of many everyday purchases, which might now require two coins instead of one. According to the *Tamworth Herald*—fittingly for the organ of Peel's old constituency—the scarcity was due to 'the unpopularity of paper money among workpeople', who tendered them as quickly as possible to get change.[29] Almost without exception, stories of coin shortages or problems with the currency notes concluded with appeals to the patriotism of those allegedly responsible.

Unlike any previous notes, currency notes were legal tender throughout the United Kingdom. This necessity had been one of the government's stated reasons for issuing its own low-denomination notes, believing that making Bank of England notes legal tender in Scotland and Ireland would be politically difficult. Instead, they made Scottish and Irish banknotes legal tender in their respective

---

[19] Hansard HC, vol. 63, c. 1992–3 (5 Aug. 1914).
[20] Hansard HC, vol. 63, c. 1999–2000 (5 Aug. 1914).   [21] *Daily Mail*, 6 Aug. 1914.
[22] See Chapter 6, p. 184, above.
[23] *Daily Record*, 17 Aug. 1914 (BNA); *Dundee Courier*, 21 Aug. 1914 (BNA).
[24] *Aberdeen Daily Journal*, 1 Mar. 1917 (BLN).   [25] *The Times*, 28 Oct. 1914.
[26] *The Times*, 28 Oct. 1914. Anderson challenged the claim that he had accused Scots of hoarding in a later letter to *The Scottish Banker's Magazine*, cited in the *Aberdeen Daily Journal*, 30 Dec. 1914 (BNA).
[27] Royal Bank of Scotland, *Economy in the Use of Gold Coin*, 9 Aug. 1915, LBGA, SBM/1/10/6/123.
[28] Challis, *Mint*.   [29] *Tamworth Herald*, 30 Oct. 1915 (BNA).

countries for the time being, on condition that they be convertible into currency notes at the issuing bank's head office. Like English joint-stock banks, the Scottish and Irish banks were permitted to borrow currency notes from the Treasury to an amount equal to 20 per cent of their deposits. Instead of circulating the currency notes as the English banks did, they issued their own notes in their place. For the banks, this was a clear second best to having their notes made inconvertible, which the Scottish representatives in particular pressed hard during their session with the inner circle on 5 August.[30] But Lloyd George was adamant that inconvertibility was now out of the question for any part of the United Kingdom.

The consideration of Scottish and Irish monetary differences did not extend to the design of the notes. While the short-lived first-series notes had featured a vignette of the king, as befitted state-issued notes for the whole of the United Kingdom, the addition of St George on the second-series notes aroused the ire of the St Andrew Society, who regarded him as a 'purely English and sectional' symbol. Ire turned to outrage on the appearance of the third-series notes in 1917, where he was featured far more prominently. In letters of protest to the Chancellor, Bonar Law (himself a Scot), the society refused to accept excuses 'for an act which is in essence unconstitutional' at a time when 'Scotland is pouring out blood and treasure for Britain'. While acknowledging the presence of the rose, thistle, shamrock, and daffodil 'in somewhat microscopic proportions' in the watermark, they regarded the use of St George in 'the most important issue of British currency in the history of the Empire' as 'an outrage to the non-English peoples of the United Kingdom'. They suggested instead 'the beautiful figure of Britannia—the personification of Britain', which in their view could 'not offend the national sentiment of any loyal subject of the British crown'.[31] One wonders what Irish nationalists fighting on the Western Front might have thought about this claim, but it is possible that by 1917, in the aftermath of the Easter Rising, the St Andrew Society regarded all Irish nationalists as beyond the pale of loyalty. In any case Irish nationalists seem to have had bigger fish to fry; the designs of the notes attracted little or no comment in Ireland.

The third-series notes featured the most warlike iconography ever to appear on any money in Britain or Ireland. St George dominated the one-pound note, slaying the dragon far more comprehensively than he ever had on the sovereign. The ten-shilling note featured an equally bellicose Britannia—presumably to the satisfaction of the St Andrew Society. (See Figure 8.1.) Unlike the Britannia of Bank of England notes, she did not carry an olive branch, nor did she sit. Rather,

---

[30] TNA T170/56 f. 109–18.
[31] St Andrew Society (Glasgow) to Chancellor of the Exchequer, 20 Feb. 1917; St Andrew Society (Edinburgh) to Chancellor of the Exchequer, 10 Apr. 1917, TNA, T/172/591; *The Thistle*, Apr. 1917, p. 67.

Figure 8.1 Britannia for a nation at war: a third-series currency note, 1917.
© The Trustees of the British Museum

she stood on a beach, feet apart, chest out, her trident planted firmly in the sand, looking out defiantly across the waves.

Currency notes were essential to the United Kingdom's capacity to fight the war. They ensured the government's access to bullion as security for foreign expenditure, while providing funds directly for dramatically increased domestic expenditure.[32] They thus served the same functions as James II's 'gun money' in Ireland; Bank of England notes, exchequer notes, tallies, and clipped silver coin during King William's war; and inconvertible banknotes and tokens during the Napoleonic wars. As we have seen, the regulation of these forms of currency and the enforcement of their use varied widely, from naked coercion to various combinations of legal terror and patriotic suasion. The use of currency notes in the early days of the war, before almost all the gold coins disappeared into the Bank of England or private hoards, depended almost entirely on the latter, buttressed by their legal tender status. Later in the war it was secured by the fact that banks other than the Bank of England and the Bank of Ireland retained only tiny stocks of gold, and that only the respective head offices of those banks were required to exchange their notes for coin in any case. None of this, however, prevented commentators from attributing the continued circulation of currency notes entirely to the 'patriotism and common sense' of the people.[33]

Currency notes were also essential to the government's raising of war loans. To ensure the success of the first war loan of 1914, the Bank of England lent currency notes to purchasers of war loan at 1 per cent below bank rate. What this meant was

---

[32] Strachan, *Financing*, pp. 145–6.   [33] *Land and Water*, 7 Nov. 1918.

that individuals, as well as banks, insurance companies, and other financial operators, could lend the government, at an effective net rate of ¼ per cent, money it had issued itself on its own security, while retaining money in hand to use for any other purpose.[34] While the terms of successive war loans differed, the fundamental point remained that the government was borrowing money it had created itself on terms that were attractive to the lenders. Lloyd George duly praised the 'patriotism' of those who subscribed to the loan.[35]

The extensive use of currency notes increased the volume of paper money from £73 m in 1913 to £492 m in 1919. This included an additional £48 m of Bank of England notes, £20.7 m of Scottish notes and £17.3 m of Irish notes, all issued on the basis of holdings of currency notes.[36] To show that the use of currency notes was purely a wartime measure and that the path of monetary orthodoxy would be resumed as soon as possible, a 'currency note reserve' was duly established. Although this never represented more than a small proportion of the notes in circulation, it constituted a political declaration that the notes would be redeemed, rather like James II's promise to redeem his Irish base metal coin.

'Back to Sanity': the Price of Orthodoxy

In 1918 the government appointed a Committee on Currency and Foreign Exchange After the War. The terms of reference and composition of the committee made all but the fine details of its findings entirely predictable. The committee was directed to 'report on the steps required to bring about the restoration of normal conditions after the war'.[37] Headed by Walter Cunliffe, whose tenure as Governor of the Bank had just ended, the only two members with no direct connection with banking were A. C. Pigou, Professor of Political Economy at Cambridge, and the head of the Treasury, Sir John Bradbury, whose monetary orthodoxy was unimpeachable.[38] Among the remainder, merchant bankers and those with extensive imperial and foreign interests predominated: two of the exceptions were a former Governor of the Bank of Ireland and a director of Bank of Scotland. To such a group the benefits of the gold standard as a preserver of exchange rate stability and the international value of financial securities were self-evident, and its national importance unquestionable.

Almost all of the committee's substantive recommendations appeared in its interim report of August 1918. On the basis of a 'simple and simplistic' description of the operation of the 1844 Bank Acts, the committee urged a return to its

---

[34] Blaazer, 'Patriotism', p. 7.   [35] Strachan, *Financing*, p. 164.
[36] Capie and Webber, *Monetary History*, 1, pp. 326, Table III (1).
[37] Cunliffe, *First Report*, p. 2.
[38] Pigou's views on monetary policy shifted significantly in the years following the return to the standard. See Takami, 'Pigou'.

'automatic machinery' for regulating the exchange rate, domestic prices, currency in circulation, and the volume of purchasing power.[39] Apart from an increased fiduciary issue, it proposed only two modifications to the Act, both of which had been urged from orthodox quarters long before the war: the machinery for suspension of the limit on the fiduciary issue should be built into the Act itself, and (as Ricardo had proposed in 1816) there was no need to return to the internal circulation of gold coin, at least for the time being. Instead, the country's entire stock of monetary gold should be held at the Bank of England, and currency notes should be replaced at the earliest opportunity with low-denomination notes issued by the Bank, which would be legal tender throughout the UK. This programme entailed a contraction of the currency, to be achieved by means of the earliest possible end of government borrowing and the establishment of a sinking fund to pay down wartime debt.

The committee's final report endorsed its earlier recommendations. It also added recommendations for Scotland and Ireland that amounted to a return to the conditions of the 1845 Act with the exception that the banks could hold any legal tender—not just gold—as cover for their non-fiduciary issues. This recommendation provoked the only reservation to either report by any member, with George Stewart, the Irish representative, proposing that Ireland's return to pre-war conditions be delayed indefinitely.[40]

Released at the end of October 1918, with the newspapers' attention firmly fixed on the unfolding of the war's endgame, the interim report received very little press coverage. The final report, published more than a year after the war ended, attracted only slightly more. Most newspapers ignored it altogether; a few reported little or nothing more than that it 'made no actual reference to the restoration of the use of the sovereign', which they possibly thought was the only aspect of the report that would interest their readers.[41] Almost without exception, the very small amount of editorial commentary regarded the report's core propositions as 'incontestable'.[42] This was in keeping with the views of *The Economist*, which headed its welcome of the interim report with 'Back to Sanity', praising both its logic and its recommendations as an endorsement of 'contentions concerning inflation, war finance &c, at which we have been steadily hammering for years'.[43] Endorsements like these carried weight in governing and financial circles but it is important to bear in mind, when considering debates and dilemmas faced by experts and policymakers, that at this stage the level of general public knowledge or interest in the whole matter was close to zero.

---

[39] Flanders, 'Model', p. 226 n.14.   [40] Cunliffe, *Final Report*, p. 4.
[41] *Daily Telegraph*, 13 Dec. 1919; *Yorkshire Evening Post*, 13 Dec. 1919 (BNA); *Leicester Daily Post*, 15 Dec. 1919 (BNA); *Belfast News-Letter*, 15 Dec. 1919 (INA).
[42] *Yorkshire Post and Leeds Intelligencer*, 19 Dec. 1919 (BNA). For an exception, see *Burnley News*, 17 Dec. 1919 (BNA).
[43] *Economist*, 2 Nov. 2018, pp. 618–20.

It is impossible to discern any distinctively Irish or Scottish response to the reports except to observe that the Irish press ignored them even more thoroughly than the British. By the time of the final report, the news sections of Irish newspapers were thoroughly preoccupied with the Anglo-Irish war, which had been under way since the beginning of the year. Scottish reporting followed the same pattern as English. Such Scottish commentary as was reported was pure orthodoxy, including a speech by Allan M'Neil, lecturer in banking at Edinburgh University, who praised the 1845 Act as 'that great sheet anchor of Scottish banking'.[44]

In the immediate aftermath of war, notwithstanding the recommendations of the interim report, the government neither reduced its borrowing nor contracted the currency. Rather, it borrowed to support housing and other social programs, officially left the gold standard early in 1919, and permitted the expansive monetary policy necessary to enable a post-war restocking boom.[45] Currency and banknotes in circulation rose rapidly, as did bank credit, prices, and wages.[46] The reasons for the government's choice are clear. Apart from its election commitments to returning soldiers (chiefly Lloyd George's 'homes fit for heroes'), the government was deeply worried by the post-war spread of the European revolutionary wave to the UK, where working class organizations in some cities were taking on an increasingly militant, often pro-Bolshevik, aspect.[47] However limited the revolutionary threat actually was, bringing the armed forces home to immediate mass unemployment was an act of recklessness that Lloyd George's government was not prepared to contemplate, whatever the consequences for the currency.

The government announced its acceptance of the report's recommendations in December 1919. The Treasury and the Bank, which had been pushing the government to contain inflation for months, now worked assiduously to ensure prompt implementation of the report by raising interest rates and contracting the currency.[48] As wartime inflation had been more severe in the UK than the US, it had become urgent that inflation be reversed as quickly as possible in order to bring the two countries' general price levels back to their pre-war relationship. Given the policy goal of restoring the pre-war gold standard, this was self-evident to all economists.[49]

The post-war boom, already slackening, abruptly turned to slump in April. At this point, the use of deflation as a means to restore the pre-war standard did

---

[44] *Scotsman*, 15 Oct. 1919 (BNA). [45] Howson, 'Dear Money', p. 89.
[46] Moggridge, 'Gold Standard', pp. 260–1; Flanders, 'Model', p. 89. Despite the sharp tightening of monetary policy in April 1920, the average of Bank of England and currency notes outstanding in that year was 140 per cent above the 1918 figure. Scottish and Irish note issues rose less steeply (entirely on the basis of increased reserves of the outstanding currency notes just mentioned) and peaked earlier. Capie and Webber, *Monetary History*, 1, pp. 326–7, Table III (1).
[47] Howson, 'Dear Money', p. 91. On the revolutionary wave see Challinor, *British Bolshevism*, ch. 9.
[48] Howson, 'Dear Money', pp. 93–8.   [49] Howson, 'Dear Money', pp. 101–3.

arouse criticism from some 'bankers, industrialists and financial journalists'.[50] Some was of the kind that invariably come from industry during periods of tight monetary policy. Others were of a piece with critiques of the finer points of currency management within the gold standard paradigm that characterized the last half of the nineteenth century, which the Cunliffe Committee had either ignored or dismissed.[51] But the desirability of the gold standard and the restoration of the pre-war parity remained virtually unchallenged. Such disputes as arose were about the route and the pace, not the destination.[52]

Support for a return to gold was by no means unique to the UK. Every country saw it as a means to end the severe inflation resulting from the need to print money to fund their respective war efforts and as the path to the exchange rate stability necessary to revive severely disrupted international trade and restore political stability.[53] Nobody, however, believed that it could be restored in all its details. Like the UK, those countries that had featured circulating gold coin as a prominent part of their domestic monetary systems realized that this was too expensive a luxury to maintain. In the international context, the large drains of gold from Europe to the USA that were bound to follow the war turned minds toward a 'gold exchange standard', whereby currencies would be pegged to gold but countries would hold a substantial portion of their reserves in foreign currency to help manage the exchanges. This proposal, which won wide support at the Genoa conference on currency in 1922, was particularly attractive to the UK, as the bulk of such reserves would inevitably be held in London, where transfers would be mediated by City institutions.[54]

The UK was unusual only in the priority it gave to restoring its pre-war parity. It was one of only six countries, and the only belligerent, to set out to do so. For others, the parity had fallen so far during the war that restoring it was simply out of the question, a possibility that even Ricardo had acknowledged. Uniquely among the currencies of belligerents and major powers, a restoration of sterling to the pre-war status quo, although difficult, at least looked feasible. The UK's unique relationship with its currency's gold parity made it deeply attractive. Fixed for just over two hundred years, it had been Great Britain's effective standard since that time. Together with the convertibility of banknotes, it had become a point of national honour and self-worth during the bank restriction period, powerfully reinforced with the dual mandates of history and nature by Peel in 1844, and reiterated to the point of platitude thereafter. The sterling–gold parity had long appeared indispensable, natural, and timeless.

---

[50] Hume, 'Gold Standard', p. 228; Boyce, 'Myth', p. 188.
[51] Hume, 'Gold Standard', p. 227; Flanders, 'Model', pp. 224–6. Boyce, 'Myth', p. 179, shows the Federation of British Industry briefly questioning the parity in 1921 but remaining committed to the principle of the gold standard.
[52] Hume, 'Gold Standard', p. 229.   [53] Tooze, *Deluge*, pp. 365, 487–8.
[54] Cain and Hopkins, *British Imperialism*, vol. 2, pp. 63–4; Roselli, 'Money', pp. 324–5.

In every other country the initial adoption of the gold standard, and therefore a specific gold parity, had taken place within living memory. For them the restoration of the international gold standard was important; for the UK, restoration of its own leadership of the international gold standard was vital if its global leadership and sources of wealth were to be maintained. This would only happen if 'confidence' in sterling's gold value were maintained. The parity was never up for discussion.

Such attitudes from the mainstream of political and monetary opinion are unsurprising—especially from the gentlemanly capitalists and rentiers who made their substantial livings or unearned incomes from dealings in sterling and many of whom now had a significant interest in loans to the government. More broadly, as Ingham puts it, 'the return to gold promised the restoration of the powers of the City, Bank and Treasury, both collectively and singly'.[55] Nor is it surprising that many in the business world deferred to their opinions, even when they could see the likely harmful effects on their own business. As Robert Boyce suggests, whatever their doubts, such people 'for the most part...lacked the self-assurance of their public school and Oxbridge-educated contemporaries in the City who vigorously applauded the recommendations of the Cunliffe Committee'.[56]

Boyce also suggests that labour leaders were even more diffident, as they 'had experience only of industrial, or shop floor, issues and...lacked the resources adequately to confront the larger questions of economic, financial, and monetary policy'.[57] While pertinent, this ignores two important issues. First, the post-war Labour Party, and constituent elements like the Fabian Society and the more radical ILP, contained a significant number of intellectuals, including middle-class university graduates and products of the movement's own impressive educational networks and institutions, whose horizons were not limited to industrial issues. Secondly, it ignores the extent to which both the leadership and the rank and file actively supported gold-standard orthodoxy, convinced that no solutions to the working class's problems were to be found along the path of currency reform.

The movement's adherence to orthodoxy was reiterated just after the war by the leading Fabian intellectual Sidney Webb, later a minister in the Labour government that would be broken by the financial crisis of 1931. In a Fabian Tract on the capital levy (Labour's plan to pay for the war and fund its reform program), Webb felt the need to begin by condemning every kind of monetary heterodoxy and mocking their proponents. He concluded by affirming the 'comforting fact' that on monetary questions 'the British Labour Movement is, as Lombard Street would say, "as sound as a bell"'.[58]

---

[55] Ingham, *Capitalism Divided*, p. 181.   [56] Boyce, 'Myth', p. 178.
[57] Boyce, 'Myth', p. 179.
[58] Webb, *National Finance*, p. 3. In a strange footnote to this passage, Webb referred the reader to a work by the ultra-orthodox Cannan and to J. A. Hobson's unorthodox and confused *Gold, Prices and*

This was near the truth. With very few exceptions the labour movement shared Webb's conviction that there was no space for monetary thought between the purest gold-standard orthodoxy and 'delusions' or 'Utopian manipulation of the currency'. Such heterodox ideas as did appear seldom arose from a specifically socialist critique of the monetary system. R. B. Suthers, a socialist journalist with Robert Blatchford's *Clarion*—a highly eclectic weekly aimed expressly at a working-class audience—argued for inconvertible paper money based on the national credit, and praised the ready availability of money during the war years. But Suthers was heavily influenced by Arthur Kitson, an engineer and inventor whose decades-long campaign for radical currency reform began with advocacy of 'free banking', which he believed would be an effective antidote to socialism.[59] Kitson also found a platform in *The Clarion*.

Kitson's ideas—although not his fixation on currency reform—oscillated fairly wildly over the years, even including a brief flirtation with state socialism during and after the war.[60] Soon after, he became a convert to the 'Social Credit' theories of C. H. Douglas—another engineer—who applied some idiosyncratic cost accounting to discover that, as the embedded cost to industry of historically produced capital goods did not create current or future purchasing power, production under the current monetary system could never produce sufficient purchasing power to buy the products of industry. The solution was to release this 'social credit' in the form of a 'national dividend' paid to every individual.[61] Apart from this, business credit should be extended to any viable business that needed it. Like Kitson, Douglas would later gravitate to anti-Semitic conspiracy theories to explain his theory's failure to win universal acceptance.[62]

Social credit attracted a minor flurry of interest after the war.[63] Although it claimed to make socialism unnecessary, resolutions in its favour were moved at successive conferences of both the ILP and the Labour Party during the 1920s. These made little headway, but in 1922 the Labour Party felt that the challenge warranted appointment of a high-powered committee of party leaders and economic thinkers to demolish 'the faulty Douglas analysis'.[64] While this group acknowledged that the labour movement had neglected the importance of credit and banking for 'far too long', little would change until much later in the decade.[65]

Labour movement writers within a Marxist framework contributed little to critique of the existing monetary order. Their ideas sat comfortably with two strands of monetary thought that formed part of the movement's inheritance: one

---

Wages. Webb had either not read or not understood one or both of these texts, relying perhaps on Cannan's standing in the economics profession and Hobson's standing in the labour movement and among progressive liberals as the basis of his recommendations.

[59] Kitson, *Scientific Solution*.   [60] Kitson, *Trade Fallacies*.
[61] Kitson, *Unemployment*, pp. 10, 50–2; Douglas, *Social Credit*, Appendix.
[62] Kitson, *Unemployment*, p. 12; Kitson, *Conspiracy*, pp. 40–1; Douglas, *Social Credit*, pp. 146, 153.
[63] Finlay, *English Origins*, ch. 6.   [64] Labour Party, *Labour and Social Credit*, p. 9.
[65] Labour Party, *Labour and Social Credit*, p. 1.

represented by Ricardo via Peel, the other by Cobbett via the Chartists. At the core of all such analysis lay the idea that the value of money subsisted in the value of gold, which, according to the labour theory of value, derived from the socially necessary labour required to produce it.[66] Once such writer, John Barr, presented a version of the barter theory of the origins of money that would have pleased Bishop Fleetwood or Adam Smith. Paper money was acceptable for national circulation provided it 'conforms to the law regulating its proportions to the amount of the standard of price (gold) it would require to do the work'—in other words, provided each pound note corresponded to a pound's worth of gold.[67] Any paper issued beyond this would invariably set off an inflationary spiral, as demonstrated by John Law's Mississippi scheme and the *assignats* of revolutionary France. In support of these arguments, Barr cited Edwin Cannan, including a quotation we have encountered in an earlier chapter where he urged the people of Europe to burn their wartime paper money.[68] As well as Marx, Barr's bibliography included an assortment of highly orthodox 'hard money' economists.[69]

Webb, therefore, although not precisely accurate, was essentially correct. As would be shown by the movement's initial responses to the government's decision to return to the gold standard at the pre-war parity in April 1925, there were few intellectual resources available to help socialists develop cogent critique of current monetary problems.

'A Golden Gallipoli': the Return to Gold and Its Critics

The return to gold in April 1925 was not without critics. Apart from Keynes, whose views we will consider shortly, a number of figures in industry and banking (most conspicuously Reginald McKenna, Chairman of the Midland Bank), as well as Lord Beaverbrook, proprietor of the *Daily Express*, were critical of the timing, the chosen parity, or both. In this view, it would only be possible to fix the parity at $4.86 by keeping interest rates high, thus locking in the deflation that had been pursued since 1920 and continuing the economic slump indefinitely. Moreover, the higher exchange rate would make British exports even less competitive than they had already become.

Even the Chancellor, Winston Churchill, whose decision it was, worried about these arguments. But senior figures in the Treasury and the Bank of England left no room for doubt. Their coordinated responses to his queries were utterly contemptuous of any alternative to a 'golden 1925'. Acknowledging that 'the restoration of Free Gold will require a high Bank Rate', Montagu Norman, the

---

[66] Woodburn, *Mystery*; Barr, *Money Problem*.   [67] Barr, *Money Problem*, p. 11.
[68] Barr, *Money Problem*, p. 13. See Chapter 6, pp. 170–1, above.
[69] Barr, *Money Problem*, p. 4.

Governor, set out a stark choice: 'the government cannot avoid a decision for or against Restoration: the Chancellor will surely be charged with a sin of omission or commission. In the former case (Gold) he will be abused by the ignorant, the gamblers and the antiquated industrialists: in the latter case (not Gold) he will be abused by the instructed and by posterity.'[70] Churchill bowed to the united expertise of the City–Treasury nexus.[71]

In fact he was abused by hardly anybody—at least for the time being. His announcement appeared to be almost universally welcomed as a sign of a return to normality and as the United Kingdom's return to its proper place in the world. As Boyce has shown, it could hardly have been otherwise. Those papers and periodicals that covered financial issues at all left them to their 'City editors', who were thoroughly imbued with the deepest monetary orthodoxy and depended on their networks in the money market for their stories.[72] The more influential among them were also favoured with Montagu Norman's 'carefully-rationed attention' and his view of events and problems.[73]

The response of Labour's parliamentary leadership stayed within the mainstream of the criticisms noted above. Following secret communication with Norman, Philip Snowden responded to the announcement with a Commons resolution intended to be 'strong enough to appease party supporters without directly challenging the decision'.[74] As someone who had repeatedly supported a return to gold as soon as possible there was in any case little more Snowden could do other than move that the government had acted with 'undue precipitancy'.[75] Even this was enough to allow Conservative opponents to embarrass him with a series of his own recent pronouncements in favour of early resumption and the need to accept the sacrifices it entailed.[76]

Although the Snowden–Norman strategy was successful, it did not prevent sterner criticism in the socialist press. In *The Clarion*, Suthers had been attacking the prospect of an early return to the gold standard policy for months before the April announcement. His prescription for the troubles of the system were nationalization of the banks and abolition of the gold standard, on which topic he commended Kitson. Labour's support for the 'present basis of the money system', he believed, was completely incompatible with any part of its programme.[77]

H. N. Brailsford, editor of the ILP's weekly *New Leader*, characterized the decision as 'A Golden Gallipoli', comparing it with Churchill's disastrous strategic gambit of 1915. Like Suthers, he singled out the Labour leadership for particular criticism, arguing that 'a socialist policy should have more to say about financial

---

[70] Norman, memorandum for the Chancellor (bcc Niemeyer), 2 Feb. 1925, BE G14/312. (Emphasis original.)
[71] Moggridge, *Conquest*, pp. 94–7.   [72] Boyce, 'Myth', pp. 185–7.
[73] Boyce, 'Myth', p. 188.   [74] Boyce, 'Myth', p. 192.
[75] Hansard HC, vol. 195, c. 625 (4 May 1925).
[76] Horne, Hansard HC, vol. 195, c. 634–5 (4 May 1925).   [77] *Clarion*, 15 May 1925 (BNA).

policy' when it involved 'a gamble which may involve a heavy increase of unemployment, and an attempt to lower wages by 2s in the pound'. He also denounced the deflation pursued to enable the restoration as a 'subtle financial robbery' which had 'endowed the leisured class with a capital sum of about £2,000 millions'. Labour would make little progress until its front bench found 'adequate words to denounce this transaction ... and to create a spirit of revolt against the dictatorship of the City'.[78]

These strictures had little effect on the labour movement in the short term. The only major leader to criticize Churchill's decision or question the gold standard consistently from 1925 onwards was Ernest Bevin, the formidable head of the Transport and General Workers' Union. As his biographer notes, however, Bevin 'had no Socialist blueprint in mind for remodelling the monetary system'.[79] Given that no such thing could be said to exist within British socialism in the 1920s, it could hardly have been otherwise. Bevin apart, it took years of high unemployment, wage cuts, and bitter industrial conflict (including the 1926 General Strike) for the labour movement to begin to give any serious attention to monetary questions.

In the ILP, this translated to growing hostility to the power of the Bank of England. In 1928 it moved unsuccessfully to commit the Labour Party not merely to nationalization of the banking system but to the revision of 'the Bank Acts'.[80] The Labour Party did commit to public ownership of the Bank the following year, but even then its leaders successfully resisted pressure to include this in its 1929 election manifesto.[81] Although the labour movement as a whole, like many other sections of opinion, would become retrospectively highly critical of Churchill's decision by 1931, the gold standard and the re-established parity remained largely untouchable for the time being.[82]

The sharpest early criticism of Churchill's decision came not from the Labour leadership, on whose followers it bore most heavily, but from Keynes, a liberal whose aim was to save capitalism from itself. Even before the decision was taken, he campaigned publicly and privately to prevent it, believing that the underlying price level was still too distant from that of the USA, and maintaining that it was both unimportant and unjust to return to the pre-war parity.[83] When the decision was announced, he was furious, famously criticizing it in *The Economic Consequences of Mr Churchill*, where he emphasized the human cost of the 'adjustments' that would have to occur as a result and predicted the

---

[78] *New Leader*, 8 May 1925.   [79] Bullock, *Bevin*, 1, p. 418.
[80] ILP, *Report of the Annual Conference*, 1928, p. 34.
[81] ILP, *Report of the Annual Conference*, 1929, Appendix 4; Labour Party, *Report of the Annual Conference*, 1929, p. 226.
[82] McKibbin, 'Economic Policy', pp. 110–11.
[83] Boyce, 'Myth', pp. 174, 189, 191; Moggridge, 'Gold Standard', p. 262; Skidelsky, *Keynes*, vol. 2, pp. 197–200.

unemployment and bitter industrial conflicts that were to follow, especially in the UK's already struggling export industries.[84]

Elsewhere, he attacked the report of the Bradbury Committee, which Churchill had released as justification for his decision. Its 'few pages, indolent and jejune' had not even considered any of the difficult questions that must confront any serious attempt to assess the practicability or desirability of a return to gold, in particular the extent of the disparity between UK and US prices; nor had it attempted to consider the actual economic consequences of the increase in bank rate which it recommended as 'the panacea' to meet all difficulties that the return to gold might encounter.[85]

The report was indeed a remarkable document. Ostensibly an inquiry into whether the time had come to replace currency notes with Bank of England notes, it dwelt almost exclusively on the need for an early return to the gold standard at the former parity. The committee found ingenious ways to make light of any problems that might arise. Astonishingly, the authors cited the experience of the resumption of gold payments for their lesson: 'British experience of the restoration of the gold standard after the French wars, 100 years ago, and the recent experience of continental countries which have taken steps... to rehabilitate their currencies, have shown that a courageous policy in currency matters surmounts apparently formidable obstacles with surprising ease. We believe that on this point history will repeat itself.'[86] This was as disingenuous about recent European developments as it was ignorant, or callous, about their own country's history.

One reason for Keynes's contempt for the committee is that he had come to think that history was moving in a different direction. In his *Tract on Monetary Reform* the previous year, he had argued that the international monetary system, with active British participation, was in practice evolving into a managed gold–dollar–sterling system, not unlike the one he would help to design following the next world war.[87] In this context, the prescriptions of the Cunliffe Committee had simply become irrelevant. To read its report, he thought, was merely to be reminded of 'what a great distance we have covered since then'.[88]

Although Labour speakers after 1925 began to make use of Keynes's attacks on the restoration of the parity, the influence of his theoretical ideas on the labour movement remained slight before the 1930s. Some intellectuals, such as Brailsford, had clearly engaged with his work before 1925, and increasing numbers did so afterwards, but the movement as a whole retained its ancestral commitment to gold until after the debacle of 1931. As well as its profound distrust of all kinds of monetary heterodoxy, the movement, conceiving its mission as the overthrow of

---

[84] J. M. Keynes, *Churchill*. This first appeared as three articles in Beaverbrook's *Evening Standard*, 22–4 July 1925.
[85] Keynes, 'Bradbury', p. 304.   [86] Bradbury, *Report*, pp. 7–8.
[87] Keynes, *Monetary Reform*, ch. 5, esp. p. 204.   [88] Keynes, *Monetary Reform*, p. 194.

capitalism, and in robust electoral competition with the Liberal Party, could not but view the ideas of a committed Liberal supporter of capitalism with some suspicion. This was especially so as he proclaimed a deliberate choice not to follow the many former Liberals who had joined the Labour Party or converted to socialism since August 1914.[89]

Nevertheless, sections of the movement did begin to attach more importance to monetary questions after 1925. This was clearly on display in 1928 when the government legislated—as per the Bradbury Committee—to replace currency notes with Bank of England one-pound and ten-shilling notes. Labour's response included a demand for an inquiry into the 'constitution, powers and policy of the Bank of England'.[90] Characteristically, Snowden was unable to move this amendment without delivering an encomium on the Bank and on Norman in particular, but some of his ILP colleagues were much more assertive, demonstrating a belief largely missing from working-class movements since Cobbett's time, that monetary policy is necessarily political and is run in the interests of the powerful. The ILP's James Maxton explicitly rejected the claim—repeated by Snowden among many others—that the Bank was and should be free of 'political interference'. He asked, 'does anyone believe... that every director of the Bank of England is not a Tory and a defender of Capitalism, and that his Tory philosophy does not operate in his ruling of the Bank's affairs'. The government had only looked at currency 'as an opportunity for private enterprise to make more profits and more money'.[91] Maxton's comrade, R. C. Wallhead, gave a speech peppered with references to the rentier class, money changers, money lords, and financiers who 'put greed above the promptings of patriotism or humanity'. Citing Keynes, he spelt out the ravages of the post-war deflation and the return to gold, particularly among his own constituents, who suffered 81 per cent unemployment: 'They want to know what your juggling with currency will do for them. Will it bring them work, or bread, or give them anything that is of any value at all? Juggle with these things as you will; all your talk of what you are going to do with these marvellous manœuvrings leaves them cold. It is time that we took control of currency ourselves. It is time that the State controlled it.'[92]

The change required the design of new notes. Although the Bank broke its own traditions by using colour and printing the reverses, the front of the notes looked much as the Bank's notes had done for more than a century, as the directors had specified.[93] Despite the fact that the notes were legal tender throughout the United

---

[89] Blaazer, *Popular Front*, ch. 4. See 'Am I a Liberal' (1925) and 'Liberalism and Labour' (1926), in Keynes, *Persuasion*.
[90] Hansard HC, vol. 217, c. 703 (14 May 1928).
[91] Hansard HC, vol. 217, c. 818–22 (14 May 1928).
[92] Hansard HC, vol. 217, c. 801–3 (14 May 1928).
[93] Byatt, *Promises*, p. 123. The bank's initial plan had simply been to produce smaller versions of the white notes. Mackenzie, *Note*, pp. 149–50; Roberts, *Saving City*, p. 125.

Figure 8.2 The Bank of England combines nostalgia for circulating gold with a reassertion of its privilege of note issue: a one-pound note (reverse), 1928.
© The Trustees of the British Museum

Kingdom, Britannia's shield still bore only the cross of St George. The reverse of the one-pound note (Figure 8.2) was simultaneously novel and nostalgic, featuring two symmetrically placed images of Pistrucci's St George from the pre-war gold sovereigns, together with a picture of the facade of the Bank of England's head office where the reverses of the currency notes had depicted the Houses of Parliament—a clear reassertion of the Bank's rights in the matter of note issue.

The notes were met with something between indifference and hostility in the press. The *Daily Mail* thought that the notes lacked 'that distinctively British air which belonged to the old £1 and 10s. Treasury notes', even going so far as to worry that they looked 'as if they had been designed and printed in the United States'.[94] According to provincial reporters who tested the notes' reception, many people were suspicious of their American or more generally 'foreign' appearance.[95] A prominent artist declared that the notes were 'quite unworthy of a great country'.[96]

A more substantial complaint about the new arrangements came from the Scottish banks, who lobbied for permission to issue their own ten-shilling notes, arguing that their customers would strongly prefer the familiar Scottish notes to the new Bank of England notes. When this was denied, the bankers threatened a repeat of the campaign of 1826.[97] But no campaign followed when the government

---

[94] *Daily Mail*, 23 Nov. 1928, p. 12.
[95] *Liverpool Echo*, 22 Nov. 1928 (BNA); *Yorkshire Post and Leeds Intelligencer*, 23 Nov. 1928 (BNA); *Leicester Evening Mail*, 23 Nov. 1928 (BNA); *Dundee Evening Telegraph*, 26 Nov. 1928 (BNA).
[96] *Daily Herald*, 23 Nov. 1928 (BNA).
[97] Geo. J. Scott to Sir John Gilmour, 12 May 1928, LBGA, GB1830 SBM 1/14.

held firm, leading the president of Bank of Scotland's shareholders to denounce the Scottish banks' management as unfit representatives of Scotland.[98] The bankers' decision not to campaign was probably wise. Given that small notes remained available, it is difficult to imagine that many Scots shared the view that their source was 'of national importance'.[99] Unlike 1826, difference had been obliterated by making a UK system that resembled Scotland's in its everyday workings. That being so, especially in the context of the class politics of the 1920s, the banks' chances of inciting a mass mobilization for their right to print a particular denomination of banknote were negligible. All that was left was for Norman Hird, Chairman of the Scottish Institute of Bankers, to quote Malachi Malagrowther and lament the 'growing disposition towards uniformity without regard to past history and local or national conditions'.[100]

Apart from this, Scottish opinion followed the same lines as English. There was some questioning about the timing of the return to gold, and Hird, like other British bankers, voiced concerns before the event about the likely effects of a high bank rate on industry, but otherwise the decision was welcomed.[101] With Scottish note issues now backed by Bank of England notes, monetary differences between England and Scotland were now almost completely drained of substance. Moreover, commercial imperatives were rapidly driving convergence of their banking systems. Beginning in 1919, a movement of 'affiliation' between various Scottish banks and their now much larger English joint-stock counterparts foreshadowed an eventual amalgamation of capital, management, and practices that by the end of the century would leave little distinctive about Scottish money but the curio of three private issues, each articulating its own themes of 'Scottishness', including portraits of Sir Walter Scott.[102]

Union (Partially) Undone: Creating an Irish Currency

It is also surprisingly difficult to find much deviation from British monetary opinion in Ireland, even in the aftermath of Ireland's bitter war of independence and the consequent separation of twenty-six Irish counties from the United Kingdom to form Saorstát Éireann. Indeed, the process of creating a new currency for the new state demonstrated a desire on both sides of the Irish Sea to reintroduce as little monetary difference as possible. This was made possible by a shared commitment to the gold standard and the principles of Peel's legislation.

---

[98] *Dundee Evening Telegraph*, 3 Apr. 1929 (BNA).
[99] *Dundee Evening Telegraph*, 23 May 1928 (BNA).   [100] *Scotsman*, 5 June 1928 (BNA).
[101] Speech of Norman Hird, General Manager of the Union Bank of Scotland, *Glasgow Herald*, 21 Apr. 1925 (BNA).
[102] Checkland, *Scottish Banking*, pp. 576–81; Blaazer, 'Identities'.

That commitment came as a surprise to some. On 24 February 1922, not long after the Anglo-Irish treaty came into effect, the House of Commons debated a government proposal for financial compensation to victims of UK actions in the Anglo-Irish war. The proposal was inherently disgraceful to many Unionist MPs.[103] Sir Charles Oman, the prolific military historian, prominent numismatist, and MP for Oxford University, attacked the proposal from a novel angle. Certain that the new government would issue 'paper money in enormous quantities' and thus reduce the value of its currency to those of Germany, Austria, or Poland, Oman asked whether the government was 'prepared to guarantee that all the damages paid to the loyalists in Ireland by the Irish government will be paid in pounds sterling and not in some trashy harp-decorated stuff...We want a declaration that we shall not give a representative of gold and get back the representative of trash.' Oman could hardly have been more mistaken, for the men who were soon to set about crafting the monetary regime of Saorstát Éireann were as committed to 'sound money' as Oman himself.

Oman was correct in one respect. Like their counterparts in all newly independent states in the twentieth century, the new rulers of the Saorstát saw the issue of a distinctive currency as 'one of the indications of sovereignty'.[104] They therefore set about as quickly as they reasonably could to create their own national currency. The formal implementation of the Saorstát constitution on 6 January 1922 gave the matter some urgency. The United Kingdom's authority over currency in the new state then lapsed, leaving it with neither legal tender money nor legal units of account.[105] United Kingdom coins and currency notes, Bank of England notes, and the notes of Irish banks nonetheless continued to circulate easily because people continued to accept them and nobody had any reason to want them to fail. For the British government monetary instability or collapse in the Saorstát would have dislocated a key trading relationship. For the Irish government, still struggling for legitimacy, it would almost certainly have led to collapse of the new regime itself. For the ordinary people there was little choice; it was the only money available.

Given the circumstances of the Saorstát's birth, and the violent rejection of its legitimacy by many of its leaders' erstwhile comrades on the grounds that it remained a British dominion owing allegiance to the crown, the ongoing circulation of British money was embarrassing. The new government could not permit it to continue for long. But there was more than symbolism at stake in these

---

[103] The map of British party politics was redrawn in 1886 when the Liberal Prime Minister, William Gladstone, declared his support for the 'Home Rule' (i.e. a devolved parliament) objective of the Irish Parliamentary Party. Liberal opponents of the measure broke away under the banner of Liberal Unionism and gradually merged into the Conservative Party, which added the word 'Unionist' to its official name. 'Unionist' was frequently used to describe the party and its members until well into the interwar period, especially in Irish and Scottish contexts.
[104] Mohr, 'Coinage', p. 464. [105] Colbert, 'Currency Problem', p. 13.

decisions. A national currency confers the power to make monetary policy, a key element of economic independence.[106] Moreover, the seignorage on paper money and token coin would be more than welcome to the severely cash-strapped new regime. As we shall see, however, the Saorstát government willingly made choices that reduced these benefits.

From the beginning, the government's priority was to create an overwhelming impression of 'soundness'. Their first step in that direction was to make the silver coin of 75 per cent purity rather than the approximately 50 per cent of the current British coin. This ruled out the relatively cheap and easy option of calling in the current UK coin and reminting it at existing values. Instead, the Irish government asked the UK government to buy up the coin circulating in Ireland at its face value to provide funds for Ireland to purchase silver for its new coinage. This was costly for the UK Exchequer, and became the subject of a bitter dispute between Churchill and the Saorstát officials.[107] The resulting compromise phased the UK government's purchases and placed a limit on the total it would accept.

The Irish government was thereby foregoing significant seignorage purely in order to obtain 'a good reputation for the coins in popular estimation at the outset'.[108] This was surely fanciful; the time had long passed when popular estimation cared much about the bullion content of token coins. Nevertheless, it demonstrates that the government's need to persuade the wider world of its bottomless financial and fiscal probity was more important to the articulation of its nationalism than was its wish either to maximize its revenues or to assert its sovereign rights to the fullest possible extent. This was an abiding theme in its decisions on the currency.

The national rhetoric embodied in the coins was subtle. On the reverse there were representations of a different animal or bird for each denomination. The inscriptions were in Irish rather than English. The obverses were indeed 'harp-decorated', as had been many Irish coins since Henry VIII had introduced the device to his Irish coins. The novelty lay in the fact that the harps were not surmounted by a crown, and still more in the fact that the king did not appear anywhere. This was appalling to Unionists. As Lord Danesfort asked, 'is there any precedent of any of His Majesty's Dominions issuing coinage with the head of the King eliminated from the design?'[109] There was not, but in the disputed context of the Saorstát's creation, that was precisely the symbolic point that its authorities needed to make.

These decisions on new coin were merely a prelude to the issue of new paper money and decisions on banking and the monetary standard. This was tackled

---

[106] Helleiner, *National Money*, p. 9.   [107] Mohr, 'Coinage', pp. 466–9.
[108] NAI, DT S3875, 'Memorandum on Token Coinage', Department of Finance [1924], quoted in Mohr, 'Coinage', p. 457.
[109] Hansard HL, vol. 73, c. 509 (13 Mar. 1929).

before the new coins began to circulate. In 1926, the Finance Minister, Ernest Blythe, established a Banking Commission whose composition reflected his own views on these questions. A fire-eating republican from a Unionist background, Blythe's fiscal conservatism is a stock point of historical discussion of the Saorstát.[110] His monetary conservatism matched it. Among his commissioners were a Columbia University professor of finance, four bankers, an industrialist, a former senior executive of the Commonwealth Bank of Australia, and J. J. McElligott, shortly to become permanent secretary to the Ministry of Finance. McElligott was cut from the same cloth as Blythe. A graduate of University College Dublin, he was progressing through the Irish civil service until he fought in the 1916 Easter Rising. After a stint in jails in England he studied economics and became editor of *The Statist,* a respected, deeply orthodox London financial weekly, before joining the Saorstát civil service in 1923.[111] His fiscal and monetary ultra-orthodoxy was as profound as his commitment to the national cause.

The commission's defining recommendation was that the monetary standard of the Saorstát was to be identical to that of the United Kingdom, and that its monetary arrangements were to be designed purely in order to maintain that state of affairs.[112] There was to be no central bank, at least for the time being; instead, there would be a 'Currency Commission'. The key functions of central banking—setting interest rates, intervening in the money market, and maintaining public credit—were not to be exercised in Ireland but in London, by the Bank of England.[113]

The reasons were spelt out in the commission's reports. The Irish economy had been linked to Britain's for centuries and Britain still took 95 per cent of Ireland's exports. The establishment of a monetary system in Ireland that could give rise to the development of an exchange rate with the UK would create impediments to that trade for no benefit.[114] Control of the currency must be vested in a non-political body to prevent it from succumbing to 'changes of government', or 'the development of budget deficits and other evils from which no country has found itself immune'. Forswearing the possibility of democratic control of the monetary system by attaching Ireland's system to that of the UK would show the world that Ireland had no intention of sinking into the monetary troubles that had beset other countries during and after the war. Underpinning it all was a British monetary system based on 'sound principles'. In particular, the commission's first report noted, 'Great Britain is making the utmost effort to return to a well-established Gold Standard'.[115] The commission was as quick to condemn 'the

---

[110] Regan, *Counter-Revolution*, pp. 209–12, 218; Ó Gráda, 1995, p. 441.
[111] Cromien, 'McElligott'.   [112] Banking Commission, *Final Reports*, p. 3.
[113] Banking Commission, *Final Reports*, pp. 35–8.
[114] Banking Commission, *Final Reports*, p. 2.
[115] [Saorstát] Banking Commission, First Interim Report (TS), pp. 10, 12, TNA, T160/423.

numerous more or less fanciful proposals for relying on a different type of monetary standard' as it was to wish away the deflationary effects of 'British' policy.[116]

Such statements might have gone some way to allay 'the nervousness of the vast majority' which some believed to be present in Ireland. According to one newspaper, what 'the man in the street—or rather, the man in the fields' wanted above all was to keep the 'honest and trusted standard of value. He is not anxious to see the British pound sterling meet the fate of a sacrificial lamb upon the altar of nationalism.'[117] In the opinion of one correspondent, however, people would not trust the new, government-issued notes even if they were truly equal in value to sterling. They would hoard sterling and 'financial chaos would ensue'.[118] According to this writer, the answer was to make the familiar notes of the Irish banks legal tender.

The adherence of both countries to the pre-war gold standard ensured that the issue of paper money in both parts of Ireland could be rebuilt on the foundations of the 1845 Banking Act. The commission's report proposed the circulation of two kinds of paper money. 'Legal Tender notes' would be issued by the currency commission and would take the place of UK currency notes then in circulation. They would also replace the existing Irish banks' so-called 'excess issues' which under the terms of the 1845 Act were permitted if wholly backed by bullion. The legal tender notes were an absolute obligation of the state, and would be backed pound for pound by holdings of Bank of England notes, of gold, or of British Government Securities held in London.[119] They would be freely convertible at par in London to Bank of England notes, which in turn were freely convertible into legal tender notes in Dublin. 'Consolidated Notes' would be issued by the currency commission to the Irish banks for issue to the public. These would have a common design, but would bear the name of the relevant bank, and would replace their existing fiduciary issue. They would be convertible into legal tender notes at the head office of the issuing bank. The total fiduciary issue would remain the same, which is to say the total amount the existing banks of issue had been permitted in the 1845 legislation.[120]

The image the Currency Commission chose for the consolidated banknotes articulated a concept of national identity which was clearly a product of its historical context. Eschewing any reference to national struggles, the 'ploughman' notes present an image of tranquil labour, proclaiming Ireland's return to peace after long years of armed conflict. (See Figure 8.3.) But it was a very particular vision of Ireland whose peace was proclaimed: an Ireland built on a vision of the

---

[116] Banking Commission, *Final Reports*, pp. 3–4, 19.
[117] *Westmeath Independent* 3 Apr. 1926 (BNA).
[118] H. Walker, letter to *Freeman's Journal*, 20 Sept. 1924 (INA).
[119] [Saorstát] Banking Commission, First Interim Report (TS), p. 11, TNA, T160/423.
[120] Banking Commission, *Final Reports*, pp. 38–9.

Figure 8.3 A nationalist vision of Ireland: an Irish Currency Commission note, 1929.
© The Trustees of the British Museum

Irish peasant which lay at the centre of the blood-and-soil myths promoted by exponents of the 'Gaelic revival' of the turn of the century: a movement that inspired both the leaders of the Saorstát and their republican enemies.[121] The legal tender notes also featured tranquil national symbolism, with a vignette of a modern-looking, robed, and somewhat languid Erin leaning on a harp, with images of Irish rivers in the background.

The commission's recommendations faced thorny problems of implementation. Of Ireland's six banks of issue only the Belfast Bank confined its business to the six counties of what was now Northern Ireland. The others issued notes at their offices throughout the whole of Ireland. These banks' fiduciary issues now also had to be partitioned, as some would remain part of the currency of the UK while the rest would form part of the currency of the Saorstát. But there was no obvious way to decide how many of its fiduciary notes a bank could now issue on each side of the border. The negotiations around this question were inevitably quite technical, with the banks finding ingenious arguments for maximizing their issues.

Negotiations on the Saorstát side were conducted by McElligott and his friend and superior at finance, Joseph Brennan, who was shortly to become the founding head of the Currency Commission. Their monetary views were almost indistinguishable. Sir Otto Niemeyer acted for the UK Treasury. The key figure in the Northern Irish government was Sir Wilfrid Spender—a member of the Ulster

---

[121] See Hutchinson, *Cultural Nationalism*, chs. 4 and 7; Foster, *Modern Ireland*, pp. 446–56, 518–21.

Volunteer Force. Although head of the Ministry of Finance, Spender, unlike any of the others, had no background in finance at all. While this meant that his correspondence on this question lacked the stamp of strongly held theoretical views that permeated the work of his counterparts, it also meant that he was easily persuaded by the banks that an increase in their issues was in Northern Ireland's interests. His letter to Niemeyer, suggesting that the banks' ideas were 'logical' called forth a stinging, didactic response:

> The monopoly right to issue notes is exceedingly valuable to a private bank. Under modern conditions it is a complete anachronism and ought not to be allowed except to a central bank. Where, as in Northern Ireland, it cannot at the moment be abolished, (the only 'logical' solution), it should in no circumstances be extended. The Banks, guided by their own interests, of course take the opposite view, and that is behind the many ingenious suggestions which they produce to you.[122]

The only discernible difference between the UK and Saorstát officials was that the latter treated their banks more gently than Niemeyer would have liked. Certainly their policy of allowing the right of issue (of consolidated notes) to three banks that had not been in existence in 1845 was at odds with Niemeyer's view that the right of issue should not be extended. It was acceptable only because the new banks' issues were to be carved out of the existing total, rather than added to it, and were therefore not inflationary.[123]

This difference, however, was at the margins, and reflected merely that the fledgling state's officials were in a weaker position vis-à-vis the Irish banks than was the financial controller of the UK Treasury in relation to the banks of Northern Ireland. Niemeyer's correspondence with Brennan and McElligott, unlike his correspondence with Spender, shows a clear sense of common purpose, which in their view transcended national or parochial self-interest. That common purpose was, in the first instance, the long-term monetary stability of the Saorstát and the United Kingdom, which were intimately connected owing to the sterling basis of the Irish currency. But that was only a brushstroke on a much bigger canvas. What was also at stake for all of them was the health and stability of the whole international monetary order, which they believed could only be guaranteed by the gold standard.

The commission's report and the legislation modelled on it inevitably attracted criticism from militant republicans, who argued that the currency was insufficiently independent, while criticizing recent UK monetary policy. The decision 'to

---

[122] Spender to Niemeyer, 3 June 1926; Niemeyer to Spender, 22 June 1926, TNA, T160/423.
[123] Note of Interview with Messrs Campion, Galloway and McElligott, 23 July 1926, TNA, T160/423.

adopt the English currency system was in fact a surrender of our fiscal autonomy', which had put Ireland 'in pawn to Great Britain'.[124] *The Nation* argued that the Bank of England, with the Irish banks 'acting as its agents', had ruined Irish farmers through the deflation mandated by the Cunliffe Committee. By means of this 'financial juggling' Irish farmers had been robbed, 'while the bank shareholders, the old ascendancy gang, have been enriched.... Yet it is to the same banks that the Cosgrave Government is handing over the management of the Currency Commission.' Speaking at a large meeting of Fianna Fáil—the main political party of the opponents of the Anglo-Irish treaty—its leader, Eamonn de Valera, criticized this 'bankers' report' and demanded an inquiry with full representation from farming and industry. The report meant that Ireland would be 'tied financially, instead of being allowed to cut themselves free, to England' and thus subject to the damaging monetary policy of the Bank of England. Speaking next, Seán MacEntee offered an alternative policy: 'Currency in this country', he argued, 'should be based on Irish gold, not English paper'.[125]

In a memorandum to Cosgrave, McElligott repudiated such criticisms. After cautioning that national considerations had no place and no significance in the money market, and that 'nothing can or ought to be attempted to alter the existing condition of affairs', McElligott concluded: 'The tendency today is against monetary nationalism not towards it, to endeavour to achieve stability and security by currency and banking cooperation and united effort. The Saorstát must align itself with this movement.'[126] This argument was, of course, only valid if the UK's monetary order could be understood as representing something international rather than merely national, or worse still from an Irish point of view, imperial.

The more frequent response to such concerns was analogous to Michael Collins's defence of the Anglo-Irish Treaty—that it had given Ireland the freedom to achieve freedom. In the case of money, Ireland chose to exercise its monetary sovereignty by pegging its currency to sterling only because it was in its interest to do so. The evidence of sovereignty was that Ireland could choose some different arrangement at will. For example, if at some time in the future 'Great Britain ... began to inflate, as it did during the war', Ireland could 'cut adrift from sterling'.[127] In the fifty years that the arrangement lasted, faith that the sterling peg was in Ireland's best interests, or that it represented a link to a wholesome monetary internationalism, faced many tests. The first—only three years after Ireland's paper currency came into being—was the United Kingdom's abandonment of the gold standard.

---

[124] *Honesty*, 9 Nov. 1929 (INA).
[125] *Drogheda Independent*, 5 Feb. 1927 (BNA). Five years later, as Finance Minister in a Fianna Fáil government, MacEntee ran a conservative fiscal and financial policy in partnership with McElligott as Department Secretary.
[126] [Oct. 1929,] NAI TSCH/3/S2355 A.   [127] *Irish Statesman*, 16 Apr. 1927 (INA).

1931: Power, Patriotism, and the Discourse of Catastrophe

The international gold standard was already in trouble by the time the first Irish notes appeared in September 1928. Within a year the system would begin to 'crumble from the periphery' as Argentina, Australia, and New Zealand were forced to abandon key elements by the end of 1929.[128] The crisis had its roots in fundamental weaknesses that were present from the beginning, chiefly a serious maldistribution of gold resulting from the United States' massive trade surplus and flows of payments of war debts and reparations, including large transfers of gold from London to New York.[129]

The UK's central role in the international financial system ensured once again that it would be affected by every phase of the developing international crisis. Unlike in 1914, however, by the time the crisis reached its crescendo in mid-1931 the UK was already facing major economic and financial difficulties. In addition to mass unemployment and chronic balance of payments problems, its traditional and much-cherished leadership role in the world's financial system obliged it to provide loans to struggling countries, thus depleting reserves it might have used to sustain its overvalued currency. As Eichengreen argues, these factors, combined with its decision to abandon the gold standard only twelve years earlier, meant that its commitment to defend the standard at any cost lacked the credibility it had enjoyed before the war, affecting the behaviour not only of speculators but also of the international and domestic lenders whose support was required to defeat them.[130]

For as long as the UK was committed to remaining on the gold standard at the existing parity, its monetary authorities had no choice but to enact policies congenial to the British and American financiers on whose decisions the fate of sterling ultimately depended. These reflected not only the pecuniary interests and ideological prejudices of the investing classes but also, in the garb of 'sound finance', the considered opinions of academic economists, financial journalists, senior Treasury officials, and senior staff of the Bank of England.

Commitment to the preservation of the gold standard remained as deeply and widely held in the United Kingdom as any proposition in political economy can ever be, even as commitment to free trade disintegrated, sector by sector.[131] Snowden was close enough to the truth when he told the Labour conference in October 1929 that 'there is no one... who does not admit, now that the Gold Standard has been universally re-established, that it must be maintained until the wisdom of man has devised some better substitute for it'.[132] This consensus included not only the Labour minority government that had taken office in June

---

[128] Eichengreen, *Globalizing*, p. 47. [129] Tooze, *Deluge*, pp. 349–50, 359.
[130] Eichengreen, *Golden Fetters*, p. 282. [131] Trentmann, *Free Trade*, pp. 335–6.
[132] Labour Party, *Report of the Annual Conference*, 1929, p. 228.

(with Snowden as Chancellor) but those who had argued for alternative courses in 1925. Thus the professionally and politically diverse Macmillan Committee on the financial system, which Snowden established reluctantly in November 1929, categorically ruled out devaluation on the grounds that a decision by the 'greatest creditor nation' to lower the value of its currency would shatter the confidence essential to international trade, commerce, and finance.[133] For good measure, an addendum signed by six of the least orthodox in the committee's ranks, including Keynes, Bevin, and McKenna, ruled it out again.[134]

The commitment to maintain the gold standard at the existing parity severely limited the government's options to tackle unemployment, the main plank of its successful election campaign. It not only ruled out devaluation itself, which might have made export industries more competitive; it also ruled out proto-Keynesian solutions such as deficit funding of large-scale public works. Historians have often stressed the importance of Snowden's orthodox commitment to balanced budgets, but deficit funding was not an option for any government committed to the gold standard.

In fact, the government was under intense pressure to expunge a deficit that continued to grow as unemployment increased due to the deepening global slump. It was in response to such pressure that the government appointed the May Committee in March 1931 to recommend 'all possible reductions' to government spending.[135] The publication of its report on 31 July worsened an already serious financial crisis and extended it into a major political one. In effect it set a public test of the government's commitment to 'saving the pound' by itemizing a programme of draconian budget cuts focussed on unemployment benefits, education, and the salaries of government employees, including the armed services.[136]

The accelerating global crisis that would end the gold standard had already begun to hit the UK with full force. Bank failures in Austria and Germany drove lenders needing liquidity to withdraw funds from London. As well as having £140 m of its own frozen in Central Europe, the Bank in the course of July lost £55 m in gold and £33 m of foreign exchange, requiring it to seek loans in New York and Paris to support sterling.[137] This task was made more difficult by the May Report's revelation of the extent of the budget deficit, which weakened international confidence in the government's capacity and commitment to defend the pound.[138]

The gold standard thus became the point of leverage for relentless pressure to force the government to implement cuts that were anathema to the labour movement. Evidence of this pressure is overwhelming, both in communications to the government and more private communications in the circles of high

---

[133] Macmillan, *Report*, p. 110.   [134] Macmillan, *Report*, p. 199.
[135] Kynaston, *City*, vol. 3, p. 234; Skidelsky, *Slump*, pp. 331–5; May, *Report*, p. 4.
[136] May, *Report*, pp. 215–19.
[137] Kynaston, *City*, vol. 3, pp. 233–8; Eichengreen, *Golden Fetters*, pp. 281–3.
[138] Skidelsky, *Slump*, p. 379.

finance. The gist of the Bank's strategy was summed up in Norman's private remark on 15 August that the country would 'pull through', 'if we can get [the government] frightened enough'.[139] Ernest Harvey, who was in the governor's chair for most of the crisis owing to Norman's nervous collapse from stress and overwork, was relentless in pursuit of this strategy. On 6 August, in a letter to Snowden emphasizing the need for urgent action, he left no doubt what was required and why: 'As I tried to explain to you last week,...the sign which foreigners expect from this country is the readjustment of the budgetary position, and this attitude has again been forcibly expressed in messages from both Paris and New York.'[140] On one level this was mere reporting of facts, but Harvey was at least as zealous for a balanced budget as any nervous overseas lender. Indeed, James Morrison has argued that Harvey released information and operated policy levers to increase the pressure on the government at critical moments, even when this came at the expense of sterling's position, while another historian, Adam Tooze, suggests that the Bank 'wanted a showdown with the Labour cabinet and secretly encouraged American and French lenders to stiffen their conditions'.[141]

On 23 August, Harvey advised that the Bank had only a few days' reserves left with which to defend the gold standard. This brought weeks of agonized debate within the government and the labour movement to a climax. Following the Trades Unions Congress leaders' decision not to support any of the proposed cuts, the ministry was divided between MacDonald, Snowden, and others who supported cuts to the full extent of the May Report and a minority who could agree only to a smaller programme of reductions, which the Bank had already declared 'wholly unsatisfactory' and likely to further diminish 'confidence'.[142] Unable to resolve the impasse, the cabinet resigned on 23 August. Enjoying the support of the king and leaders of the other parties, MacDonald formed a 'National' government, with Snowden remaining as Chancellor and the remaining cabinet posts distributed between Conservatives, Liberals, and two other members of the former Labour government. Its advent was greeted rapturously by both the press (apart from Labour's *Daily Herald*) and the City.

Within days, elements of the labour movement began to describe these events as a 'bankers' ramp', alleging that financiers had exaggerated and manipulated the situation to destroy the Labour government.[143] Notwithstanding Harvey's behaviour, few historians now support these claims. Indeed, as Philip Williamson suggests, it is likely that bankers in the UK generally preferred that a socialist

---

[139] Kynaston, *City*, vol. 3, p. 236.   [140] Kynaston, *City*, vol. 3, p. 235.
[141] Morrison, 'Intellectual Austerity', esp. pp. 189, 194; Tooze, *Deluge*, p. 500.
[142] Morrison, 'Intellectual Austerity', p. 189.
[143] Numerous historians claim that the *Daily Herald* used the term the following day. Kynaston, *City*, vol. 3, p. 240, asserts that it was the headline of the City Editor's story that day. The actual headline was 'Put the Country before the Bankers'. The first reference to the term I can find in the paper is in a report on 27 August in a report of a speech by MacDonald in which he claimed that the formation of the government was 'no banker's ramp'.

government implement the cuts.[144] But arguments about conspiracies merely distract from the fact that the crisis was shaped throughout by the exercise of monetary power by those who possessed it both institutionally and culturally.[145]

It was inevitable that the defence of sterling would be framed in terms of patriotism, especially after the publication of the May Report. As early as 4 August, a reflective piece in a provincial newspaper on the anniversary of the war invoked 'the spirit of 1914', arguing that if the danger to 'our standard of life' were better explained, 'hard fighting and resolute effort' would 'in the end triumph over our difficulties'.[146] A few weeks later, Field Marshal Lord Methuen told a regimental reunion that 'what they had to do during the great crisis through which they were passing was to maintain that same spirit that carried them through the great war'. He called on the men to show the 'patriotism under great difficulties' that would 'keep England [sic] at the top'.[147]

Such appeals were obviously intended to reconcile their readers and listeners to the hardships that the May Committee's cuts would mean for many of them. They were 'innocent' in that they did not overtly seek advantage for one political party or another. But what is striking about these and other appeals for patriotism in the first few weeks of August is that they did not translate—as they had, for example, in the first few weeks of the war—into support for the government of the day. Rather, it was the government's patriotism that was on trial. It was not until after the formation of the National government that readers were enjoined to support the government in its ultimately unsuccessful efforts to 'save the pound'. At the same time, a flood of editorial comment emphasized the patriotism of all the ministers who had 'put country before party', especially MacDonald and Snowden. Their erstwhile colleagues, however, 'had deserted their posts in the hour of national need'.[148] The *Yorkshire Evening Post* carried a headline, 'The T.U.C. shows its hand. Class preferred to patriotism.'[149] The *Western Mail* contrasted the Conservative and Liberal parties' unanimous endorsements of the government with the attitude of the 'Socialist party' which had proved that it was 'not animated by... patriotic motives'.[150]

This was the reverse of the trajectory of the *Daily Herald*, which during the life of the Labour government rehearsed the full repertoire of conventional monetary patriotism, emphasizing both the foreign origins of the pound's problems and the deep national necessity to overcome them. In terms reminiscent of 1914 it explained that while 'French and other Continental investors ha[d] withdrawn millions of pounds at a panic rate', 'British calm ha[d] provided an example to the rest of the world'. Underlying it all was 'the proud fact that Britain has never paid

---

[144] Williamson, 'Bankers' Ramp?', p. 805. [145] Williamson, 'Bankers' Ramp?', p. 805.
[146] *Lincolnshire Echo*, 4 Aug, 1931 (BNA). [147] *North Wilts Herald*, 21 Aug. 1931 (BNA).
[148] *Daily Express*, 26 Aug. 1931. [149] *Yorkshire Evening Post*, 25 Aug. 1931 (BNA).
[150] *Western Mail*, 29 Aug. 1931 (BNA).

its creditors less than 20 shillings in the pound'. Preserving this state of affairs by balancing the budget was a 'patriotic duty' which the *Herald* was sure would have the support of the City and the other parties.[151] As Conservatives began to mobilize patriotism behind the newly formed National government, the *Herald* tried hard to turn such arguments. 'Where is the patriotism', it asked, in allowing American bankers to dictate policy? The labour movement was 'fulfilling a high national duty' by 'defending the nation' against 'a fatal policy, which blinded by regard for the interests of one small but powerful section, ignores the interests of the whole nation'. Resisting this policy was 'the highest patriotic duty of the moment'.[152]

The formation of the National government was not enough to save the gold standard. The Bank quietly stopped defending sterling on 18 September, and the decision was formally announced two days later. This required more rhetorical twists. Now it was the turn of the Conservative press and politicians to emphasize the international origins of the crisis. Like the *Herald,* many papers began to stress the opportunities presented by being liberated from maintaining the parity at such a high rate. Like the *Herald* at a much earlier phase of the crisis, the *Express* deployed an image of a muscular John Bull rolling up his sleeves to confront the crisis. Beside him, the 'Little Man' also rolls up his sleeves, saying 'Say John, do you remember that shell hole in 1914?'[153] (See Figures 8.4 and 8.5.) *The Belfast News-Letter* explained in lurid terms why the end of the socialist government made it safe to abandon gold. Previous, thus warnings that the end of the gold standard would send the pound 'fluttering into the gutter after the mark and the rouble' were largely forgotten.[154]

The domestic monetary consequences of the end of the gold standard were remarkably undramatic. Over the next few months the Bank and the Treasury managed the currency down to $3.24, and maintained a 'managed float' for the rest of the decade, with target exchange rates determined primarily by domestic economic objectives.[155] As many had predicted, however, the UK's departure from the gold standard did mean the rapid unravelling of the system internationally, with catastrophic economic and political consequences across the globe.[156]

The Glasgow Herald was characteristically sober in its assessment. It accepted that the abandonment of the gold standard was 'in a sense humiliating, but there it is'. It acknowledged that the global power of sterling and 'British' finance would be lost 'for a time'. What was required now was calm and unity 'in a supreme effort to retrieve our position'. The 'essential condition' of this recovery was to retain the balanced budget that the National government had achieved: 'It restores

---

[151] *Daily Herald*, 8 Aug. 1931 (BNA).   [152] *Daily Herald*, 31 Aug. 1931 (BNA).
[153] *Daily Express*, 21 Sept. 1931.
[154] *Belfast News-Letter*, 22 Sept. 1931 (INA); *Orkney Herald, and Weekly Advertiser and Gazette for the Orkney & Zetland Islands*, 16 Sept. 1931 (BNA).
[155] Howson, 'Management', p. 55.   [156] Tooze, *Deluge*, pp. 501–4.

Figure 8.4 With the Labour Government still in power, John Bull faces the crisis in the *Daily Herald*, 19 August 1931.
With thanks to the British Newspaper Archive, http://www.britishnewspaperarchive.co.uk

Figure 8.5 With the Labour Government gone, John Bull faces the crisis in the *Daily Express*, 21 September 1931.
Source: Strube/Daily Express/Mirrorpix

confidence in ourselves, and possessed once more... of the initiative in our own financial affairs, we can again hold up our heads.'[157]

This was an instinctively 'British' response to the crisis, which rehearsed similar arguments in a similar tone to commentary in *The Times*, *Financial Times*, and *Economist*. It was left to the small-circulation monthly of the Scottish National Party to try to articulate a distinctively 'Scottish' response. It regarded MacDonald (a Scot) merely as 'an official charged with the unpleasant duty of cutting down the Scottish services and votes in accordance with the decrees of his English masters'. It compared Scotland's level of taxation unfavourably with that of other small European countries, including the Irish Free State. More fundamentally, it asked, 'would the problem of the crisis have arisen at all in Scotland but for the Union?' The 'only effective remedy' was 'complete financial autonomy and a real National Government in Scotland'.[158]

However an independent Scotland might have fared, financial autonomy and a National government did not insulate Saorstát Éireann from the crisis. Publicly, the Saorstát government 'put the best face on matters' by stressing the increased competitiveness of Irish agricultural products in British markets. Privately, it was aggrieved not only by the change but by the fact that it had not been consulted.[159] Brennan felt it as a betrayal of the gold standard internationalism that had driven his and McElligott's approach to the currency question from the beginning. It was also a direct blow to the Saorstát's interests. In a memorandum he shared with the UK Trade Commissioner, he explained that Ireland, 'in the common interest of gold standard countries', had followed the Genoa resolution to economize gold by keeping its balances in London in paper, whose value in terms of gold was now depreciated. He called for an international conference to find a way to restore a 'rehabilitated monetary mechanism'. Ideally, this meant repairing the 'largely automatic' gold standard system, which was far easier to manage than 'the vagaries of unrelated units of unaccountable inconvertible currencies'.[160]

The Fianna Fáil newspaper, *The Irish Press*, welcomed the end of 'the sacrifice of human and economic interests in order to maintain the gold standard' and acknowledged the likely benefits to Irish trade.[161] The crisis also revived Fianna Fáil's criticisms of the sterling peg. A cartoon the following week, ironically captioned 'FREE STATE CURRENCY: "Safely anchored to the pound,"' captured this view concisely (Figure 8.6). The same paper pointed out the significant loss of value in gold terms of UK securities held by both the Irish government and its citizens, which it estimated at about thirty million pounds. The more important point was that if the Saorstát had its own gold reserve and central bank, it could act

---

[157] *Glasgow Herald*, 21 Sept. 1931; 22 Sept. 1931 (BNA).
[158] *Scots Independent*, vol. 12 (Oct. 1931), p. 177.
[159] W. Peters to E. R. Eddison, 1 Oct. 1931, TNA T241/14 (9071/1 f. 5).
[160] W. Peters to E. R. Eddison, 12 Oct. 1931 (encl.), TNA T241/14 (9071/2).
[161] *Irish Press*, 19 Sept. 1931 (INA).

FREE STATE CURRENCY : "Safely anchored to the pound."

Figure 8.6 A sardonic comment on Saorstát Éireann's sterling peg: *Irish Press*, 26 September 1931.
With thanks to the Irish Newspaper Archive, http://www.irishnewsarchive.com

'in accordance with what we thought to be our own best interests, instead of allowing the Bank of England and the British government to make the decision for us, without consulting us, or even recalling our existence'.[162] In response to similar criticisms in the Seanad, Blythe rehearsed the familiar argument that the Saorstát's trading relationships 'would have made it impossible for us, if we were to have any regard for the economic interests of the country, to remain on a gold standard if Britain went off it'. Meanwhile, its holdings of securities continued to earn interest that gold in a vault would not.[163]

Even without the gold standard, Ireland remained committed to some version of monetary internationalism. Despite its pursuit of a damaging 'economic war' against the UK, the Fianna Fáil government that took office in 1932 left Ireland's currency arrangements untouched. Successive Irish governments did likewise

---

[162] *Irish Press*, 26 Sept. 1931 (INA).   [163] Seanad Éireann Debate, vol. 14, 32 (14 Oct. 1931).

until 1978, when Ireland, along with every country of the European Economic Community except the United Kingdom, joined the European Monetary System to prepare for the creation of a much larger monetary union. In England and Scotland, although not in Northern Ireland, the press observed that Ireland's decision 'left Britain out in the cold alone'.[164]

---

[164] *Birmingham Daily Post* (BNA); *Daily Mirror* (BLN); *Aberdeen Press and Journal* (BNA), 16 Dec. 1978.

Epilogue

The Burdens and Uses of the Past

> The event illuminates its own past; it cannot be deduced from it.
> Hannah Arendt, 'Understanding and Politics' (1994)

Debates over the euro revealed divergent attitudes to currency among past and present constituent nations of the United Kingdom that continued to evolve long after it became clear that the UK was not going to join the single currency. Subsequent monetary events and debates have shed further light not only on these differences but also on the disposition of monetary power and the unequal nature of the struggle between the monetary order's critics and its leaders and key beneficiaries. While I make no claim to have shown any kind of linear 'causation' to account for these events, the underlying premise of this book has been that many of these phenomena have historical roots and therefore can be better understood through the study of their history. In this Epilogue, which I present by way of conclusion, I will examine how recent phenomena help to make sense of the history presented in the preceding pages and evaluate some of the ways that participants in recent debates have tried to use (or ignore) history to support their positions.

The United Kingdom and the Republic of Ireland represent the absolute extremes in the spectrum of responses to a European single currency. Not only did Ireland adopt the euro with little controversy, but its citizens consistently express more positive attitudes towards it on every dimension than their counterparts in any, or almost any, other member state.[1] In stark contrast, the UK not only declined to adopt the euro, but the very proposal triggered a backlash against the whole European project that was eventually powerful enough to carry the UK out of the EU altogether, spawning new political parties, shattering the unity of two others, and destroying and fulfilling political careers while stoking deep cultural and social acrimonies along the way.[2] At the same time the vicissitudes of the euro have had significant consequences for the Scottish National Party's posture on Scotland's currency future, leaving it vulnerable to questions about the relationship between currency, sovereignty, and nationality.

---

[1] See, for example, *Flash Eurobarometer 501: The Euro Area. Summary* (2012), p. 12.
[2] Adonis, 'Ming Vase'; Gamble and Kelly, 'Britain and Emu'.

While Ireland has been unusual in its enthusiasm for the single currency, the UK has been exceptional in not just the degree, but the nature, of its hostility. Quantitative studies by social and economic psychologists during the 1990s confirmed the general impressions generated by political debate and press commentary that questions of identity were at stake in the UK in uniquely powerful ways. Such studies applied a variety of conceptual frameworks to understanding attitudes to the euro and came to similar conclusions. Every variable identified as having a strong correlation with negative attitudes to the euro was more prominent in the UK than in other countries. Moreover, the correlations themselves were stronger there than anywhere else.

The most striking findings come from a study by Anke Müller-Peters conducted in 1997, which shows that 'fundamentally, the introduction of a single European currency cannot be reconciled with the British self-image, no matter how this self-image is framed in concrete terms'.[3]

Müller-Peters's findings make it clear that the euro was not merely collateral damage in a larger anti-European struggle, as some have suggested, but was objectionable in and of itself.[4] In a number of countries, including the UK, she found that 'the currency is apparently a part of the national culture and as integral to cultural-historical pride [in one's country] as language or history is'. She also found a significant negative correlation between 'pride in one's own currency and acceptance of the euro'. Her results make it clear that this correlation was stronger in the UK than in any other country and much stronger there than in Europe as a whole. 'Cultural and historical pride' in one's country showed a similar pattern. While six countries (including Ireland) showed stronger cultural and historical national pride than the UK, the negative correlation between that pride and support for the euro was overwhelmingly stronger in the UK than in any other member country. Indeed, in only one other country, Finland, was the correlation even statistically significant. In Ireland there was a very weak *positive* correlation.[5] In other words, Irish people's cultural and historical pride in their country was marginally more likely to be accompanied by *support* for the euro than by opposition.

Memory, History, and the 'Decline' of Sterling

Considering these findings in the light of the UK's monetary history during the lifetimes of the respondents, we can only conclude that the pride in sterling that was so important to their attitudes to the euro was derived from their understanding of history rather than personal memory. An 80-year-old respondent to

---

[3] Müller-Peters, 'National Pride', pp. 704, 713. [4] Risse, 'Euro', p. 492, makes this argument.
[5] Müller-Peters, 'National Pride', pp. 709–10, 714 (Table 5).

Müller-Peters's 1997 survey could have had no recollection of any national monetary event earlier than the crisis of 1931. The national monetary memories throughout their adult years were similarly traumatic. From the convertibility crisis of 1947 to 'Black Wednesday' in 1992, the story of the UK's currency—at least as presented by politicians and the press—was of permanent vulnerability and periodic failure and humiliation. By the later 1950s, sterling duly took its place in burgeoning accounts of 'British decline'.[6]

Remarkably, this 'decline' of sterling did not diminish the identification of the worth of the currency with that of the nation. Indeed, something like the reverse seems to have occurred. By the time of the 1967 sterling devaluation, politicians, journalists, and writers of letters to newspapers took the association for granted. By 1990, when the European single currency emerged as a topic of general public debate, the equation of the continuation of the pound sterling with the United Kingdom's very existence as a sovereign nation was easily asserted and widely accepted. And despite determined attempts to move the question onto narrow grounds of economic costs and benefits, questions of identity, sovereignty, and history became more rather than less prominent as the debate went on. Again, this is paradoxical, for the history that the participants in those debates had experienced at first hand saw sterling crushed under the weight of its own history in a series of episodes that demonstrated just how limited the UK's monetary sovereignty had become. The more things slip away, the more tightly they are grasped.

Sterling's problems after the Second World War were an amplified version of those it faced after the previous war: its role in the global economy was far greater than the UK's ravaged economy could now sustain, especially in the light of the overwhelming strength of the US economy and global demand for dollars. Its global importance, inherited from the period of the UK's unquestioned financial hegemony, nevertheless remained enormous. Half of global trade was denominated in sterling, and it still accounted for 80 per cent of all foreign exchange reserves.[7]

The new international monetary architecture established at Bretton Woods in July 1944 therefore assigned sterling a crucial structural role. The agreement established fixed exchange rates whereby global currencies would be pegged either directly to the dollar or to sterling, which itself would be pegged to the dollar in a narrow band around a par of $4.03. Separately, the United States fixed its gold parity at $35 per ounce. In normal circumstances, central banks would be responsible for ensuring that their currencies stayed within the agreed range. If this was temporarily impossible, international cooperation would assist with access to

---

[6] For an account of the emergence of economic decline as a theme in political and public discourse see Tomlinson, 'Inventing Decline'. Coates, *UK Decline*, provides a stimulating critical interpretation of the arguments as they had developed to the early 1990s.

[7] Schenk, 'Sterling Area', p. 775.

credits from the newly created International Monetary Fund. If the problem was agreed to be due to 'fundamental disequilibrium', countries could seek the IMF's permission to change the parity officially. This system would operate in the context of exchange controls that would be progressively liberalized as the international economy recovered from the war.[8] Among other things, these controls would prevent any flight from sterling that would imperil the entire system by massively increasing demand for dollars in a world in which they were already in severely short supply.

The 1947 convertibility crisis simultaneously demonstrated sterling's weakness and importance, as well as the UK's lack of effective monetary sovereignty. It was precipitated by a $3.75 bn loan the UK was obliged to negotiate with the USA following the abrupt ending of wartime Lend-Lease arrangements in 1945. One of its terms stipulated that the UK would resume sterling convertibility by 15 July 1947, much sooner than agreed at Bretton Woods. When this was implemented, international holders of sterling rapidly exchanged it for much-needed dollars with which to buy American products, causing the UK's dollar reserves to fall precipitately and consuming a large proportion of the loan. The USA, eventually understanding that the collapse of sterling would be harmful to its own interests, agreed that convertibility could be suspended on 20 August.[9] The UK chose not to suspend convertibility unilaterally, convinced that the long-term cost of American displeasure would be too high.

The crisis saw the updated use of two tropes familiar from previous crises, including 1931, 1797, and the 1690s. One blamed foreigners; the other emphasized domestic 'luxury' and laziness. As in 1929–31, the latter concern was focussed on the Labour government's allegedly excessive generosity towards the working class. According to the Opposition and the government's usual critics in the press, the crisis was due largely to the government's refusal to properly acknowledge that the country was living beyond its straitened post-war means. People would need to work harder for less to solve the problem. In the context of tight rationing and widespread shortages, however, this was not an easy proposition to sell. Only *The Economist* fully faced its implications and openly relished the salutary effects of hunger on workers.[10]

In this instance, blaming foreigners was much more persuasive. Unlike 1931 (before the formation of the National government), even the government's most severe critics acknowledged not only that the global shortage of dollars and imbalance of demand was a formidable problem beyond the government's control but that the Americans' insistence on early convertibility had been unreasonable and unrealistic. The scope to blame the government or enemies within was correspondingly limited.

---

[8] Kugler and Straumann, 'Bretton Woods', pp. 26–7.
[9] Newton, 'Sterling Crisis', p. 400.
[10] *Economist*, 9 Sept. 1947, pp. 1–2.

The end of convertibility averted immediate disaster, but the drain of dollar reserves left sterling further weakened. In September 1949, in the light of recurring difficulties earning dollars, the government obtained agreement from the IMF to devalue the pound by 30 per cent to $2.80. Although this was the biggest single devaluation in the history of sterling, it met a remarkably muted political response. Of course, the government's opponents blamed 'reckless' spending and general failure of socialist economic policies for the decision. But these attacks were blunted by ministers contrasting the government's priorities with those of the interwar period. As one minister put it, the current government had chosen to 'devalue the pound rather than devalue the man'. He explained that the government would work to solve the country's economic problems 'on the basis of full employment', whereas 'in the interwar years the Tories tried to solve this problem by devaluing the worker'.[11] In the subsequent Commons debate, speaker after speaker hammered home the point, stressing the horrors they believed to have arisen from placing the sterling parity above human needs, and stressing Churchill's responsibility for the overvaluation of sterling in 1925.[12]

From the Conservative point of view the argument was lost when they fell back on defence of the interwar record and attempts to blame the period's problems on the policies of the second Labour government. Notably, they were not prepared to question the binary that the government presented. Even their claim that the devaluation was a 'a blow to Britain's pride' was highly qualified by the suggestion that it need not be if it achieved its aim of increasing British exports. For this to occur government spending had to be reduced and everybody had to work harder.[13] On this occasion, though, devaluation itself was not humiliation, and the parity was not identical with the nation's worth. On some level at least, the government's rhetorical strategy was successful. In the election held just over one year later, Labour was returned with only a slightly smaller percentage of votes than in the landslide of 1945.

But the government's capacity to mobilize such a defence was the product of a unique historical moment that left little trace on the monetary priorities of either of the major parties or on the terms in which the currency was discussed in the press. It was also unique in that its international consequences were limited by the existence of the sterling area and the absence of convertibility. The sterling area countries, consisting of the Empire and Commonwealth (except Canada) and a number of other countries, including Ireland, with especially close economic links with the UK, held their currency reserves in sterling and transacted much of their trade with the UK and other sterling area countries. While the devaluation

---

[11] *Manchester Guardian*, 20 Sept. 1949; *Devaluation. The Facts*, Issued at the Labour Party Rally, Filey, 22 Sept. 1949.
[12] Hansard HC (series 5), vol. 468, c. 25 (27 Sept. 1949).
[13] Conservative Party, *Your Pound* (1949).

reduced the dollar value of their reserves, much of which consisted of debts owed to them by the UK in exchange for wartime supplies, the practical damage this did them was diminished by the lack of convertibility. The fact that they all followed sterling down meant that they too gained export competitiveness against dollar countries while maintaining parity with the rest of the area. Nonetheless, the devaluation aroused considerable resentment and distrust within the sterling area, especially as the UK authorities had not discussed it with them beforehand. It was the USA and the IMF (dominated by the USA) whose prior blessing was required.

The Suez crisis of 1956 showed that a clear consensus had emerged that the UK should maintain the sterling parity at almost any cost. While the government was prepared to proceed with its military attack on Egypt in the face of diplomatic opprobrium from its friends and military threats from its enemies, it was the USA's pointed decision not to support the pound against speculative attacks that made it impossible for the venture to continue. The fact that the vulnerability of sterling made independent military action impossible was perhaps the most galling aspect of the general humiliation of the whole episode, especially when followed by the need to seek a waiver on the next repayment of the 1946 loan.

Despite widespread bitter criticism of the government's actions from the press and the opposition, there was complete unity on the currency. The shadow chancellor, Harold Wilson (one of the three ministers who had decided on the 1949 devaluation), promised Labour's cooperation with the government's defence of sterling. When sterling again came under pressure the following year, the Opposition, although highly critical of the government's economic policies and its 'sacrifice' of industry and employment to 'City finance', again pledged its support to 'the defence of sterling', emphasizing that the pound was 'a national, Commonwealth and world asset'.[14]

One of the prices of eventual IMF support for sterling and the French franc in the wake of the Suez crisis was British and French agreement to make their currencies convertible by 1958. All other major currencies followed, marking a significant reduction in the monetary autonomy of their respective states.[15] For the UK, convertibility made the defence of sterling both more difficult and more important. While the dollar shortage had eased greatly, there was now no bar to any country that wanted to exchange its sterling for dollars, and the fear of devaluation would be a powerful motive to do so.[16] It thus became essential for British governments to make holding sterling as attractive and as secure as possible. This meant high interest rates, continuous nursing of the balance of

---

[14] Hugh Gaitskell, speech to members of the American Chamber of Commerce, London, *Guardian*, 21 Sept. 1956; Harold Wilson, speech to Labour Party Conference, *The Times*, 1 Oct. 1957. It is perhaps not a coincidence that it was in 1957 that the mint first began to issue 'commemorative' Pistrucci sovereigns of the kind depicted on the cover of this book—a practice it continues to the present day.
[15] Kugler and Straumann, 'Bretton Woods', p. 672.
[16] Kugler and Straumann, 'Bretton Woods', p. 671.

payments, and the sternest rhetorical denunciations of even the thought of devaluation.[17] This posture came at a heavy cost to growth and industrial redevelopment, as governments were obliged to put a sharp stop to economic growth to prevent balance of payments deficits making sterling the target of speculative attacks. It has often been cited as a key reason for the UK's failure to modernize its economy and hence for its economic 'decline' in the long post-war period.[18]

Scholars have offered various explanations for the absolute priority given to the preservation of the exchange rate and the sterling area, including an anachronistic instinct to maintain an empire and otherwise play a much larger role in world affairs than the UK could afford, possibly linked to a Kiplingesque belief that sterling's role presented an inescapable burden of responsibility to preserve the international monetary system. More persuasive than these are explanations based on the historically ingrained desire of the City, the Bank of England, and the Treasury to preserve the City as a major financial centre, even when this was in conflict with ambitions to expand the domestic economy.[19] What all of these explanations imply is that the UK suffered in one way or another from the mismatch between sterling's historical legacy as a hegemonic global currency and the capacity of the UK's economy to sustain it in such a role.

As the mismatch between role and capacity grew, so did the bellicosity of sterling's defence and the association of its decline with that of the nation. Both reached their culmination with the 1967 devaluation from $2.80 to $2.40.[20] Facing a serious balance of payments crisis when it first took office in 1964, the Wilson Labour government immediately decided not only that it would not devalue but that it would not even discuss the possibility. So strong was this taboo that the Bank of England's committee to plan purely technical aspects of any possible devaluation was designated the 'FU [Forever Unmentionable] Committee'. The government therefore spent three years exhausting its energy and electoral goodwill in a doomed effort to maintain the sterling–dollar parity. Meanwhile, Wilson and other ministers deployed histrionic military metaphors to underline sterling's strength and the government's and people's determination to defend it. When the devaluation duly occurred, it was a short and easy step for the government's opponents to compare it with national humiliations such as the Munich agreement.[21]

This was standard grist to the political mill, as was the general claim—mobilized again during the euro debate—that it showed (together with 1931 and

---

[17] According to Strange, 'Sterling', p. 306, the need to offer special inducements to foreign holders is a characteristic of currencies that have fallen from the status of 'master currency' owing to their loss of political and military power.

[18] Strange, 'Sterling', esp. pp. 303, 310. See also Coates, *UK Decline*; Blank, 'Economic Problems'. This view is contested by Schenk, 'Sterling Area'.

[19] Ingham, *Capitalism Divided*, pp. 202–5.   [20] Blaazer, 'Devalued'.

[21] Blaazer, 'Devalued', p. 127.

1949) that Labour could not be trusted with the currency. But the genuinely anguished tone of newspaper opinion and letters columns shows a far deeper pain and anxiety. Britain was held to be a 'sick nation' and devaluation was a 'profound and far-reaching judgment' on its people.[22] Many such comments echoed centuries of diagnosis of monetary problems, encapsulated in a widely reprinted and discussed *Times* editorial at the beginning of the 1966 election campaign: love of luxury, frivolity, and ease, and excessive government spending abroad coupled with a reluctance to face or tell the truth.[23] Foreigners, whether the so-called 'gnomes of Zurich' or hard-working and determined Germans, French, and Italians, were also held to blame.

As many had feared, the devaluation of sterling saw the beginning of the end not only of the sterling area but of the whole Bretton Woods system. International cooperation ensured that the former was managed in an orderly fashion, but the pressure on the dollar continued until August 1971, when President Nixon abruptly ended its convertibility to gold. The long epoch of commodity money thus came to its end. Within twelve months sterling became the first currency to 'float' against the dollar, ending for the time being its attachment to any system of fixed exchange rates. This did not 'liberate' sterling, as some suggested; rather, it acknowledged that the capacity of governments to control their currencies without the sanction of 'the market' was even more constrained than it had ever been. Governments that attempted to operate fiscal policies or industrial relations or welfare systems that threatened the profits or offended the ideological sensibilities of the people who operated those markets would be punished by self-reinforcing flights of speculative capital, with devastating effects on government budgets, employment, the cost of living, and social cohesion.

The sterling crisis of 1976 made this clear, although not quite in the way that it was presented at the time. It is true that the Labour government, as a condition of a $3.9 billion loan from the International Monetary Fund, was obliged to implement a package of expenditure cuts, tax increases, and high interest rates that were odious to the labour movement as a whole and incompatible with the government's stated social objectives. But what is more significant is that the Treasury and senior ministers had already determined that such measures were necessary before they sought assistance from the IMF, that they sincerely believed that the consequences of not implementing them would be much worse than accepting them, and that they understood that convincing the IMF of the credibility of their projections and plans was merely (as Prime Minister Callaghan candidly admitted) a proxy for convincing 'millions of bankers around the world'.[24]

---

[22] *Daily Mail*, 20 Nov. 1967; *Sun*, 24 Nov. 1967.   [23] *The Times*, 10 Mar. 1966, 11.

[24] Rogers, 'IMF Crisis', pp. 966, 988, *et passim*; John Holloway, 'Global Capital', p. 36, cites this episode as one instance of a general tendency of governments to present IMF terms as 'externally imposed, whereas in reality they are part of the seamless integration of "national" and global political conflict'.

Money, Sovereignty, and Identity in Ireland and the UK

Globally, the 1970s were a period of chronically unstable exchange rates and powerful inflationary pressures, especially in the wake of enormous increases in the price of oil triggered by the OPEC crisis of 1973. The UK experienced these problems more severely than most comparable countries. The European Monetary System (EMS), and the Exchange Rate Mechanism that was its key feature, was one of a number of devices proposed to create at least some islands of exchange rate stability in an increasingly disordered world. In the minds of some of its supporters it was also an important first step towards the long-discussed goal of Economic and Monetary Union (EMU) of the EEC, the plan that would eventually transform the community into the European Union and see the establishment of the euro.

As noted in Chapter 8, Ireland, after much hesitation, decided to enter the EMS, while the UK, also after much hesitation, chose not to. In both countries there were cogent economic arguments on either side of the question. Apart from anything else, there was considerable doubt about whether the EMS itself would survive. An earlier attempt at keeping European currencies within narrow bands—the so-called 'snake in the tunnel'—had fairly quickly shrunk to a small Deutsche Mark zone. The UK and Ireland had managed to adhere to it for only six weeks early in 1972 before the pound was floated. But even if it were to survive, the EMS presented risks and opportunities of uncertain size and probability. Naturally these were different for Ireland's small, mainly agricultural economy than for the UK's large economy dominated by manufacturing and financial services. Nonetheless, the system's main attractions were similar for both countries. Stable exchange rates are always attractive to those involved in international trade; in addition, the EMS offered an external mechanism, derived ultimately from the rigid monetary discipline of the West German Bundesbank, to impose strong anti-inflationary pressure. The latter point raised serious objections in both countries, especially among trade unionists, who had good reason to fear that deflation would produce unemployment and that 'discipline' would take the form of downward pressure on real wages and reduced social spending.

The economic debate in each country had different contours, but the more striking difference was that the Irish debate was almost exclusively about those economic issues, while the public debate in the UK was dominated by questions of the surrender of sovereign power to the EEC, especially West Germany. In fact, much of the debate in the Commons was not about the EMS at all but about the prospect of EMU. It thus foreshadowed many themes that were to dominate the euro debate in the 1990s and early 2000s.

The biggest difference between the debates in the two periods was less the content than the political orientation of the strongest critics. In 1978 these came overwhelmingly from the left of the Labour Party rather than, as in the 1990s and beyond, the right of the Conservative Party. Thus in 1978 we find Labour backbenchers and former and future ministers deeply concerned about sovereignty and warning that the EMS was a thinly veiled plot by EEC bureaucrats and their enablers in the government to achieve monetary union on the way to a federal Europe. We find them denouncing German attempts to dominate Europe economically through a Faustian bargain with the French. Most remarkable of all, Winifred Ewing, a leading Scottish Nationalist, used the example of Scotland's economic and monetary union with England to show the 'ravages' that must follow any such union with Europe.[25]

By contrast, Conservative frontbenchers welcomed the import of German monetary and fiscal discipline to the UK, while some on their back benches looked forward to a common currency and proudly proclaimed their hopes for a federal Europe. One Conservative MP went so far as to argue that partnership with Europe was the path to recovering a monetary sovereignty that had been lost to the markets. This was a stronger version of the claim of the Chancellor, Denis Healey, that the UK had 'no independence to surrender' if it wanted exchange rate stability. The question was simply 'whether we can get more stability at less cost inside the system than outside the system'.[26]

One line of argument raised by some opponents of the EMS that was not pursued by their counterparts in the euro debate related directly to sterling's twentieth-century experience. Douglas Jay, who had held economic portfolios during both the 1949 and 1967 devaluations, pointed to those episodes as well as 1931 to argue that 'all experience... when we have had fixed limits, is that we indulge in a long, agonised struggle to stick to them and finally give way in an atmosphere of disaster'.[27] Similar points were made by speakers from the Labour left as well as by the right-wing Conservative Enoch Powell, who claimed that controlled exchange rates would always be unworkable and that the attempt to work such a system had had 'a devastating effect upon the life of this country and upon its morale in the past 30 years'. To make the point clearer, he reminded the Labour Party of the 'grinding deflation' imposed after 1925.[28] In the 1990s, when EMU became a live issue in European politics, its opponents put this history to a different use. According to Margaret Thatcher it simply showed that the Labour Party had 'no competence on money' and therefore would be glad 'to hand it all over'.[29]

No such agonies, and no anxieties about sovereignty, figured in the debate on the EMS in the Dáil or in commentary in the Irish press. In contrast to Healey, who had to deny repeatedly that the proposal would lead to monetary union, the

---

[25] Hansard HC (series 5), vol. 959, c. 544. (29 Nov. 1978).
[26] Hansard HC (series 5), vol. 959, c. 468 (29 Nov. 1978).
[27] Hansard HC (series 5), vol. 959, c. 491 (29 Nov. 1978).
[28] Hansard HC (series 5), vol. 959, c. 507, 508 (29 Nov. 1978).
[29] Hansard HC (series 6), vol. 178, c. 873 (30 Oct. 1990).

Taoiseach, Jack Lynch, not only admitted that it did but gave this as a reason for supporting it. This was uncontroversial. There was no opposition to monetary union in itself. As for questions of sovereignty, it was universally accepted that, as a small open economy, 'Ireland's freedom of action in currency matters is inevitably restricted'.[30] Accordingly, there was no dissent from the idea that Ireland would not have the option of staying out if the rest of the EEC went in.

The tricky question was what Ireland should do if the UK stayed out. Although the government had begun to consider ending the sterling peg when sterling became highly unstable in the mid-1970s, it was not until the EMS was proposed that this began to be seen as a viable option.[31] Even so, as it began to look increasingly as if the UK would not join the EMS, concerns about the consequences of breaking the sterling peg mounted in official and political circles as well as the press. It was widely—although incorrectly—assumed that the punt would soon appreciate against sterling, making Irish exports less competitive in what was still by far Ireland's largest export market.

These concerns were more powerful than any historic nationalistic urge to break the link with the UK, which had hardly any purchase in either the public debate or the government's deliberations. The eventual decision to join the EMS even when the UK decided not to was driven by other factors, principally a judgment that it would be more beneficial to be linked to a stable currency regime than to the unstable and crisis-ridden pound, and a belief that Ireland would benefit from strengthening relations and a positive profile within the EEC. This was encapsulated in a parliamentary committee report on the EMU proposals which pointed out that while Ireland had 'little influence on British monetary institutions', it would at least participate in policy decisions in a European Monetary Union.[32] Of more concrete appeal was the fact that Ireland was able to negotiate grants and cheap loans from the EEC to a total equivalent of about 3 per cent of its annual GDP to help it manage the anticipated tendency of the EMS to draw capital towards its economically stronger members.[33]

When Ireland joined the EMS, it became the last country to leave the sterling area, a point that was barely noted at the time. While there is some small evidence of satisfaction at breaking this link with the former colonial ruler, it was far outweighed by practical anxieties at the economic price it may incur. Among those anxieties, the effect the break might have on the border with Northern Ireland and the prospects for reunification was a very long way down the list. An internal memorandum concluded that a separation of the currencies would be of little importance compared to the existing obstacles to unification.[34] The issue also

---

[30] Dáil Éireann Debates, vol. 308, 3 (17 Oct. 1978).
[31] Honohan and Murphy, *Sterling Link*, p. 1.
[32] Ireland. Oireachtas, *Report on Commission's Proposals*, 28 June 1978, p. 20.
[33] Honohan and Murphy, *Sterling Link*, p. 33.   [34] Honohan and Murphy, *Sterling Link*, p. 31.

received little press coverage in the Republic, apart from a fairly light-hearted story about possible problems for shopkeepers and publicans in border towns, and a more serious story about risks to tourism in Donegal.[35] There was more serious interest among Unionists in Northern Ireland, who welcomed the reinforcement of difference and anticipated a rise in the punt as an opportunity to strengthen the province's economic ties with Britain at the expense of the Republic.[36]

In short, currency questions in the Republic of Ireland lacked almost any capacity to arouse patriotic or nationalistic sentiment. This is hardly surprising. If such sentiment was subordinate to purely economic considerations and a commitment to monetary internationalism in the immediate aftermath of independence, it was hardly likely to figure prominently half a century later.

The EMS did not work well for Ireland. Despite perennially high interest rates, the currency was devalued repeatedly (although without the anguish that devaluations aroused in the UK).[37] Instead of making any monetary link with the EU unpopular, as it might have, this experience made the decision to adopt the euro uncontroversial. In the referendum to ratify the Maastricht Treaty, which included agreement to a single currency, the main point of controversy was the treaty's possible effects on Irish laws on abortion. This had only a minor effect on the result, which saw a 2:1 majority in favour based largely on economic arguments supported by every significant party.[38] There is no evidence of any regret at giving up the punt and no sense that a fully independent national currency (whatever that might mean at the turn of the twenty-first century) was indispensable to national sovereignty, much less national identity. Given the history of currency in Ireland, it could hardly have been otherwise.

The contrasts with the UK were even starker than in the debate over the EMS. They need hardly be laboured. The tone was set in the Commons debate of 30 October 1990 following Margaret Thatcher's combative performance at the European Council meeting in Rome. In the debate, Thatcher did not just repeatedly link currency with national identity but described 'the pound sterling' as 'the greatest expression of sovereignty'.[39] These themes remained central to the case against the euro throughout, from UKIP's adoption of a logo designed around a £ symbol in the aftermath of 'Black Wednesday', to the Conservatives' 2001 election campaign slogan of 'Save Britain – Save the Pound'. As we have seen, these themes resonated powerfully with large sections of the UK populace.

In the euro debate—in contrast to the debate over the EMS—sterling's twentieth-century history was invoked in support of monetary union. It was not a reading of history that monetary nationalists could entertain. In 1990, Anthony

---

[35] *Irish Press*, 4 Dec. 1978 (INA); *Donegal Democrat*, 8 Dec. 1978 (INA).
[36] *Belfast News-Letter*, 10 Nov. 1978 (INA). [37] Honohan and Murphy, *Sterling Link*, p. 35.
[38] Holmes, 'Maastricht Referendum', p. 109.
[39] Hansard HC (series 6), vol. 178, c. 874 (30 Oct. 1990).

Nelson, a Conservative, Europhile backbencher (and banker by profession), asked Thatcher whether she agreed 'that the prospects for the British people enjoying a higher standard of living and sharing in greater prosperity will depend in no small part on securing a currency that is strong and stable—something that has dogged us in the postwar years? Is that not more likely to be achieved if we have a common currency based on the great economies of western Europe rather than relying on our going it alone?'

Thatcher's reply makes clear the notion of 'history' that she and other defenders of sterling had in mind: 'We will have a stronger sterling, with all its history.... We shall trade better with the great history behind sterling than we possibly could with a single currency.' Sterling's history had thus become ancient and non-specific—shuffled off into the national pantheon with the Empire, Magna Carta, and other empty totems of the national past. It was a fetishized version of the monetary history of the UK's construction as a nation state and rise to global hegemony, which had somehow made sterling's 'greatness' immanent. It was 'the story of the currency that ruled the world', to borrow the subtitle of a populist, Eurosceptic 'biography' of the pound.[40] It was a history in which sterling had never struggled to 'look the dollar in the face', and certainly not one in which the pound was less stable and secure than the Deutsche Mark. This version of history, which necessarily obliterates the twentieth century, provides an answer to the brutal question put by Hugh Dykes, another veteran Conservative backbencher, as conflict over the euro was tearing the Major government apart: 'As the pound has been repeatedly devalued since the war,' Dykes wondered, 'what fantasy are we defending?'[41]

History and Forgetting in the Scottish Currency Debate

The future of Scotland's currency is widely acknowledged to have been the most damaging single issue for the 'yes' case in the 2014 independence referendum.[42] Remarkably, despite half a century of developing and defending proposals for an independent Scotland's currency arrangements, the SNP was repeatedly wrong-footed on this issue by an otherwise defensive and lacklustre anti-independence campaign. As in the euro debate, the relationship between currency and sovereignty was crucial. Unlike the euro debate, however, references to history of any kind—concrete or idealized, recent or remote—were few and far between. Nevertheless, it is possible to discern differences between the approaches of Scottish nationalists and UK nationalists to this question that reflect differences between the historical monetary experience of Scotland and Britain.

[40] Sinclair, *Pound*.   [41] Hansard HC (series 6), vol. 237, c. 264 (12 Dec. 1994).
[42] Liñeira, Henderson, and Delaney, 'Voters' Response', pp. 181–2.

The currency options for an independent Scotland boil down to four. With a pragmatic flexibility that would have been familiar to their pre-Union forebears, the SNP has advocated or entertained all of them at different points since the beginning of its resurgence in the 1970s. In 1976, in the midst of some of sterling's heaviest travails, it argued that an independent Scotland should have an independent currency, which, given the massive export earnings and revenues from North Sea oil, would be stronger than sterling.[43] This became less appealing as oil earnings began to fall from the mid-1980s. More importantly, a radical reorientation of the party's approach to the EC, which saw it adopt a platform of 'independence in Europe', did not long predate the signing of the Maastricht Treaty.[44] With increasing conviction during the 1990s and to the following decade, the SNP therefore advocated the earliest possible adoption of the euro, not only for an independent Scotland but also for the UK. But when the Global Financial Crisis produced a crisis in the eurozone, with especially grim consequences for small, peripheral economies, this policy faded from view and was replaced with a plan to maintain a monetary union with the UK until conditions were right for a referendum on adopting the euro. As the eurozone crisis deepened, the second part of this plan was jettisoned.[45] The SNP-led Scottish government officially adopted a plan for a sterling union in April 2013, which its leaders actively promoted during the following months.[46] According to opinion polls it was then the preferred option of a clear majority of Scots.[47] The fourth option, forced into prominence during the referendum campaign, is for Scotland to continue to use sterling without a formal monetary union, in the same way that a few small countries use the US dollar or the euro.[48]

It was immediately clear that UK authorities would reject the Scottish plan for monetary union.[49] As the referendum campaign proceeded, the entire Unionist establishment, including the leaders and financial spokespeople of the three main parties, ruled it out emphatically. In this they were eagerly and repeatedly supported by the Treasury and the Bank of England, whose comments were widely reported and discussed.

In the light of this development the SNP leadership was repeatedly challenged to explain their 'plan B'. Instead, they accused their opponents of bullying and bluff, arguing that monetary union was so clearly in the UK's interest as well as Scotland's that negotiations would begin as soon as independence was voted in. This aspect of the SNP campaign had some success. Interviewed three months after the vote, more people (in a fixed sample) believed that a 'yes' vote would

---

[43] *Aberdeen Press and Journal*, 3 Nov. 1976 (BNA).
[44] Laible, 'Europeanizing', pp. 112–13; Dardanelli, 'Europeanisation', pp. 276–9.
[45] Swan and Petersohn, 'Currency Issue', p. 71.
[46] Swan and Petersohn, 'Currency Issue', p. 67.
[47] ICM/Scotland on Sunday poll, *Guardian*, 12 Apr. 2014.   [48] See Kay, 'Options'.
[49] *Scotsman*, 24 Apr. 2013.

probably have produced a formal monetary union than had believed it three months before the vote. They were not, however, prepared to bet on it. The most common reason for voting 'no' was because there were too many unanswered questions. And when hypothetical scenarios were offered in which uncertainty on various issues was removed, the positive assurance that produced the strongest 'yes' response was 'the UK government allows Scotland to keep the pound'.[50]

Despite the leadership's reticence on the question, it became reasonably clear that 'plan B' was 'sterlingization'—the continued use of the pound without a formal monetary union. This provided easy pickings for the Unionist side, who pointed to countries from Panama to Montenegro that used similar arrangements and did not arouse a keen desire to emulate them. Nor did they have large financial services sectors to maintain, as Scotland did.[51]

More fundamentally, sterlingization was even more vulnerable than monetary union to attacks that questioned the value of independence in such circumstances. Unionists argued that Scotland in a monetary union would have no capacity to set interest rates and would have to submit to fiscal rules and oversight from England that would severely constrain its capacity for independent economic action. Sterlingization would multiply these problems, leaving Scotland with no capacity to influence decisions about the money it used, and no way of obtaining it except through the vagaries of commerce. For these critics, monetary and political union were corollaries. Control of the currency was the hallmark of sovereignty, which could not be shared or pooled. It was the vision of sovereignty that had driven much of the opposition to the euro.

Swan and Petersohn have framed the Scottish currency debate largely in these terms, seeing it as stemming from rival understandings of independence and sovereignty. Unionists advanced a 'traditional' view in which currency was central, while the independence leaders held a view of sovereignty 'that could be shared, so long as partners chose to do so willingly. This was a fact of life in an interdependent world.'[52] Paolo Dardanelli has advanced a similar view of the evolution of the SNP's view of sovereignty.[53] This is illuminating, but it is also worth observing that the 'traditional' view closely reflects England's historical experience of currency, including its experience as the hegemonic nation of the United Kingdom.

Scotland's historical experience was different. Parliamentary sovereignty was still in an early state of evolution when monetary union took place, meaning that

---

[50] Liñeira, Henderson, and Delaney, 'Voters' Response', pp. 178–81, figs 10.7, 10.8, and 10.9. Two 'negative' scenarios that produced a stronger yes result were 'The UK government reduced the powers of the Scottish parliament' and 'The Conservative Party was certain to win the 2015 UK general election'.
[51] *Scotsman*, 15 May 2014.   [52] Swan and Petersohn, 'Currency Issue', pp. 66, 82.
[53] Dardanelli, 'Europeanisation', p. 281.

Scotland had never exercised monetary sovereignty in the sense that it exists in modern parliamentary regimes. At the time of the Union of the Crowns, the coinage was still understood in both England and Scotland to be a royal prerogative. A century later, on the eve of the political union that ended Scotland's separate coinage, the Scottish executive still required royal permission to make changes to the currency. In practice, authority over Scotland's currency was negotiated between the executive in Edinburgh, the Scottish Parliament, and the Privy Council in London. Most such changes were made in response to developments south of the border, where Scots also looked for models for their monetary institutions.

The small-notes fracas of 1826 suggests that Scots understood Westminster's sovereignty over Scottish money to be constrained by Scottish usages and wishes. The echo of the controversy in 1844–5, and Peel's speech introducing the 1845 legislation, suggest that this was accepted as an element of the Union. When it was clear in 1928 that Scots could not be mobilized behind Edinburgh-headquartered banks over the issue of ten-shilling notes, this did not show that Scots had acquired a different understanding of the limits of Westminster's power, merely that they did not care whether the notes they used in their everyday life were produced by a quasi-public UK bank or by joint-stock banks, most of which were by then Anglo-Scottish in any case. Such monetary patriotism as existed in Scotland was 'British', focussed on sterling in terms common to the rest of the UK.

It could be argued that some serious reflection about the historical relationship between currency and history in the UK and its constituent parts might have improved the quality of the referendum debate. But politicians are in the business of winning polls, not improving debates, and these fairly arcane historical points are not obviously helpful to either side. It might also be suggested that the past under discussion here is far too remote to be of any relevance. Perhaps so, although mere remoteness has seldom stopped nationalist movements from mobilizing aspects of the past. Scottish nationalists, for example, have regularly deployed the language of the Declaration of Arbroath (1320) to support their claims. Indeed, the SNP's own 'independence in Europe' campaign drew on historical claims that pre-Union Scotland had been more outward-looking and Europe-focussed than England, and that Union had pushed it into an uncharacteristic insularity.[54] In the context of the outbreak of xenophobia that accompanied the euro debate in England, this had obvious appeal, whatever its merits as history.

On the specific question of currency, however, the SNP made only one substantive historical claim. Denying the assumption that a post-independence UK would have the right to stop Scotland using the pound, nationalist leaders replied

---

[54] Laible, 'Europeanizing', p. 117. See also Dardanelli, 'Europeanisation'.

with some variant of Alex Salmond's claim during the first televised debate: 'it is our pound as well as England's pound. This is Scotland's pound... It has been built up by Scotland over a long time.' Counter to this were claims that the pound belonged to the Bank of England, which belonged to the Parliament, and would therefore 'remain with the rest of the UK'.[55] This is at least open to question on historical grounds. The Bank of England was created by the charter of a dual monarch and the Act of a Parliament that ceased to exist at the Act of Union. The same can be said of Bank of Scotland. The Bank of England's functions as a central bank—which was the actual point at issue– clearly evolved under the Parliament of Great Britain, and then of the United Kingdom, enterprises in which Scotland might reasonably claim to have had some historical share, although whether this could be constructed into a claim for shared rights in the event of independence is a question of constitutional law that is beyond the scope of this book and the expertise of its author.

Claims about 'the pound', taken as a synecdoche for the currency, are more difficult to disentangle. When surveyed closely, this historical terrain becomes unhelpful to both sides. As we have seen, the framers of the Treaty of Union understood themselves to be legislating for the currency by legislating for the coinage. While in theory the English and Scottish coinages were replaced by a British coinage, in practice the English currency became the British and the Scottish currency disappeared. But this is to emphasize those incorporating aspects of the Union that Unionists wished to downplay during the referendum debate. On the other hand, the history of the independent Scottish coinage, and the apparent eagerness of the Scottish political elite to give it up, does not provide any fertile ground for nationalist narrative. Once again, the historical record is nuanced, untidy, and full of snares for both sides. Far better to confine the history to the odd glib claim and counterclaim.

The debate did stray into one other quasi-historical area. At various points between early 2012 and 2014, the Treasury, the Bank of England, and the Chancellor all threatened that 'sterlingization' would mean an end to Scottish banknotes, as the Scottish banks only printed notes under licence from the Bank of England. Quite how such a licensing provision would be enforced was never made clear. George Osborne also made the point that if Scottish banks wished to print notes under sterlingization, they could only do so on the basis of pound-for-pound holdings of Bank of England notes. Interestingly, although *The Scotsman* observed that the notes, with their images of famous Scots, were 'symbolic of Scottish identity', these threats did not arouse as much mortification as Osborne might have hoped.[56] While the SNP described them as 'churlish' and asserted their

[55] Alistair Darling, quoted in *The Scotsman*, 26 Aug. 2014; Michael Moore, quoted in *The Scotsman*, 17 May 2013.
[56] *Scotsman*, 13 Jan. 2012.

general point that such issues would form the topic of negotiations after a 'yes' vote, there was little reaction from the press. More generally, the history of Scottish banking was only available for Unionists in this debate. Scots were reminded repeatedly that an independent Scotland would not have had the resources to bail out the Royal Bank of Scotland and Bank of Scotland when they threatened to break during the financial crisis. The result would have been a multidimensional disaster for Scotland, allegedly far worse than the one that actually transpired. To show what a cruel twist of history this was, one need only imagine the independence debate taking place sometime in the second half of the twentieth century. In such a scenario, Scotland's history of banking stability and world-leading innovation would surely have figured prominently in any debate about its future monetary system.

In the aftermath of the 'no' vote, the SNP's stance on currency was in some disarray. Even during the campaign, many members and supporters were highly critical of the plan for monetary union, arguing that it largely defeated a major goal of independence, which was to escape from the clutches of post-Thatcherite fiscal austerity. Given developments in the eurozone, there was clearly no escape there either. In 2019, the SNP membership forced their reluctant leaders to accept a policy of adopting a separate currency as soon as possible. As well as being less popular than monetary union with the UK, this plan is also fraught with difficulties. It is likely that Scotland will be obliged to operate its monetary and fiscal policies within very narrow parameters to maintain the 'confidence' of lenders and to shield its currency from speculative attacks based on the possibility of devaluation if it chooses to maintain a peg with sterling. The difficulties and costs for a freely floating currency would be different but at least as formidable. As John Kay explains—and as Irish governments have understood since the beginning of Irish independence—the extent to which a small country can exercise monetary independence is very limited.[57]

Final Thoughts: the Global Financial Crisis and Its Aftermath

The history of sterling since the First World War suggests that the monetary independence even of large countries is also severely constrained. This became abundantly clear in 1931 and repeatedly during the post-war period. And while most of these episodes can be framed in terms of the UK's dependence on the USA, the much larger Global Financial Crisis (GFC) that began in 2007 can only be understood in terms of dependence on and constraint by financial networks and institutions operating across national boundaries.

---

[57] Kay, 'Options', p. 118.

The GFC was the biggest purely financial crisis in the history of the world.[58] Unlike the comparably serious crisis of July–August 1914, or the lesser crisis of February 1797, it was caused entirely by failures within financial markets. It nonetheless immediately became a problem for states and their citizens to solve to an extent only rivalled in the unique context of 1914, and for obviously quite different reasons. The crisis echoes many of the financial crises we have seen in the book. At bottom, the fundamental problem in all of them concerns money creation and the capacity of private entities to effectively create money in the pursuit of profit. In the current dispensation central banks issue 'high-powered' state money (or 'public money') in response to the demands of financial institutions' creation of 'deposits' through lending.[59] This is merely a new version of the old 'inverted pyramid' of credit resting on a narrow point of high-powered money, with the difference from Bagehot's day being that the small, commodity-based portion of the high-powered money is absent, meaning that all of the high-powered money is based on triangles of credit relationships between lenders, issuers, and users.[60]

The GFC left governments and monetary authorities with very few meaningful choices of response. Many of the institutions that had stocked themselves with 'toxic assets' were 'too big to fail', and while governments made some attempts to impose conditions on the process, these were mostly trivial and easily sidestepped. Largely at the expense of taxpayers, the financial institutions were bailed out, and their structures at most temporarily disrupted, for example through quasi-nationalizations. And while there has been some minor revision of the 'financial deregulation' mania of the 1980s and 1990s, little has changed. In the aftermath, central banks around the world embarked on massive programmes of money creation under the aegis of 'quantitative easing', whose central aim was the injection of liquidity into banks and other financial institutions and whose central mechanism was the creation and manipulation of government debt.[61]

In the United Kingdom, as in parts of the eurozone, the serious problems these processes have presented to state finances have been blamed in many quarters on extravagant government social spending (the modern version of old complaints about extravagance and love of ease) which has been sharply curtailed in a long-running programme of austerity that has frozen the wages of government employees, increased unemployment, and brought untold suffering to the most vulnerable, inflaming social conflict, anger, despair, and cynicism. Such programmes have been justified publicly by the claim that governments cannot simply create money. As Prime Minister Theresa May put it in response to a nurse complaining that her real wage had been frozen, 'there is no magic money tree'. The many critics who have pointed out the obvious dissonance between this claim and the

[58] Capie, 'Crises', p. 11.
[59] McLeay, Radia, and Thomas, *Money Creation*.
[60] Ingham, *Nature*, p. 135.
[61] Benford et al., *Quantitative Easing*.

quantitative easing programme miss part of the point. Governments (or rather central banks) can create money, but, in an echo of an old refrain, they can only do so on terms that are acceptable to the rational self-interest, irrational prejudices, and dominant economic doctrines of financial markets. To do otherwise is to endanger 'confidence' and thus to incur a very real risk of financial and economic catastrophe.

The GFC has rekindled interest in the nature of money and the economics and politics of its creation to an extent only exceeded by the 1690s and the bank restriction period. Echoes of earlier debates, half-forgotten heresies, and defunct theories may be clearly heard. At one extreme, enthusiasts for cryptocurrencies combine modern technology and extreme individualism with an eclectic mix of old monetary ideas.[62] Central to their thinking is a conflation of the concept of money and means of payment, with a corresponding disregard of the concept of units of account—the same confusion that dominated the recoinage debate and that shaped the terms of Anglo-Scottish monetary union. It is this that allows them to believe that cryptocurrencies are money.[63] Moreover, the inbuilt limitation on the quantity of cryptocurrencies that can be 'mined', and the need for ever-increasing computing power consuming enormous amounts of electricity, are predicated on the obsolete 'hard money' notions that the value of money arises from a combination of scarcity and the 'labour' required to produce it that will be familiar from the preceding pages.[64]

At the other extreme, advocates of Modern Money Theory (MMT) have attracted significant public notice since 2008. Drawing explicitly on long traditions of credit and state theories of money, they argue that 'government spends currency into existence and taxpayers use that currency to pay their obligations to the state'.[65] This is a flat repudiation of the sanctity of balanced budgets, based on the idea that both governments and private lenders not merely do, but must, create money out of thin air. These are arguments that would be intelligible to the credit theorists of the sixteenth century as well as to many of the nineteenth-century monetary heretics. MMT theorists argue that while state money creation should be constrained only by inflation, private money creation is necessary to provide sufficient funds in a modern capitalist economy. More stringent regulation would ensure that it funds productive activity rather than the kinds of speculation in financial instruments and existing assets (such as housing) that precipitated the GFC.[66]

Advocates of 'sovereign money' challenge MMT chiefly by arguing that private money creation, once permitted, can never be reliably regulated to prevent practices damaging to the public good. Informed by socialist traditions, they insist

---

[62] Golumbia, 'Bitcoin as Politics'.   [63] Dodd, 'Social Life'.
[64] Brunton, *Digital Cash*, pp. 69, 111.   [65] Wray, *Modern Money*, p. 2.
[66] Wray, *Modern Money*, pp. 6–7.

that money creation should once again be the sole prerogative of the state.[67] This can be read as a return to early modern monetary regimes (minus the fatal constraint of a supply of precious metals) or, viewed from a different angle, to the 'Currency School' doctrines underpinning Peel's 1844 Bank Act. Critics make similar points to those made by the 'Banking School'. Private markets will always find alternative ways of creating liquidity, and the state's institutional disregard of these processes would, as Peel's critics argued, make the system not only more expensive but more dangerous.[68]

It remains to be seen whether either MMT or sovereign money ideas will achieve more lasting or widespread influence on monetary thought than the monetary heretics of previous centuries. Both face similarly formidable challenges in attracting support from a public still convinced of long-defunct notions of the nature and history of money. More formidable still would be the challenges presented to their implementation within the capitalist economy that MMT embraces and sovereign money seeks to challenge. What is clear is that even if one holds—to paraphrase James VI and I—that nothing is more appropriate to the sovereign dignity of states than the ordering of their money, one must also acknowledge that in the current global dispensation few things are more difficult to attain.

---

[67] See the outline in Jackson and Dyson, *Modernising*, and the resources at 'Positive Money', https://positivemoney.org/.
[68] Goodhart and Jensen, 'Commentary', pp. 22–3.

Select Bibliography

Note on internet sources: URLs are shown only where they are likely to be stable and where the source (in the version I have cited) does not require a personal or institutional subscription.

1. Contemporary Sources

(i) Manuscript Repositories and Collections
Bank of England Archive, London.
British Library Additional Manuscripts (Huskisson Papers).
British Museum Coins and Medals Department.
Lloyds Banking Group Archives, Edinburgh (Bank of Scotland Archive).
National Archives of Ireland, Dublin.
National Records of Scotland, Edinburgh.
NatWest Group Archives, Edinburgh (Royal Bank of Scotland Archive).
Public Record Office of Northern Ireland, Belfast.
Senate House Library, London (Goldsmiths Manuscripts).
The National Archives (UK), Kew.

(ii) Published Archival Materials
Note: volume is specified when only a single volume has been used.
Archives of the Independent Labour Party Series 1, Pamphlets and Leaflets (microform).
Calendar of State Papers, Domestic [1547–1704], 92 vols (1856–1972).
Calendar of State Papers, Ireland [1586–1614], 13 vols (1872–1912).
Calendar of the Manuscripts of the Marquess of Ormonde, K.P., preserved at Kilkenny Castle, ed. John Thomas Gilbert, 8 vols (1902–1920).
Calendar of Treasury Books, 1660–[1718], 31 vols (1904–1962).
Calendar of Treasury Books and Papers, 1729–[1745], 5 vols (1897–1903).
Records of the Coinage of Scotland, from the Earliest period to the Union, collected by R. W. Cochran Patrick, 2 vols (1876).
Royal Commission on Historical Manuscripts, *Report on the manuscripts of Mrs. Stopford-Sackville, of Drayton House, Northamptonshire*, vol. 1 (1904).
Royal Commission on Historical Manuscripts, *The Manuscripts of the Duke of Portland, preserved at Welbeck Abbey*, vol. 3 (1894).

(iii) Parliamentary Proceedings and Legislation
Great Britain. Parliament. House of Commons. *Journal of the House of Commons*, British History Online, https://www.british-history.ac.uk/.
Great Britain. Parliament. House of Commons. *Proceedings 1660–1740*, 14 vols (1742).
Great Britain. Parliament. House of Lords. *Journal of the House of Lords*, British History Online, https://www.british-history.ac.uk/.
Hansard (UK).

Ireland. Houses of the Oireachtas. Debates, https://www.oireachtas.ie/en/debates/.
Ireland. Parliament. House of Commons. *Journals of the House of Commons of the Kingdom of Ireland*, 19 vols (1796-1800).
Ireland. Parliament. House of Commons. *Proceedings*, 15 vols (1784-1795).
Ireland. Parliament. House of Lords. *Journals of the House of Lords of the Kingdom of Ireland*, 8 vols (1779-1800).
Parliamentary Register, 1796-1802, 18 vols (1797-1802).
Records of the Parliaments of Scotland to 1707, https://www.rps.ac.uk/.
Statutes of the United Kingdom of Great Britain and Ireland 56 George III (1816)

(iv) Online Primary Source Databases

British History Online https://www.british-history.ac.uk/.
British Library Newspapers (Gale Newsvault).
British Newspaper Archive.
Burney Newspaper Collection.
Eurobarometer: Public Opinion in the European Union, https://europa.eu/eurobarometer/screen/home.
Irish Newspaper Archive.
Proceedings of the Old Bailey, https://www.oldbaileyonline.org/.

(v) Newspapers & Periodicals (not sourced from databases listed above)

Daily Express
Economist
Financial News
Financial Times
Financial World
Guardian
Illustrated London News
Land and Water
London Gazette
New Age
New Leader
Scotsman
Times
Westminster Journal

(vi) Contemporary Publications

Anderson, William. *The Iniquity of Banking*, 2 vols (London, 1797).
Anon. *Advice to the Industrious Tradesmen and Manufacturers of Ireland, Upon the Present Regulation of the Coin, with Some Reasons for the Present Reduction of the Gold* (n.p., 1737).
Anon. *Considerations on the Present Calamities of This Kingdom; and the Causes of the Decay of Public Credit with the Means of Restoring It* (Dublin, 1760).
Anon. *A Defence of the Conduct of the People of Ireland in Their Unanimous Refusal of Mr. Wood's Copper-Money* (Dublin, 1724).
Anon. *Dialogues on Corn and Currency Between Sir John Thickscull, M.P. And Mr. Wiseacre* (London, 1827).
Anon. *A Discourse of Money. Being an Essay on That Subject, Historically and Politically Handled* (London, 1696).

Anon., *For Encouraging the Coining of Silver Money in England, and after for Keeping It Here* (n.p., 1692).
Anon. *The Last Speech and Dying Words of the Bank of Ireland Which Was Executed at College-Green on Saturday the 9th Inst* ([Dublin,] 1721).
Anon. *A Letter from a Gentleman in the North of Ireland, to His Friend in Dublin in Relation to the Regulation of the Coin* (Dublin, 1736).
Anon. *A Letter to a Member of Parliament Touching the Late Intended Bank* (Dublin, 1721).
Anon. *An Overture for Supplying the Present Scarcity of Money* ([Edinburgh,] 1705).
Anon. *A Proposal for the Relief of Ireland, by a Coinage of Monies, of Gold, and Silver and Establishing a National Bank* (London, 1733).
Anon. *Proposals Humbly Offered to Parliament for the Restoration of Cash and Public Credit to Ireland* (Dublin, 1760).
Anon. *A Short View of the Apparent Dangers and Mischiefs from the Bank of England* (London, 1707).
Anon. *Some Considerations Offered against the Continuance of the Bank of England: In a Letter to a Member of the Present Parliament* ([London,] 1694).
Anon. *Some Reflections Concerning the Reduction of Gold Coin in Ireland: Upon the Principles of the Dean of St. Patrick's and Mr. Lock* (Dublin, 1737).
Anon. *A Word in Season About Guineas* (London, [1695]).
Arbuthnot, Harriet. *The Journal of Mrs. Arbuthnot, 1820–1832* (London, 1950).
Asgill, John. *Remarks on the Proceedings of the Commissioners for Putting in Execution the Act Past Last Sessions, for Establishing of a Land-Bank* (London, 1696).
Attwood, Thomas. *A Letter to the Earl of Liverpool on the Reports of the Committees of the Two Houses of Parliament on the Questions of Bank Restriction Act* (Birmingham, 1819).
Attwood, Thomas. *The Scotch Banker* (London, 1828).
Bagehot, Walter. *Lombard Street: A Description of the Money Market* (London, 1873).
Banking Commission. [Saorstát Éireann]. *Final Reports of the Banking Commission* (Dublin, 1926).
Barbon, Nicholas. *A Discourse Concerning Coining the New Money Lighter in Answer to Mr. Lock's Considerations About Raising the Value of Money* (London, 1696).
Barr, John. *Labour and the Money Problem* (Merthyr Tydvil, [1920]).
Benford, James, et. al. *Quantitative Easing*. Bank of England Quarterly Bulletin ([London,] 2009).
Bindon, David. *An Essay on the Gold and Silver-Coin Currant in Ireland* (Dublin, 1729).
Bindon, David. *Some Reasons Shewing the Necessity the People of Ireland Are under, for Continuing to Refuse Mr. Wood's Coinage* (Dublin, 1724).
Boulter, Hugh. *Letters Written by His Excellency Hugh Boulter*, 2 vols (Oxford, 1770).
Bradbury, John Swanwick. 'Report of the Committee on the Currency and Bank of England Note Issues' (London, Cm 2393, 1925).
Bray, John Francis. *Labour's Wrongs and Labour's Remedy* (Leeds, 1839).
Briscoe, John. *A Discourse on the Late Funds of the Million-Act, Lottery-Act, and Bank of England* (London, 1694).
Briscoe, John. *To the Honourable the Knights, Citizens, and Burgesses in Parliament Assembled* (n.p., 1695).
Broadloom, Isaac. *The Hue and Cry of the Poor of Ireland for Small Change* (Dublin, 1731).
Cannan, Edwin, ed. *The Paper Pound of 1797–1821: A Reprint of the Bullion Report* (London, 1919).
Cantillon, Richard. *An Essay on Economic Theory*, tr. Chantal Saucier, ed. Mark Thornton (Auburn, AL, 2010 [1755]).

Carr, John. *The Stranger in Ireland* (Shannon, 1970 [1806]).

[Chamberlen, Hugh.] *A Present Remedie for the Want of Money* ([Edinburgh,] 1705).

Chamberlen, Hugh. *Some Remarks Upon a Late Nameless and Scurrilous Libel, Entituled, a Bank-Dialogue between Dr. H.C. and a Country-Gentleman* (London, 1696).

[Chamberlen, Hugh.] *Some Useful Reflections Upon a Pamphlet Called a Brief Account of the Intended Bank of England* (n.p., 1694).

[Charles II of Scotland.] *A Proclamation Concerning the Coyn* (Edinburgh, 1681/2).

A Chartist (of ten years' standing, and a Christian). *To the Oppressed and Mystified People of Great Britain* [n.p. 1849?].

Citizen of Dublin. *The Question Relative to the Petitions of the Cities of Dublin and Corke, and the Town of Belfast, for a New Regulation of the Portugal Gold Coin* (Dublin, 1760).

Cobbett, William. *Gold for Ever!: Real Causes of the Fall of Funds* (London, [1825]).

Cobbett, William. *Paper against Gold* (London, [1820]).

Cobbett, William. *Rotten Rag Manufactory!!! The Threadneedle-Street Catechism* (London, [1818]).

Colquhoun, Patrick. *A Treatise on the Police of the Metropolis* (London, 1796).

Combe, William. *Plain Thoughts of a Plain Man Addressed to the Common Sense of the People of Great Britain* (London, 1797).

Cunliffe, Walter, 'Final Report of the Committee on Currency and Foreign Exchanges after the War' (Cm 464, 1919).

Cunliffe, Walter, 'First Interim Report of the Committee on Currency and Foreign Exchanges after the War' (Cm 9182, 1918).

Davies, Sir John. *A Report of Cases and Matters in Law, Resolved and Adjudged in the King's Courts in Ireland* (Dublin, 1762).

The De Moneta of Nicholas Oresme and English Mint Documents, tr. Charles Johnson (London, 1956).

Dickens, Charles, *Little Dorritt* (Harmondsworth, 2003 [1857]).

Douglas, C. H. *Social Credit* (London, 1933).

Drummond, David. *An Historical Account of the Establishment, Progress and State of the Bank of Scotland* (Edinburgh, 1728).

Fleetwood, William. *A Sermon against Clipping* (London, 1694).

Forbes, William. *Memoirs of a Banking-House* (London, 1860).

Ford, Sir Edward. *Experimented Proposals: How the King May Have Money...* (London, 1666).

Fortune, T. *The History of the Bank of England, from the Establishment of That Institution to the Present Day* (London, 1797).

Foster, J. L. 'Select Committee on State of Ireland as to Circulating Paper, Specie and Current Coin, and Exchange between Ireland and Great Britain. Report', HC (1804).

Gaskell, Elizabeth. *Cranford* (Oxford, 1980 [1853]).

A Gentleman in Trade, *Observations on, and a Short History of Irish Banks and Bankers* (Dublin, 1760).

Gissing, George, *The Whirlpool* (Harmondsworth, 2015).

Gold Standard Defence Association. *General Statement* [London, 1895].

Gooch, Thomas Sherlock. 'Select Committee on Petitions complaining of Depressed State of Agriculture of United Kingdom. Report', HC (London, 1821).

Gray, John. *An Essay Concerning the Establishment of a National Bank in Ireland* (London, 1774).

Gray, John. *A Letter to the Earl of Nugent: Relative to the Establishment of a National Bank in Ireland* (London, 1780).

Great Britain. Parliament. House of Commons. 'List of Petitions Presented to House of Commons Complaining of Agricultural Distress, 1820-22' (London, 1822).
Great Britain. Parliament. House of Commons. 'Return of Number of Banks in England, Ireland and Scotland, Discount Houses and Bill Brokers Which Have Become Bankrupt or Stopped Payment, 1844-75' (London, 1876).
Harrowby, 'Secret Committee of House of Lords on State of Bank of England, with reference to Resumption of Cash Payments. First and Second Reports', HL (London, 1819).
Hobson, J. A. *The War in South Africa: Its Causes and Effects* (London, 1900).
Holland, John. *A Short Discourse on the Present Temper of the Nation with Respect to the Indian and African Company, and of the Bank of Scotland* (Edinburgh, 1696).
Holt, Richard. *Seasonable Proposals for a Perpetual Fund or Bank in Dublin* ([Dublin,] 1696).
Hume, David. 'Of the Balance of Trade'. In *Hume: Political Essays*, ed. Knud Haakonssen, pp. 136-49 (Cambridge, 1994).
Hutchinson, Francis. *A Letter to the Gentlemen of the Landed Interest in Ireland Relating to a Bank* (Dublin, 1721).
Ireland. Oireachtas. Joint Committee on the Secondary Legislation of the European Communities. *Report on Commissions' Proposals on Economic and Monetary Unio* (Dublin, 28 June 1978).
Irwin, John. *To the Nobility, Gentry and Commonalty of This Kingdom of Ireland* [Dublin, 1718?].
[James I, King of England.] *A Proclamation declaring at what values certaine Moneys of Scotland shal be currant within England* (London, 1603).
[James I, King of England.] *A Proclamation for Coynes* (London, 1604).
[James II, King of England.] *Whereas for Remedy of the Present Scarcity of Money...* (Dublin, 1689).
[James II, King of England.] *Whereas We Are Informed That Several Covetous Persons...* (Dublin, 1690).
Jebb, Frederic. *Considerations on the Expediency of a National Circulation Bank at This Time in Ireland* (Dublin, 1780).
J. R. *Short Reasons Why Our Gold-Money in Ireland Should Not Be Lowered* (n.p., 1737).
Keynes, J. M. 'The Committee on the Currency', *Economic Journal* 35, no. 138 (1925): p. 299.
Keynes, J. M. *The Economic Consequences of Mr. Churchill* ([London,] 1925).
Keynes, J. M. *Essays in Persuasion* (London, 1931).
Keynes, J. M. *A Tract on Monetary Reform* (London, 1924).
Keynes, J. M. *A Treatise on Money*, 2 vols (London, 1933).
Keynes, J. M. 'War and the Financial System, August, 1914', *Economic Journal* 24, no. 95 (1914): p. 460.
King, Peter. 'On the Second Reading of Earl Stanhope's Bill Respecting Guineas and Bank Notes'. In *A Selection from the Speeches and Writing of the Late Lord King* (London, 1844).
King, Peter. 'Speech on the Bank Restriction Bill'. In *A Selection from the Speeches and Writing of the Late Lord King* (London, 1844).
King, Peter. 'Thoughts on the Effects of the Bank Restrictions'. In *A Selection from the Speeches and Writing of the Late Lord King* (London, 1844).
Kitson, Arthur. *The Banker's Conspiracy Which Started the World Crisis* (London, 1933).
Kitson, Arthur. *A Scientific Solution of the Money Question* (Boston, MA, 1895).

Kitson, Arthur. *Trade Fallacies: A Criticism of Existing Methods, and Suggestions for a Reform Towards National Prosperity* (London, 1917).
Kitson, Arthur. *Unemployment, the Cause and a Remedy* (London, 1921).
Labour Party. *Labour and Social Credit* (London, 1922).
Laing, David. *Historical Notices of Scottish Affairs: Selected from the Manuscripts of Sir John Lauder of Fountainhall, Bart.*, ed. John Lauder Fountainhall (Edinburgh, 1848).
Lawrence, Richard. *The Interest of Ireland in Its Trade and Wealth Stated* (Dublin, 1682).
Leslie, Charles. *On the Scarcity of the Copper Coin. A Satyr* ([Edinburgh], 1739).
Liverpool, Earl of. *A Treatise on the Coins of the Realm in a Letter to the King* (Oxford, 1805).
Lloyd George, David. *War Memoirs of David Lloyd George*, vol. 1 (London, 1933).
Locke, John. *Further Considerations Concerning Raising the Value of Money* (London, 1696).
Locke, John. *Locke on Money*, ed. Patrick Kelly, 2 vols (Oxford, 1991).
Lockhart, George. *Memoirs Concerning the Affairs of Scotland* (London, 1714).
London Corresponding Society. *A Narrative of the Proceedings at the General Meeting of the London Corresponding Society, Held on Monday* (London, 31 July, 1797).
Lowndes, William. *A Report Containing an Essay for the Amendment of the Silver Coins* (London, 1695).
McCulloch, John Ramsay. *A Supplement to the Edition of Mr. McCulloch's Commercial Dictionary Published in 1844* (London, 1846).
Macmillan, Hugh, 'Committee on Finance & Industry. Report' (Cm 3897, 1931).
Macneill of Carskey: His Estate Journal, 1703-1743, ed. Frank Forbes Mackay (Edinburgh, 1955).
May, George Ernest, 'Committee on National Expenditure. Report' (Cm 3920, 1931).
A Member of the Said Corporation. *A Letter to a Friend Concerning the Credit of the Nation* (London, 1697).
Miller, Hugh. *Words of Warning to the People of Scotland on Sir R. Peel's Scotch Currency Scheme* (Edinburgh, 1844).
Misolestes, Patriophilus. *Objections against the General Bank in Ireland as It Stands Now Circumstanciated Whether It Do's or Do's Not Receive a Parliamentary Sanction* (Dublin, 1721).
Morgan, William. *An Appeal to the People of Great Britain, on the Present Alarming State of the Public Finances and of Public Credit* (London, 1797).
Mun, Thomas, and John Mun. *England's Treasure by Forraign Trade* (London, 1664).
Murray, Robert. *A Proposal for a National Bank Consisting of Land or Any Other Valuable Securities or Depositums...* (London, 1695).
National Currency Reform Association Tracts (London, 1850).
Owen, Robert. *Report to the County of Lanark* (Glasgow, 1821).
Paine, Thomas. *The Decline & Fall of the English System of Finance* (London, 1796).
Paterson, William. *A Brief Account of the Intended Bank of England* (London, 1694).
Peacock, Thomas Love. *The Works of Thomas Love Peacock,* ed. H. F. B. Brett Smith and C. E. Jones. vol. 7 (London, 1924).
Pease, Edward R. *Gold and State Banking: A Study in the Economics of Monopoly* (London, 1912).
Peel, Robert, 'Secret Committee on State of Bank of England with Reference to Expediency of Resumption of Cash Payments. Second Report', HC (London, 1819).
Peel, Robert, 'Select Committee on State of Circulation of Promissory Notes under Five Pounds in Scotland and Ireland. Report' HC (London, 1826).

Petty, William. *The Political Anatomy of Ireland* (London, 1691).
Petty, William. *Quantulumcunque Concerning Mony* (London, 1695).
Petty, William. *A Treatise of Taxes & Contributions* (London, 1667).
Pope, Simeon. *Scarcity of Specie No Ground for Alarm, or, British Opulence Unimpaired* (London, 1797).
Potter, William. *The Trades-Man's Jewel* (London, 1650).
Prior, Thomas. *Observations on Coin in General with Some Proposals for Regulating the Value of Coin in Ireland* (London, 1729).
Publicola. *A Letter to the Author of a Pamphlet Entitled Some Thoughts on the Nature of Paper Credit* (Dublin, 1760).
Quelch, Harry. *The Bimetallic Bubble* (London, 1895).
Ricardo, David. *The High Price of Bullion a Proof of the Depreciation of Bank Notes* (London, 1810).
Ricardo, David. *Proposals for an Economical and Secure Currency; with Observations on the Profits of the Bank of England, as They Regard the Public and the Proprietors of Bank Stock* (London, 1816).
Rowley, Hercules. *An Answer to a Book, Intitl'd, Reasons Offer'd for Erecting a Bank in Ireland* (Dublin, 1721).
Scott, Sir Walter (Malachi Malagrowther, pseud.). *Thoughts on the Proposed Change of Currency, and Other Late Alterations, as They Affect, or Are Intended to Affect, the Kingdom of Scotland* (Edinburgh, 1826).
Secundus, Junius. *Junius Secundus's Letters to the People of Ireland, against the Establishment of a National Bank* (Dublin, 1782).
Sharp, R. *A Letter to the People of Ireland; on the Present State of the Kingdom. Relative to the Banks, &C* (Dublin, 1755).
Simon, James. *An Essay Towards an Historical Account of Irish Coins, and of the Currency of Foreign Monies in Ireland* (Dublin, 1749).
Smith, Adam. *An Inquiry into the Nature and Causes of the Wealth of Nations*, ed. Edwin Cannan, 2 vols (London, 1904).
S. R. *A Letter to a Member of Parliament, from His Friend at Oxford: Concerning the Settling Gold and Silver* (n.p. [1696]).
Swift, Jonathan. *The Eyes of Ireland Open* (London, 1722).
Swift, Jonathan. *Fraud Detected, or, the Hibernian Patriot: Containing All the Drapier's Letters to the People of Ireland* (Dublin, 1725).
Swift, Jonathan, and Thomas Sheridan. *The Intelligencer* [1728–29], ed. James Woolley (Oxford, 1990).
T—w, J.-n. *Paper-Credit Considered Particularly Relative to the Late Failures of Bankers and Receivers in Ireland* (Dublin, 1760).
Taylor, John. *An Essay on Money, Its Origin and Use* (London, 1833).
Taylor, John. *What Is a Pound: A Letter to the Premier on His New Currency Measure*, 2nd ed (London, 1844).
Temple, Richard. *Some Short Remarks Upon Mr. Lock's Book, in Answer to Mr. Lounds, and Several Other Books and Pamphlets Concerning Coin* (London, 1696).
Thornton, Henry. *An Enquiry into the Nature and Effects of the Paper Credit of Great Britain* (London, 1802).
Trollope, Anthony, *The Way We Live Now* (Ware, 1995).
Turner, Thomas. *The Diary of Thomas Turner, 1754–1765*, ed. David Vaisey (Oxford, 1984).
Vallavine, Peter. *Observations on the Present Condition of the Current Coin of This Kingdom* (London, 1742).

Violet, Thomas. *An Appeal to Cæsar Wherein Gold and Silver Is Proved to Be the Kings Majesties Royal Commodity* (London, 1662).
Wakefield, Edward. *An Account of Ireland, Statistical and Political.* 2 vols (London, 1812).
Webb, Sidney. *National Finance and a Levy on Capital: What the Labour Party Intends* (London, 1919).
Withers, Hartley. *War and Lombard Street* (New York, 1915).
Wood, Charles. 'Select Committee of Secrecy on Banks of Issue: Second Report', HC (London, 1841).
Woodburn, Arthur *The Mystery of Money* (London, 1931).

2. Secondary Sources

Acheson, Graeme G., and John D. Turner. 'The Death Blow to Unlimited Liability in Victorian Britain: The City of Glasgow Failure', *Explorations in Economic History* 45, no. 3 (2008): p. 235.
Adamson, John. 'The English Context of the British Civil Wars', *History Today* 48, no. 11 (Nov. 1998): p. 23.
Adonis, Andrew. 'Tony Blair and Europe: Shattering the Ming Vase', *Prospect*, 11 Nov. 2017.
Alborn, Timothy L. *All That Glittered: Britain's Most Precious Metal from Adam Smith to the Gold Rush* (New York, 2019).
Alborn, Timothy L. 'Coin and Country: Visions of Civilisation in the British Recoinage Debate, 1867–1891', *Journal of Victorian Culture* 3, no. 2 (1998): p. 252.
Alborn, Timothy L. *Conceiving Companies: Joint-Stock Politics in Victorian England* (London, 1998).
Alborn, Timothy L. 'Money's Worth'. In *The Victorian World*, ed. Martin Hewitt (2012).
Allen, Martin. 'The First Sterling Area', *Economic History Review* 70, no. 1 (2017): p. 79.
Allen, Martin. 'The Groats of Edward I', *British Numismatic Journal* 74, no. 5 (2004): p. 28.
Allen, Martin. 'The Proportions of Denominations in English Mint Outputs, 1351–1485', *British Numismatic Journal* 77 (2007): p. 190.
Allen, Martin. 'The Volume of the English Currency, 1158–1470', *Economic History Review* 54, no. 4 (2001): p. 595.
Andreades, Andreas Michael. *History of the Bank of England,* tr. Christabel Meredith (London, 1909).
Appleby, Joyce Oldham. *Economic Thought and Ideology in Seventeenth Century England* (Princeton, 1978).
Appleby, Joyce Oldham. 'Locke, Liberalism and the Natural Law of Money', *Past & Present* 71 (1976): p. 43.
Arendt, Hannah. 'Understanding and Politics (the Difficulties of Understanding)'. In *Essays in Understanding 1930-1954*, ed. Jerome Kohn (New York, 1994).
Armitage, David, and M. J. Braddick. *The British Atlantic World, 1500–1800* (New York, 2002).
Asch, Ronald G. '"Obscured in Whiskey, Mist and Misery" the Role of Scotland and Ireland in British History'. In *Three Nations—a Common History?: England, Scotland, Ireland, and British History, c. 1600–1920*, ed. Ronald G. Asch (Bochum, 1993).
Asch, Ronald G., ed., *Three Nations—a Common History?: England, Scotland, Ireland, and British History, c. 1600–1920* (Bochum, 1993).
Ashton, Robert. *The Crown and the Money Market, 1603–1640* (Oxford, 1960).

Aylmer, G. E. 'Vyner [Viner], Sir Thomas, First Baronet (1588–1665), Goldsmith and Banker', *ODNB* (2008).
Barnard, T. C. 'British History and Irish History'. In *The New British History: Founding a Modern State 1603–1715*, ed. Glenn Burgess (London, 1999).
Barry, Kevin. 'The Suspension of Cash Payments and Ireland's Narrative Economy: The Contexts of Maria Edgeworth's "National" Novels'. In *The Empire of Credit: The Financial Revolution in the British Atlantic World, 1688–1815*, ed. Daniel Carey and Christopher Finlay (Dublin, 2011).
Beattie, J. M. *Crime and the Courts in England, 1660–1800* (Princeton, 1986).
Beattie, J. M. 'London Juries in the 1690s'. In *Twelve Good Men and True: The Criminal Trial Jury in England, 1200–1800*, ed. J. S. Cockburn and Thomas Andrew Green (Princeton, 1988).
Bennett, Rachel E. *Capital Punishment and the Criminal Corpse in Scotland, 1740–1834* (Basingstoke, 2018).
Blaazer, David. '"Devalued and Dejected Britons": The Pound in Public Discourse in the Mid-1960s', *History Workshop Journal* 47 (Spring 1999): p. 121.
Blaazer, David. '"Not Only Patriotism but Self-Interest": War, Money and Finance in British Public Discourse 1914–1925', *War and Society* 23, Special Issue (2005): p. 1.
Blaazer, David. *The Popular Front and the Progressive Tradition: Socialists, Liberals, and the Quest for Unity, 1884–1939* (Cambridge, 1992).
Blaazer, David. 'Sharks and Shylocks: Englishness and Otherness in Popular Discourse on "the City" 1870–1914', *National Identities* 18, no. 2 (2016): p. 139.
Blaazer, David. 'Sterling Identities', *History Today* 52, no. 1 (January 2002): p. 12.
Blank, Stephen. 'Britain's Economic Problems: Lies and Damn Lies'. In *Is Britain Dying? Perspectives on the Current Crisis*, ed. Isaac Kramnick (Ithaca, 1979).
Bolton, James. *Money in the Medieval English Economy 973–1489* (Manchester, 2012).
Bolton, James. 'Reply to Pamela Nightingale's "a Crisis of Credit"', *British Numismatic Journal* 83, no. 11 (2013): p. 164.
Bolton, James. 'Was There a "Crisis of Credit" in Fifteenth-Century England?', *British Numismatic Journal* 81, no. 5 (2011): p. 144.
Bonar, J. 'Ricardo's Ingot Plan', *Economic Journal* 33, no. 131 (1923): p. 281.
Bordo, Michael D., and Eugene N. White. 'A Tale of Two Currencies: British and French Finance During the Napoleonic Wars', *Journal of Economic History* 51, no. 2 (1991): p. 303.
Bourke, Richard. 'Pocock and the Presuppositions of New British History', *Historical Journal* 53, no. 3 (2010): p. 747.
Boyce, Robert. 'Creating the Myth of Consensus: Public Opinion and Britain's Return to the Gold Standard in 1925'. In *Money and Power: Essays in Honour of L.S. Pressnell*, ed. P. L. Cottrell and D. E. Moggridge (Basingstoke, 1988).
Boyne, William D. *Trade Tokens Issued in the Seventeenth Century in England, Wales, and Ireland, by Corporations, Merchants, Tradesmen, etc.*, 2 vols (New York, 1970).
Bradbury, Jill Marie. '"Interest" and Anglo-Irish Political Discourses in the 1720-21 Bank Pamphlet Literature,' *Eighteenth-Century Ireland/Iris an dá chultúr* 29 (2014).
Bradshaw, Brendan, and J. S. Morrill, eds. *The British Problem, c. 1534–1707: State Formation in the Atlantic Archipelago* (New York, 1996).
Bragge, Charles, 'Committee of Secrecy on Outstanding Demands of Bank of England: Reports', House of Commons (1997).
Brewer, John. *The Sinews of Power: War, Money and the English State, 1688–1783* (London, 1989).

Briggs, Asa. *The Age of Improvement 1783–1867* (London, 1959).
Briggs, Chris. *Credit and Village Society in Fourteenth-Century England* (Oxford, 2009).
Brock, Michael. *The Great Reform Act* (London, 1973).
Brown, Keith M. *Kingdom or Province?: Scotland and the Regal Union, 1603–1715* (London, 1992).
Brown, Keith M. 'Seducing the Scottish Clio: Has Scottish History Anything to Fear from the New British History?'. In *The New British History: Founding a Modern State 1603–1715*, ed. Glenn Burgess (London, 1999).
Broz, J. Lawrence, and Richard S. Grossman. 'Paying for Privilege: The Political Economy of Bank of England Charters, 1694–1844', *Explorations in Economic History* 41, no. 1 (2004): p. 48.
Brunhoff, Suzanne de. *Marx on Money,* tr. Maurice J. Goldbloom (New York, 1976).
Brunton, Finn. *Digital Cash. The Unknown History of the Anarchists, Utopians and Technologists Who Built Cryptocurency* (Princeton, 2019).
Bullock, Alan. *The Life and Times of Ernest Bevin,* 3 vols (London, 1960–83).
Burgess, Glenn, ed., *The New British History: Founding a Modern State 1603–1715* (London, 1999).
Byatt, Derrick. *Promises to Pay: The First Three Hundred Years of Bank of England Notes* (London, 1994).
Caden, Mara H. 'Mint Conditions: The Politics and Geography of Money in Britain and Its Empire, 1650–1730', PhD dissertation, Yale University, 2017.
Caffentzis, Constantine George. *Clipped Coins, Abused Words and Civil Government. John Locke's Philosophy of Money* (New York, 1989).
Cain, P. J., and A .G. Hopkins. *British Imperialism,* 2 vols (London, 1993).
Calvocoressi, Peter. *The British Experience 1945–1975* (London, 1965).
Cameron, Rondo E. *Banking in the Early Stages of Industrialization; a Study in Comparative Economic History* (Oxford, 1967).
Campbell, Martha. 'Marx and Keynes on Money'. *International Journal of Political Economy* 27, no. 3 (1997): p. 65.
Campbell, Ruth. 'Sentence of Death by Burning for Women', *Journal of Legal History* 5, no. 1 (1984): p. 44.
Canny, Nicholas. 'The Attempted Anglicization of Ireland in the Seventeenth Century: An Exemplar of "British History"'. In *Three Nations—a Common History?: England, Scotland, Ireland, and British History, c. 1600–1920*, ed. Ronald G. Asch (Bochum, 1993).
Capie, Forest. 'British Financial Crises in the Nineteenth and Twentieth Centuries'. In *British Financial Crises since 1825*, ed. Nicholas H. Dimsdale and Anthony Hotson (Oxford, 2014).
Capie, Forest, and Alan Webber. *A Monetary History of the United Kingdom, 1870–1982,* Vol. 1 (London, 1985).
Carey, Daniel, and Christopher Finlay, eds. *The Empire of Credit: The Financial Revolution in the British Atlantic World, 1688–1815* (Dublin, 2011).
Carruthers, Bruce G. *City of Capital. Politics and Markets in the English Financial Revolution* (Princeton, 1996).
Cassis, Youssef. *City Bankers, 1890–1914,* tr. Margaret Rocques (Cambridge, 1994).
Challinor, Raymond. *The Origins of British Bolshevism* (London, 1977).
Challis, C. E. 'Debasement: The Scottish Experience in the Fifteenth and Sixteenth Centuries'. In *Coinage in Medieval Scotland (1100–1600)*, ed. D. M. Metcalf (Oxford, 1977).
Challis, C. E. 'Lord Hastings to the Great Silver Recoinage, 1464-1699'. In *A New History of the Royal Mint*, ed. C. E. Challis (Cambridge, 1992).

Challis, C. E., ed., *A New History of the Royal Mint*. (Cambridge, 1992).
Chart, David Alfred. *An Economic History of Ireland* (Dublin, 1920).
Checkland, S. G. *Scottish Banking: A History, 1695-1973* (Checkland, 1975).
Clancy, Kevin. 'The Recoinage and Exchange of 1816-17', PhD dissertation, University of Leeds, 1999.
Clapham, J. H. *The Bank of England: A History*, 2 vols (Cambridge, 1945).
Coates, David. *The Question of UK Decline: State, Society and Economy* (London, 1994).
Colbenson, Peter Dahle. 'British Socialism and Anti-Semitism, 1884-1914', PhD dissertation, Georgia State University, 1977.
Colbert, John P. 'The Free State Currency Problem', *Journal of the Statistical and Social Inquiry Society of Ireland* XV, No. 2 (1931/2).
Cole, G. D. H. *The Life of William Cobbett* (London, 1947).
Colella, Silvana. 'Monetary Patriotism: The Letters of Malachi Malagrowther, the Antiquary and the Currency Question', *Nineteenth-Century Studies* 17 (2003): p. 53.
Colley, Linda. *Britons: Forging the Nation, 1707-1837* (New Haven, 1992).
Connolly, S. J., ed., *Kingdoms United? Great Britain and Ireland since 1500: Integration and Diversity* (Dublin, 1999).
Coppieters, Emmanuel. *English Bank Note Circulation 1694-1954* (The Hague, 1955).
Corish, Patrick J. 'The Cromwellian Regime, 1650-1660'. In *A New History of Ireland*, ed. T. W. Moody, F. X. Martin and F. J. Byrne (Oxford, 1976).
Craig, J. H. M. *The Mint: A History of the London Mint from A.D. 287 to 1948* (Cambridge, 1953).
Craig, John. *Newton at the Mint* (Cambridge, 1946).
Cromien, Seán, 'McElligott, James John (Jimmy)', *DIB*, https://creativecommons.org/licenses/by/4.0/legalcode.
Cuddy, Neil. 'Anglo-Scottish Union and the Court of James I, 1603-1625', *Transactions of the Royal Historical Society* 5th Series, 39 (1989): pp. 107-24.
Cullen, L. M. *An Economic History of Ireland since 1660* (London, 1972).
Cullen, L. M. 'The Irish Economy in the Eighteenth Century'. In *The Formation of the Irish Economy*, ed. L. M. Cullen (Cork, 1968).
Cullen, L. M. 'Landlords, Bankers and Merchants: The Early Irish Banking World, 1700-1820', *Hermathena* 135 (1983): p. 25.
Cullen, L. M., and T. C. Smout. *Comparative Aspects of Scottish and Irish Economic and Social History, 1600-1900* (Edinburgh, 1977).
Dalrymple, William. *The Anarchy: The Relentless Rise of the East India Company* (New York, 2019).
Dardanelli, Paolo. 'Ideology and Rationality: The Europeanisation of the Scottish National Party', *Österreichische Zeitschrift für Politikwissenschaft* 32, no. 3 (2003): p. 271.
Davies, Glyn. *A History of Money: From Ancient Times to the Present Day* (Cardiff, 1994).
Davis, Mike. *Late Victorian Holocausts El Niño Famines and the Making of the Third World* (London, 2002).
Day, John. 'The Great Bullion Famine of the Fifteenth Century', *Past & Present* 79, no. 1 (1978): p. 3.
de Cecco, Marcello. *Money and Empire: The International Gold Standard, 1890-1914* (Oxford, 1974).
De Krey, Gary Stuart. *A Fractured Society: The Politics of London in the First Age of Party, 1688-1715* (Oxford, 1985).
Dell, Edmund. 'Britain and the Origins of the European Monetary System,' *Contemporary European History* 3, no. 1 (1994).

Desan, Christine. *Making Money: Coin, Currency, and the Coming of Capitalism* (Oxford, 2015).
Devenney, Andrew D. 'Joining Europe: Ireland, Scotland, and the Celtic Response to European Integration, 1961–1975,' *Journal of British Studies* 49, no. 1 (2010).
Devine, T. M. *The Scottish Nation, 1700–2000* (London, 2000).
Dick, Alexander. *Romanticism and the Gold Standard: Money, Literature, and Economic Debate in Britain 1790–1830* (London, 2013).
Dickinson, W. Calvin. 'The Sword of Gold: Sidney Godolphin and War Finance, 1702–1710', *Albion* 6, no. 1 (1974): p. 12.
Dickson, David, and Richard English. 'The La Touche Dynasty'. In *The Gorgeous Mask, Dublin, 1700–1850*, ed. David Dickson (Dublin, 1987).
Dickson, P. G. M. *The Financial Revolution in England: A Study in the Development of Public Credit, 1688–1756* (London, 1967).
Dimsdale, Nicholas, and Anthony Hotson. 'Financial Crises and Economic Activity in the UK since 1825'. In *British Financial Crises since 1825*, ed. Nicholas Dimsdale and Anthony Hotson (Oxford, 2014).
Dodd, Nigel. 'The Social Life of Bitcoin', *Theory, Culture & Society* 35, no. 3 (2018): p. 35.
Dodd, Nigel. *The Social Life of Money* (Princeton, 2014).
Dodd, Nigel. *The Sociology of Money. Economics, Reason and Contemporary Society* (Cambridge, 1994).
Dolley, Michael. 'Coinage to 1534'. In *A New History of Ireland*, vol. 2, ed. Art Cosgrove (Oxford, 1993).
Dolley, Michael. 'The Irish Coinage, 1534-1691'. In *A New History of Ireland*, vol. 3, ed. T. W. Moody, F. X. Martin and F. J. Byrne (Oxford, 1991).
Dowell, Stephen. *A History of Taxation and Taxes in England, from the Earliest Times to the Present Day* (New York, 1965).
Dresser, Madge. 'Britannia'. In *Patriotism: The Making and Unmaking of British National Identity*, vol. 3, ed. Raphael Samuel (London, 1989).
Dudley, Rowena. 'The Failure of Burton's Bank and Its Aftermath', *Irish Economic and Social History* 40 (2013): p. 1.
Dyck, Ian. 'From "Rabble" to "Chopsticks": The Radicalism of William Cobbett', *Albion: A Quarterly Journal Concerned with British Studies* 21, no. 1 (1989): p. 56.
Dyer, Christopher. *A Country Merchant, 1495–1520: Trading and Farming at the End of the Middle Ages* (Oxford, 2012).
Dyer, Christopher. *Making a Living in the Middle Ages: The People of Britain 850–1520* (New Haven, 2003).
Eichengreen, Barry J. *Globalizing Capital: A History of the International Monetary System* (Princeton, 2008).
Eichengreen, Barry J. *Golden Fetters: The Gold Standard and the Great Depression, 1919–1939* (New York, 1992).
Einaudi, Luigi. 'The Theory of Imaginary Money from Charlemagne to the French Revolution'. In *Enterprise and Secular Change: Readings in Economic History*, ed. Frederic Chapin Lane and Jelle C. Riemersma (London, 1953).
Einzig, Paul. *The History of Foreign Exchange* (London, 1970).
Einzig, Paul. *Primitive Money in Its Ethnological, Historical and Economic Aspects* (Oxford, 1966).
Elliott, J. 'A Europe of Composite Monarchies', *Past & Present* 137 (1992): p. 48.
Ellis, Steven G. 'Crown, Community and Government in the English Territories, 1450–1575', *History* 71, no. 232 (1986): 187.

Ellis, Steven G. 'The Struggle for Control of the Irish Mint, 1460-C. 1506', *Proceedings of the Royal Irish Academy. Section C: Archeology, Celtic Studies, History, Linguistics, Literature* 78 (1978): p. 17.
Ellis, Steven G. *Tudor Frontiers and Noble Power: The Making of the British State* (Oxford, 1995).
Emsley, Clive. *Crime and Society in England* (Harlow, 1987).
Fay, C. R. 'Newton and the Gold Standard,' *Cambridge Historical Journal* 5, no. 1 (1935).
Feavearyear, Albert. *The Pound Sterling: A History of English Money*, rev. Victor E. Morgan (Oxford, 1963).
Ferguson, William. *Scotland's Relations with England: A Survey to 1707* (Edinburgh, 1977).
Fetter, Frank Whitson. 'The Authorship of Economic Articles in the Edinburgh Review, 1802–47', *The Journal of Political Economy* 61, no. 3 (1953): p. 232.
Fetter, Frank Whitson. *Development of British Monetary Orthodoxy, 1797–1875* (Cambridge MA, 1965).
Fetter, Frank Whitson. *The Irish Pound, 1797–1826: A Reprint of the Report of the Committee of 1804 of the British House of Commons on the Condition of the Irish Currency* (London, 1955).
Fetter, Frank Whitson, ed., *Selected Economic Writings of Thomas Attwood* (London, 1964).
Finlay, John L. *Social Credit: The English Origins* (Montreal, 1972).
Firmstone, Julie. *'Britain in the Euro?' British Newspaper Editorial Coverage of the Introduction of the Euro*. European Political Communications. Working Paper Series 5/03 (2003).
Flanders, M. June. 'A Model of Discretion: The Gold Standard in Fact and in Fiction', *World Economy* 16, no. 2 (1993): p. 213.
Flick, Carlos T. 'Thomas Attwood, Francis Place, and the Agitation for British Parliamentary Reform', *Huntington Library Quarterly* 34, no. 4 (1971): p. 355.
Forbes, Thomas R. 'A Jury of Matrons', *Medical History* 32, no. 1 (1988): p. 23.
Ford, A. G. 'International Financial Policy and the Gold Standard, 1870–1914'. In *The Cambridge Economic History of Europe from the Decline of the Roman Empire*, vol. 8, ed. Peter Mathias and Sidney Pollard (Cambridge, 1989).
Forster, E. M. *Marianne Thornton 1797–1887: A Domestic Biography* (London, 1956).
Foster, R. F. *Modern Ireland 1600–1972* (London, 1989).
Fox, David. 'The Anglo-Scots Monetary Union of 1707', *Edinburgh Law Review* 23, no. 3 (2019): p. 360.
Fox, David. 'The Case of Mixt Monies (1604)'. In *Money in the Western Legal Tradition: Middle Ages to Bretton Woods*, ed. David Fox and Wolfgang Ernst (Oxford, 2016).
Fox, David. 'The Enforcement of Nominal Values to Money in the Medieval and Early Modern Common Law'. In *Money in the Western Legal Tradition*, ed. Wolfgang Ernst (Oxford, 2016).
Francis, John. *History of the Bank of England, Its Times and Traditions*, 2 vols (London, 1847).
Galloway, Bruce. *The Union of England and Scotland, 1603–1608* (Edinburgh, 1986).
Gamble, Andrew, and Gavin Kelly. 'Britain and EMU'. In *European States and the Euro: Europeanization, Variation, and Convergence*, ed. Kenneth H. F. Dyson (Oxford, 2002).
Gamble, Andrew, and Gavin Kelly. 'The British Labour Party and Monetary Union,' *West European Politics* 23, no. 1 (2000).
Gardner, William B. 'The Later Years of John Maitland, Second Earl and First Duke of Lauderdale', *Journal of Modern History* 20 (1948): pp. 112–22.
Gaskill, Malcolm. *Crime and Mentalities in Early Modern England* (Cambridge, 2000).

Gemmill, Elizabeth, and Nicholas Mayhew. *Changing Values in Medieval Scotland: A Study of Prices, Money, and Weights and Measures* (Cambridge, 1995).
Gibson, A. J. S., and T. C. Smout. *Prices, Food and Wages in Scotland 1550-1780* (Cambridge, 1995).
Gilbert, John M. 'The Usual Money of Scotland and Exchange Rates against Scottish Coins'. In *Coinage in Medieval Scotland (1100-1600): The Second Oxford Symposium on Coinage and Monetary History*, ed. D.M. Metcalf (Oxford, 1977).
Gillespie, Raymond. *The Transformation of the Irish Economy 1550-1700* ([Dublin], 1991).
Giuseppi, John. *The Bank of England. A History from Its Foundation in 1694* (London, 1966).
Golumbia, David. 'Bitcoin as Politics. Distributed Right-Wing Extremism'. In *Moneylab Reader: An Intervention in Digital Economy*, ed. Geert Lovink, Nathaniel Tkacz, and Patricia de Vries (2015).
Goodhart, Charles A. E., and Meinhard A. Jensen. 'A Commentary on Patrizio Lainà's "Proposals for Full Reserve Banking: A Historical Survey from David Ricardo to Martin Wolf". Currency School Versus Banking School: An Ongoing Confrontation', *Economic Thought* 4, no. 2 (2015): p. 20.
Goodspeed, Tyler Beck. *Legislating Instability: Adam Smith, Free Banking, and the Financial Crisis of 1772* (Cambridge, MA, 2016).
Goodwin, A. 'Wood's Halfpence', *English Historical Review* 51, no. 204 (1936): p. 647.
Graeber, David. *Debt: The First 5,000 Years* (New York, 2011).
Graham, Aaron. 'Credit, Confidence and the Circulation of Exchequer Bills in the Early Financial Revolution,' *Financial History Review* 26, no. 1 (2019).
Grampp, William D. 'Scots, Jews, and Subversives among the Dismal Scientists', *Journal of Economic History* 36, no. 3 (1976): p. 543.
Grant, Alexander. *Independence and Nationhood: Scotland 1306-1469* (London, 1984).
Grant, Alexander, and K. J. Stringer, eds. *Uniting the Kingdom? The Making of British History* (London, 1995).
Green, E. H. H. 'The Bimetallic Controversy: Empiricism Belimed or the Case for the Issues', *English Historical Review* 105, no. 416 (1990): p. 673.
Green, E. H. H. 'Rentiers Versus Producers? The Political Economy of the Bimetallic Controversy C. 1880-1898', *English Historical Review* 103, no. 408 (1988): p. 588.
Grierson, Philip. *The Origins of Money* (London, 1977).
Griffiths, Clare. 'G.D.H. Cole and William Cobbett', *Rural History* 10, no. 1 (1999): p. 91.
Grueber, Herbert A. *Handbook of the Coins of Great Britain and Ireland in the British Museum* (London, 1899).
Guinan, Joe. 'Modern Money and the Escape from Austerity,' *Renewal* 22, no. 3/4 (2014).
Hall, F. G. *History of the Bank of Ireland 1783-1946* (Dublin, 1949).
Hamilton, Henry. *An Economic History of Scotland in the Eighteenth Century* (Oxford, 1963).
Hamilton, Henry. 'The Failure of the Ayr Bank, 1772', *Economic History Review* 8, no. 3 (1956): p. 405.
Handley, Stuart. 'Fleetwood, William (1656-1723), Bishop of Ely', *ODNB* (2011).
Handley, Stuart. 'Harbord, William (1635-1692), Politician and Diplomat', *ODNB* (2011).
Harris, Tim. 'Critical Perspectives: The Autonomy of English History'. In *The New British History: Founding a Modern State 1603-1715*, ed. Glenn Burgess (1999).
Harvie, Christopher. *Scotland and Nationalism: Scottish Society and Politics, 1707-1977* (London, 1977).
Hay, Douglas. *Albion's Fatal Tree: Crime and Society in Eighteenth-Century England* (New York, 1975).

Hayton, D. W. 'The Stanhope/Sunderland Ministry and the Repudiation of Irish Parliamentary Independence', *English Historical Review* 113, no. 452 (1998): p. 610.
Helleiner, Eric. *The Making of National Money: Territorial Currencies in Historical Perspective* (2003).
Helleiner, Eric, and Emily Gilbert, eds. *Nation-States and Money: The Past, Present and Future of National Currencies* (Ithaca, 1999).
Hewitt, Virginia H. 'Applegarth's Answers: Anti-Forgery Note Designs for the Bank of England, 1818-1821', Paper presented at the XIth International Numismatic Conference, Brussels (1993).
Hewitt, Virginia H. 'Beware of Imitations: The Campaign for a New Bank of England Note, 1797-1821', *Numismatic Chronicle* 158 (1998): p. 197.
Hilton, Boyd. *Corn, Cash, Commerce: The Economic Policies of the Tory Governments, 1815-1830* (Oxford, 1977).
Hirshfield, Claire. 'The British Left and the "Jewish Conspiracy": A Case Study of Modern Antisemitism', *Jewish Social Studies* 43, no. 2 (1981): p. 95.
Hobsbawm, E. J. *Industry and Empire; an Economic History of Britain since 1750* (London, 1968).
Holloway, John. 'Global Capital and the National State', *Capital & Class* 18, no. 1 (1994): p. 23.
Holmes, Colin. *Anti-Semitism in British Society, 1876-1939* (London, 1979).
Holmes, Michael. 'The Maastricht Treaty Referendum of June 1992', *Irish Political Studies* 8, no. 1 (2007): p. 105.
Holmes, Richard. 'English Whigs and Irish Patriots: Archbishop Boulter and the Politics of Party in Hanoverian Ireland,' *Eighteenth-Century Ireland* 31 (2016).
Honohan, Patrick, and Gavin Murphy. *Breaking the Sterling Link: Ireland's Decision to Enter the EMS* (Dublin, 2010).
Hoppit, Julian. 'Financial Crises in Eighteenth-Century England', *Economic History Review* 39, no. 1 (1986): p. 39.
Hoppit, Julian. 'The Landed Interest and the National Interest 1660-1800'. In *Parliaments, Nations, and Identities in Britain and Ireland, 1660-1850*, ed. Julian Hoppit (Manchester, 2003).
Hoppit, Julian. 'The Myths of the South Sea Bubble', *Transactions of the Royal Historical Society* 12 (2002): p. 141.
Horsefield, J. K. 'The Beginnings of Paper Money in England', *Journal of European Economic History* 6, no. 1 (1977): 117.
Horsefield, J. K. *British Monetary Experiments, 1650-1710* (1960).
Horsefield, J. K. 'Inflation and Deflation in 1694-1696', *Economica* 23, no. 91 (1956): p. 229.
Horsefield, J. K. 'The Origins of the Bank Charter Act, 1844', *Economica* 11, no. 44 (1944): p. 180.
Horsefield, J. K. 'The "Stop of the Exchequer" Revisited', *Economic History Review* 35, no. 4 (1982): p. 511.
Howarth, David. 'The Domestic Politics of British Policy on the Euro,' *Journal of European Integration* 29, no. 1 (2007).
Howe, A. C. 'Bimetallism, c. 1880-1898: A Controversy Re-Opened?', *English Historical Review* 105, no. 415 (1990): p. 377.
Howson, Susan. 'The Management of Sterling, 1932-1939', *Journal of Economic History* 40, no. 1 (1980): p. 53.
Howson, Susan. 'The Origins of Dear Money, 1919-20', *Economic History Review* 27, no. 1 (1974): p. 88.

Hume, L. J. 'The Gold Standard and Deflation: Issues and Attitudes in the Nineteen-Twenties', *Economica* 30, no. 119 (1963): p. 225.

Hutchinson, John. *The Dynamics of Cultural Nationalism: The Gaelic Revival and the Creation of the Irish Nation State* (London, 1987).

Hutton, Gordon. 'Archbishop King, the Bank Scheme (1720–21), and Wood's Halfpence (1722–25)', *Éire-Ireland* 35, no. 3 (2000): p. 81.

Ingham, Geoffrey. *Capitalism Divided? The City and Industry in British Social Development* (London, 1984).

Ingham, Geoffrey. 'Money Is a Social Relation.' *Review of Social Economy* 54, no. 4 (1996): p. 507.

Ingham, Geoffrey. *The Nature of Money* (Cambridge, 2004).

Jack, R. I. *Medieval Wales* (London, 1972).

Jackson, Alvin. *The Two Unions* (Oxford, 2011).

Jackson, Andrew, and Ben Dyson. *Modernising Money: Why Our Monetary System Is Broken and How It Can Be Fixed* (London, 2012).

Jackson, Clare. 'Maitland, Charles, Third Earl of Lauderdale (*c.* 1620–1691), Politician and Judge', *ODNB* (2008).

James, John A. 'Panics, Payments Disruptions and the Bank of England before 1826', *Financial History Review* 19, no. 3 (2012): p. 289.

Jenkinson, Hilary. 'Medieval Tallies, Public and Private', *Archaeologia: or Miscellaneous Tracts relating to Antiquity* 74 (1925): p. 289.

Johnston, Joseph. 'Irish Currency in the Eighteenth Century', *Hermathena* 27, no. 52 (1938): p. 3.

Johnston-Liik, E. M. *History of the Irish Parliament, 1692–1800: Commons, Constituencies and Statutes* (Belfast, 2002).

Jones, Dwyryd. *War and Economy in the Age of William III and Marlborough* (Oxford, 1988).

Jones, W. Douglas. '"The Bold Adventurers": A Quantitative Analysis of the Darien Subscription List (1696)', *Scottish Economic & Social History* 21, no. 1 (2001): p. 22.

Kay, John. 'Currency and Monetary Policy Options for an Independent Scotland'. In *Scotland's Future: The Economics of Constitutional Change*, ed. Andrew Goudie (Dundee, 2013).

Kelly, E. M. *Spanish Dollars and Silver Tokens: An Account of the Issues of the Bank of England 1797–1816* (London, 1976).

Kelly, Patrick. 'Berkeley and the Idea of a National Bank', *Eighteenth-Century Ireland/Iris an dá chultúr* 25 (2010): p. 98.

Kelly, Patrick. 'The Politics of Political Economy in Eighteenth Century Ireland'. In *Political Ideas in Eighteenth-Century Ireland*, ed. S. J. Connolly (2000).

Kenny, Seán, and John D. Turner. 'Wildcat Bankers or Political Failure? The Irish Financial Pantomime, 1797–1826', *European Review of Economic History* 24, no. 3 (2020): p. 522.

Kenyon, J. P., Jane H. Ohlmeyer, and J. S. Morrill, eds. *The Civil Wars: A Military History of England, Scotland, and Ireland 1638–1660* (Oxford, 1998).

Kindleberger, Charles Poor. *A Financial History of Western Europe* (London, 1984).

King, Peter, and Richard Ward. 'Rethinking the Bloody Code in Eighteenth-Century Britain: Capital Punishment at the Centre and on the Periphery,' *Past & Present* 228, no. 1 (2015).

Klamer, Arjo, Donald McCloskey, and Robert M. Solow, eds. *The Consequences of Economic Rhetoric* (Cambridge, 1988).

Kleer, Richard A. '"The Ruine of Their Diana": Lowndes, Locke, and the Bankers', *History of Political Economy* 36, no. 3 (2004): p. 533.

Knafo, Samuel. *The Making of Modern Finance. Liberal Governance and the Gold Standard* (Abingdon, 2013).
Kosmetatos, Paul. *The 1772-73 British Credit Crisis* (Cham, 2018).
Kugler, Peter, and Tobias Straumann. 'International Monetary Regimes: The Bretton Woods System'. In *Handbook of the History of Money and Currency*, ed. Stefano Battilossi, Youssef Cassis, and Kazuhiko Yago (Singapore, 2020).
Kynaston, David. *The City of London*, 4 vols (London, 1994-2001).
Laible, Janet. 'Europeanizing the Nationalist Agenda: The Scottish National Party'. In *Separatism and Sovereignty in the New Europe: Party Politics and the Meanings of Statehood in a Supranational Context*, ed. Janet Laible (New York, 2008).
Lanchester, John. *Whoops! Why Everyone Owes Everyone and No One Can Pay* (Rearsby, 2010).
Lang, Andrew. *A History of Scotland from the Roman Occupation*, 4 vols (Edinburgh, 1907).
Lenman, Bruce P. 'A Client Society: Scotland between the '15 and the '45'. In *Britain in the Age of Walpole*, ed. Jeremy Black (Basingstoke, 1984).
Lenman, Bruce. *An Economic History of Modern Scotland, 1660-1976* (London, 1977).
Levack, Brian P. *The Formation of the British State: England Scotland and the Union 1603-1707* (Oxford, 1987).
Leyshon, Andrew, and Nigel Thrift. *Money/Space: Geographies of Monetary Transformation* (London, 1997).
Li, Ming-Hsun. *The Great Recoinage of 1696 to 1699* (London, 1963).
Linebaugh, Peter. *The London Hanged: Crime and Civil Society in the Eighteenth Century* (Cambridge, 1992).
Liñeira, Robert, Ailsa Henderson, and Liam Delaney. 'Voters' Response to the Campaign: Evidence from the Survey'. In *Debating Scotland*, ed. Michael Keating (Oxford, 2017).
Lipson, E. *The Economic History of England* (London, 1959).
Lloyd, T. H. 'Early Elizabethan Investigations into Exchange and the Value of Sterling, 1558-1568', *Economic History Review* 53, no. 1 (2000): pp. 60-83.
Lloyd-Jones, Naomi, and Margaret M. Scull, eds. *Four Nations Approaches to Modern 'British' History: A (Dis)United Kingdom?* (London, 2017).
Lloyd-Jones, Naomi, and Margaret M. Scull. 'A New Plea for an Old Subject? Four Nations History for the Modern Period'. In *Four Nations Approaches to Modern 'British' History: A (Dis)United Kingdom?*, ed. Naomi Lloyd-Jones and Margaret M. Scull (London, 2017).
Lynch, Michael. *Scotland: A New History* (London, 1991).
Lyons, F. S. L., ed., *Bicentenary Essays, Bank of Ireland 1783-1983* (Dublin, 1983).
Macaulay, Thomas Babington. *The History of England from the Accession of James the Second*, 2 vols (London, 1899).
MacDonagh, Oliver. *Ireland. The Union and Its Aftermath* (London, 1977).
McDowell, J. Moore. 'The Devaluation of 1460 and the Origins of the Irish Pound', *Irish Historical Studies* xxv, no. 97 (1986): p. 19.
McGowan, Padraig. *Money and Banking in Ireland: Origins, Development and Future* (Dublin, 1990).
McGowen, Randall. 'From Pillory to Gallows: The Punishment of Forgery in the Age of the Financial Revolution,' *Past & Present* 165 (1999).
McGowen, Randall. 'Managing the Gallows: The Bank of England and the Death Penalty, 1797-1821', *Law and History Review* 25, no. 2 (2007): p. 241.
McGrath, Charles Ivar. '"The Public Wealth Is the Sinew, the Life of Every Public Measure": The Creation and Maintenance of a National Debt in Ireland, 1716-45'. In *The Empire of Credit: The Financial Revolution in the British Atlantic World, 1688-1815*, ed. Daniel Carey and Christopher J. Finlay (Dublin, 2011).

McGrath, Charles Ivar, and Christopher J. Fauske, eds. *Money, Power, and Print: Interdisciplinary Studies on the Financial Revolution in the British Isles* (Newark, 2008).

Macinnes, Allan I. *Union and Empire: The Making of the United Kingdom in 1707* (Cambridge, 2007).

Mackenzie, A.D. *The Bank of England Note* (Cambridge, 1953).

McKibbin, Ross. 'The Economic Policy of the Second Labour Government 1929–1931', *Past & Present* 68, no. 1 (1975): p. 95.

McKillop, Andrew, and Micheál Ó Siochrú. *Forging the State: European State Formation and the Anglo-Scottish Union of 1707* (Dundee, 2009).

McLeay, Michael, Amar Radia, and Ryland Thomas. 'Money Creation in the Modern Economy', *Bank of England Quarterly Bulletin* (London, 2014).

Macleod, Emma Vincent. 'Craig, Sir James Gibson, First Baronet (1765–1850), Lawyer and Politician', *ODNB* (2004).

McNally, Patrick. 'Wood's Halfpence, Carteret, and the Government of Ireland, 1723–6', *Irish Historical Studies* 30, no. 119 (1997): p. 354.

Maddicott, J. R. *The English Peasantry and the Demands of the Crown, 1294–1341* (Oxford, 1975).

Magennis, Eoin. 'Whither the Irish Financial Revolution? Money, Banks and Politics in the 1730s'. In *Money, Power, and Print. Interdisciplinary Studies on the Financial Revolution in the British Isles,* ed. Charles Ivar McGrath and Chris Fauske (Newark, 2008).

Malcolm, Charles Alexander. *The Bank of Scotland, 1695–1945* (Edinburgh, 1945).

Martin, Felix. *Money: The Unauthorised Biography* (London, 2013).

Marwick, Arthur. *The Deluge: British Society and the First World War* (London, 1965).

Mason, Roger A. 'Debating Britain in Seventeenth-Century Scotland: Multiple Monarchy and Scottish Sovereignty', *Journal of Scottish Historical Studies* 35, no. 1 (2015): p. 1.

Mate, Mavis. 'Monetary Policies in England, 1272–1307,' *British Numismatic Journal* 41, no. 8 (1972): 34.

Mathias, Peter. 'Official and Unofficial Money in the Eighteenth Century: The Evolving Uses of Currency. The Howard Linecar Memorial Lecture 2003', *British Numismatic Journal* 74, no. 8 (2004).

Mayhew, N. J. 'From Regional to Central Minting, 1158–1464'. In *A New History of the Royal Mint*, ed. C. E. Challis (Cambridge, 1992).

Mayhew, N. J. 'The Monetary Background to the Yorkist Recoinage', *British Numismatic Journal* 44, no. 9(2) (1974).

Mayhew, N. J. 'Money and the Economy'. In *Money and Coinage in the Middle Ages*, ed. Rory Naismith (Boston, 2018).

Mayhew, N. J. 'Money in England from the Middle Ages to the Nineteenth Century'. In *Money, Currency and Crisis: In Search of Trust, 2000 BC to 2000 AD*, ed. R. J. van der Spek and Bas van Leeuwen (Abingdon, 2018).

Mayhew, N. J. 'Money in Scotland in the Thirteenth Century'. In *Coinage in Medieval Scotland (1100–1600): The Second Oxford Symposium on Coinage and Monetary History*, ed. D. M. Metcalf (Oxford, 1977).

Mayhew, Nicholas. *Sterling: The Rise and Fall of a Currency* (London, 1999).

Mayhew, Nicholas. 'Wages and Currency: The Case in Britain up to c. 1600'. In *Wages and Currency: Global Comparisons from Antiquity to the Twentieth Century*, ed. Jan Lucassen (Bern, 2007).

Mellor, Mary. *Money* (Bristol, 2019).

Mellor, Mary. 'Money—the Neglected Agent of Change.' *Capitalism Nature Socialism* 27, no. 4 (2016): p. 28.

Miller, Henry. 'Radicals, Tories or Monomaniacs? The Birmingham Currency Reformers in the House of Commons, 1832–67', *Parliamentary History* 31, no. 3 (2012): p. 354.
Mitchison, Rosalind. *Lordship to Patronage: Scotland, 1603–1745* (London, 1983).
Moggridge, D. E. 'The Gold Standard and National Financial Policies, 1919–39'. In *The Industrial Economies: The Development of Economic and Social Policies*, ed. Peter Mathias and Sidney Pollard (Cambridge, 1989).
Moggridge, Donald Edward. *British Monetary Policy, 1924–1931: The Norman Conquest of $4.86* (Cambridge, 1972).
Mohr, Thomas. 'The Political Significance of the Coinage of the Irish Free State', *Irish Studies Review* 23, no. 4 (2015): p. 451.
Morrill, J. S. 'The British Problem c. 1534–1707'. In *The British Problem, c. 1534–1707: State Formation in the Atlantic Archipelago*, ed. Brendan Bradshaw and J. S. Morrill (New York, 1996).
Morrison, James Ashley. 'Shocking Intellectual Austerity: The Role of Ideas in the Demise of the Gold Standard in Britain', *International Organization* 70, no. 1 (2016): p. 175.
Moseley, Fred, ed., *Marx's Theory of Money: Modern Appraisals* (London, 2005).
Moss, D. J. 'Banknotes Versus Gold: The Monetary Theory of Thomas Attwood in His Early Writings, 1816–19', *History of Political Economy* 13, no. 1 (1981): p. 19.
Moss, D. J. *Thomas Attwood: The Biography of a Radical* (Montreal, 1990).
Moynihan, Maurice. *Currency and Central Banking in Ireland, 1922–1960* (Dublin, 1975).
Muldrew, Craig. *The Economy of Obligation: The Culture of Credit and Social Relations in Early Modern England* (New York, 1998).
Muldrew, Craig. '"Hard Food for Midas": Cash and Its Social Value in Early Modern England', *Past & Present* 170 (February 2001): p. 78.
Müller-Peters, Anke. 'The Significance of National Pride and National Identity to the Attitude toward the Single European Currency: A Europe-Wide Comparison', *Journal of Economic Psychology* 19, no. 6 (1998): p. 701.
Murray, Athol L. 'Administration and the Law'. In *The Union of 1707: Its Impact on Scotland*, ed. T. I. Rae (Glasgow, 1974).
Murray, Athol L. 'The Scottish Recoinage of 1707–9 and Its Aftermath', *British Numismatic Journal* 72, no. 8 (2002): p. 115.
Murray, Athol L. 'The Scottish Treasury 1667–1708', *Scottish Historical Review* 45, no. 139 (1966): p. 89.
Nelson, Anitra. *Marx's Concept of Money: The God of Commodities* (London, 1999).
Newton, C. C. S. 'The Sterling Crisis of 1947 and the British Response to the Marshall Plan', *Economic History Review* 37, no. 3 (1984): p. 391.
Nightingale, Pamela. 'A Crisis of Credit in the Fifteenth Century, or of Historical Interpretation?', *British Numismatic Journal* 83, no. 10 (2013): p. 149.
Nightingale, Pamela. *Enterprise, Money and Credit in England before the Black Death 1285–1349* (Cham, 2018).
Nightingale, Pamela. 'Gold, Credit and Mortality: Distinguishing Deflationary Pressures on the Late Medieval English Economy', *Economic History Review* 63, no. 4 (2010): p. 1081.
Nightingale, Pamela. 'Money and Credit in the Economy of Late Medieval England'. In *Medieval Money Matters*, ed. Diana Wood (Oxford, 2004).
O'Brien, Patrick K. 'The Political Economy of British Taxation, 1660–1815', *Economic History Review* 41, no. 1 (1988): p. 1.
Officer, Lawrence H., and Samuel H. Williamson, 'The Price of Gold, 1257–Present,' *MeasuringWorth* (2021), http://www.measuringworth.com/gold/ (accessed 1 Aug. 2021).
Ó Gráda, Cormac. *Ireland: A New Economic History, 1780–1939* (Oxford, 1995).

Ó Gráda, Cormac. 'The Last Major Irish Bank Failure before 2008', *Financial History Review* 19, no. 2 (2012): p. 199.
Ó Gráda, Cormac. 'Reassessing the Irish Pound Report of 1804', *Bulletin of Economic Research* 43, no. 1 (1991): p. 5.
Ohlmeyer, Jane. 'Seventeenth-Century Ireland and the New British and Atlantic Histories', *American Historical Review* 104, no. 2 (1999): p. 446.
Oldham, James C. 'On Pleading the Belly: A History of the Jury of Matrons', *Criminal Justice History* 6 (1985 1985): p. 1.
O'Regan, Philip, 'King, William', *DIB*, https://creativecommons.org/licenses/by/4.0/legalcode.
Osborne, John Walter. *William Cobbett; His Thought and His Times* (New Brunswick, 1966).
Palk, Deirdre. '"Fit Objects for Mercy": Gender, the Bank of England and Currency Criminals, 1804–1833', *Women's Writing* 11, no. 2 (2004): p. 237.
Palk, Deirdre, ed. *Prisoners' Letters to the Bank of England, 1781–1827* (London, 2007).
Patrick, John. 'A Union Broken? Restoration Politics in Scotland'. In *Scotland Revisited*, ed. Jenny Wormald (1991).
Paul, Helen J. *The Darien Scheme and Anglophobia in Scotland* (Southampton, 2009).
Paul, Helen J. *The South Sea Bubble: An Economic History of Its Origins and Consequences* (Hoboken, 2010).
Pawlisch, Hans S. *Sir John Davies and the Conquest of Ireland: A Study in Legal Imperialism* (Cambridge, 1985).
Peters, John. 'The British Government and the City-Industry Divide: The Case of the 1914 Financial Crisis', *Twentieth Century British History* 4, no. 2 (1993): p. 126.
Photos-Jones, Effie, Richard Jones, and Donal Bateson. '"Light on Many Journeys": A Crisis in Charles II's Scottish Silver Leading to the Closure of the Mint.', *British Numismatic Journal* 87 (2017): p. 163.
Pincus, Steve. *1688: The First Modern Revolution* (New Haven, 2009).
Pocock, J. G. A. 'British History: A Plea for a New Subject', *Journal of Modern History* 47, no. 4 (1975): p. 601.
Pocock, J. G. A. *The Discovery of Islands: Essays in British History* (Cambridge, 2005).
Polanyi, Karl. *The Great Transformation* (Boston, 1985).
Poovey, Mary. *Genres of the Credit Economy: Mediating Value in Eighteenth- and Nineteenth-Century Britain* (Chicago, 2008).
Postan, M. M. *Essays on Medieval Agriculture and General Problems of the Medieval Economy* (Cambridge, 1973).
Prebble, John. *The Darien Disaster* (Harmondsworth, 1970).
Pressnell, Leslie Sedden. *Country Banking in the Industrial Revolution* (Oxford, 1956).
Pugh, Martin. *State and Society: A Social and Political History of Britain since 1870* (London, 2017).
Quinn, Stephen. 'Gold, Silver, and the Glorious Revolution: Arbitrage between Bills of Exchange and Bullion', *Economic History Review* 49, no. 3 (1996): p. 473.
Quinn, Stephen. 'Goldsmith-Banking: Mutual Acceptance and Interbanker Clearing in Restoration London', *Explorations in Economic History* 34, no. 4 (1997): p. 411.
Rawnsley, Andrew. *Servants of the People: The inside Story of New Labour* (London, 2000).
Reddy, William M. *Money and Liberty in Modern Europe: A Critique of Historical Understanding* (Cambridge, 1987).
Redish, Angela. *Bimetallism: An Economic and Historical Analysis* (Cambridge, 2000).
Redish, Angela. 'The Evolution of the Gold Standard in England', *Journal of Economic History* 50, no. 4 (1990): pp. 789–805.

Regan, John M. *The Irish Counter-Revolution 1921–1936* (Dublin, 1999).
Richards, Eric. 'Darién and the Psychology of Scottish Adventurism in the 1690s'. In *Imperial Expectations and Realities*, ed. Andrekos Varnava (Manchester, 2015).
Richards, R. D. *The Early History of Banking in England* (London, 1929).
Richards, R. D. 'The Evolution of Paper Money in England', *Quarterly Journal of Economics* 41, no. 3 (1927): p. 361.
Risse, Thomas. 'The Euro between National and European Identity', *Journal of European Public Policy* 10, no. 4 (2003): p. 487.
Roberts, Peter, and Brendan Bradshaw, eds. *British Consciousness and Identity: The Making of Britain, 1533–1707* (Cambridge, 1998).
Roberts, Richard. *Saving the City: The Great Financial Crisis of 1914* (Oxford, 2013).
Roberts, Richard, and David Kynaston, eds. *The Bank of England: Money, Power, and Influence 1694–1994* (Oxford, 1995).
Robertson, John. 'Union, State and Empire: The Britain of 1707 in Its European Setting'. In *An Imperial State at War: Britain from 1689 to 1815*, ed. Lawrence Stone (London, 1993).
Rogers, Chris. 'The Politics of Economic Policy Making in Britain: A Re-Assessment of the 1976 IMF Crisis', *Politics & Policy* 37, no. 5 (2009): p. 971.
Rogers, James E. Thorold. *The First Nine Years of the Bank of England* (Oxford, 1887).
Rose, Craig. *England in the 1690s: Revolution, Religion and War* (Oxford, 1999).
Roselli, Alessandro. 'Money: The Long Twentieth Century'. In *Money, Currency and Crisis: In Search of Trust, 2000 BC to AD 2000*, ed. R. J. van der Spek and Bas Van Leeuwen (Abingdon, 2018).
Rowlinson, Matthew Charles. *Real Money and Romanticism* (Cambridge, 2010).
Royle, Edward. *Modern Britain. A Social History* (London, 1987).
Rubini, Dennis. 'Politics and the Battle for the Banks, 1688–1697', *English Historical Review* 85, no. 337 (1970): p. 693.
Russell, Conrad. 'The British Problem and the English Civil War', *History* 72, no. 236 (1987): p. 395.
Russell, Conrad. *The Fall of the British Monarchies, 1637–1642* (Oxford, 1991).
Russell, Conrad. 'John Bull's Other Nations', *Times Literary Supplement*, 12 March 1993.
Russell, Norman. *The Novelist and Mammon: Literary Responses to the World of Commerce in the Nineteenth Century* (Oxford, 1986).
Ryder, Michael. 'The Bank of Ireland, 1721: Land, Credit and Dependency', *Historical Journal* 25, no. 3 (1982): p. 557.
Sacks, David Harris. *The Widening Gate: Bristol and the Atlantic Economy, 1450–1700* (Berkeley, 1991).
Sargent, Thomas J., and Francois R. Velde. *The Big Problem of Small Change* (Princeton, 2002).
Saville, Richard. *Bank of Scotland: A History, 1695–1995* (Edinburgh, 1996).
Sayers, R. S. *The Bank of England 1891–1944*, 3 vols (London, 1976).
Schenk, Catherine. 'The Sterling Area 1945–1972'. In *Handbook of the History of Money and Currency*, ed. Stefano Battilossi, Youssef Cassis, and Kazuhiko Yago (Singapore, 2020).
Scott, Paul Henderson. *Walter Scott and Scotland* (Edinburgh, 1994).
Selgin, George. 'Steam, Hot Air, and Small Change: Matthew Boulton and the Reform of Britain's Coinage', *Economic History Review* 56, no. 3 (2003): p. 478.
Sharpe, J. A. '"Last Dying Speeches": Religion, Ideology and Public Execution in Seventeenth-Century England', *Past & Present* 107 (1985): p. 144.
Shaw, W. A. 'The "Treasury Order Book"', *Economic Journal* 16, no. 61 (1906): p. 33.

Shin, Hiroki. 'The Culture of Paper Money in Britain: the Bank of England Note during the Bank Restriction Period, 1797–1821', PhD Dissertation, Cambridge University, 2008.
Shin, Hiroki. 'Paper Money, the Nation, and the Suspension of Cash Payments in 1797', *Historical Journal* 58, no. 2 (2015): p. 415.
Simpson, Kathryn. 'The Model EU Citizen? Explaining Irish Attitudes Towards the EU,' *Political Insight* 9, no. 1 (2018).
Sinclair, David. *The Pound: A Biography: The Story of the Currency That Ruled the World* (London, 2001).
Sinclair, John. *Memoirs of the Life and Works of the Late Right Hon. Sir John Sinclair, Bart* (Edinburgh, 1837).
Skidelsky, Robert. *John Maynard Keynes: A Biography*, 3 vols (London, 1983–2000).
Skidelsky, Robert. *Politicians and the Slump* (Harmondsworth, 1970).
Smith, David L. *A History of the Modern British Isles, 1603–1707: The Double Crown* (Oxford, 1998).
Smout, T. C. 'The Anglo-Scottish Union of 1707. I. The Economic Background', *Economic History Review* 16, no. 3 (1964): p. 455.
Smout, T. C. 'The Anglo-Scottish Union of 1707. II. The Economic Consequences, *Economic History Review* 16, no. 3 (1964): p. 468.
Spang, Rebecca L. *Stuff and Money in the Time of the French Revolution* (Cambridge, MA, 2015).
Spence, C. 'Accounting for the Dissolution of a Nation State: Scotland and the Treaty of Union', *Accounting, Organizations and Society* 35, no. 3 (2010): p. 377.
Spufford, Peter. *Money and Its Use in Medieval Europe* (Cambridge, 1988).
Spufford, Peter, Wendy Wilkinson, and Sarah Tolley, *Handbook of Medieval Exchange* (London, 1986).
Steel, Anthony. *The Receipt of the Exchequer: 1377–1485* (Cambridge, 1954).
Stevenson, David. 'The Covenanters and the Scottish Mint, 1639–1641', *British Numismatic Journal* 42, no. 10 (1972).
Stevenson, John. 'William Cobbett: Patriot or Briton?', *Transactions of the Royal Historical Society* 6 (1996): p. 123.
Strachan, Hew. *Financing the First World War* (Oxford, 2004).
Strange, Susan. 'Sterling and British Policy: A Political View', *International Affairs* 47, no. 2 (1971): p. 302.
Styles, John A. '"Our Traitorous Money Makers": The Yorkshire Coiners and the Law, 1760–83'. In *An Ungovernable People: The English and Their Law in the Seventeenth and Eighteenth Centuries*, ed. John A. Styles and John Brewer (London, 1980).
Swan, Coree Brown, and Bettina Petersohn. 'The Currency Issue: Contested Narratives on Currency Union and Independence'. In *Debating Scotland*, ed. Michael Keating (Oxford, 2017).
Takami, Norikazu. 'Pigou on Business Cycles and Unemployment: An Anti-Gold-Standard View', *European Journal of the History of Economic Thought* 18, no. 2 (2011): p. 203.
Thompson, E. P. *The Making of the English Working Class* (1963, repr. Harmondsworth, 1980).
Thompson, E. P. *The Poverty of Theory, & Other Essays* (London, 1978).
Thompson, F. M. L., ed., *The Cambridge Social History of Britain, 1750–1950*. 3 vols (Cambridge, 1990).
Thompson, James. *Models of Value: Eighteenth-Century Political Economy and the Novel* (Durham, 1996).
Tomlinson, Jim. 'Inventing "Decline": The Falling Behind of the British Economy in the Postwar Years', *Economic History Review* 49, no. 4 (1996): p. 731.

Tooze, Adam. *The Deluge: The Great War, America and the Remaking of the Global Order, 1916-1931* (New York, 2015).
Trentmann, Frank. *Free Trade Nation: Commerce, Consumption, and Civil Society in Modern Britain* (Oxford, 2008).
Turner, Michael J. *Radicalism and Reputation: The Career of Bronterre O'Brien* (East Lansing, 2017).
Valenze, Deborah M. *The Social Life of Money in the English Past* (Cambridge, 2006).
Von den Steinen, Karl. 'In Search of the Antecedents of Women's Political Activism in Early Eighteenth Century Scotland: The Daughters of Anne, Duchess of Hamilton'. In *Women in Scotland: c.1100—c.1750*, ed. Elizabeth Ewan and Maureen M. Meikle (1999).
Waddell, Brodie. 'The Politics of Economic Distress in the Aftermath of the Glorious Revolution, 1689-1702', *English Historical Review* 130, no. 543 (2015): p. 318.
Walsh, Patrick. 'The Bubble on the Periphery: Scotland and the South Sea Bubble', *Scottish Historical Review* 91, no. 1 (2012): p. 106.
Walsh, Patrick. *The South Sea Bubble and Ireland: Money, Banking and Investment, 1690-1721* (Woodbridge, 2014).
Watt, Douglas. *The Price of Scotland* (2008).
Wennerlind, Carl. *Casualties of Credit: The English Financial Revolution, 1620-1720* (Cambrdige, MA, 2011).
Wennerlind, Carl. 'The Death Penalty as Monetary Policy: The Practice and Punishment of Monetary Crime', *History of Political Economy* 36, no. 1 (2004): p. 131.
Whatley, Christopher A. *Bought and Sold for English Gold?: Explaining the Union of 1707* (East Linton, 2001).
Whatley, Christopher A. *The Scots and the Union: Then and Now* (Edinburgh, 2014).
White, Nicholas J. *Decolonisation: The British Experience since 1945* (London, 2014).
Whiting, J. R. S. *Trade Tokens: A Social and Economic History* (Newton Abbot, 1971).
Wiener, Martin J. 'The Changing Image of William Cobbett', *Journal of British Studies* 13, no. 2 (1974): p. 135.
Williams, Raymond. *Culture and Society, 1780-1950* (Harmondsworth, 1963).
Williamson, Oliver E. 'Transaction Cost Economics and Organization Theory'. In *The Handbook of Economic Sociology*, ed. Richard Swedberg and Neil J. Smelser (Princeton, 1994).
Williamson, Philip. 'A "Bankers' Ramp"? Financiers and the British Political Crisis of August 1931', *English Historical Review* 99, no. 393 (1984): p. 770.
Wood, John H. *A History of Central Banking in Great Britain and the United States* (Cambridge, 2005).
Woodmansee, Martha, and Mark Osteen, eds. *The New Economic Criticism: Studies at the Intersection of Literature and Economics* (London, 1999).
Wormald, Jenny. 'The Creation of Britain: Multiple Kingdoms or Core and Colonies?', *Transactions of the Royal Historical Society* 2 (1992): p. 175.
Wormald, Jenny. '"O Brave New World?" The Union of England and Scotland in 1603'. In *Anglo-Scottish Relations from 1603 to 1900*, ed. T. C. Smout (Oxford, 2005).
Wray, L. Randall. *Modern Money Theory: A Primer on Macroeconomics for Sovereign Monetary Systems* (London, 2015).
Yeates, F. Willson. 'The Coinage of Ireland During the Rebellion 1641-1652', *British Numismatic Journal* 15, no. 11 (1919): p. 185.
Zelizer, Viviana A. *The Social Meaning of Money* (New York, 1994).

Index

For the benefit of digital users, indexed terms that span two pages (e.g., 52–53) may, on occasion, appear on only one of those pages.

Act for Encouraging of Coinage (1666) 54
African Company. *See* Company of Scotland Trading to Africa and the Indies
Alborn, Timothy 19, 234
Anglocentrism 12–13
Anglo-Dutch Wars 64
Anglo-Irish monetary union. *See* monetary union (England and Ireland)
Anglo-Irish Nine Years War (1594–1603) 35
Anglo-Irish war (20th century) 245, 255–6
Anglo-Scottish monetary union. *See* monetary union (England and Scotland)
Anti-Gold-Law League 228
Anti-semitism 183, 218, 229. *See also* Jews
Arbuthnot, Harriet 203
Armitage, David 14
Armstrong, Thomas 63
army pay. *See* military expenses and army pay difficulties
Asgill, John 87–9
Assignats 167, 184, 219–20, 248–9
assignments (treasury orders). *See* exchequer orders (treasury orders, assignments); tallies
Attwood, Matthias 200, 218
Attwood, Thomas 200, 218, 220–2
Ayr Bank (Douglas, Heron and Company) 132–3, 150

Bagehot, Walter 227–8
Bank Charter Act (1844) 216–17, 222–6
bank notes (cashier's notes, running cash notes) 81–3
Bank of England 78–9, 105–6, 117. *See also* monetary system (England); monetary system (United Kingdom)
   Bank Charter Act (1844) provisions 222–6
   cash payment restriction (1797) 135, 166–78
   cash payment resumption Act (1819) 188–9, 195–9
   charter 81, 127–8, 204
   contrasted with Bank of Scotland 109
   cooperation with Royal Bank of Scotland 127
   departments 222–3, 226
   and exchequer bills 121–5
   foundation 78, 81, 83–5, 146–7
   gold reserves 167–8, 196–7, 219–20, 237, 264–5
   holding of coin (1696) 102
   legal tender notes proposal 83–4
   loans to support sterling 236, 264
   management of government's remittances 85, 92, 144
   notes 8–9, 81–3, 101–2, 164–5, 168
   'old lady of Threadneedle Street' epithet 178
   opposition to and criticism of 84–7
   paper money 78–9
   political economists' distrust of 216–17
   public debt held 143–4
   relationship with state 13, 142, 144, 183–4, 187, 194, 197–9, 216–17, 222–3, 253
   reputation 229
   role 85–7, 92, 134, 142, 144, 194, 226–8, 237–8
   'sealed bills' 81–2
   securities 223–4
   tokens 172–3, 192
Bank of Ireland 208
   cash payment restriction (1797) 135, 169
   cash payment resumption Act (1819) 195–6
   foundation (1783) 149–52
   notes (*see* banknotes (Bank of Ireland))
   proposal and opposition (1721) 142, 144–9
   proposal and opposition (1780–82) 150–3
   purpose 151–2
   resemblance to Bank of England 149, 151–2
Bank of Scotland 90, 105–6, 108–12, 116, 120, 134, 205
   branches 110–11
   charter 110–11, 122–3, 127
   contrasted with Bank of England 109
   difficulties 110–12, 116, 128
   foundation 108–9, 148
   note exchanges 132
   notes 110–11, 115–16, 119–20
   paper credit 125
   perceived political disaffection of 122–3, 127
   resists English exchequer bills 120, 122–3

318 INDEX

Bank of Scotland (*cont.*)
  role 109–10, 112, 117
  security for issues 110
'bank wars' (Scotland) 128–9
Banking Acts (1844 and 1845) 216–17, 222–7, 229–30, 234–5, 243–5, 255, 259, 287, 291–2
banknotes. *See also* banks and banking; paper money
  as business loans 129–30
  common usage 9–10, 120
  convertibility 129–30, 246
  forgery of 193–4
  note issues extinguished (other than Bank of England) 224
  optional clauses 129–30, 132
  origin 8
  Scottish and Irish notes banned in England 210–11
  small notes 115–16, 120, 128–32, 168–78, 187, 202, 224–5
  small notes bans 130, 168, 203–10
banknotes (Bank of England) 8, 81–4, 103, 164–5, 230
  and British patriotism 144
  convertibility 83, 102, 168, 196–7, 234–5
  denominations 104, 115–16, 133, 168–9
  'excessive issue and depreciation' question 181–3
  forgery of 193–4
  legal tender 183, 217
  pound as means of exchange and unit of account 168, 222
  reduction of volume in circulation (1819) 196–7, 199
  in Saorstát Éireann (Irish Free State) 256–7
  small notes introduced as money 168–78
  small notes reintroduction proposals 234–5
  small notes replacing currency notes 253–5
  small notes withdrawal 199, 202–3
  uniform equivalency of notes to coin 222–4
  value basis 101–2, 104
  volume in 1919 243
banknotes (Bank of Ireland) 151–2, 179, 214–15
  as legal tender 240–1
  denominations 151–2
  volume in 1919 243
banknotes (Bank of Scotland) 110–11, 119–20, 254–5, 288–9
  denominations 115
  as legal tender 240–1
  small notes exchange for new silver 192
  value basis 110
  volume in 1919 243

banknotes (Royal Bank of Scotland) 128–9
banks and banking 6, 16, 80–90. *See also* Bank of England; Bank of Ireland; Bank of Scotland; banknotes; Royal Bank of Scotland; trading companies
  bank failures 127–8, 132–3, 150–1, 202–3, 205, 215–16, 227, 230–1, 264
  Banking Acts (1844 and 1845) 216–17, 222–7, 229–30, 234–5, 243–5, 255, 259, 287, 291–2
  banks of issue banned 222–5
  central banks 8–9, 15–16
  country banks in England 133, 164–5, 202–4, 215
  debates about money and banking (1820s to 1840s) 216–22
  difference in England and Scotland 127–8, 204
  First World War (1914–19) 237–43
  historiography 16
  in Ireland 144–53, 180, 207–8, 224–5, 260–2
  joint-stock banks in England 216
  land banks 51, 84, 87–90
  Saorstát Éireann (Irish Free State) 257–62
  in Scotland 126–30, 132–4, 149, 174, 204–6, 208–11, 224–6
  Scottish banks' acceptance of each other's notes 132, 230
  state banks 84–6
Barbon, Nicholas 87–9
Baring, Alexander 183–4
Baring Brothers bank 229
Barnard, Toby 12
Barr, John 248–9
barter myth 7–8, 15–16, 248–9
Beaverbrook, Lord 249
Bellingham, Daniel 60–3
Bentham, Jeremy 221
Berkeley, George 150–1
Bevin, Ernest 251, 263–4
bills of exchange 8–9, 26–7, 81, 110, 123, 132–4, 182, 228
bimetallism 223, 231–4
Bindon, David 159–60
Bird, William Wilberforce 172
Birmingham School of currency reformers 200, 218, 220, 228
Bland, John 50–1
Blondeau, Pierre 51
Blythe, Ernest 257–8, 269–70
borrowing. *See* credit; government borrowing
Boulter, Hugh (Archbishop) 156–61
Boulton, Matthew 173, 180, 190
Boyce, Robert 247, 250

Bradbury, John 243
Bradbury Committee (Committee on the Currency and Bank of England Note Issues) 252–3
Braddick, M. J. 14
Brailsford, H. N. 250–3
Bray, John 202, 219
Brennan, Joseph 260–1, 269
Bretton Woods agreement 274–5, 279
Brewer, John 58, 77
Briscoe, John 87–9
Britain. *See also* United Kingdom of Great Britain and Ireland (from 1801)
  Britishness 11
  'King of Great Britain' legend on coins 38, 40–1, 48
  terminology 11
Britannia imagery 83, 172–3, 208, 241–2, 253–4
  parodies of 193, 195
'British' history as subject of study 10–14
  Anglocentric approach 12–13, 51
  terminology 11–12
Brougham, Henry 184
Broz, J. Lawrence 87
bullion exports 26, 52–4, 90–1, 136
bullion shortages 27–8, 31, 46, 50, 69
bullion value 4–5, 23–9, 52, 54, 91, 162, 189–90, 196–7. *See also* gold standard; silver standard
bullionism 181–3, 185–9, 192–3, 195–201, 215–22, 225
Burdett, Francis 221
Burgess, Glenn 14
Burke, Edmund 164
Burns, Robert 117–18
Burton's Bank 150–1

Caden, Mara 156
Cannan, Edwin 170–2
Cantillon, Richard 136–7
Carteret, John (Viscount) 156
cartoons 177–8
cash credit system 128–9
cashier's notes 81–3. *See also* banknotes
central banks
  monetary decision-making 15–16
  money creation 8–9
Chamberlain, Austen 238–9
Chamberlain, Joseph 234
Chamberlen, Hugh 50–1, 87–9, 115
Charles I
  coinage 40–3
Charles II
  coinage 44, 47–9
  interest-bearing tallies 56

Chartists 186, 219–21, 233, 248–9
cheques 8–9, 224, 228, 231
Churchill, Winston 249–52, 257, 276
'cis-archipelagic' history 14
'cis-Atlantic' history 14
City. *See* London money market
City of Glasgow Bank 230
Clancy, Kevin 191
clipped coins 5, 24–5, 52, 60, 78, 91–7
  English, in Scotland 106–7
  functional role 91–2
  lucrative nature of clipping 91, 162–3
  negative consequences 92, 96–7
  prosecutions for currency offences 92–6
  treasonable 94, 96
Cobbett, William 185–9, 192–4, 211, 215, 217–18, 221–2, 233, 248–9
coin shortages 31, 46, 52–5
  copper coin 157–8
  credit and 31–2, 54–5, 141
  England 30–2, 75, 77, 82, 89
  gold coin 161–4
  Ireland 32–3, 46, 59–61, 73, 138–9, 144–5, 158–9, 161
  Scotland 32, 61, 68–9, 106–7, 111–16, 130–2
  silver coin 24, 52–3, 69, 90–1, 103, 120, 135–7, 161, 240
  United Kingdom 240
coin value 56–8, 219. *See also* bullion value
  legal valuation 24–5, 37
  tale (face) value 5, 24–6, 75
Coinage Act (1816) 188–9
coining offences. *See* currency offences
coins. *See also* English coins; foreign coin; gold coin; Irish coins; mint charges; minting techniques; mints; Scottish coins; silver coin
  counterfeit (*see* counterfeiting)
  demonetized 5–6, 30, 34–5, 37
  disadvantages of coin 219
  early standards 27–8
  free coinage 54, 71–2, 107
  milled coins 52
  origins 219
  quality 51–2
Cole, G. D. H. 186
Colebrooke's Bank 150–1
Colley, Linda 11, 184–5
Colquhoun, Patrick 157–8
Combe, William 176
Committee on Currency and Foreign Exchange After the War (Cunliffe Committee) 243–5, 247, 252, 261–2
Committee on the Currency and Bank of England Note Issues (Bradbury Committee) 252–3

Commonwealth of England, Scotland and Ireland.
  See Cromwellian period (Protectorate)
Company of Scotland Trading to Africa and the
  Indies 108–15, 118, 123–7
contract payments 25, 37, 41
Conway, Viscount 59
  tenants' rents 63
Cooperative Movement 218–19
Cope, John 122–3, 125
copper coin 48, 69, 131, 138–9, 173
  counterfeit 131, 153–4, 157–8
  for Ireland 153–8
  scarcity 157–8
Corn Laws 199, 221
corruption 49, 69–71, 76
counterfeiting 5, 76, 162–3
  coins 52, 75, 92, 103, 131, 153–4, 157–8,
    162–3, 180
  tokens 173
  as treason 94, 96
Craig, Gibson 206–7
credit. *See also* banks and banking
  coin shortages and 31–2, 54–5, 141
  money and 7–9
  non-regulation of 224
  personal credit 44–5 (*see also* tradesmen's
    tokens)
  public 79, 81
credit instruments 8–9, 27, 50–1, 77, 112, 128–9,
  224, 228. *See also* banknotes; bills of
  exchange; cheques; exchequer orders
  (treasury orders, assignments)
  paper credit 81–2, 128–9, 134, 163–5
Cromwellian period (Protectorate) 41–5, 47, 65
Cruikshank, George
  'Bank Restriction Note' 193–4
  'Restriction Barometer' 195
cryptocurrencies 291
Cunliffe, Walter 243
Cunliffe Committee (Committee on Currency
  and Foreign Exchange After the
  War) 243–5, 247, 252, 261–2
currency, forms of 55–8, 103, 242. *See also* coins;
  tallies
currency notes (state-issued) 239–45
  replaced by Bank of England notes 253–5
currency offences 157–8. *See also* clipped coins;
  counterfeiting; forgery of banknotes
  England 52–3, 92–8
  Scotland 26, 107
currency reform associations 228

Dardanelli, Paolo 286
Darien venture 112–15

Davies, Glyn 16
de Valera, Eamonn 261–2
depression. *See* financial crises
Desan, Christine 18, 24–5, 29, 32, 54, 78, 96,
  100–1, 138
Dickson, P. G. M. 79
Dodd, Nigel 3–4, 17–18
Douglas, C. H. 248
Douglas, Heron and Company
  (Ayr Bank) 132–3, 150
Downing, George 53
Drummond, David 127
Dunfermline, Lord 225
Dungannon Convention 152
Dykes, Hugh 284

East India Company 113, 132–3, 136, 142–3
Economic and Monetary Union of the European
  Economic Community 280
economics (discipline) 15–16
Edinburgh mint 40, 42–4, 49
  closure and re-opening (1680s) 71
  corruption of officers 49, 69–71
  reopening (1664) 46, 68–9
  revenue for the Crown 30
Edward I
  military expenses 29
Edward VI 34
Eichengreen, Barry J. 263
Einzig, Paul 1
Elizabeth I 34–5, 37
Ellice, Edward 200
England
  in 1720s 147
  army pay (*see* army pay difficulties)
  economic interests predominant over
    Ireland's 60
  monetary system (*see* monetary system
    (England); monetary system (United
    Kingdom))
  political union with Scotland (*see* political
    union (England and Scotland, 1707);
    United Kingdom of Great Britain and
    Ireland (from 1801))
  regal union with Scotland (*see* regal union
    (England and Scotland, 1603))
  terminology 11
  Williamite revolution and war (1689–91) 75
English coins 27–8, 52. *See also* English tokens;
  gold coin; silver coin
  bullion coin disappearance (20th century) 236
  Charles I coinage 40–3
  Charles II coinage 47–8
  clipped (*see* clipped coins)

debasement 34
demonetization (1696) 102-3, 107
demonetized in Ireland 35, 37
demonetized in Scotland 107-8
designs 36-43
exchange rates with Scottish coins 23-4, 29-30, 72-3
free coinage 54
gold to silver price ratio (1717) 136
high bullion content 29, 43-4
high denominations 30-1
James I coinage 36-40
'laurel' coins 47-8, 168
legal tender in three kingdoms 43-4 (*see also* legal tender)
milled coins 52
overstamped foreign coins 172-3
Protectorate (Cromwellian period) 42-4, 47
push to return to circulating gold coin 178-89
reduction in silver content 28
replaced Irish coin (1826) 211-15
silver recoinage (1696) 78, 89, 97-104, 106-7
silver recoinage (1817) 103, 189-93
small payments 172-3
standards 34-5, 61-2
union (1707) 114-25
'unite' coins 38-41, 168
withdrawal from Ireland 35
English Privy Council 37, 59-61, 66, 107-8, 155, 286-7
English tokens 172-3, 192
 tradesmen's tokens 44-5, 59, 62-3, 173
Equivalent 114-27, 134
Equivalent Company 126-7
European Central Bank 6, 13
European Economic and Monetary Union 280-2
European Monetary System 270-3, 280-4
Ewing, Winifred 280-1
exchange rates 6-7, 27. *See also* units of account
 England-Ireland 39-40, 179-81
 expression of 26
 Scotland-England 23-4, 29-30, 39, 68-9, 72-3
 stability 231
Exchequer, establishment of 32
exchequer bills 90
 in Scotland 120-5
exchequer orders (treasury orders, assignments) 56-9
exotic coins. *See* foreign coins

Fabian Society 233-4, 247
Falconer, John 69-71
Feavearyear, Albert 16-17, 54, 86

Fetter, Frank Whitson 216
Fielding, Henry 144
financial crises 226-9, 274-80
 1754-9 crisis 150-1
 1772 crisis 132-4, 150-1
 1820s depression 199-201
 1825 crisis 202-11
 1914-19 (First World War) 237-43
 1930s 264-71, 275
 1970s 279-80
 2007-8 (Global Financial Crisis) 285, 289-92
financial revolution (England) 79-80. *See also* monetary revolution (England)
First World War 237-43
Fleetwood, William 93-7, 100-1
Flood, Henry 151
Florentine gold florin 27
Folkestone, Lord 198
Forbes, William 170-1
Fordyce, Alexander 132-3
foreign coins 27, 36, 40-1, 60, 64
 French 189
 Portuguese 140-1, 158-9, 162
 Spanish 35, 68-9, 75, 140-1, 162, 172-3
foreign exchange 6-7, 179, 195-6, 203, 216-17, 223-4, 243, 264, 274. *See also* international trade
forgery of banknotes 193-4
Fox, Charles James, and the Foxite Whigs 171-2, 174, 176-8
Fox, David 25, 114, 117
France, war with 73-5, 83, 106, 115, 166-8, 182-5, 188
fraud 69-71, 228-9. *See also* counterfeiting; currency offences; forgery of banknotes
Frazer, James 174
free trade
 doctrines 204, 234
 Ireland participation in British mercantile system 152
French coins 189
French Mississippi scheme 143-5

gendered aspect of currency crime prosecutions 93-6
Gilchrist, Ebenezer 196
Gillray, James 177-8
Global Financial Crisis (2007-8) 285, 289-92
Godolphin, Sidney 89
gold
 discoveries 231
 exports (*see* bullion exports)
 imports 136
 monetary standard (*see* gold standard)

322 INDEX

gold (*cont.*)
  reserves (*see* gold reserves (Bank of England))
  value (*see* bullion value)
gold coin 8–9, 24–5, 31, 38–9, 75–7, 103–4
  'angels' 27
  circulating gold coin not sustainable 246
  circulating gold coin versus paper money 178–89, 192–3
  counterfeiting 162–3
  designs 188–9, 229
  deterioration 234
  Florentine gold florin 27
  guinea revaluations 68, 136–7, 140
  guinea scarcity 161–4
  guinea worth 136–7
  hoarding 139, 237, 239–40, 242
  in Ireland 139–41, 158–62, 181
  legal tender status 154
  Portuguese 140–1, 158–9, 162
  ratings 75, 140–1
  recoinage (1891) 234–5
  Scottish 40–1
  sovereigns 188–9, 229, 234, 239
  'unite' coinage 38–9
Gold Coins and Bank Notes Act. *See* Stanhope's Act (1811)
gold reserves (Bank of England) 167–8, 196–7, 219–20, 237, 264–5
gold standard 78–9, 170–1, 188–90, 229–32, 246. *See also* bullionism
  advocated 189–90
  de facto 78–9, 104, 136–8, 140
  'economic theology' 216
  end of 263–71
  India 232
  official 188–9, 202
  replaced by US currency 236
  Saorstát Éireann (Irish Free State) 255–62, 269–71
  support for 231–5, 245–7, 252–3, 263–4
  UK departures from 236, 245, 263, 267–71
  UK return to pre-war standard (1820s) 196–201, 252
  UK return to pre-war standard (1925) 246–7, 249–55, 263–4, 276
goldsmith minting syndicate proposal (Ireland) 60–3
goldsmiths' notes 55–8, 83
Gordon, Robert 46, 72
Goschen, George 234–5
government borrowing 55–8, 81, 245
government debt
  and Bank of England 81–3
  and Global Financial Crisis 290–1
  and South Sea Company 142–4
  stock of Bank of Ireland 152
  stock of Royal Bank of Scotland 126–7, 134
Graham, Aaron 90
Gray, John 151
Great Britain. *See* Britain; political union (England and Scotland, 1707); United Kingdom of Great Britain and Ireland (from 1801)
Green, E. H. H. 232–3
Grossman, Richard S. 87
guineas. *See* gold coin
Gurney, Hudson 198

Halifax, Lord (Charles Montagu, Lord Halifax) 90, 105, 121–3
Haltoune, Lord (Charles Maitland, Lord Haltoune) 69–71
Hamilton, Archibald 190–1
Hamilton, James 111–12
Harbord, William 76
Hardie, Keir 233
Harley, Robert 142–3
Hartlib Circle 50
Harvey, Ernest 264–6
Hay, John 226
Healey, Denis 281–2
Heathcote, Gilbert 92
Helleiner, Eric 9–10, 17
Henry VII
  Irish minting 33
Henry VIII
  debasement of coinage 34
  and English mint 30
Hibernia imagery 151–2, 172–3, 208
Hird, Norman 254–5
historiography of money 15–19, 51
historiography of nations of the Atlantic archipelago 10–15
Hollow Sword Blade Company 142–4
Hoppit, Julian 133
Horner, Francis 190
Horsefield, J. K. 99
Houblon, John 92
Hume, David 199–200, 223
Huskisson, William 203, 209–10
Hutchinson, Francis 135, 149

Independent Labour Party 233, 247, 250–1
India 229, 231–2
inflation 90–2, 245–6
Ingham, Geoffrey 8, 15, 17, 55–6, 247
Innes, Gilbert 205
interest-bearing securities 55–7

International Monetary Fund 274-9
international trade 29, 31, 53-4, 64, 97, 100-3, 232. *See also* foreign exchange
international transactions 26-9, 51
Ireland. *See also* monetary system (Ireland); monetary union (England and Ireland)
  in 1720s 147
  Anglocentric approach of historians of Britain 12-13
  banks (*see* Bank of Ireland; banks and banking)
  constitutional relationship with Britain 152, 155-6
  dependent kingdom 33-6, 48-9, 59, 148-9, 152
  economic interests subordinated to England's 60
  'free trade' 152
  governance 33, 59, 62, 148-9, 152-3, 180-1
  historiography 16-17
  opposition to Wood's copper coin 154-6
  poverty and hardship 63-4, 152-3, 180, 212-13
  trade with the king's enemies 64
  Williamite revolution and war (1689-91) 73-4, 76
Ireland (Free Irish State). *See* Saorstát Éireann (Irish Free State)
Ireland (Republic). *See* Republic of Ireland
Irish coins 28, 32-5, 44, 63, 153-8. *See also* Irish tokens
  central tool of Norman government 32
  Charles II 44
  during civil war 44
  currency inquiry (House of Commons) 179-81
  debasement 34
  minted in London 33, 37, 59, 138-9, 157, 181
  mixed money 35, 37
  reduction in silver content 28, 34
  replaced with English coin (1826) 211-15
  Saorstát Éireann (Irish Free State) coinage 257
  standards 33, 41
  sterling silver (James VI and I) 39-40
  valuation 66-7, 138-9
  Wood's patent for copper coin 154-7
Irish Free State. *See* Saorstát Éireann (Irish Free State)
Irish Privy Council 155-9
Irish tokens 44-5, 74, 106-7, 172-3, 180, 191

James VI (Scotland) and I (England)
  coinage 36-40
  proclamation on currency 23-4, 36-7

James VII (Scotland) and II (England)
  coin rating in Ireland 73-4
  flight and defeat 73-4
  Scottish coins 72-3
Jay, Douglas 281
Jenkinson, Charles (1st Earl of Liverpool) 189-90, 192-3
Jews 136, 183, 187, 192, 211
'Jewish financiers' 233
Jones, Dwyryd 92
Junto Whigs 88-9

Kay, John 289
Keynes, J. M. 231, 239, 251-3, 263-4
Killigrew, William 50-1
King, Peter (Lord King) 178-9, 182-7, 215, 221
King, William (Archbishop) 148-9, 154, 156
Kitson, Arthur 248, 250
Knatchbull, Edward 200-1
Kosmetatos, Paul 134

La Touche, David 151-2
labour movement 233-4, 247-53, 265-6
Labour Party 233-4, 247, 250-1
  government 263-4
Lambe, Samuel 50-1
land banks
  National Land Bank 87-90
  proposals 51, 84, 87-8
Lauderdale, Duke of (1680s) 69-71
Lauderdale (Lord, 1840s) 185
'laurel' coins 47-8, 168
Lawrence, Richard 51, 65-7, 72
lawsuits 25, 37
legal tender 37. *See also* banknotes; coins
  Bank of England notes 183, 217, 253-4
  Bank of England notes proposal 83-4
  currency notes (UK state-issued) 240-3
  English coins in three kingdoms 43-4
  precious metal coins 24-5, 154
  Scottish and Irish banknotes legal tender in respective countries 240-1
  small notes 168-72
  status of silver coin 137-8
Leyshon, Andrew 17
Li, Ming-Hsun 99, 103
Liverpool, first Earl (Charles Jenkinson) 189-90, 192-3
Liverpool Borough bank 230
Lloyd George, David 238-43, 245
Lloyd-Jones, Naomi 14
Locke, John, and Lockean dogma 8, 96-8, 100-3, 138, 141, 159-60, 162-3, 198, 201, 222, 234

London
  as global financial centre 229, 236, 246–7, 263, 278
  mint (Tower mint) 33–4, 42–4, 46, 52
London money market 129, 132–4, 229, 232–3
  'saving the City' (1914) 237–9
Londonderry, Lord 200–1
Lowndes, William 52, 100–2

MacDonald, (James) Ramsay 265–6, 269
McElligott, J. J. 257–8, 260–2, 269
MacEntee, Seán 261–2
McGowen, Randall 194
McKenna, Reginald 249, 263–4
Maitland, Charles (Lord Haltoune) 69–71
Mar, Earl of 121
marke (merk) (Scottish coin) 23–4
  half-merk coin 23, 40–1
market value of silver and gold. *See* bullion value
Martin, Felix 16
Mary I 34
Mason, Colin 13–14
May, Theresa 290–1
May Committee 264, 266
Mayhew, Nicholas 16, 25
M'Neil, Allan 245
Melville, Viscount 205–6, 225
military expenses and army pay difficulties 29, 75, 85, 89, 98
  in Ireland 58–9, 64–5, 74, 76, 139, 162
  in Scotland and Flanders 108
mint charges 5, 24–5, 54, 135–6
minting techniques 24–5, 52, 173, 190
mints 41–2
  Aberystwyth 42
  American colonies 62
  Edinburgh (*see* Edinburgh mint)
  Ireland mint proposals 60–1, 140, 156–7, 159–60
  Ireland mintless 33–4, 46
  London (Tower) 33–4, 42–4, 46, 52
  provincial 102–3
Modern Money Theory 291–2
moidores. *See* Portuguese coins
monetary patriotism. *See* patriotism
monetary power 6–9, 49, 53, 96. *See also* sovereignty
  royal monetary authority 27–30, 43–4, 49, 84–5
  Scottish monetary autonomy 67–73
monetary revolution 78–80
monetary revolution (England) 78–80
  banks 80–90
  coinage crisis 90–8, 108
  recoinage (1696) 97–104, 106–7

monetary revolution (Scotland) 79–80, 105–6, 134. *See also* political union (England and Scotland, 1707)
  Bank of Scotland foundation 108–12
  (*see also* Bank of Scotland)
  Company of Scotland failure 112–14
  (*see also* Company of Scotland Trading to Africa and the Indies)
  money crisis 106–8
  union of coins 114–25
monetary standards 135–41, 236. *See also* gold standard; silver standard; sterling
monetary system (England) 23–35, 178–89. *See also* Bank of England; banknotes (Bank of England); English coins; gold standard; monetary system (United Kingdom); silver standard
  coin shortages (*see* coin shortages)
  hegemonic 105–6
  imperial policy and 140–1, 232
  James VI (Scotland) and I (England) proclamation on Scottish coins 23–4, 36–7
  London money market 129, 132–4
  monetary revolution (*see* monetary revolution (England))
  'pound' as means of exchange and unit of account 168–9, 222
  Protectorate (Cromwellian period) 42–4, 47
  royal monetary authority 27–9, 43–4, 84–5
  silver recoinage (1696) 78, 89, 97–104, 106–7
  structural issues 46–7, 50, 55
  Williamite revolution and war (1689–91) 75
monetary system (Europe) 270–1, 280–4
monetary system (Ireland) 11, 23–35, 134, 138–41, 225–6. *See also* Bank of Ireland; Irish coins; monetary union (England and Ireland)
  in 17th century 44–5, 58–67, 73–4
  ban on export of sterling money to 138–9, 161–2
  circulation of English coin 33–5, 47–8
  civil war and Cromwellian period 43–5
  coin problems (18th century) 153–8
  coin shortages (*see* coin shortages)
  currency inquiry (House of Commons) 179–81
  exclusion of Ireland from 1817 recoinage 191
  foreign coin 35, 60, 64, 73, 139–41, 161–2
  Irish Free State (*see* Saorstát Éireann (Irish Free State))
  mint proposals 60–3, 140, 156
  mintless 33–4, 46
  monetary power in 49, 65–6
  money calculated in sterling 41
  rating of silver coin 140–1
  replacement of Irish coin with English (1826) 211–15

INDEX 325

Republic (*see* Republic of Ireland)
standards 138, 140, 158–61 (*see also* gold standard)
Stanhope's Act and 185
terminology in monetary history 11
tokens (*see* Irish tokens)
Williamite revolution and war (1689–91) 73–4, 76
withdrawal of English coin 35
monetary system (Scotland) 11, 23–32, 106, 225–6, 254–5. *See also* Scottish coins
banking (*see* banks and banking)
coin shortages (*see* coin shortages)
community transactions 130–2
crisis 106–12, 114–15
currency options for an independent Scotland 284–9
foreign coin 40–1, 68–9
monetary autonomy (17th century) 49, 67–73
monetary union with England (*see* monetary union (England and Scotland))
paper money 117–18, 127–9, 131–2, 134
Protectorate (Cromwellian period) 43–4
response to Bank of England suspension of cash payments 169–71
royal monetary authority 28–30, 43–4, 49
standards 28, 71–3, 106
Williamite revolution and war (1689–91) 74–5
monetary system (United Kingdom) 236. *See also* Bank of England; banknotes (Bank of England); English coins
Banking Acts (1844 and 1845) 216–17, 222–7, 229–30, 234–5, 243–5, 255, 287, 291–2 (*see also* banks and banking)
Bradbury Committee 252–3
bullion coin disappearance 236
cash payment resumption Act (1819) 188–9, 195–9
cash payment suspension (1797) 135, 166–78
contraction of money supply (1820s) 196–203, 218
Cunliffe Committee 243–5, 247, 252, 261–2
currency notes (state-issued) 239–45, 253
debates about money and banking (1820s to 1840s) 216–22
decline of sterling 273–9
and European Monetary System 280–4
financial crises (1820s) 199–211
financial crisis (1914–19) 237–43
financial crisis (1930s) 264–71
financial crisis (2007–8) 289–92
and gold standard (*see* gold standard)
London money market 229, 232–3
May Committee 264, 266

silver coin shortages 240
US currency as UK monetary standard 236
monetary union (England and Ireland) 41, 225–6. See also United Kingdom of Great Britain and Ireland (from 1801)
civil war and Protectorate (Cromwellian period) 42–5
not implemented at 1801 union 180–1
replacement of Irish coin with English (1826) 211–15
Restoration reversal of 47–9
steps towards (1812) 185
monetary union (England and Scotland) 125–34, 225–6, 254–5, 286–9. *See also* monetary system (Scotland); monetary system (United Kingdom); United Kingdom of Great Britain and Ireland (from 1801)
Charles I approach 40–1
currency options for an independent Scotland 284–9
economic case for 113–14
James VI (Scotland) and I (England) approach 36–41
Protectorate (Cromwellian period) 42–5
Restoration period reversal of 40–1, 47–9
silver recoinage (1817) 189–93
union of coins (18th century) 114–25
money
and credit 7–9 (*see also* credit; credit instruments)
debates about (1820s to 1840s) 216–22
definitions and functions 2–9, 56
notions of 291–2
origins myth 8, 248–9
types 219
Montagu, Charles (Lord Halifax) 90, 105, 121–3
Montrose, Duke of 121–3
Moore, Roger 154
Morgan, William 174
Morrison, James 264–5
Muldrew, Craig 18
Mun, Thomas and John 53
Munster Bank 230
Murray, Robert 78, 86

National Land Bank 87–90, 142
nationalism. *See* patriotism; Scots nationalist feeling
Neale, James, Fordyce and Down 132–3
near money 8–9, 56–8. *See also* credit instruments
Nelson, Anthony 283–4
New British History 10–14
New York 236–7, 264–5
Newport, John 185

Newton, Isaac 93, 136-7, 140
Niemeyer, Otto 260-1
Norman, Montagu 249-50, 253, 264-5
Norman conquest of England 32
Northern Ireland 11, 13, 260-1, 282-3

O'Brien, Bronterre 219
offences. *See* currency offences
Oman, Charles 256
O'Neill, Hugh 35
Ormond (Lord-Lieutenant of Ireland) 58-62, 64-7
overdrafts 128-9
Overend, Gurney and Co. 227-8
Owen, Robert, and Owenite ideas 218-19, 233-4

Paine, Thomas 187
Palmer, J. Horsley
  Palmer rule 223-4
paper credit 81-2, 125, 128-9, 134, 163-5
paper money. *See also* banknotes
  circulating gold coin versus paper money 178-89, 192-3
  currency notes throughout UK 236
  currency notes (UK state-issued) 239-45, 253
  debates about money and banking (1820s to 1840s) 216-22
  denunciations of 185-9, 192-4, 211, 215, 217-18, 221-2, 248-9
  exchequer bills 90, 120-5
  forgery of 193-4
  in Ireland 207-8
  Saorstát Éireann (Irish Free State) 257-62
  in Scotland 117-18, 127-9, 131-2, 134, 224-5
  small notes bans 130, 168, 203-10, 216
  small notes in England 168-78, 187, 202, 204
  volume in 1919 243
Paris 236, 264-5
Parnell, Henry 185, 211-12
Paterson, William 83-6, 88, 109-11
patriotism 144, 166, 174-6, 182-5, 266-7
  pride in sterling 273-4, 277, 283-4
payment in kind 31-2
Peacock, Thomas Love 210-11
Peel, Robert 197-8, 201, 209, 215, 246, 248-9. *See also* Banking Acts (1844 and 1845)
Perceval, Spencer 183
Peters, John 238
Petersohn, Bettina 286
Petty, William 51, 53, 66-7, 72
Pigou, A. C. 243
Pistrucci, Benedetto, image of St George 188-9, 229, 253-4, 277
Pitt, William 168, 174, 177-8

Pocock, John 10-14
Polanyi, Karl 199-200
Pole, Thornton & Co 203
Pole, William Wellesley 190-1
political economy as a system of thought 217-18
political union (England and Scotland), attempt by James VI (Scotland) and I (England) 36-40
political union (England and Scotland, 1707) 105-6, 108-9, 134. *See also* United Kingdom of Great Britain and Ireland (from 1801)
  economic arguments for 113-14
  Scottish and British money 125-34
  union of coins 114-25
Ponsonby, George 185
Poovey, Mary 19, 182, 217-18, 230
Pope, Simeon 166, 175-6
popular attitudes to money 186, 215, 220-2
Portuguese coins 140-1, 158-9, 162
Potter, William 50-1
pound. *See also* sterling
  means of exchange and unit of account 168, 222
  synecdoche of the British currency 169, 288
  terminology 168-9
Powell, Enoch 281
Poynings, Edward 33
Poynings' Law 59, 152
Prior, Thomas 160
prosecutions for currency offences 92-6, 193-4
Protectorate (Cromwellian period) 41-5, 47, 65
Provincial Bank (Ireland) 208

Quelch, Harry 233-4

Rawdon, George 59
regal union (England and Scotland, 1603) 23, 36, 48-9. *See also* James VI (Scotland) and I (England); James VII (Scotland) and II (England)
rents 29
  coin versus paper payment 182-6
Republic of Ireland 11, 13, 270-3, 280-3
Restoration period 47-9
Ricardo, David 181, 196-7, 199-200, 215, 233-4, 243-4, 246, 248-9
Rothschilds 229
Rowley, Hercules 148-9
Royal Bank of Scotland 126-30, 205
  Bank of England cooperation 127
  charter 127
  note exchange 132
  notes 128-9
running cash notes 81-3. *See also* banknotes

INDEX   327

Russell, Lord John 220-2
Ryder, Michael 145-7

Saorstát Éireann (Irish Free State) 11, 236, 257-8
  coinage 257
  monetary standard 255, 258-9, 261-2, 269-71
  paper money and banking 257-62
  UK money circulation 256-7
Saville, Richard 112
Scotland
  in 1695 147-8
  Anglocentric approach of historians of Britain 12-13
  banks (see banks and banking)
  governance 110, 149, 286-7
  monetary union with England (see monetary union (England and Scotland))
  political union with England (see political union (England and Scotland, 1707); United Kingdom of Great Britain and Ireland (from 1801))
  regal union with England (see regal union (England and Scotland, 1603))
  terminology 11
Scots nationalist feeling 205-7, 224-6, 269, 280-1
Scott, Walter 205-7, 255
Scottish coins 23-4, 28, 38, 68-9. See also monetary union (England and Scotland)
  assimilation with England (proposed) 71-3
  Charles I coinage 40-1
  Charles II coinage 48
  designs 38-41, 48, 72-3, 116
  exchange rates with English coins 23-4, 29-30, 72-3
  free coinage 71-2, 107
  James VI (Scotland) and I (England) coinage 36-40
  James VI (Scotland) and I (England) proclamation on 23-4, 36-7
  James VII (Scotland) and II (England) coinage 72-3
  marke (merk) and half-merk 23-4, 40-1, 48
  recoinage (1707) 103, 118-20
  recoinage (1817) 189-93
  reduction in silver content 28-30
  revaluation 68-9
  small money 30, 44-5, 174
  standards 28, 71-2
  union of coins 114-25
  'unite' coins 38-41
Scottish National Party
  on currency options for an independent Scotland 13, 272, 284-9
  on financial crisis (1931) 269

Scottish Privy Council 43-4, 49, 68-71, 106-7, 116
Scull, Margaret M 14
Seafield, Lord 121, 124-5
seigniorage 5, 24-5, 27, 106-7
  abolition (England) 54
  Saorstát Éireann (Irish Free State) 256-7
Sheridan, R. B. 177-8
Shin, Hiroki 175
silver
  bullion backing for Bank of England notes 223
  exports (see bullion exports)
  monetary standard (see silver standard)
  value (see bullion value)
silver coin. See also English coins; Irish coins; Scottish coins
  clipped (see clipped coins)
  counterfeit (see counterfeiting)
  deterioration 5, 137-8
  foreign coins 140-1
  hoarding 52, 76, 106-7, 237
  legal tender status 137-8, 154
  loss of/scarcity 24, 52-3, 69, 90-1, 103, 120, 135-7, 161, 240 (see also coin shortages)
  milled coins 52
  minting cessation 137-8
  recoinage (1696) 78, 89, 97-104, 106-7
  recoinage (1707) 103, 118-20
  recoinage (1817) 103, 189-93
  reduction in silver content 28-30, 33, 91
  standards 28, 33
  value in circulation (1805) 189-90
silver exports. See bullion exports
silver standard 24-5, 75, 78-9, 91, 104, 136-8, 140, 173
  bimetallism 223, 231-4
  India 232
Sinclair, John 195-6
Sketchley, John 233-4
slave trade 142-3
small payments 30-1, 44-5, 54-5, 115, 128-31, 157-8, 172-3, 192
Smith, Adam 8, 129-30, 132, 144-5, 206
Snowden, Philip 250, 253, 263-6
social credit theories 248
South Sea Bubble 141-5
'Sovereign money' proposals 291-2
sovereignty and national currency 5, 13, 25, 32, 256-7, 262, 279-84, 286-7, 291-2. See also monetary power
Spanish coins 35, 68-9, 75, 140-1, 162, 172-3
specie. See coins
Spence, Crawford 117
Spender, Wilfrid 260-1

St Andrew Society 241–2
St George imagery 42–3, 188–9, 229, 241–2, 253–4, 277
Stanhope's Act (1811) 183–6, 221
state, the
  Bank of England relationship with 13, 142, 144, 183–4, 187, 194, 197–9, 216–17, 222–3, 253
  role of 290–2
  sovereignty and national currency 5, 13, 25, 32, 256–7, 262, 279–84, 286–7, 291–2
sterling. *See also* English coins; monetary system (England); monetary system (United Kingdom); pound
  decline of 273–9
  global importance 274
  pride in 273–4, 277, 283–4
sterling area 28, 276–9, 282–3
'sterling peg' 68–9, 262, 269–70, 274–5, 282, 289
'stop of the exchequer' (1672) 57–8
Stuart monarchy. *See* Charles I; Charles II; James VI (Scotland) and I (England); James VII (Scotland) and II (England)
Styles, John 163
Suez crisis (1956) 277–8
Suthers, R. B. 248, 250
Swan, Coree Brown 286
Swift, Jonathan 148, 156, 160

tale value (face value) 5, 24–6, 75
tallies 28–9, 51, 55–8, 77, 82, 85
tax collection 29, 55–6, 75–7, 79–82, 154–5
Taylor, John 218–20, 228
Thatcher, Margaret 281, 283–4
Thrift, Nigel 17
Tipperary Bank 230
tokens 44–5, 59, 62–3, 74, 103, 106–7, 172–3
  English 44–5, 172–3, 192
  Irish 44–5, 74, 106–7, 172–3, 180, 191
  tradesmen's 44–5, 59, 62–3, 173
  Welsh 44–5
tontines 55
Tooze, Adam 264–5
town pieces 44–5
tradesmen's tokens 44–5, 59, 62–3, 173
trading companies 112. *See also* international trade
  Company of Scotland 108–15, 118, 123–7
  East India Company 113, 132–3, 136, 142–3
treason 94, 96, 175, 239–40
treasury orders. *See* exchequer orders (treasury orders, assignments)
Treaty of Union (1707). *See* political union (England and Scotland, 1707)

Trentmann, Frank 234
Tudor monarchy. *See* Elizabeth I; Henry VII; Henry VIII; Mary I
Turner, Thomas 164–5

Union of the Crowns. *See* regal union (England and Scotland, 1603)
'unite' coins 38–40, 168
United Kingdom of Great Britain and Ireland (from 1801) 11, 134, 202. *See also* monetary revolution (Scotland); monetary system (United Kingdom)
  creation 180–1
  currency notes (UK state-issued) 239–45, 253
  decline of sterling 273–9
  and European Monetary System 280–4
  financial crises (*see* financial crises)
  gold standard (*see* gold standard)
  Irish coins 181
  loan from International Monetary Fund 279
  loan from United States 275, 277
  London money market 229, 232–3, 237–9
  'National' government (1931) 265–9
  opposition to the euro 272–3
  pride in sterling 273–4, 277, 283–4
  silver recoinage (1817) 189–93
United States 276–7
  dollar 274–5, 277–9
  economy 263, 274–5
  loan to United Kingdom 275, 277
units of account 3–6, 9–10, 27–8, 168. *See also* exchange rates

Valenze, Deborah 17–18
Violet, Thomas 43, 53
Vyner, Robert 57–8, 60–3
Vyner, Thomas 60–3

Wales 12, 28, 44–5, 168
Wallace, Thomas 212
Walpole, Robert 127, 143–4
Walsh, Patrick 145
war
  Anglo-Dutch Wars 64
  Anglo-Irish Nine Years War (1594–1603) 35
  Anglo-Irish war (20th century) 245, 255–6
  First World War 237–43
  with France 73–5, 83, 106, 115, 166–8, 182–5, 188
  between and within kingdoms 35, 41–4, 48–9, 73
war loans 242–3, 263
Webb, Sidney 247–9
Wellington, Duke of 217

Wennerlind, Carl 18, 50, 92
Western, Charles 201
Western Bank of Scotland 230
William III and Mary II reign 73–4
Williamite revolution and war (1689–91) 73
Williamson, Philip 265–6

Wilson, Harold 277
Wood, William 153–7
wooden tallies. *See* tallies
Wren, Christopher 99–100

Yarranton, Andrew 50–1